D0977312

Tracking the Axis Enemy

MODERN WAR STUDIES

Theodore A. Wilson
General Editor

Raymond A. Callahan
J. Garry Clifford
Jacob W. Kipp
Jay Luvaas
Allan R. Millett
Dennis Showalter
Series Editors

Tracking the Axis Enemy

The Triumph of Anglo-American Naval Intelligence

Alan Harris Bath

University Press of Kansas

© 1998 by the University Press of Kansas
All rights reserved

Published by the University Press of Kansas (Lawrence, Kansas 66049), which was organized
by the Kansas Board of Regents and is operated and funded by Emporia State University,
Fort Hays State University, Kansas State University, Pittsburg State University, the University
of Kansas, and Wichita State University

Library of Congress Cataloging-in-Publication Data

Bath, Alan Harris.
    Tracking the axis enemy : the triumph of Anglo-American naval
intelligence / Alan Harris Bath.
        p.   cm. — (Modern war studies)
    Includes bibliographical references and index.
    ISBN 0-7006-0917-2 (alk. paper)
        1. World War, 1939–1945—Secret service—United States. 2. World
War, 1939–1945—Secret service—Great Britain. 3. Military
intelligence—United States—History—20th century. 4. Military
intelligence—Great Britain—History—20th century. I. Title.
II. Series.
D810.S7B35   1998
940.54'8673—DC21   98-18726

British Library Cataloguing in Publication Data is available.

Printed in the United States of America

10 9 8 7 6 5 4 3 2 1

The paper used in this publication meets the minimum requirements of the American
National Standard for Permanence of Paper for Printed Library Materials Z39.48-1984.

To the memory of my father,
Gerald Horton Bath

Nations don't have permanent friends or permanent enemies, they only have permanent interests.

—Chaim Herzog, president of Israel

Contents

Preface

Anglo-American cooperation during the Second World War has been characterized as "not only very close, but perhaps unique in the history of war."[1] Recent writers, however, have pointed out that while Sir Winston Churchill may have seen this cooperation as the result of a "special relationship" between the British Commonwealth and the United States—"the political expression of an underlying cultural unity"—it was affected more by the political differences and the economic rivalries that marked the shift of power from England to America than by cultural influences.[2] This work examines the history of the development and the interactions of both American and British naval intelligence before and during the Second World War to determine the extent to which the concept of the "special relationship" was present in the field of intelligence—particularly naval intelligence—and to identify the political, military, and human factors that either aided or hindered the process of cooperation. To what extent did the external influences affect naval intelligence cooperation? Did the process of cooperation proceed at the same pace in all theaters of the war? What was the role of Allied intelligence, specifically that of Canada, Australia, New Zealand, and France, in the Anglo-American cooperative process? To what extent did intragovernmental rivalries affect Allied intelligence efforts? Since British naval intelligence had time to make mistakes and to grow in the two years prior to America's entry into the war, to what extent did the U.S. Navy's intelligence effort profit from British experience?

Naval intelligence, or the lack thereof, played a major role for both the Allies and the Axis in determining strategy during the key battles of the Atlantic and throughout the Pacific war. Yet its role has often been overshadowed in intelligence literature by concentration on one of its components: the Allied breaking of German and Japanese codes—ULTRA and

Magic. This study goes beyond examining the work of the code breakers, in that it attempts to put in perspective the total contribution of Allied naval intelligence to the successful prosecution of the war—a contribution made in great measure by overcoming national and individual rivalries to achieve a common goal. The development of Anglo-American naval intelligence is traced as it progressed from disparate, underfunded, and understaffed prewar national entities to a closely knit, multinational organization that rose above parochial interests to make a major contribution to the Allied victory.

Much of the information contained in this book, especially that concerning Allied intelligence relationships in the Pacific from 1942 to 1945, is derived from previously classified documents newly released by the British Public Records Office and from examination of Canadian, Australian, and New Zealand archives seldom utilized by American and British historians. These documents offer a new perspective on the often-told tale of wartime Allied cooperation and reveal with a new frankness some of the strains that beset the cooperative effort.

Anglo-American naval intelligence cooperation took place at all levels of decision making, in all theaters of war, and at all points in the intelligence process: collection, analysis, and dissemination. The progress of Anglo-American naval intelligence cooperation—with its ups and downs—and its contributions to the winning of the war are the major themes of this volume.

Many people provided assistance and support on the long road from dissertation topic, through archival research, to finished book, and of these, several were of particular importance. First, Dr. Ira D. Gruber of Rice University shaped my ideas on military history, led me firmly—but with great enthusiasm—through the mysteries of dissertation writing, and encouraged me to expand the result into a book. Edward Drea of the U.S. Army Center of Military History was particularly helpful in providing information on code breaking during the Pacific war from his files and in suggesting contacts in Australia and Canada that would prove helpful in my research. Bradley Smith, in London, provided much useful information on new releases of material at the British Public Record Office.

I am particularly indebted to Professors John Ferris of the University of Calgary and Wesley K. Wark of the University of Toronto, whose careful reading and detailed comments on the manuscript led to a much better finished product. Of course, all errors in fact or interpretation are mine alone.

Finally, I owe a debt of gratitude to my wife, Connie Belle, my research associate and chief cheerleader, whose faith never weakened that "all those little bits of paper" would eventually turn into a book.

Part One
The Road to Cooperation

I.
Uneasy Beginnings

What American spymaster Allen W. Dulles, echoing Britain's Lord Palmerston, called "the craft of intelligence" has had a long, if not always savory, history. Moses, an early advocate of intelligence collection, sent men "to spy out the land of Canaan . . . and see the land, what it is; and the people that dwelleth therein, whether they be strong or weak, few or many."[1] The more specialized field of naval intelligence developed somewhat later. In England, its roots extended back to Queen Elizabeth I and Sir Francis Walsingham, her secretary of state, and his successful "agent operations" in Spain against the Armada of 1588.[2] A similar American tradition can be traced back to colonial times.[3]

Anglo-American cooperation in naval intelligence dated from the First World War, and many themes present in 1916–1918 were replicated in the "special relationship" of 1940–1945—among them the Admiralty's lead in championing the cause of Anglo-American naval cooperation, sensitivity of both governments to anti-British sentiments in domestic American politics, American naval leaders' unwillingness to accept a status inferior to that of the "Senior Service," and British concern over the American inability to keep secret matters a secret.

Intelligence sharing during the interwar years did not cease but was limited in great part to informal exchanges between American and British naval representatives overseas; it was rarely part of a coordinated navy-to-navy cooperative program. A diminished interest in intelligence, coupled with depression-era limitations on funds in Britain and America, restricted cooperative growth, as did the fears of isolationists and pacificists on both sides of the Atlantic that preparations for defense would lead to war. However, by 1938, concern over German and Japanese aggression caused leaders in both the U.S. and Royal Navies to look to the condition of their respective intelligence establishments and to consider areas for mutual support.

Surprisingly, in view of Britain's reputation as a longtime naval and intelligence power, the first naval intelligence organization to be officially chartered on either side of the Atlantic was in the United States. On 23 March 1882, the Navy Department issued an order, signed by the secretary of the navy, establishing an Office of Naval Intelligence (ONI) within the Bureau of Navigation, "for the purpose of collecting and recording such information as may be useful to the Department in time of war, as well as peace."[4] Lieutenant Theodorus B. M. Mason became the first director of ONI on 15 June and, with a staff of three, began to implement the directive of the secretary of the navy "to collect, compile, record and correct" information on such subjects as the fleets of foreign powers; their armaments, personnel, and facilities; their coasts and ports; and their merchant navy[5]—much the same mission that ONI has today.

In Britain, the Royal Navy lagged behind the Army in recognizing the need for an intelligence department. The lack of basic information on the Crimea at the start of the war with Russia in 1854 gained the reluctant attention of the War Office, and the following year it created the Topographical and Statistical Department, which eventually became its first intelligence entity.[6]

The Board of the Admiralty began preparatory committee examination of the intelligence problem in 1879, established the Foreign Intelligence Committee in 1882, and officially created the Naval Intelligence Department in January 1887.[7] The instructions to the Foreign Intelligence Committee were essentially the same as those given to ONI. They were to "collect, classify and record, with a complete index, all information which bears a naval character . . . to keep up our knowledge of progress made by foreign countries in naval matters and to preserve the information in a form readily available for reference." Well before the start of World War I, the Admiralty had fashioned colonial officials and Royal Navy representatives overseas into a worldwide reporting net to monitor the movements of foreign merchant ships and warships.[8]

At their inception, both the American and the British naval intelligence organizations were roughly equal in size, but the position of each in its respective naval hierarchy was vastly different. ONI lacked direct access to the naval policy makers, a situation that continued throughout the Second World War. Although it was consulted from time to time, it was unable to convince leaders in the Navy Department of the need for intelligence or of its significance in decision making.[9] This subordinate organizational position coupled with a lack of acceptance of its product, continued to limit ONI's growth in both size and influence during the 1930s and beyond.

At the time of its formation, the British Department of Naval Intelligence (NID)[10] was made responsible not only for the collection and dissemination of information but also for mobilization and naval war planning. Its director had direct access to the Admiralty's first sea lord and first lord (titles of the military and political heads of the British naval establishment, similar to the offices of the chief of naval operations and the secretary of the navy in the American system), giving the incumbent great authority both in the Admiralty staff and in the Fleet.[11] NID "was in fact a Naval Staff in embryo."[12] Although its nonintelligence functions were later transferred to other staff sections, NID retained its preeminent position in the Admiralty until the end of the First World War.

Formal intelligence cooperation between the American and British navies originated during World War I. However, rivalries internal to both naval staffs, as well as external personal, political, and military relationships between the two countries, intervened to limit or impede the cooperative effort.

The subject of cooperation in naval matters was first raised by the British ambassador in Washington in January 1917. He reported that the president "would not consent to naval agreement in anticipation of joint defensive measures," which presumably would have to await the formal entry of the United States into the war.[13] Prior to that time, the ambassador recommended that the British naval attaché in Washington make highly secret proposals to the U.S. Navy Department concerning coordination of patrols along shipping lanes. These proposals were "not to be written down," nor was the British ambassador himself to be informed of their content. The reason given for this sub rosa approach was fear of its discovery by "Germans in the Navy Department,"[14] but one must not rule out the possibility that the ambassador was preparing what has more recently been termed "plausible denial" of the proposals in case of a leak. Both the secrecy of the approach and the reluctance of the president to become involved in open cooperation were to be reprised in the events of the late 1930s. In February 1917, the British Foreign Office indicated that no secret information was to be exchanged officially with the Americans, "as secrecy [is] impossible with Congress."[15]

Although the American naval attaché in London had been supplied copies of British intelligence publications on German warships as early as February 1917, the first specific reference to intelligence cooperation was contained in a March naval staff memo in which NID suggested "co-operation between the two Intelligence Divisions."[16] The type of cooperation was not specified; however, a month earlier, the Admiralty had indicated that the U.S. naval attaché in London was not to be informed of "the most secret methods"—an undoubted reference to Admiralty code-breaking activities that were then providing such impressive results.[17] Room 40 of NID, under the close supervision of the director of naval intelligence, Admiral Sir Reginald ("Blinker") Hall, was the hub of the decoding operation. Room 40 began operations in 1914 with a small staff drawn mainly from the faculties of the Royal Naval Colleges of Osborne and Dartmouth. Some of these early recruits were German linguists, among them Alastair Denniston, who was to achieve discreet fame in the early years of World War II as head of the Government Code and Cypher School (GC&CS), better known as "Bletchley Park," the center of British code-breaking activities during the Second World War.[18]

Admiral Hall maintained an extraordinary control over the dissemination of Room 40's output, a situation that did not always work to the betterment of cooperation between NID and ONI. Hall did not choose to pass information to the U.S. Navy Department through the usual intelligence channel— the U.S. naval attaché in London; he preferred to pass specific items of "most secret" information to Mr. Edward Bell of the American embassy in London, who was charged with maintaining liaison with the various British intelligence agencies.[19] It was Bell that Hall summoned to Room 40 to see the decrypted translation of the famous Zimmermann telegram. On 16 January 1917, German Foreign Minister Arthur Zimmermann sent a coded telegram to the German ambassador in Washington announcing Germany's intention to resume unrestricted submarine warfare and to attempt to bring Mexico into an alliance with Germany that would provide Mexico with "generous financial support and an undertaking on our part that Mexico is to reconquer the lost territory in Texas, New Mexico and Arizona."[20] Once Bell had been convinced of its authenticity, he and Hall took the telegram to the American ambassador, who transmitted it to Washington, where the president was said to have "showed 'much indignation' on reading it."[21] The story was published in the American press on 1 March and aroused in Congress and in the American public the wrath that Hall and the British government had anticipated. David Kahn, doyen of modern American cryptographic historians, has commented that "no other single cryptanalysis has had such enormous consequences. . . . For those few moments in time, the codebreakers held history in the palm of their hand."[22]

Following the United States' formal entry into the war in April 1917, Admiral William F. Sims was ordered to London to command American naval forces in Europe. Sims, who in the course of his career had held several intelligence-related assignments, including naval attaché in Paris and briefly in London (in 1898), considered himself fully as competent in intelligence matters as was the director of naval intelligence in Washington. Sims soon took control of American naval intelligence in Europe at the expense of ONI's efforts in the area and built in his Planning Section an intelligence team that "resembled a second Office of Naval Intelligence."[23]

Team members included Commander (later Commodore) Dudley Knox, who subsequently became head of the Office of Naval Records and Library and curator for the Navy Department,[24] and Lieutenant (junior grade) Tracy B. Kittredge, who, twenty-five years later, became both command historian and a close adviser to Admiral Harold R. Stark, commander of U.S. naval forces in Europe during World War II, who had also served on Sims's London staff. In a 1942 memo to Stark, Kittredge outlined the organization of the American naval staff in Europe in 1917–1919 and reminded him that "complete information [i.e., intelligence] was available only in London. The intelligence sources available to the British were placed at the disposal of the American Naval Headquarters."[25]

British Director of Naval Intelligence (DNI) Hall had formed a friendship with Lieutenant Commander John R. Roys, the local ONI representative in London, and had assured the American DNI "of the close cooperation in Naval Intelligence matters which exists between your people and myself."[26] Nevertheless, Hall tended to deal more often with Admiral Sims. The Admiralty provided confidential books and periodicals "to Sims, to Benson [Admiral William S. Benson, U.S. chief of naval operations] and to Roy [sic]. Day to day matters to Sims for transmission to Benson, also weekly appreciation."[27]

During a 1918 visit to London, Benson designated Sims as naval attaché in order to reduce the friction caused in both Washington and London by differing assessments of British naval policy by Sims and by the incumbent attaché.[28] This appointment was another blow to ONI's prestige, since traditionally, naval attachés reported to the chief of naval operations via the DNI and not directly, as Sims did. Hall continued to provide Sims with large amounts of information, particularly of the type derived from decrypts, yet he refused all requests from Sims or from ONI for access to the technical secrets of Room 40, perhaps because the United States had nothing to offer in return.[29] Hall's reticence may have contributed to the delay in the U.S. Navy's development of its own code-breaking capability, which did not begin until the 1920s.

During the period 1914–1918, the Admiralty had but one DNI, Rear Admiral "Blinker" Hall—so called because of his habit of rapidly blinking his eyes. NID's great reputation rested as much on the influence of its leader as on its preeminent position in the British Naval Staff. Hall was a vigorous activist, "building up his own espionage system, deciding for himself when and how to release intelligence to other departments, and acting on intelligence independently of other departments in matters of policy that lay beyond the concerns of Admiralty."[30]

Hall's "opposite number" in Washington, Captain Roger Welles, was appointed DNI in April 1917 and served in that post until January 1919. The pressures of attempting to meet increased wartime demands for intelligence with inadequate resources, particularly personnel, took their toll on Welles's health, which was a problem throughout his tenure as DNI and was given as the reason for his being passed over in 1918 for promotion to rear admiral—although he was retained as DNI.[31] Welles was successful in building a viable wartime intelligence organization, but his reputation never approached that of Hall.

Despite Hall's great personal influence, NID exhibited weaknesses that limited its effectiveness during the First World War. NID was considered more a source of raw information than of evaluated intelligence. Assessment was the prerogative of the Admiralty's Operations Department, and the close association between Intelligence and Operations that developed during the Battle of the Atlantic in the Second World War did not exist during the First.[32] A second weakness that existed at the start of World War I and gradually disappeared during its course was the lack of an operational intelligence capability—the ability to provide the tactical commander with timely information on the strength and location of enemy forces.[33]

Immediately following the United States' entry into World War I, Great Britain dispatched its foreign secretary, Arthur James Balfour, with a diplomatic mission that arrived in Canada on 20 April 1917, held conversations with—among others—the British naval commander in chief, North America and West Indies Squadron, then proceeded to Washington on 22 April, where the British diplomats prepared the groundwork for subsequent Anglo-American naval cooperation.[34] After conversations with President Wilson's adviser, Colonel Edward M. House, the British ambassador informed London that the "best plan" would be an exchange of naval missions, but that the British mission should not be headed by a "prominent person" and should operate in an "inconspicuous way" so as not to further fuel presidential sensitivity to public charges that the United States was fighting an "English war"—a sensitivity that reappeared as the war against Japan drew to a close in 1945.[35]

In British eyes, cooperation did not mean full partnership. The proposal for establishment of the British mission emphasized that "it is of the greatest importance that the development of their [U.S.] Sea Forces should proceed along lines dictated by British War experience and be co-ordinated with British policy" and that the officer in charge of the mission "should encourage the Navy Bureau to make use of British standard of guns, ammunition and weapons and machinery generally."[36] Although the subordinate role proposed by the British had little effect on naval intelligence activities during the First World War, it colored attitudes of U.S. naval leaders toward British leadership, leaving impressions that were to influence the development of American naval intelligence in 1941–1943.

The British ambassador's proposal to establish a naval mission in Washington made provision for an intelligence liaison organization under the general supervision of the deputy chief of mission, but there is no indication in the British record that this body ever played an active part in intelligence cooperation. The primary British naval intelligence representative in the United States during World War I was Captain Guy Gaunt, RN, the naval attaché. In addition to his duties in Washington, Gaunt, who reported directly to Admiral Hall in London, was busy in New York on counterintelligence duties directed against German agents in the United States.[37] In a 1937 conversation with the British ambassador, President Roosevelt indicated that while he had been assistant secretary of the navy between 1915 and 1917, a mechanism for the systematic sharing of intelligence had been organized and that Gaunt and Captain William V. Pratt, USN, Benson's assistant, had been the mediums for effecting the exchange.[38]

Perhaps the president exaggerated when he called the ad hoc and informal arrangements between Gaunt and Pratt "systematic sharing of intelligence," but at the very least, a precedent had been established for future Anglo-American cooperative actions. Also, "sharing" may have been a misnomer. The United States had little intelligence on Germany to offer the British, especially after diplomatic relations with Berlin were severed when America entered the war, and the British were highly selective about the material passed to the United States—information often chosen for its political or propaganda impact rather than its military value. There is little to indicate that the navy-to-navy intelligence sharing that did take place had any great impact on the prosecution of the war by either Great Britain or the United States.

The interwar years saw the dismantling of both the American and the British naval intelligence organizations. At the end of the First World War, the Office of Naval Intelligence had 306 officers in Washington. By 1 July 1920 "just 42 remained, and many of these faced imminent detachment."[39] In 1935, ONI employed twenty civilian clerks and had an officer allowance of twenty-one.[40]

British naval intelligence was similarly reduced. Hall, who was replaced as DNI by Admiral Hugh Sinclair in 1919, retired from the navy and later became a member of Parliament. His influence on British intelligence was once again felt on the eve of the Second World War when he provided both his vast experience and his London flat to Admiral John Godfrey, who had just joined the naval staff as DNI, Hall's old job.

In 1919, the British Cabinet, prompted at least in part by a desire to see that no future DNI could exercise the unbridled authority possessed by "Blinker" Hall, directed Admiral Sinclair to form a permanent code-breaking body under civil administration in the Admiralty. The new organization, named the Government Code and Cypher School (GC&CS), was assigned both public and secret functions: "*Public:* advise on the security of government cyphers. *Secret:* 'to study the methods of cypher communications used by foreign powers.'"[41] In 1921, control of GC&CS passed from the Admiralty to the Secret Intelligence Service,[42] which was under the loose supervision of the Foreign Office.

Although documentary evidence is scanty,[43] intelligence cooperation between the two navies did not completely cease in the interwar years but consisted mainly of low-level operational exchanges carried out informally by American or British naval officers in the fleet or by naval attachés on foreign station. In 1928, American intelligence officers in the Far East discussed possible joint activities with their British counterparts in the event of hostilities in Asia.[44] Again, in 1938, American marines in China gave the British staff officer (Intelligence) in Shanghai their intelligence reports on Japanese landing craft and operations in the Yangtze Delta "in exchange for two sketches of the [Japanese] landing craft carrier which were produced by this office."[45]

Evidence of British interest in rekindling the cool embers of wartime cooperation was first reported early in January 1937. Robert W. Bingham, American ambassador to Britain, wrote to President Roosevelt that "official orders have been given in the British Army and Navy that good relations with their American opposite numbers at home and abroad must be established and maintained. Similarly, the attitude of government officials in their daily contacts with the Embassy . . . is marked with a progressive and almost bewildering friendliness that cannot pass unnoticed."[46] Although the ambassador did not speculate on the reason for this change in attitude, a growing awareness by British leaders of the sad state of Britain's military defenses and of the need to cultivate allies may have prompted the change.

Intelligence cooperation between sovereign nations depends to a great extent on the attitudes, prejudices, and motives of their leaders. Therefore, in any study of intelligence relationships, it is necessary to examine the dispositions of the leaders toward intelligence—judgments formed in the main by the leader and by his personal experience with intelligence. However, other factors, such as a leader's perception of the relative strength or weakness of his country vis-à-vis that of a potential enemy, also play a part. Military historian Michael Handel emphasized this point in writing that Britain's weakness in 1940 "made its very survival dependent on the quality of its intelligence. Almost any British leader at that moment would have shown a keen interest in intelligence."[47] While accepting Handel's argument, it must be noted that Churchill was singularly well prepared, by reason of both background and inclination, to require the maximum effort from the British intelligence establishment. Churchill's knowledge of intelligence and its uses dated back to the Boer War and to his tenure as first lord of the Admiralty in 1911–1915. From this experience he developed an appreciation for the importance of intelligence in war.

Churchill's great skill in the acquisition and use of intelligence was counterbalanced by what British intelligence historian Christopher Andrew termed "his fascination with cloaks and daggers and his exaggerated expectations of what they could achieve."[48] This predilection certainly influenced his decision in 1940 to form the Special Operations Executive (SOE), which he ordered to operate on the Continent as a clandestine sabotage organization and which prompted his oft-quoted exhortation to Hugh Dalton, SOE's first chief, to "set Europe ablaze!"[49]

Churchill's enthusiasm for "cloaks and daggers" was shared in great measure by Franklin Roosevelt. A case in point occurred in the coordination of Plan Catherine. "Catherine" was the code name for an operation, strongly backed by Churchill, who was then first lord of the admiralty, in which the British fleet would penetrate the Baltic, then gain control of the area through a series of rapid, massive strikes. The plan was first discussed in October 1939 but was overtaken by events before it could be carried out. Churchill briefed the American ambassador, Joseph. P. Kennedy, on the details of Catherine and asked him to lay the plan before President Roosevelt for his endorsement during the ambassador's planned visit to Washington in December. Churchill wrote to Kennedy on 10 December, "if you cable 'my wife cannot express an opinion,' I shall take it in a favourable sense. If you cable 'Eunice had better not go to the party,' I shall take it as forecasting bad trouble." Kennedy replied by commercial cable on 23 December, "My wife cannot express an opinion but is much more friendly to the idea than I had anticipated."[50]

The famous Roosevelt-Churchill wartime correspondence had begun at the invitation of the president who, in an 11 September 1939 letter to Churchill, expressed his pleasure at Churchill's return to the Admiralty and wrote that "I shall at all times welcome it if you will keep me in touch personally with anything you want me to know about."[51] Churchill accepted with alacrity, and a regular flow of operational and intelligence information was opened to the president. On 16 October 1939, Churchill sent a memorandum to Admiral Sir Dudley Pound, the first sea lord, requesting material for one such message and commenting, "I think I ought to send something more to my American friend in order to keep him interested in our affairs," then added in a handwritten postscript, "We must not let this liaison lapse."[52]

Like Churchill's, Roosevelt's involvement in naval intelligence dated from the First World War and from civilian service with the navy. Roosevelt's interests had ranged much more widely than were necessary to fulfill his duties as assistant secretary of the navy, which were essentially those of management and were concerned with civilian personnel matters and with the running of the Navy's large shore establishment. In 1917, when the director of naval intelligence was forced to turn to reserve officers to fill vacant positions in his organization, Roosevelt aided him with nominations. Roosevelt had been instrumental in the initiation of the naval reserve system a year earlier. Through this experience, he was aware of the numbers of qualified young men who were eager to serve in naval intelligence, many of whom came from backgrounds similar to his own—old money, Yankee aristocracy, prep school, and Ivy League education.[53] ONI's recruitment effort was not unlike that of British intelligence organizations, particularly NID and GC&CS, which depended heavily on the "Old Boy" network to fill key positions as war neared.

When he became president of the United States, Roosevelt brought with him a management style that required his receiving a flow of information from a number of sources, both official and personal. "Roosevelt's persistent effort therefore was to check and balance information acquired through official channels by information acquired through a myriad of private, informal, and unorthodox channels and espionage networks."[54] "Roosevelt seemed at times like a sponge soaking up information and ideas indiscriminately."[55]

Vincent Astor, millionaire businessman, yachtsman, and friend of the president, was an early recruit to Roosevelt's private information network. Astor, a commander in the naval reserve who had been appointed by the president to the post of coordinator of intelligence in the New York area, wrote to Roosevelt in April 1940 that he had made informal contact with Sir James Padget, a retired Royal Navy officer who directed the British Passport Control Office in New York. Paget was the top British Secret Intelligence

Service representative in the United States and the Passport Control Office was his somewhat transparent "cover." Astor reported that Padget had "gladly accepted" his offer of cooperation, but, Astor noted, the arrangement was one-sided, since "we, for obvious reasons, could not return the compliment in the sense of turning over to them any of our confidential information."[56]

The same concerns that led the British government to seek closer cooperation with the American military in 1937 also prompted the Admiralty to examine the condition of its own intelligence organization for war. The previous year, Admiral Sir William James, who in 1917 had been in charge of Room 40 and, by 1936, had become deputy chief of the naval staff, sent a series of memos to the DNI reminding him of the success achieved in World War I by combining the work of cryptographers and direction-finding stations in "a proper intelligence section" that "put two and two together" and passed the results to the operators. In a subsequent memo, James reiterated to the DNI that an operational intelligence capability was "essentially a wartime requirement," but one that must be planned in peacetime. Again, on 11 February 1937, James urged the naval staff to draw upon the experience gained during the First World War to "see how near we can get in peace time to the organization as it existed at the end of the war."[57]

To implement James's directive, the DNI chose Lieutenant Commander Norman Denning, who was later to serve as DNI himself and subsequently as the first deputy chief of the defence staff (Intelligence). In June 1937, he was given the task of "creating an all source intelligence center" that was later to play a major role in Anglo-American intelligence cooperation.[58] According to Patrick Beesly, wartime deputy to Roger Winn in the Admiralty's submarine tracking room, Denning started the Operational Intelligence Centre in a corridor of the Admiralty with one clerk and was at first chiefly concerned with following the movements of Italian submarines and German warships supporting the Nationalists in the Spanish Civil War.[59]

Perhaps reflecting some of the concern felt by his British colleagues, the American naval attaché in London, at a luncheon with the British DNI a few days before Denning's appointment, raised the subject of a closer exchange of information between the two navies. This remark prompted the Admiralty to review its policy, set the previous year, on information exchange with the United States. At the time, it had been determined that "Great Britain could not participate in any arrangement for the exchange of information against a third power."[60] In urging reconsideration of this policy, the DNI quoted a March 1937 telegram from the British ambassador in

Washington to the Foreign Office in which he commented, "It seems to me that, for us, a nice balancing of information given against information received is entirely unimportant. What we want is the goodwill of the American General Staff just as much as their information."[61]

At roughly the same time, the U.S. Navy was not much more forthcoming on the question of information exchange than were the British. In August 1937, the State Department asked the Navy Department if it had any objection to a British engineer's proposed visit to the Bell Telephone Laboratories and to the Radio Corporation of America in connection with a grant he had been awarded by the Carnegie Corporation of New York to study shortwave and ultra-shortwave radio-telephone transmissions. The Office of the Director of Naval Communications replied rather ungraciously that, while it could "raise no specific objections" to the visit, "it is considered an undesirable practice for this country to disclose its technical secrets to foreigners while getting nothing in return."[62]

By 1937, American and British attention had become focused on the Far East and the Sino-Japanese conflict. Throughout the 1930s, the Royal Navy had seen Japan, much more so than Germany, as its chief threat at sea.[63] In London, the American ambassador called on Prime Minister Chamberlain to discuss Anglo-American cooperation in Asia. Both agreed that cooperation in naval matters had been "satisfactory and beneficial." However, Chamberlain indicated that he felt "there should be other ways in which we might most usefully cooperate."[64]

In November, Sir Ronald Lindsay, the British ambassador in Washington, told Undersecretary of State Sumner Welles that the British government was considering "an overwhelming display" of naval strength in the Far East and wished to know if the United States would entertain the idea of staff conversations to discuss combined actions. Admiral William Leahy, who had become chief of naval operations in January 1937, favored the conversations, but Welles rejected the concept.[65]

It was the president who, perhaps stirred by the Japanese sinking of the USS *Panay* on 12 December 1937, unexpectedly revived the idea of Anglo-American staff discussions. After a 16 December reception at the White House, Roosevelt met privately with Ambassador Lindsay and the secretary of state, "plunged at once into the question of staff conversations," and recalled his own contribution to the intelligence exchange between Gaunt and Pratt during World War I.[66] Lindsay's cable sent Admiralty archivists scurrying to the files for evidence of presidential involvement in the exchange, which Lindsay "clarified" in a 2 January telegram quoting the president as having "begun with exchange of naval information" and having "gone on to

exchange of all sorts of intelligence."[67] No record of the details of this exchange or of Roosevelt's involvement has been found in Admiralty files.

"I want Admiral Leahy and Captain Ingersoll to be there [the president's
office] at 1:30 and to come in the back way—through the White House."[68]
Thus did Roosevelt secretively set out on the path that would lead to
pre–World War II naval cooperation with Great Britain. At that meeting, it
was decided to send Ingersoll, chief of the Navy Department's Plans Division,
to London immediately to arrange for "parallel action in the Far East." Accordingly, he sailed for Great Britain on Christmas morning. Captain Ingersoll registered at a London hotel under his own name and later commented
ingenuously in his memoirs, "There was nothing secret about it, except that
the newspaper reporters didn't know about it until some time after I left
Washington."[69]

The Admiralty saw it somewhat differently. "Captain Ingersoll was sent to
this country direct by the President of the U.S.A. without the matter being
handled in the normal way by the State Department or the American Embassy. . . . The only ministers informed were the First Lord, the Prime Minister and the Secretary of State for Foreign Affairs. The more secret part of the
conversations was contained in a Plans Division paper which was not circulated in the ordinary manner, and the subject of the conversations was never
referred to either the Cabinet or the C.I.D. [Committee of Imperial Defence].
This procedure was adopted at the special request of the U.S.A."[70]

Ingersoll's conversations were mainly with Captain Tom Phillips, his counterpart as director of plans on the naval staff. Their talks were informal and exploratory, and little concrete agreement was achieved—but the ice had been
broken. Ingersoll wrote a memorandum to the U.S. chief of naval operations
concerning his discussions with Phillips and with Admiral Chatfield, chief of
the naval staff, a copy of which has survived in the Admiralty's records. Concerning intelligence, Ingersoll noted that an informal agreement was currently
in effect between the British DNI and the American naval attaché for exchange of information on Japanese activities in the Mandated Islands, and he
reported that "the British believe this should be extended now to include
movements and locations of Japan's naval units." Admiral Chatfield also indicated that he thought it desirable for the British and American fleets in the
Pacific to exchange intelligence, "whenever it became necessary."[71]

Meanwhile, back in Washington, the chief of naval operations was busy as-
suring the press that Ingersoll's mission, news of which had leaked by this time,
had nothing to do with "joint Anglo-American action in any part of the
world."[72] Ingersoll completed his visit to London on 18 January 1938, returned
to the United States, and reported verbally to the president on 29 January

1938. Admiral Leahy also provided Roosevelt with a written report of the discussions. A year later, Leahy still considered the topic so sensitive that he asked Roosevelt's naval aide to retrieve the presidential copy, "if [it] can be found . . . in order to destroy [it]."[73] This penchant for secrecy in matters involving Great Britain, generated in great part by concern over the reaction of American isolationist politicians, was to become the hallmark of the president's approach to Anglo-American military cooperation in any form from 1937 until the United States' entry into the war.

Many of the underlying differences in attitude between the American and British navies during World War I continued into the Second World War, coloring Anglo-American naval intelligence relationships. American political sensitivity to any type of overt military alliance with England, the British perception that Americans were unable to keep secrets, the lack of American material to make intelligence exchange mutually advantageous, and the U.S. Navy's fear of being maneuvered into a subordinate position in the partnership all impeded development of an intelligence "special relationship." On both sides of the Atlantic, interwar reductions in funding and manpower for intelligence served as an additional brake on cooperative development. Despite these problems, by the start of 1938, the groundwork had been prepared for the cooperation that was to come.

2.

Changing Attitudes

In 1938, Hitler moved closer to the war he sought, first by annexing Austria to Germany in March, then by instigating the "Munich crisis" of September, in which Britain and France agreed to the partition of Czechoslovakia. The Second World War began officially in September 1939 with Hitler's invasion of Poland and subsequent British and French declarations of war against Germany. After Poland's rapid defeat, a lull in the war on land—but not at sea—ensued. The period of "phony war" ended with German attacks in Norway in April 1940, followed by the invasion of France and the Low Countries. After the collapse of France in June 1940, Hitler began preparing for an invasion of the British Isles. He undertook first to destroy the Royal Air Force and to soften up British defenses and morale. During the ensuing Battle of Britain, England stood alone in Europe to face the German challenge.

As war came to Europe, Anglo-American cooperation in naval intelligence grew, but at an irregular rate. Belligerent Britain looked with misgiving at neutral America's attempts to obtain hard-won British information while offering little in return. The cooperative process was overshadowed by the course of the war and by the United States' concern, which fluctuated with the ebb and flow of the war, over Britain's ability to continue resistance against Germany. Canada, accepting British leadership but wanting to be recognized as a sovereign ally, entered the Battle of the Atlantic. Both British and American attitudes toward Anglo-American cooperation were to change as the war deepened and spread.

The seeds of cooperation sown during the Ingersoll discussions in London in early 1938 were slow to germinate. The Admiralty cautiously continued to explore the possibility of giving the U.S. naval attaché a type of "most favored nation" status. On 17 February 1938, the British director of naval intelligence, Rear Admiral James A. C. Troup, had cautioned against the embarkation in wartime of neutral observers in Royal Navy ships, but added, "Should the United States remain neutral, the case of the U.S. naval attaché should be given special consideration."[1]

For his part, the U.S. naval attaché in London continued to generate a high volume of information during the late 1930s, dispatching 1,400 to 1,700 reports to ONI annually.[2] However, the record is silent both on the sources of these reports and on their quality. There is no indication during 1938 that exchange of intelligence extended beyond that already discussed concerning the situation in the Pacific. The Admiralty's files from January to March 1938 suggest that one possible reason for this slow growth in cooperation may have been reluctance on the part of the technical divisions of the Admiralty to exchange technical (i.e., nonintelligence) "information laboriously acquired at great expense and trouble," even on a quid pro quo basis.[3] The Admiralty's Plans and Intelligence Divisions, recognizing the politics of the question, recommended a much more forthcoming attitude.

Reluctance to exchange technical information was equally strong on both sides of the Atlantic. The technical bureaus of the U.S. Navy were quick to deny the British information on experimental American weapons or those under development for the fleet. These restrictions continued in force well after the fall of France in June 1940 and even later with regard to certain items deemed to be of critical national importance, such as the details of the United States' Norden bombsight.[4]

Despite Admiral James's exhortations to the British DNI to prepare his organization for war, a prewar recruit to Naval Intelligence Division commented that when he "joined the division [in March 1938] then under the directorship of Admiral Troup, it must surely have plumbed its greatest depth of inefficiency and no effort was being made to prepare for the war that by then seemed inevitable to all of us."[5] This criticism seems somewhat harsh in light of the fact that NID's Operational Intelligence Centre (OIC), arguably the single most effective intelligence organization of the Second World War, had been developed and brought to its wartime personnel strength under Troup's direction.

The OIC was the all-source intelligence center previously mentioned that had originally been given the task of tracking the movements of potential enemy men-of-war. With the commencement of hostilities and of the Battle of the Atlantic, the OIC evolved into the primary intelligence weapon against U-boats, providing Royal Navy operational commanders with up-to-the-minute information on strength and locations of German wolf packs. Spurred perhaps by a 6 October 1938 directive from the Committee of Imperial Defence calling on the services to identify shortcomings brought to light by the Czech crisis, Troup increased the manning of the OIC from a skeleton crew of four to fifty and put the center on a wartime footing in October, nearly a year before formal declaration of hostilities.[6] That same month, he encouraged the establishment of a similar OIC in Singapore to serve the intelligence needs of the commander in chief, Far East, and strengthened the naval intelligence organization in Capetown, South Africa. In addition, he proposed a plan for the retention in intelligence assignments of naval officers with special skills such as "good language qualifications" and the ability "to deduce correct conclusions as to the future movements of foreign forces."[7]

Despite Troup's organizational improvements, the Admiralty's intelligence system in 1938 suffered from a shortage of sources of information on the activities of potential enemy fleets. Overt material was obtained from quasi-official publications such as Lloyd's *Register of Shipping*, which tracked merchant vessel activities worldwide, and from naval attaché reports that were in great part based on official foreign government handouts. Covert material from the Secret Intelligence Service or other government agencies was minimal and communications (signals) intelligence was unavailable.[8]

The American naval intelligence establishment was in no better condition. A British student of naval intelligence noted that prior to 1939, "Unlike its British counterpart the American Naval Intelligence Division failed to develop a clear plan for its own organization, nor did it establish a workable scheme for classifying the type of information deemed necessary for determining the purposes and capabilities of potential enemies."[9] In other areas, however, progress was being made. Rear Admiral Ralston Holmes, USN, who had become American director of naval intelligence in May 1937, inherited an organization that was preoccupied with matters of domestic security and counterintelligence and was hampered by lack of adequate funds and by personnel shortages. Holmes revitalized the American naval attaché system, which had been allowed to decline in the mid-1930s, reopening key offices that had been closed and pressing for the establishment of new ones. In addition, Holmes bettered the lot of his attachés by improving relations with the Department of State and by providing additional funds and equipment for attaché use in their collection and reporting efforts overseas. Professor Jeffery M. Dorwart, who has written extensively on the history of ONI, commented that, "Just in time, ONI realized that the greatest menace to the United States came not from internal enemies but from foreign aggressors."[10]

In 1939, two naval officers, one British and one American, were transferred to London, where they were to play major roles in Anglo-American naval intelligence cooperation. Rear Admiral John H. Godfrey, RN, became British DNI, and Captain Alan G. Kirk, USN, became the American naval attaché. Captain S. W. Roskill, author of the official history of the Royal Navy in World War II, described Godfrey as "not only a man of unusually wide interests, but also gifted with an exceptionally powerful and original intellect." Roskill also recognized that Godfrey was "highly-strung . . . which made him unnecessarily combative and so created enemies."[11] Both these facets of his personality—superior intellect and ill temper—were evident in his direction of NID and in his relations with the service intelligence chiefs, his peers on the Joint Intelligence Committee.

John Godfrey was born in 1888 and entered the Royal Navy as a cadet in 1903. Upon receiving his commission, Godfrey served a pre–World War I tour on the China Station as navigator on a British gunboat on the Yangtze River, then returned to England and the Home Fleet. He spent most of the war in the Mediterranean and took part in the abortive British attempt to take the Gallipoli peninsula from the Turks, after which he was posted to the staff of the commander in chief, Indies and Egypt, and subsequently to the staff of the commander in chief, Mediterranean. Godfrey's interwar assignments followed the path of an upwardly mobile Royal Navy officer: increasing responsibility and finally command at sea, interspersed with shore duty in such places as the Plans Division of the Admiralty and as deputy director of the Naval Staff College in Greenwich. Godfrey's career at sea culminated in command of the battle cruiser HMS *Repulse* in the Mediterranean just prior to becoming DNI and receiving a promotion to rear admiral.[12]

By his own admission, Godfrey knew little about intelligence when he became DNI. Nor, he said, did his colleagues on the naval staff, "because the subject was swept out of sight during the twenty years of peace."[13] Godfrey chose to adopt much of the good counsel offered by Admiral "Blinker" Hall, of World War I fame. Hall saw to it that Godfrey met key government officials as well as business and financial leaders." These men would later prove to be of inestimable value in assisting Godfrey to recruit the bright young people he required to staff his rapidly expanding organization. Hall also gave warning of the political dangers and lingering jealousies that surrounded the position of DNI. "When in doubt," Godfrey said later, "I often asked myself what would Hall have done."[14]

Hall was also willing to share some of the tricks of the intelligence trade with the fledgling DNI. According to Ian Campbell, who headed NID 1 under Godfrey and later rose to the rank of vice admiral, Hall suggested that

Godfrey revive an old trick that had been useful to Hall. He told Godfrey to obtain an obsolescent code or one that could be broken easily and sell it to the enemy, so that it could be used to plant false information and other deceptive material. Shortly thereafter, "C," head of the British Secret Intelligence Service, informed Godfrey that he had a chance to sell a naval cipher. Once the agent acting as a go-between had demonstrated a relative degree of trustworthiness, NID devised a code and used the agent's services to sell the code to the Germans. When it appeared that the Germans had taken the bait, Godfrey began a series of "Most Secret" messages, ostensibly to high-ranking Royal Navy commanders, in which harmless truth and deceptive material were intermingled. The messages continued for several years as part of the larger Allied "Double Cross System" that achieved such impressive results as the war progressed.[15]

From the beginning of his tenure as DNI, despite occasional lapses probably engendered by frustration with American neutrality policies, Godfrey was a staunch advocate of increased intelligence cooperation with the United States. In 1940, prior to the fall of France, he was a strong voice in the Admiralty urging the dropping of the requirement that intelligence be exchanged, not given freely. In this regard, Godfrey's thinking was ahead of that of his political leader, First Lord Winston Churchill, who at the time favored a strict policy of quid pro quo.[16]

Captain Alan Kirk, USN, described by Godfrey as "a modest, shrewd and kind-hearted man,"[17] arrived in London in June 1939. Like Godfrey, his previous intelligence experience was slight, but he was enthusiastic about the assignment and had sought the help of Rear Admiral Walter S. Anderson, a former naval attaché in London and at the time the American DNI, in obtaining the posting.[18] Kirk came well recommended to Joseph P. Kennedy by mutual friends who had been associated with Kennedy on the shipping board. Kirk's entry into the diplomatic world was also smoothed by his prior acquaintance with key members of the embassy staff.[19]

Godfrey went out of his way to establish a personal relationship with Kirk that was to serve both of them well in the next few years. Their paths were to cross often: in 1939–1940 when Kirk was naval attaché, in 1941 when he served briefly as DNI in Washington, and in 1942 when he returned to London as chief of staff to Admiral Harold R. Stark, commander in chief, U.S. naval forces in Europe.[20]

As was customary for newly reported foreign attachés, Kirk paid a formal call on the British DNI. Kirk later reported to the American DNI that Godfrey had been "very agreeable" and had told him that "if there was anything I wished to know, just ask him." In the course of a subsequent and less formal chat, Godfrey was at pains to separate "material matters" from intelligence, indicating that he wished to talk "most freely" about the latter. Godfrey told Kirk that in the event of war, "we will give you a dugout in the Admiralty."[21]

Although they worked well together, Kirk remained reserved in his evaluation of Godfrey. While Kirk found Godfrey to be "perfectly civil and perfectly nice, he never was what you might call a really warm and outgoing person. He was by nature inclined to be crafty."[22] Kirk later commented that when he arrived in London, British authorities were "pretty good" about providing information to the U.S. Navy and that while "in no case was there what you might call a wide-open exchange," the British were more willing to share than were the Americans.[23]

Godfrey worked diligently to get NID ready for war. Noting that "there is a great deal to be done, and perhaps not much time in which to do it," Godfrey reported his progress to the deputy chief of the naval staff on 21 June 1939. Because he considered the most important duty of naval intelligence in wartime to be providing information on enemy warships, Godfrey stressed the work that had already been accomplished in readying the Operational Intelligence Centre for war: moving critical functions underground as protection against air raids, establishing "close touch" with the cryptographers at the GC&CS in Bletchley Park to ensure timely receipt of communications intelligence, and preparing for expansion "within a few hours" to meet a crisis. Godfrey indicated that he had reorganized those sections of NID that dealt with "static" intelligence—resources, shipbuilding, ports, and so forth—to cope with the increased workload brought on by the tense political situation, by the addition of new sources of information, and by the growing numbers of short-notice tasks laid on the division. By the summer of 1939, smaller versions of the London OIC had been created in Malta and Singapore. Godfrey also commented that his campaign to enlist the support of those in the academic and business world was "beginning to bear fruit."[24]

While Anglo-American cooperation was being discussed openly in official circles in London, such was not the case in Washington. In March 1939, the director of plans in the Admiralty wrote a minute to the chief of the naval staff indicating that in the aftermath of the Ingersoll discussions in London the previous year, the United States government seemed more interested in exchanging intelligence than in sharing operational plans, a major British interest. The plans director therefore suggested that another meeting be held— this time with Kirk, after his arrival in London—to discuss "these differences of view."

According to the British record, President Roosevelt agreed to renewal of the talks, but only in Washington and only under conditions of "complete secrecy," since "leakage might seriously compromise the pending [U.S.] neutrality legislation."[25] The British government agreed and chose as its emissary Commander T. C. Hampton, RN, of the Admiralty Plans Division. "Cover" for his arrival was to be provided by a previously scheduled visit of HMS *Exeter* to Baltimore, where Hampton—unnoticed among the other British naval officers—could slip off to Washington.

The trip soon took on the trappings of a James Bond novel (Bond's creator, Ian Fleming, was a key member of Godfrey's staff in NID during the war). Instead of arriving by warship, Hampton, posing as a civilian "land agent," took passage on a merchant ship and disembarked in Montreal, Canada. Bypassing Baltimore, he arrived in Washington on 12 June 1939. There he held two meetings with Admiral Leahy, the American chief of naval operations, on 12 and 14 June at his private residence. Attendance was limited to Leahy, Hampton, and two others: Leahy's director of plans, Rear Admiral Robert L. Ghormley, USN, and the British naval attaché. Hampton subsequently reported to his superiors that "the British Minister in Washington gave instructions to the naval attaché that I was on no account to visit the Embassy or visit his [the naval attaché's] staff, and further that I was to leave Washington as soon as my business was completed."

Hampton found the talks "somewhat disappointing," because they were "very general" and because Admiral Leahy "was most unwilling to put anything in writing."[26] Although no official record of the conversations has come to light, they dealt in general with plans for disposition of the two naval forces in time of war. Hampton ended his report on a provocative note: "In this connection [security arrangements] it is of interest that the [British] naval attaché in Washington was told by Admiral Leahy to arrange our meetings direct with him and that the U.S. Director of Naval Intelligence was on no account to be informed of my visit."[27] Whether this restriction was imposed for security or for other reasons was never made clear. However, it might have been related to the growing conflict between the Plans and Intelligence Divisions of the American naval staff over which organization was to provide the chief of naval operations and the president with naval intelligence estimates for planning purposes.

During the waning months of what Neville Chamberlain called "peace in our time,"[28] naval intelligence organizations on both sides of the Atlantic were beginning to prepare for war and to seek cooperation in intelligence matters. At the moment, the British were more forthcoming in offering to share intelligence. However, their attitude was to change, at least temporarily, once actual fighting started and the United States remained neutral.

Great Britain declared war on Germany on 3 September 1939. Since there was no immediate clash between British and German forces, within a few weeks, some circles in London began making reference to the "Bore War."[29] Not so His Majesty's government. The naval staff moved quickly onto a wartime footing, and by early 1940, Godfrey had accomplished most of the restructuring of NID to meet expected wartime demands. Kirk, in his report for the second half of 1939, indicated that relations with the Admiralty "are considered to be on as satisfactory, close, and amiable a basis as wartime conditions permit." Nevertheless, he admitted "that the obtaining of information has been more difficult due to the belligerent status of this country." Later in the report, he noted that "war conditions make all very guarded in their conversations" and concluded by saying that "the above applies equally to the Air Ministry—even with greater emphasis."[30]

With the coming of hostilities, security became a major concern of the British chiefs of staff. The Emergency Powers (Defence) Act, which strengthened the government's ability to act against espionage, sabotage, and subversion, was passed on 24 August 1939 and was implemented by a series of defense regulations. These regulations provided for close controls over the travel, employment, and activities of both enemy and neutral aliens. Notwithstanding these restrictions, there was concern in the Admiralty and elsewhere in the British government that information on military activities within the United Kingdom was reaching Germany.[31] John Colville, who had recently left the Foreign Office to become a junior secretary to the prime minister, wrote in his diary on 5 November 1939, "we never seem to have accurate or certain information about German fleet and troop movements, whereas the Germans know all our movements within a few hours of their taking place."[32] As was the case in 1917, many officials in the Admiralty felt that poor U.S. security might be at least an indirect cause of this perceived leakage of information to the enemy. Doubtless this nagging worry served as a brake on British willingness to release secret information to the American government, especially that "Most Secret" type of intelligence derived from enemy communications.

Code breaking, so important to the Royal Navy in the First World War, had again started to bear fruit. British code breakers, who had been assembled in great secrecy at a country estate near London named Bletchley Park, scored their first major success against Germany during the Norwegian campaign of April 1940. For this operation, the German Army and Air Force had introduced a special series of settings for their Enigma machine, the coding device in general use throughout the German armed forces and the government. These settings were used only for Norway, but from 15 April until the middle of May, the British continuously broke and read German Air Force operational messages from that region. By the time of the Battle of Britain, which followed a few months later, British cryptographers were providing timely access to much of the German Air Force operational traffic; however, similar success in penetrating the German Army and Navy systems was not to be achieved until later in the war.[33]

The British slowdown in the exchange of information with the United States may have been prompted in great measure by concerns over American security practices, but it also may have been used to express a hint of pique. In October 1939, Kirk radioed Washington that "intimation received (of British) willingness to exchange full Orange (i.e., Japanese) cryptographic information if you agreeable." After respectful prodding from Kirk, the Navy Department replied in November that since it was "unable offer equitable exchange at present" it must "therefore regretfully decline for time being."[34] It is probable that this refusal stemmed from objections by army and navy cryptographers, who felt that they were ahead of their British counterparts in solving Japanese codes and that they would gain little "quid" in return for their "quo." How this rebuff was received is not known. Six months later, however, Godfrey produced a minute in which he stated, "in my opinion it would be most unwise to give the Americans details of our 'most secret' material."[35]

During the slowdown period, Kirk continued to encourage the Navy Department to exchange information with the British and to press Godfrey for release of more intelligence. In an attempt to gain high-level support on the exchange matter, the Navy Department sent the commander in chief, U.S. Fleet, Admiral Claude C. Bloch, extracts from a Kirk letter in which he invited attention to the fact that "as the British Navy gains in war experience they will gradually out distance us in many technical subjects" and urged that the department "seize any opportunity for making exchanges."[36] Judging from Godfrey's remarks, Kirk made little progress in obtaining the release of technical material but was more successful in the intelligence field. Godfrey wrote in February 1940 that the Americans "have already helped us a good deal, though not technically," and commented that they have been "thoroughly unneutral" in providing attaché reports from Berlin, information on the Japanese Navy, and sighting reports from U.S. Navy ships.[37]

In the end, even Godfrey started to lose patience with Kirk's complaints about the Admiralty's foot-dragging on his requests for information. The DNI informed him that the delays were necessary and warned that "some British officers were asking why they should do anything for the Americans."[38] Following the fall of France in June 1940, as Britain stood alone against the Axis, the reasons for "doing anything for the Americans" became somewhat clearer.

As the war continued into the second half of 1940, official British attitudes began to shift from a feeling of irritation that the United States was not playing a greater role in the fight against Germany to a search for measures that would encourage rapid American intervention. One such initiative was to seek ways to increase technical and intelligence cooperation between the two navies. British distrust of American security, especially their concern over the unregulated American press, continued unabated. Martin Gilbert reflected this pervasive attitude in his study of the Second World War, in which he commented that "a considerable amount of German information . . . came not from an individual spy, but from a careful reading of the uninhibited American press."[39] British fears could not have been much allayed by Roosevelt's June 1940 appointment of Frank Knox, publisher of the *Chicago Daily News*, to the post of secretary of the navy. There was, however, good reason for both the United States and Great Britain to keep secret their joint activities. As one military historian pointed out, "At this time [summer 1940] the political situation in the United States and national pre-occupation with the Presidential Campaign of 1940 made it necessary for the administration and for the Navy to maintain complete secrecy on discussions of detailed arrangements for American-British Naval cooperation."[40]

As British interest in wooing the United States increased, so did American interest in assessing the course of the European war and in estimating the survivability of England. Following the defeat of France in June 1940, American strategic thinking had to take into account the possibility that Germany would invade the British Isles. Could the British successfully defend themselves against such an attack? If defeated, would they sue for peace or elect to continue the fight from bases elsewhere in the empire? To aid him in addressing vital questions such as these, Roosevelt utilized the "myriad of private, informal and unorthodox channels" previously mentioned.[41]

In addition to the normal official sources—State, War, and Navy Department assessments and telegrams from overseas—Roosevelt received information on the situation in England directly from Churchill, both when he was first lord of the Admiralty and later when he became prime minister. Personal emissaries, acting in either a quasi-official capacity (Undersecretary of State Sumner Welles's March 1940 London visit) or unofficially (World War I military hero William J. Donovan's July 1940 London visit), provided the president with direct channels of information. Of course, Ambassador Kennedy wrote directly to the president, bypassing official channels, but so did his naval attaché Kirk, sometimes without telling the ambassador. The White House received the Admiralty's papers from the U.S. naval attaché in London (via ONI), direct from the British embassy in Washington, and from the British naval attaché, Washington (also via ONI).[42]

One month after the government of France had asked Hitler for an armistice, and during the first month of massive German air attacks against Britain, a visit took place that was critical both to President Roosevelt's evaluation of Great Britain's chances of survival and to Anglo-American naval intelligence cooperation. On 14 July 1940, Colonel William J. "Wild Bill" Donovan, successful attorney, Republican, and subsequently the founder and director of the American Office of Strategic Services, departed for London. A recognized, if unofficial, direct representative of the president, Donovan was charged with two responsibilities: to seek ways to encourage greater cooperation between the American and British naval intelligence organizations and, more significantly, to assess and report to the president on the British ability and will to resist Germany.

In London, the American ambassador was less than sanguine about prospects for the trip's success. In response to instructions from the secretary of state to make such arrangements "as will facilitate Col. Donovan's mission," Kennedy replied tartly, "to send a new man here at this time, with all due respects to Col. Knox is to me the height of nonsense and a definite blow to good organization."[43] British officials were already concerned about weakening resolve in Washington and defeatist attitudes among American officials in London. Godfrey, who saw to it that all important English doors were open to Donovan, commented in a 2 August report that Ambassador Kennedy "has for some time been preaching the gospel of 'all is lost'" and that his influence "has unfortunately spread to the Embassy staff."[44]

To counteract this defeatist attitude, the British were determined to put on a good show for the unofficial representative of the president of the United States. Donovan's schedule was arranged to include calls on King George VI, the prime minister, the chiefs of staff, and Stewart Menzies, head of the Secret Intelligence Service. Godfrey and Kirk jointly planned the military portion of the visit, providing Donovan with a carefully calculated mix of meetings, social events, and visits to operational military units, all designed to show Britain's capabilities and resolve in the most favorable light.[45]

From both American and British viewpoints, Donovan's mission was highly successful. Roosevelt gained the personal insights he sought concerning the morale of British leadership. Britain gained some assurance that its pressing economic and military needs would receive a sympathetic hearing in the United States. After the military visits, Godfrey reported that Donovan would take back a "message to the effect that there is still time for American aid, both material and economic, to exercise a decisive effect on the war."[46]

Kirk, too, was impressed. He wrote to Donovan on 14 August that "it has been very evident here that your return [to the United States] produced lots of action," and Donovan himself seemed pleased. "I think that so far as the restoration of morale here was concerned the trip was worthwhile," he wrote to Kirk from Washington on 27 August.[47] Concerning intelligence, Godfrey reported that Donovan "will urge full intelligence collaboration and the placing at our disposal of reports by U.S. consular officers especially in French ports, direct liaison between myself and the U.S. D.N.I., and the establishment of Secret and direct methods of communication."[48]

Following Donovan's visit, personal diplomacy was, at least for the time being, to give way to more institutionalized contacts. The rules of the game were beginning to change. The Admiralty was now more interested in strengthening its ties with the U.S. Navy than in worrying about the potential security risks involved therein. Kirk had been quick to note the shift in policy. On 24 June 1940 he wrote to the American DNI, "It is perfectly evident now, not only to me but to many others attached to the Embassy, that the British Government, the Armed Forces, and the people as a whole are counting on intervention by the United States."[49] ONI's administrative history offers further indication of the British change in attitude. In the section detailing liaison with British agencies in Washington, reference was made to an aide-mémoire given to Roosevelt by the British ambassador on 8 July 1940 that requested an interchange of secret technical information. According to ONI, it was not the wish of the British government to make the exchange "the subject of a bargain," but to give the United States "full details . . . without pressing the United States for information," hoping that it would reciprocate.[50] Reciprocity was not immediate, but by the end of the year, the effects of British openhandedness in information exchange would be seen.

In the late summer of 1940, following the defeat of France and at the height of the Battle of Britain, a major concern on both sides of the Atlantic was the future of the Royal Navy. Churchill had assured Roosevelt that the Royal Navy would never be allowed to fall into enemy hands, but the prime minister was adamantly opposed to permitting the subject of transfer of the fleet to the western Atlantic to become a bargaining chip in discussions with the United States. Churchill was equally concerned about the adverse effect on British morale of any consideration of withdrawing the fleet from home waters.[51] Despite Churchill's reluctance to discuss removal of Royal Navy units to safer havens, the issue had been raised in Canada, and active preparations undertaken to receive all or part of the British fleet.[52] As early as 14 June

1940—coincidentally, the day that Paris fell to the Germans—Canadian prime minister Mackenzie King had discussed with the newly accredited American minister Jay Pierrepoint Moffat some of the practical problems that both countries would face if a portion of the British fleet were moved to Canada. Previous defense talks, which had started in 1938, had tended to concentrate more on the threat posed by Japan.[53]

As might have been expected, relations between the Royal Canadian and Royal Navies were extremely close. The Admiralty's status as primus inter pares among the fleets of the British Empire was accepted without question in Canada, although at times with irritation, which tended to increase as the Canadian navy grew in size and experience during the course of the Battle of the Atlantic. Traditionally, British naval officers filled some of the key positions on the Canadian naval staff, including that of Canadian director of naval intelligence.[54] Although Canada had moved from colonial to a more independent status as a dominion in 1867, it was not until 1910 that it took the first steps toward forming its own naval service.

Shortly after the establishment of the Canadian navy, the deputy minister of the Canadian Naval Service, G. T. Desbarats, wrote to the Admiralty asking its advice on placing an Intelligence Branch in the newly formed Naval Service Department of Canada. The Admiralty was cool to the suggestion, replying that the Canadian navy had not yet reached a state of development that would call for a separate naval intelligence organization, and noting with implied condescension that the Royal Navy had not felt the need for a separate intelligence staff until 1886. In the past, the Royal Navy had provided naval intelligence as it saw fit to Canada and apparently saw no reason why the system should be changed. The Admiralty recommended that should the Canadian navy wish to provide information to the Royal Navy, it could easily do so by including the material in a monthly diary of naval and military intelligence prepared by the Canadian Militia Department and sent to the War Office and the Admiralty in London. Canadian naval authorities would not be put off. Thanking the Admiralty for its advice and accepting its offer "to send periodically to this Department such intelligence as they [the Admiralty] consider will be of use to the Canadian Naval Forces," the Canadians proceeded to establish an independent naval intelligence capability. However, a separate Naval Intelligence Branch was not formed until 1913.[55]

When first established, naval intelligence in Canada consisted of three local centers: Ottawa; Halifax on the east coast; and Esquimalt on the outskirts of Victoria, British Columbia, in the west. In 1913, Canada joined the worldwide naval intelligence organization maintained by the Royal Navy for reporting the movements of foreign shipping but was not given a specific area to cover in either the Atlantic or the Pacific. With the coming of the First World War, the Admiralty allocated Esquimalt a definite area of responsibility extending from Siberia to Mexico and selected Halifax as the intelligence center for the Royal Navy's North American and West Indies Command, borrowing the Canadian navy's local intelligence staff as its nucleus.[56] The years of wartime experience being an integral part of the Royal Navy's world structure only sharpened the Canadian navy's desire for local autonomy, giving rise to a problem that was to be a recurring irritant in Anglo-Canadian naval relations until the end of the Second World War. The root of the problem was stated in a 1917 memo from the deputy chief of staff of the Canadian navy to his director: "The Admiralty has, of course, full command on the high seas, but in Canadian waters it is necessary that the Department should be supreme in all circumstances if the Department is to be anything but a name only."[57]

In intelligence, the problem was exemplified by the Royal Navy's 1917 attempt to gain control of the Canadian-staffed intelligence center in Halifax and have it report directly to the Admiralty, on the grounds that the majority of work done by the center was for use by the Royal Navy. In light of strong objections raised by its director of the naval service, the Canadian government asked the Admiralty to "reconsider" its proposal, and the center remained in Canadian hands.

The interwar years were as unkind to the Canadian Naval Service as they were to the U.S and Royal Navies. Described derisively as a "five trawler navy," it struggled for its existence amid public apathy and interservice rivalry. Canadian naval intelligence did not grow appreciably between the time of its establishment and the start of the Second World War. The Admiralty provided a small number of Royal Navy officers for intelligence duties, trained a few Canadians in intelligence in England, and furnished a certain amount of foreign strategic intelligence to Canada. In return, Canada provided the Admiralty limited information on North American trade and on the composition and movements of the U.S. Navy.[58]

Today, when one looks back on the Battle of the Atlantic, so nearly won by Germany in 1942–1943, it is difficult to remember how few U-boats the German navy possessed at the war's start. On 1 September, the navy's U-boat strength stood at fifty-seven total. According to the German U-boat war diary, in the first year of the war, there were generally no more than thirty U-boats available for patrol. It was unusual for more than six to eight to be on station in the Atlantic at any given time, and their operating areas were generally limited to the waters around the British Isles and between them and Iceland. To counter U-boat depredations, and in view of the very real possibility of a

German invasion, Britain requested maximum support from Canada, and by October 1940, virtually all of the Royal Canadian Navy (RCN) was at the disposal of the Admiralty. Once French ports in the Bay of Biscay had been captured in the summer of 1940, Hitler's U-boats moved westward into the Atlantic to cut the British supply lines from North America.[59]

With the coming of the war, the Royal Canadian Navy and its intelligence component expanded rapidly. In the early months, the director of naval intelligence's responsibilities for control of shipping in North American waters overshadowed his intelligence duties; however, as antisubmarine warfare became a major concern of the RCN, direction finding (D/F) and operational intelligence derived from enemy communications—better known as "Y" intelligence—predominated. Direction finding was the process of locating a radio transmitter at sea by having several sites on shore take a series of lines of bearing, or "cuts," on the same transmission. The point of intersection of the lines of bearing gave the approximate location of the sending unit. "Y" intelligence, better known as traffic analysis in the United States, was the art of studying the nonencrypted portions of messages sent in Morse code, such as lists of addressees, to gain information from the use and frequency patterns that emerged. Later, the term "Y" intelligence was expanded to include information derived from cryptanalysis of low-grade, that is, relatively simple, codes and ciphers.[60]

Those D/F resources that existed in Canada in the interwar years were controlled by the Department of Marine and Fisheries and later by the Department of Transport, which undertook naval assignments at the request of the British government in mid-1939. A "Y" intercept station had been operating at Esquimalt, British Columbia, since 1925, but it was operated solely for and by the British Admiralty, and the RCN was not privy to its secrets. The idea of creating a signals intelligence capability within the RCN probably originated with Commander Eric S. Brand, RN, who, as Canadian director of naval intelligence–designate, was briefed on the Admiralty's "Y" organization and capabilities in 1939 while en route to his new assignment.[61]

A few months before Brand's arrival in Canada, British authorities began to alert Royal Navy Reserve officers resident in Canada of a possible recall in the event of war. Among those notified was Lieutenant Commander J. M. ("Jock") deMarbois. DeMarbois's career had been colorful, both in and out of the Royal Navy. He was born on an island in the Indian Ocean off Madagascar in 1888 and joined the Royal Naval Reserve at the start of the First World War. In 1915, he took a special course taught by the Italian Navy at Taranto in the use of direction finding equipment and, in 1917, was assigned to the Russian cruiser *Askold* for communications duties, then loaned to the Russian

Navy as an instructor. DeMarbois was to have served as British assistant naval attaché in Petrograd, but the Russian Revolution intervened and, after a sojourn in northern Lapland in 1918 installing D/F equipment to track British transports bringing troops to Murmansk, he was assigned to the Naval Intelligence Division of the Admiralty until his retirement in 1921. Following his departure from the navy, he tried farming in Africa, then moved to Canada, where he became an instructor in modern foreign languages, including Russian and German, at Upper Canada College, Toronto, Ontario.[62]

In September 1939, the Admiralty recalled deMarbois and sent him to Naval Headquarters in Ottawa, one of four officers earmarked to fill positions in the expanding Intelligence Division. After extensive questioning about his naval background and probably because of his World War I experience in communications and direction finding, he was put in charge of the Foreign Intelligence Section, the forerunner of the Operational Intelligence Centre, which was not officially established until June 1943.[63] With little guidance except that received informally from members of the staff of the Admiralty's OIC and Signals Division, but with the full support of the Canadian DNI and the chief of the Canadian naval staff, Admiral Percy W. Nelles, RCN, deMarbois proceeded to build a modern and efficient Canadian intercept network.

The Admiralty was particularly interested in encouraging development of D/F sites in eastern Canada, because it needed their input to assist in triangulating positions of U-boats operating in British home waters. The Royal Navy's commander in chief, America and West Indies, with his headquarters in Bermuda, was equally concerned with bettering Canadian capabilities to locate enemy forces in the western Atlantic. In the fall of 1939 Ottawa began passing some admittedly not always accurate D/F bearings to London and Bermuda.

The year 1940 was marked by a continuing three-way tussle among the Admiralty, Naval Staff Headquarters, Ottawa, and Commander in Chief, America and West Indies, for control of Canadian signals intelligence capabilities. Once again, Canadian naval intelligence strove to break away from its dependence on the Royal Navy. The Admiralty wished to establish an intercept site and high-frequency direction finding (HF/DF) stations in Bermuda and Jamaica. Under the Admiralty's plan, bearings from Canadian facilities would no longer go directly to England, but would be passed to the control station in Bermuda, where they would be combined with other intercepts and the product sent to London. Tasking of Canadian stations would also come not from Ottawa or Halifax but from Bermuda. Various compromise solutions were attempted during the year, but the problem of control of the net was not finally resolved in favor of the RCN until May 1941.

Canada's fledgling "Y" service was given an additional responsibility after the fall of France, when the Admiralty asked the RCN to cover and report on French naval communications.[64]

Naval leaders in Washington, London, and Ottawa saw it as almost axiomatic that their efforts to counter the growing German U-boat threat in the western Atlantic would have to be fully integrated and that the intelligence with which to conduct the anti-U-boat war would have to be equally well coordinated. Despite this realization, little meaningful exchange of naval intelligence took place between Ottawa and Washington until the summer of 1941 and the expansion of U-boat operations into the central and western Atlantic. As will be seen later, despite problems in other areas of naval cooperation, the anticipated close working relationship among the three operational intelligence centers did eventuate, and Canada made a substantial contribution to Allied naval intelligence in both the Atlantic and the Pacific wars. By 1943, deMarbois, now promoted to captain in the RCN, was able to claim with pardonable hyperbole that his center "had become, if I may say so, the best organized 'Y' and D/F Operation Division among our great allies even far ahead of our grandmother 'the Admiralty.' "[65]

At the same time that the Canadians were testing the waters of U.S.-Canadian naval cooperation, the British were pursuing a similar course. In Washington, the British ambassador initiated a campaign to gain presidential approval of an Anglo-American naval conference, while in London, the Admiralty attempted to come to grips with questions of how much and what kind of cooperation should be sought and what should be offered in return.

On 11 June 1940, the British ambassador presented Secretary of State Cordell Hull with a proposal from Churchill, who had become prime minister on 10 May, for naval staff conversations. Hull was cool to the idea but agreed to pass the "suggestion" on to the president. The secretary of state had also reacted unfavorably to the ambassador's inquiry whether members of the War Department might talk to British attachés in Washington about the effects of British and French bombing of Germany, saying that "of course, we [presumably the U.S. officially] could not be connected with any exchange of information of that nature." Two weeks later, the ambassador again raised with Hull the subject of confidential military and naval staff conferences, saying that "it might be very important to have conversations with respect to these possible future [military] movements so each government would know what was in the mind of the other." Hull once again agreed to bring the matter to the attention of the president but suggested that the talks might better be pursued through diplomatic rather than army and navy channels and emphasized that "it was all important to avoid publicity."[66]

Roosevelt was more forthcoming than was his secretary of state. On 12 July, he discussed the matter with Secretary of the Navy Knox and Admiral Harold R. "Betty" Stark, who had replaced Leahy as chief of naval operations in August 1939. They suggested sending Rear Admiral Robert L. Ghormley, USN, former head of the Navy Department's planning staff and one of the attendees of the secret meetings with the Admiralty's Commander Hampton and CNO Leahy the previous year in Washington. The president agreed, but chose to expand the group to include representatives of the army and army air corps, although for a shorter visit than that proposed for Ghormley. Brigadier General George V. Strong, a War Department planner who was later to become the chief of army intelligence (G-2) for the greater part of the war, and Major General Delos C. Emmons, head of Army Air Corps Headquarters in Washington, were selected.[67] Ghormley was told of his new assignment on 15 July, and on 6 August, he sailed with Strong and Emmons for England on board the SS *Britannic*.[68] As prerequisites to the meeting, the United States had imposed requirements for secrecy and for nonbinding decisions. This guarded and low-key American response to the British initiative was driven in great part by domestic political considerations stemming from the forthcoming November presidential election.

In June, at much the same time that the British ambassador in Washington made his first representation to Hull for naval discussions, Churchill's War Cabinet directed the Admiralty to form a special committee "to examine all aspects of problems of America-British naval cooperation."[69] Admiral Sir Sidney R. Bailey, RN, had been selected to chair the committee that henceforth would bear his name. The Bailey Committee first met on 20 June 1940 and produced its report on 6 August, just in time for the arrival of Ghormley and his party. To prepare and gain approval of a major policy paper such as this in less than two months was a signal accomplishment, and one that indicated how vital such cooperation was to the British government.

Bailey was an excellent choice to head the committee. A former head of the Admiralty Plans Division, he had been recalled to active duty for this critical assignment. At his death in 1942, the *Times* commented that "his connections with and knowledge of the United States [his wife was American, daughter of a U.S. Army colonel] made him the ideal liaison officer with the United States Naval Observers in this country, an appointment he held to the time of his death."[70]

There is no doubt that Bailey's great stature at the Admiralty worked to the advantage of the U.S. Navy. Ghormley's administrative assistant, Lieutenant

Commander (later Vice Admiral) Bernard F. Austin, USN, recalled an incident in which Ghormley had been directed by the Navy Department to obtain urgently needed information thought to be in the Admiralty's files concerning the Japanese Mandated Islands in the Pacific. When approached on the problem, Godfrey demurred, saying that the only way he could provide the information would be to turn his department's entire portfolio on the area over to Ghormley, and this Godfrey could not do without approval of the board of the Admiralty. Austin took the problem to Bailey, who saw no reason that the files could not be loaned to Ghormley and agreed to approach the board on the matter. "Later that afternoon," Austin recounted, "sirens sounded, and up to the Embassy drove a couple of motorcycles with sidecars and riders around them to guard them. And in came this officer messenger and plunked down on my desk the entire portfolio of the Far East from the British Admiralty, and asked me to sign a receipt for it. . . . Admiral Bailey was, throughout our dealing with him, one to inspire confidence and to promote real smooth cooperative effort."[71] Bailey's openness and his effectiveness in spurring unprecedented action from the bureaucratic machinery of the Admiralty were indicative of the magnitude of British government interest in making common cause with the United States during England's dark days in the summer of 1940.

The Bailey Committee began its task by directing the major sections of the naval staff to submit a "wish list" of those items of support they desired from the U.S. Navy and what specific points of cooperation they were prepared to offer in return. Although the resulting report covered all aspects of Anglo-American naval cooperation, a significant portion of the committee's findings dealt with intelligence relationships. In response to the Bailey Committee's direction, Godfrey prepared a memorandum in which he stated that, while he did not want to reveal the whole of the British naval intelligence organization to the United States, he did wish to exchange lists containing the locations of "reporting officers," i.e., those individuals at locations around the world who were specifically tasked to collect and provide information to NID and ONI. He did not desire local cooperation between British and American reporting officers but would encourage liaison between U.S and Royal Navy intelligence centers that were located in the same general area.

When he specified "intelligence centers," Godfrey was either unaware that the U.S. Navy had none or was thinking of those British and American units in the Pacific that were separately engaged in communications intelligence collection against the Imperial Japanese Navy. The Admiralty was particularly interested in obtaining cooperation among British and American direction finding stations scattered throughout the world.

In addition to sharing some information on their respective intelligence organizations, Godfrey desired a full exchange of intelligence generated by the two navies. This exchange could best be achieved, he believed, by stationing American naval officers in NID and British naval officers in ONI to transmit information back and forth. He urged that "as soon as United States co-operation is envisaged, a U.S. Naval Intelligence Officer be appointed to work in N.I.D., . . . where he will be in a position to study our Intelligence organization, sources of information, and to assist in establishing close co-operation prior to the arrival of the Staff advocated [in his recommendation to assign U.S naval officers to NID]."[72]

Admiral Bailey signed the final report of his committee on 6 August 1940. It is clear from the wording of the report that the drafters did not assume that the War Cabinet had decided on a policy of expanded Anglo-American cooperation. The recommendations were offered should such a policy be adopted. What was assumed, however, was that at some point the United States would enter the war on the Allied side. Section VII of the report dealt with intelligence cooperation, enlarging on and making more precise the Godfrey recommendations. The section detailed cooperative initiatives that could be undertaken prior to the United States' entry into the war and other initiatives that would be more appropriate afterward.

No new sources or types of information were to be offered for exchange when the transition from peace to a wartime relationship took place. The embryo intelligence liaison channels that were recommended for immediate opening were to be greatly expanded in both Washington and London once the United States entered the war. In wartime, ONI and NID would continue to operate as separate (as opposed to combined) intelligence centers and would function in close coordination with each other and with the intelligence department of the Naval Service Headquarters in Ottawa. Perhaps fearing the Monroe Doctrinaire attitude of the United States toward foreign intelligence activities in Latin America, the British felt that "it would be undesirable at present to refer to our intelligence centers at Montevideo and Callao."[73]

The Bailey Committee report was an internal British government document that in more recent times would have been stamped "Not Releasable to Foreign Nationals." It was meant to be used by Admiralty representatives at the forthcoming talks with Ghormley and the others in his delegation. However, after Ghormley's arrival in London and prior to the start of the talks, the document was apparently leaked. Austin, Ghormley's assistant, recalled that "Admiral Pound [the first sea lord] inadvertently or advertently, I don't know; disclosed the existence of the paper." Bailey did not want to give the Americans a copy of the report but eventually did so, and it became, according to Austin, "a sort of departure for each phase of our talks with the British." In Austin's view, "the ABC conference, which took place later [beginning officially on 29 January 1941], was shorter and smoother and produced more agreement as a result of the conversations which we had had with the British on the chapters of this paper."[74]

In deference to Secretary of State Hull's desire to avoid publicity concerning Ghormley and his "observers," the British chiefs of staff directed their intelligence subcommittee to examine ways of providing "cover" (their word) for the planned program of visits. The subcommittee adopted the suggestion of Colonel Raymond Lee, the U.S. Army attaché, that the group should be treated "as ordinary visitors coming to this country to study war conditions. It was inadvisable for them to be met, or in any other way treated as out of the ordinary."[75] To disguise their true purpose, the meetings were to be called those of the "Anglo-American Standardization of Arms Committee," and to provide even greater security, Standardization of Arms Committee matters would be referred to only by the code word "Buffalo."[76]

Ghormley and the "observers" arrived in London on 15 August and spent the next few days closeted with American embassy officials and the naval and military attachés. While Ghormley was en route, his title changed. He had originally been assigned as a naval attaché, but since he was senior to Kirk, there was no way that he could assume the title without dealing a significant blow to Kirk's standing in the eyes of the Royal Navy and therefore to his effectiveness. Evidently, Kirk had discussed the problem with Donovan during his late July visit to London. Kirk wrote to Donovan the day before Ghormley's arrival that "the decision to call Rear Admiral Ghormley 'Special Naval Observer' was a good answer. It saves face—which is quite important over here."[77] In later years, Kirk admitted that Ghormley's arrival was "a little awkward" and indicated that perhaps the Navy Department had considered "that a young captain of 50 or so was not competent to deal with the British authorities at a high level."[78] With the protocol problem solved, the two American naval officers worked well together, and as Kirk later said of Ghormley, "he is a fine man, a friend, and we never had any friction of any sort."[79]

Ghormley's first official contact with the Admiralty began on 19 August with a call on A. V. Alexander, who had replaced Churchill as first lord. Alexander, Ghormley reported to Secretary of the Navy Knox, "was most considerate and cooperative," and he said that "if there was any hesitation in giving me information on the part of officers in the Admiralty to let him know and I would obtain any information I desire."[80] This offer appears somewhat ironic in the light of postwar revelations that Alexander, presumably

with the concurrence of Churchill, was not on the list of those cleared to receive communications intelligence; nor was he privy to the secrets of the Operational Intelligence Centre or the Lower War Room, which, during his
visits, had to be "suitably camouflaged for his benefit."[81]

The Anglo-American Standardization of Arms Committee met during the
last two weeks of August and completed its deliberations on the thirty-first.
Since the Americans were merely "observers," they were not empowered to
reach agreements, and no joint document was issued. However, many sensitive areas of potential cooperation were explored "in principle." Just how sensitive the talks became was illustrated in the minutes of the final meeting, in
which it was recorded that General Strong indicated that he felt the time had
come for exchange of intelligence "on a regular basis." "He outlined certain
methods by which the sources of information at the disposal of the United
States might be placed at the disposal of the British Government"—a near-
certain reference to communications intelligence—since the matter was to
be taken up with the prime minister.[82]

By the late summer of 1940, the imminent threat of a German invasion of
the British Isles had receded. American concerns over the British will to continue the war had been in great measure laid to rest, and the first steps toward
a mutual understanding on Anglo-American naval intelligence cooperation
had been taken.

More rapidly in Britain than in the United States, the weak interwar intelligence departments of the Admiralty and the U.S. Navy were strengthened
by infusions of talent and money. The Canadian naval intelligence organization, starting from near zero, began expanding to support the RCN in meeting an anticipated U-boat threat to Allied convoys in the western Atlantic.

Driven by considerations of wartime security and by a sense that sharing information with the United States would be essentially a westbound one-way
street, the British were reluctant to provide information to the neutral United
States. For its part, Washington's response to the principle of Anglo-American
cooperation was tempered by fears that too overt support of the British cause
would have political repercussions at home that would be detrimental to
Franklin D. Roosevelt's unprecedented bid for a third term as president. Following the defeat of France, British disinclination to share gave way to the realization that cooperative intelligence arrangements would help lead the
United States to increased involvement in European affairs, which was vital to
British conduct of the war. What had been in early 1939 a mutually suspicious
acceptance in principle of the need for quid pro quo information exchange

arrangements had, by late August 1940, given way to a search for ways to realize the goal of complete intelligence exchange with no strings attached.

The meetings of the Standardization of Arms Committee marked a significant milestone on the road to Anglo-American intelligence cooperation. Historian Martin Gilbert summed up the importance of the "observers" in the cooperative process: "Under the guise of being a relatively low grade mission to discuss the standardization of arms, the three Americans constituted in fact the first Staff Conversations between Britain and the United States, the one belligerent, the other neutral, but both united in a common and ever closer purpose. Not only were British and American military, naval and air matters becoming more closely interwoven, but in the sphere of Intelligence there was a growing realization of the need to share what was known."[83]

3.

Forging Ahead

The period from the start of Hitler's blitz against England until the Japanese attack on Pearl Harbor saw the war spread from Western Europe to Egypt and North Africa in the fall of 1940, to Yugoslavia and Greece the following spring, and to Russia in the summer and autumn of 1941. Having failed to gain mastery in the air over the British Isles—a necessary prelude to invasion—Hitler shelved plans to attack England and began to look eastward. In the Far East, the threat of war grew as Japan eyed European colonial holdings in Southeast Asia as potential sources for badly needed raw materials.

As the military situation became grimmer, Anglo-American relationships in naval intelligence began to take shape and grow from informal liaison to formal intelligence cooperation. This expansion was accomplished through a series of conferences of American and British military leaders and through subsequent agreement on administrative measures to implement the policy decisions that the conferences had produced. Intelligence organizations on both sides of the Atlantic were fine-tuned to fulfill their wartime responsibilities through critical self-examination of their own operations and through a series of visits by U.S. and Royal Navy intelligence officers to each other's organizations to observe, learn, and prepare.

The Anglo-American Standardization of Arms Committee finished its deliberations at the end of August 1940. Although the talks had been exploratory and the decisions nonbinding on either nation, there remained a mutual sense that the essential first steps toward creating the machinery for formal military cooperation had been taken, especially in the field of intelligence. A year of war had pointed up weaknesses in the British intelligence structure and had provided the impetus for needed changes. Improvements in intelligence techniques and organizations, derived from lessons learned "the hard way," would take place. During the months to come, the foundation of the future Anglo-American intelligence edifice would be put in place. Planning for future intelligence liaison would proceed from the general to the specific. The U.S. Army and Army Air Corps representatives at the Standardization of Arms discussions would return home, but Ghormley would remain in London working with the Bailey Committee.

As the Royal Air Force and Luftwaffe fought for control of the skies over London, Ghormley, Bailey, and their staffs began the painstaking task of turning the "wish list" embodied in the committee report and the "agreements in principle" of the Standardization of Arms Committee into concrete agreements that both sides could accept. They approached the problem on two levels. In early September 1940, Kirk was invited to a meeting of the Bailey Committee to discuss implementation of the Standardization of Arms Committee agreements. He was asked to clarify what General Strong had meant by his call for an exchange of "information." Kirk replied that "he understood the reference was to Intelligence information, particularly cryptography, rather than information on war experience or technical matters." It was explained to him that henceforth "on technical matters"—nonintelligence questions, such as those concerning operations or weapon systems—he was to address the Bailey Committee. The committee would in turn make the necessary representations to the other divisions of the naval staff and expedite their replies. Other official correspondence would continue to go to the secretary of the Admiralty, and liaison on intelligence matters apparently would continue unchanged with the DNI.[1] Three days later, Kirk informed Washington that a "special committee headed by Admiral Sidney Bailey [has been] formed in Admiralty for ALUSNA's consultation in order [to] expedite and assist collection [of] information" and that "this [is] entirely their own idea and I believe in good faith and for [the] purposes stated." Kirk also indicated that "this procedure appears very satisfactory from our point of view."[2]

While conducting what in later years would become known as "working-level" discussions with Kirk, the Bailey Committee was also preparing for "high-level" negotiations with Ghormley. The first item of business was to produce an updated copy of its 6 August report. Section VII of the resulting document, which was dated 11 September 1940, was essentially the same as that issued in August. The potentially sensitive references to British intelligence activities in South America were excised, and a few terms were more fully defined. The term "Anglo-American" of the first iteration was replaced throughout with "British-U.S.," perhaps for greater precision. Finally, some of the actions recommended for inauguration in the first version were now shown as ongoing programs.[3]

Ghormley began his review of the 11 September document the following day. Subsequent meetings were essentially one-on-one. Ghormley and his aide Bernard Austin attended for the American side, and Bailey and one or two experts in the specific topic under discussion represented the Admiralty. Upon completion of the review, the committee sent the first sea lord twelve specific proposals. The seventh dealt with liaison between the intelligence services of the Admiralty and the Navy Department and reiterated the provisions of the 11 September paper.[4]

The Navy Department, presumably following instructions from Roosevelt and Knox, carefully restricted the scope of Ghormley's power to reach an agreement with the British. Should any hint of Anglo-American military concert become public, the ensuing political repercussions could be unfortunate, especially on the eve of the presidential election year. In answer to Ghormley's request for guidance as to the extent of his authority, Admiral Harold R. Stark, the chief of naval operations, added a handwritten postscript to a letter of 16 October that cautioned, "get in on any and all staff conversations you can—go as far as you like in discussions—with the full understanding that you are expressing only your own views as what best to do—'if & when'—but such must not be understood to commit your government in any manner or to any degree—whatsoever."[5] The British, who were pressing for cooperative measures in order to increase the United States' stake in the war, must have found these instructions as irksome as Ghormley probably did.

Detailed discussions on the implementation of the proposals dealing with intelligence began on 23 September 1940 during the sixth meeting of what was by then being referred to in British minutes as the "Joint Bailey Committee." Ghormley and Bailey examined the specifics of Section VII and made recommendations as to those actions that could be undertaken immediately and those that must wait until official American entry into the war. For example, sharing of information on U.S.-British intelligence centers was marked "Exchange now," while cooperation between direction finding stations was marked "Discuss now. Action on intervention."[6] Regarding the agreement to exchange locations of direction finding stations, Austin made a note to himself to "send [the list] to Dept as soon as possible. Br. *Specially* anxious to know where our high freq. stations are."[7]

The fourteenth meeting of the committee dealt with the specific question of intelligence cooperation in the Far East. As the war at sea intensified in both the Atlantic and Mediterranean areas, the British were forced to withdraw ships from the Pacific, thus lessening the Royal Navy's ability to deal with the growing Japanese threat in Asia. Of primary concern was Singapore, considered by the British to be the key to the defense of the Malay Barrier and in turn to the protection of the Imperial lifeline to Australia and New Zealand. Japan's signing of the Tripartite Pact with Germany and Italy on 27 September 1940 had done nothing to lessen British anxiety.

As early as 1939, the Admiralty had asked the United States about the possibility of exchanging information on Japanese activities derived from communications intelligence but had been, as we have seen, rebuffed. British naval intelligence remained eager to tap this source of information and to gain access to other types of intelligence produced by the U.S Asiatic Fleet's listening posts in China and in the Philippines. Because the United States had something of value to offer, intelligence cooperation in the Far East became a major goal of the Admiralty in implementing the informal agreements made by the Standardization of Arms Committee. The participants in the 16 October meeting urged their governments to establish both intelligence liaison mechanisms and secure communications channels in advance of potential hostilities. They suggested that these ends could best be met by a prompt exchange of liaison officers between the U.S. Asiatic Fleet staff and the Royal Navy chief of intelligence staff, Singapore. Additionally, "the importance of inter-change of information between British and United States naval attachés at Tokyo was mentioned."[8]

By November 1940, Ghormley's proposals and those of the Bailey Committee had reached Washington. Section VII, which dealt with communications as well as intelligence matters, was sent for comment to both the director of naval communications and the director of naval intelligence, and their responses were to be coordinated by the director of war plans. Whether it was because of the ongoing feud between Plans and Intelligence for hegemony in the intelligence field or because of a reluctance to commit himself, the DNI's response was cool. Concerning the recommendation that information be shared now on intelligence centers, the DNI huffed that "steps will be taken to effect any further exchange which may appear necessary or desirable." Regarding direction finding stations, the DNI deferred to the director of naval communications on the question of "what further information, if any, should be furnished the British and requested from them."[9] Despite the attitude of the DNI, by 26 November, Ghormley had been informed by the chief of naval operations that he was in general agreement with Section IV (intercommunication) and the communication portions of Section VII, which included exchanging codes for intelligence use as well as sharing direction finding site information.[10]

Once consensus had been reached and the resulting agreements passed to the British naval staff and the American Navy Department for ratification, the long-term work of the committee began. Until it was disbanded in September 1941, the Bailey Committee received and processed requests for operational, technical, and intelligence information from the U.S. naval attaché. Conversely, it levied on the naval attaché British requests for information from American sources. By 6 May 1941, Bailey was able to report to the first sea lord that, "So far 433 memoranda have been addressed by the Committee to the U.S. naval attaché, and 331 memoranda have been received from him."[11]

Unfortunately, the numbers are not a good indicator of which side received the greater benefit from the exchange. Memoranda were numbered consecutively without regard to whether they were a request or a response, so there is no way of telling how many actual requests were made by either side. For example, in Memorandum 16 of 19 September 1940, the United States requested copies of interrogations of captured U-boat crews, and in Memorandum 381 of 9 June 1941, the United States provided data on the Japanese naval building program, "specifically requested by the Admiralty."[12] The relative value of the exchange to either side becomes even more difficult to assess when one remembers that, under the terms of Section VII of the Bailey Committee agreements, the British naval attaché in Washington was also providing information to the Department of the Navy and was receiving requests for information from it. The British certainly felt that it more blessed politically to give. After several months of the program, Bailey recommended to his superiors that, "in order to emphasize in higher places the wealth of hardly bought information which the Navy Department are getting from us . . . the British Ambassador in Washington be informed."[13] Bailey's superiors agreed.

It would be difficult to overstate the importance of the Bailey Committee to the development of Anglo-American naval intelligence cooperation. What had been an informal modus vivendi reached between the British and American naval attachés and their respective host governments for the exchange of intelligence in London and Washington had become formalized by the terms of Section VII. Henceforth, it was agreed that "the British and the U.S. Naval Liaison Missions in Washington and London respectively should . . . include an officer solely for intelligence duties and liaison."[14]

Despite the improvement in intelligence exchange brought about through the efforts of the Bailey Committee, snags appeared from time to time in the system—on both sides. In January 1941, the British naval attaché in Washington complained to his DNI, Godfrey, that he had to depend on the "spontaneous disgorging" of handouts from the War and Navy Departments. "As yet there is no offer from the Navy Department to see their files of documents and information is received on unsigned, unheaded slips of paper, the same method being employed by the War Department."[15] This unstructured, almost clandestine provision of information to the Admiralty's representatives in Washington was indicative of the U.S. Navy Department's determination to avoid becoming too involved with the British at a time when the United States was at least nominally neutral.

At the same time in London, the U.S. military attaché, newly promoted Brigadier General Raymond Lee, was complaining, apparently to anyone in the British intelligence establishment who would listen, about the withholding of information from his office. On 6 January 1941, he approached the new British director of military intelligence, General Francis Davidson, and asked for special treatment for U.S. military attachés and for daily reporting on the general situation.[16] Two days later, Lee again raised the intelligence flow question, this time with General Hastings "Pug" Ismay, military secretary to the War Cabinet. Ismay told him that one of the reasons for the reduction in information was that "the Prime Minister is completely rampant on the question of secrecy and is cutting down the number of people in the British government who know anything about what is going on."[17] Since the efforts of the Joint Bailey Committee were relatively unpublicized, naval intelligence was able to maintain a low profile and escape this particular round of the prime minister's periodic security purges.

In late January 1941, presidential confidante Harry Hopkins arrived in London on a mission similar to that undertaken by Donovan in July 1940. The avowed reason for the trip was to determine what immediate aid the United States could provide Great Britain. President Roosevelt, perhaps triggered by a stream of pessimistic telegrams in the final weeks of 1940 from Joseph Kennedy, the American ambassador in London, had sent Hopkins to England with the underlying purpose of assessing Churchill's and the nation's will to continue resistance to the Germans.[18]

As they had in Donovan's case, British leaders prepared carefully for the visit. The Admiralty canvassed its various divisions for items to be considered for discussion with Hopkins. While most responses dealt with military equipment, NID wished to ask Hopkins "to try to get a better U.S. intelligence service organized in places where we cannot keep consuls ourselves, e.g. French ports." Admiral T. S. V. Phillips, vice chief of the naval staff, concurred and recommended that U.S. "naval officers in a civilian capacity" be assigned to ports in metropolitan France and North Africa.[19] Apparently, previous British appeals to Donovan to provide American consular reporting from French ports had been only marginally productive.[20] The abortive British attempt to seize the Vichy-controlled port of Dakar in September 1940 and the Royal

Navy's July bombardment of the French fleet at Mers-el-Kebir (near Oran) had—as Martin Gilbert noted in a masterpiece of understatement—"caused considerable bitterness in France."[21] As a result, most British sources of intelligence in French territories had dried up.

In March 1941, the U.S. government concluded the Murphy-Weygand Agreement, an economic accord with Vichy France that provided for American shipment of food and raw materials to North Africa in return for a French promise that these goods would not be transshipped to Europe or be allowed to fall into German hands.[22] The agreement was negotiated by Robert D. Murphy, counselor of the U.S. embassy in Vichy, and General Maxime Weygand, Vichy's proconsul in North Africa. To insure that the terms of the accord were carried out, the French permitted the United States to station "control officers" at various ports in North Africa. By agreement among the State, War, and Navy Departments, these new vice-consular positions were filled by military officers. They were to operate in civilian clothes and were to "observe the military and naval situation in North Africa while carrying on their control work."[23]

Robert Murphy remained in North Africa to supervise the intelligence collection team that not only provided current information to the Anglo-American intelligence community but also collected basic information on terrain, coast and landing beaches, and ports and harbors that was later used in the November 1942 American landings in North Africa.[24] The seed of an idea, planted by Admiralty intelligence, seemed to have germinated.

By the spring of 1941, with the exception of reports resulting from the Murphy-Weygand Agreements, the British had acquired little new intelligence from increased cooperation with the United States. In British eyes, the significance of cooperative efforts such as the Bailey-Ghormley negotiations was not so much in the value of the information gained but in the development of the sharing process itself. For one country to share its intelligence secrets with another involves what is in effect a surrender of a portion of national sovereignty, a step not lightly taken. In the secret world of intelligence, to expose sources, to share methods, is to make oneself vulnerable. With vulnerability comes dependence. For Britain, early wartime exigencies made the risks inherent in Anglo-American interdependence in intelligence acceptable.

As the British rushed preparations to withstand the German invasion expected in the fall of 1940, the government became intensely concerned with its intelligence organizations' ability to fulfill their wartime responsibilities. On the Continent, the agent networks of the Secret Intelligence Service were in a state of disarray. Ever since the start of hostilities in September 1939, Britain's Secret Intelligence Service had lost ground on the Continent. First to go were SIS stations in Berlin, Vienna, and Warsaw, followed in due course by those in Scandinavia, the Low Countries, and France. By the fall of 1940, SIS had stations only in the neutral capitals of Stockholm, Bern, Madrid, and Lisbon.[25] Communications intelligence, while helpful, was spotty. Even the intelligence prowess of the Royal Navy was in question. "It is most galling," the commander in chief, Home Fleet, wrote to the Admiralty in June 1940, "that the enemy should know just where our ships, from battleships to cruisers, always are, whereas we generally learn where his major forces are when he sinks one or more of our ships."[26]

Concerned by this dearth of secret information the Chamberlain government directed Maurice Hankey, the supervising minister of both the SIS (MI-6) and the Counter-Intelligence Service (MI-5), to conduct a "full and searching inquiry" into the activities of the two organizations. The report that resulted was considered so sensitive that "during the invasion scare in the fall of 1940 an order was given to destroy all copies—lest they should fall into the enemy's hands."[27] By the summer of 1940, SIS had begun rebuilding in those countries overrun by Germany, and its chief, Colonel Stewart Menzies, was able to inform the British Joint Chiefs of Staff of his "considerable hope of being able to provide a rapid and efficient intelligence service."[28]

As the British examined their intelligence needs, they grew to realize that no single type of information could, without integration of data from many other sources, provide a sufficiently authoritative picture of what to expect from their enemies. The mechanism for coordination of multisource intelligence had existed since 1936 in the form of the Joint Intelligence Committee (JIC), which the British chiefs of staff had created to provide intelligence support to its planning staff. For a variety of reasons, including individual service hostility toward any intelligence not produced "in-house" and the JIC's failure to take the initiative in providing assessments on important questions, the committee did not play a major role in the prewar intelligence process.[29]

As had been done in the case of the Secret Intelligence and Counter-Intelligence Services, Churchill ordered a review of naval and military intelligence and its role in governmental decision making. As a result of the inquiry, "the JIC was given new terms of reference which confirmed it as the central agency for producing operational intelligence appreciations and for bringing them to the attention of the Prime Minister, the War Cabinet and the Chiefs of Staff." The role of the JIC was to provide "the principal and critical place in the central British war machine where intelligence from all Bureaus and Ministries is considered for application to Joint War Plans."[30]

In essence, the British government had opted for a single central point for intelligence analysis instead of accepting the uncoordinated inputs of the individual service intelligence organizations. This move to provide coordinated intelligence "appreciations" to top-level British leaders was extremely significant to the development of Anglo-American intelligence cooperation. From the autumn of 1940 onward, the British, convinced that a joint intelligence product was superior to that achieved by the American way of allowing each service to provide its own intelligence, lost no opportunity to urge the United States to adopt the British system. Dissimilar national intelligence structures probably retarded overall Anglo-American intelligence cooperation but may have worked to the advantage of navy-to-navy intelligence ties, since, in the absence of an American JIC, there was really no other path to choose. As we shall see, later intelligence cooperation between the two naval staffs began to suffer as a more structured joint and combined system for direction of the war emerged.

Contributing to America's delay in adopting the British JIC system was the inability of the U.S. War and Navy Departments' intelligence organizations to work together. Lacking the stimulus of an enemy poised to invade, American military leaders were much slower than their British counterparts to embrace the concept of coordinated decision making generally and coordinated intelligence specifically. A Joint Army Navy Board had existed in the United States since 1903. However, the board's chief weakness, and one that persisted until the formation of the Joint Chiefs of Staff in 1942, was that its authority was limited to making policy recommendations that could be ignored by either service if it so chose. In 1938, a Standing Liaison Committee, consisting of the undersecretary of state and the two service chiefs, was created to ensure that military and diplomatic policies were coordinated. This body, too, lacked binding authority. It met sporadically. "During 1940, for instance, it met only nine times."[31]

Unlike the Admiralty's NID, ONI had been unsuccessful in convincing Navy Department leaders of the need for its intelligence in their decision making. What intelligence was used in planning was provided by the planners themselves. Even the CNO, Admiral Harold R. Stark, looked to the War Plans Division rather than to ONI for intelligence and analysis.[32] Because of this de facto shift in intelligence responsibility, the British were faced with the vexing problem of which administrative entity to approach on questions of information exchange—Plans or Intelligence.

The first formal attempt to systematize American intelligence activities did not originate with the military, nor did it involve foreign intelligence. In addition to the Federal Bureau of Investigation (FBI) and the military departments, most of the major U.S. government agencies by the late 1930s had their own investigative organizations examining domestic subversive activities. There was no clearly defined coordinating agency, and the FBI's attempts to establish its primacy among the various warring civilian departments—State, Treasury, and Post Office, to name but a few—met with predictable bureaucratic opposition. Finally, on 26 June 1939, President Roosevelt sent a directive to the Cabinet in which he indicated that "investigation of all espionage, counterespionage and sabotage matters was to be controlled and handled only by the FBI and the Intelligence Divisions of the War Department and the Navy" and that "the heads of these three agencies were to constitute an Interdepartmental Intelligence Coordinating Committee."[33] This committee functioned only with regard to matters internal to the U.S. government, and there is no indication that it ever conducted liaison with any foreign intelligence agencies. Foreign cooperative arrangements, such as those between the FBI and the British Secret Intelligence Service and between ONI and the same Secret Intelligence Service, were carefully compartmented on an agency-to-agency basis and the relationships jealously guarded—to the detriment of Anglo-American intelligence cooperation.

As the conflict in Europe deepened and spread in 1940, extension of the formal domestic coordination machinery to the field of foreign intelligence activities soon became a necessity. Vincent Astor, Roosevelt's private intelligence agent in Manhattan, may have acted as a catalyst in bringing intelligence coordination problems to the president's attention. He wrote to Roosevelt in April 1940 that the Department of State had lodged a complaint in London that a British Secret Intelligence Service representative, under diplomatic "cover" in New York, was passing information directly to U.S. intelligence agencies rather than going through State Department channels. The British government subsequently instructed the SIS to deal only through the Department of State, and this, Astor believed, was causing unacceptable delays in the material getting to those who needed it. Citing a recent example, Astor informed the president, "It is certainly a bit difficult to conduct a blitzkrieg of our own against malefactors when information becomes stymied in department files for six weeks."[34] Astor must have seen the State Department as a threat to his carefully cultivated ties with the SIS in New York, whose communications facilities were providing a secure channel for sensitive information from London to reach the Office of Naval Intelligence and, if of sufficient importance, the president.

At the end of June 1940, the president directed that foreign intelligence responsibility was to be divided among the FBI and army and navy intelligence. The FBI would be charged with foreign intelligence activities in the

Western Hemisphere, while "the existing Military Intelligence and Naval Intelligence branches should cover the rest of the world, as and when necessity arises."[35] Despite the presidential directive, no real degree of coordination was achieved, and interagency struggles over intelligence "turf" continued. However, one positive result of the president's decision was that it gave ONI official sanction to strengthen its ties with several British intelligence organizations, including the Admiralty, that heretofore had been cooperating informally in the exchange of foreign intelligence.

The final attempt to coordinate army and navy intelligence policy prior to 7 December 1941 ended in failure. On 26 September 1941, senior officers of the army and navy Plans and Intelligence Divisions met "to establish a system for coordinating and handling important strategic and tactical information." However, their hopes for a cooperative approach to intelligence analysis foundered on the refusal of Admiral Richmond K. Turner, Navy War Plans Division chief, to permit joint evaluations. "Admiral Turner, like many naval officers of his generation harbored a hearty distrust of his sister service."[36] The group ended the day deadlocked and did not meet again until 9 December 1941.

The lack of coordinated policy and the prevalence of bureaucratic infighting among members of the fledgling American intelligence community did not go unremarked in London, by both American and British observers. Brigadier General Raymond E. Lee, the American military attaché, commented on 27 May 1941 that "it has come to a pretty pass when the American Navy can come to an agreement with the British Navy and the American Army can come to an agreement with the British Army, more easily than the American Army can come to an agreement with the American Navy."[37]

Lee's sentiments were shared by Admiral Godfrey. Following a May 1941 visit to Washington, the British DNI wrote, "we already knew that the relations between the U.S. Army and Navy were bad, but we did not realize how bad until we tried to get them to see eye to eye and collaborate with each other and with the State Department about this supremely important matter of intelligence and its allied activities."[38] Unfortunately, this situation was to persist until well after United States' entry into the war. The failure of U.S. intelligence agencies to coordinate their activities and analyses not only hindered effectiveness at home but also hampered intelligence cooperation abroad. Born of wartime necessity, British achievements in the coordination of planning and of intelligence matters were not to be emulated in the United States until 1942, and even then, reluctantly.

*   *   *

While the United States was attempting to get its intelligence house in order and to promote cooperation among the several government departments engaged in intelligence matters, pressure was increasing on both sides of the Atlantic for high-level military staff talks to build on the cooperative foundation laid at the Standardization of Arms Committee meetings. On 12 November 1940, shortly after the U.S. election results were known, the chief of naval operations prepared a memorandum for the secretary of the navy in which he reviewed the current world situation and offered four alternative courses of action for the U.S. Navy. Admiral Stark designated these alternatives in military terminology as Plans ABLE through DOG. Plan DOG, the one favored by Stark, called for recognition that the Western Hemisphere and the Atlantic were the areas of paramount strategic concern to the United States and that the Pacific was of secondary import. Stark recommended staff conversations with the British and Canadians in the Atlantic and the Dutch and British in the Pacific, to implement the concept. However, it was not until January 1941 that the president agreed and issued instructions that the concepts embodied in Plan DOG be used as a basis for strategic planning.[39]

The gist of Plan DOG was made available to the Royal Navy in both London and Washington. Stark sent a copy to Ghormley and Kirk with the admonition that the document was unofficial and that "under no circumstances should the British be given a copy and in fact I [Stark] think it would probably be best for the British not to know that it is in your possession."[40] In the same letter, Stark indicated that he would let Captain Arthur W. Clarke, RN, read the plan in the Navy Department but would not permit him to make any notes. Clarke had been sent from Admiralty Plans Division to Washington in July 1940 as assistant naval attaché to advise on questions of naval cooperation.[41]

Even before the results of the American elections were known, Britain had started to consider additional initiatives that would build on the foundations laid by the Standardization of Arms Committee understandings. British naval planners began by giving thought to the selection of delegates for desired staff conferences with the Americans. The first sea lord, Admiral Sir Dudley Pound, alerted Rear Admiral R. M. Bellairs on 9 October that he should be prepared to lead the Admiralty delegation. Bellairs had retired from the Royal Navy in 1932 and had participated as an adviser in the arms limitations treaty conferences of the 1930s, thus gaining negotiating experience with the U.S. Navy. At the beginning of the war, he had been recalled to active duty in the Admiralty, where he had served primarily as a planner.[42]

Pound pressed the case for Anglo-American naval staff conferences on American special naval observer Robert Ghormley, and also urged their consideration on the British ambassador to Washington, Lord Lothian, during his visit to London in November. Following his return to the United States, Lothian was able to inform London on 29 November that the president had agreed to staff talks in Washington, to take place as soon as arrangements could be made. The resulting American-British conversations, known as ABC-1, took place from 29 January to 27 March 1941.[43]

While the American War Department and the British War Office and Air Ministry were in favor of the talks, the real impetus came from the two navies.[44] Both the Navy Department and the Admiralty prepared carefully, and both were well represented. The U.S. Navy delegation was led by Rear Admiral Ghormley, recalled temporarily from London for the discussions, and included Navy Department Plans Division chief, Rear Admiral Richmond K. Turner, who was also deeply involved in the department's intelligence process, and Captain Alan G. Kirk, who returned from London to participate but remained in Washington after the conference to become the new director of naval intelligence.

In addition to Rear Admiral Bellairs, the British delegation included Rear Admiral Victor H. Danckwerts, former director of plans in the Admiralty. Joining them in Washington was Captain Clarke, the Royal Navy coordination expert to whom Plan DOG had been revealed. Ghormley and Brigadier General Lee, the U.S. military attaché, London, traveled with the British delegation on board Britain's newest battleship, HMS *King George V*, which was transporting Lord Halifax, the new British ambassador, to Washington. At this rather low point in the war, one suspects that the pride of the Royal Navy was selected to carry the delegates more for reasons of prestige than for the relatively greater protection against U-boat attack that its speed afforded.

British positions on potential conference issues had been prepared in detail and in great secrecy. Lee noted in his diary that the British delegation had declined to give its American fellow travelers any information on what it planned to propose prior to embarkation, ostensibly for reasons of security, but agreed to do so once at sea.[45]

The U.S. Joint Planning Committee prepared with equal care. In late January 1941, the committee recommended to the Joint Board that ONI should summarize intelligence on the strength, disposition, and building programs of the British, French, German, and Italian navies. In addition, ONI should prepare brief estimates of the political, economic, and financial situations of each country with respect to its ability to sustain military operations. ONI was also asked to provide statistics on British merchant shipping losses and on the British merchant navy building program. In the same memorandum, the Joint Planning Committee recommended that the U.S. delegation adopt a firm position regarding the British proposals "because the United States can safeguard the North American Continent . . . whether allied with Britain or not," but "Great Britain cannot encompass the defeat of Germany unless the United States provides that nation with direct military assistance, plus a far greater degree of material aid than is being given now." The committee warned that "never absent from British minds are their post-war interests, commercial and military. We should likewise safeguard our own eventual interests."[46] Concern for protection of national interests was a preoccupation of U.S. Navy planners as well, even when cooperation was at its most fruitful, and it was a theme that was to recur with increasing frequency in the later years of the war.

Even as both sides prepared for a historic meeting to create the machinery for arguably the closest and most extensive cooperative effort ever achieved between sovereign nations, the seeds of discord were being sown. Mutual suspicions of seeking postwar advantage were to become a leitmotif running through the Anglo-American wartime cooperative experience, affecting intelligence as well as other cooperative ventures.

ABC-1, the short title given to the 27 March 1941 report of the U.S.-British conversations, "must be recognized as the true opening of formal permanent relations between American and British Staffs."[47] The stated purpose of the conversations was "to determine the best methods by which the armed forces of the United States and British Commonwealth, with its present Allies, could defeat Germany and the Powers allied to her, should the United States be compelled to resort to war." To realize the objective of defeating Germany, "the Atlantic and European area is considered to be the decisive theater." Were Japan to enter the war, "the Military strategy in the Far East will be defensive."[48]

To implement the agreements contained in ABC-1, the conferees agreed to exchange military missions. Provision was also made for the exchange of U.S. liaison officers with those of the Dominions: Canada, Australia, and New Zealand. By August 1941, Canadian-American cooperation had progressed to the point that a second joint defense plan had been prepared, updating the original plan of August 1940. Anglo-American talks, in which Australia and New Zealand participated, were also under way in the Far East. Representatives of the Dominions sat as members of the British ABC-1 delegation in its private meetings but were not present at the combined U.S.-U.K. discussions.

ABC-1 was to have a profound effect on the U.S., Royal, and Royal Canadian Navies. Under its terms, the United States assumed responsibility for convoy protection in the western sector of the Atlantic, and with this responsibility came operational control of all naval units—U.S., British, and Canadian—involved in convoy protection. This subordination, while agreeable to the British, did not sit well with the Canadians and later would give rise to problems in which intelligence served as an unintended catalyst. In September 1941, the U.S. Navy provided escort for its first convoy, and nearly simultaneously, Canadian Atlantic and Newfoundland naval forces passed to the operational control of the U.S. commander in chief, Atlantic Fleet.[49] Until the time of ABC-1, Canadian-American naval cooperation had been limited to informal discussions in early 1941 between the Canadian naval attaché in Washington and the U.S. Navy concerning provision of submarine support for the antisubmarine warfare training that was badly needed by the Canadian navy.[50]

Intelligence cooperation, while not a burning issue during the ABC-1 discussions, was addressed. The final report, issued on 29 March 1941, contained provisions that served to formalize existing ad hoc information exchange arrangements.[51] Once again, the British were more willing to explore the uncharted waters of full intelligence exchange than were the Americans. On 6 March, the British delegation to ABC-1 submitted the following draft paragraph for consideration. "*Intelligence*. All relevant information about enemy or neutral powers that may come into the possession of the United States or British Governments will be fully and promptly exchanged. United States and British intelligence officers will be associated with the appropriate intelligence organizations in the United States or Great Britain and in their overseas territories as required."[52]

The thrust of the British paragraph on intelligence was significantly altered through negotiation. In its final form, the ABC-1 agreement stated that "existing Military intelligence organizations of the two Powers will operate as independent intelligence agencies, but will maintain close liaison with each other in order to ensure the full and prompt exchange of pertinent information concerning war operations. Intelligence liaison will be established not only through the Military Missions but also between all echelons of command in the field with respect to matters which affect their operations."[53]

In all probability, the American negotiators were unable to accept two major points in the original British proposal. The first British version called for exchange of "all relevant information on enemy and neutral powers." If the United States had agreed, all information derived from codebreaking activities would have had to be revealed—something the Navy Department would have found premature at best, considering that the United States was not even officially in the war. Limiting the terms of intelligence exchange to "pertinent information concerning war operations" considerably narrowed the scope of the agreement. The British draft also called for Royal Navy intelligence officers to be physically located in U.S. Navy intelligence centers. Imbued with a strong traditional distrust of British motives, the U.S. Navy Department might well have seen exchange of personnel as an underlying move to gain national advantage rather than to promote wartime cooperation. In the months that followed, the United States was to be equally unresponsive to subsequent British offers to combine American and British intelligence-producing organizations.

Admiral Ghormley returned to his duties in London shortly after the conclusion of the ABC-1 agreements. On 26 April 1941, he wrote to Admiral Pound, the first sea lord, that President Roosevelt had approved "the methods envisaged by ABC-1" for Anglo-American cooperation and that the CNO desired that terms of ABC-1 be placed into effect "as rapidly as practicable."[54] In the case of intelligence, however, the CNO did not instruct his attachés and observers abroad to implement the provisions for close cooperation contained in ABC-1 until less than two weeks before the attack on Pearl Harbor.[55] Until his hand was forced by the deteriorating situation in the Far East, the CNO may have felt more comfortable retaining closer control over intelligence liaison with the British by keeping it on a headquarters-to-headquarters basis, rather than by authorizing cooperation at all echelons of command.

Ghormley's return to London in April 1941 was marked by a significant increase in his authority. Although his title remained special naval observer, he and his small staff began to operate as the nucleus of the U.S. military mission called for under the terms of the ABC-1 agreements. It will be remembered that when Ghormley first arrived in London in the early fall of 1940, he had been directed to operate in a quasi-private capacity—all views expressed by him were to be considered personal and not a commitment on the part of the U.S. government.[56] On 5 April, the chief of naval operations sent Ghormley a new letter of instruction broadening the scope of his activities. In addition to performing his purely naval duties as the representative of the CNO, he was to negotiate with the British "on military affairs of common interest" that bore on the implementation of ABC-1. All matters arising in London that required joint decisions of the U.S. and British military chiefs were to be communicated to Washington via his office and not through any other military or diplomatic channels. In the event of U.S. entry into the war, Ghormley was told to expect orders designating him the naval member of the U.S. military mission in London, as well as commander in chief of U.S. naval forces in North Europe, and to plan accordingly.[57]

Prior to Ghormley's return, changes had taken place in the American leadership in England. Kirk had remained in Washington as the new director of naval intelligence. In March, Captain Charles H. Lockwood, USN, had assumed Kirk's duties as U.S. naval attaché in London and, in addition, had been designated chief of staff to the special naval observer. This "double-hatting" had the effect of placing all American naval liaison activities—including those concerning intelligence, which previously had been within the purview of the naval attaché—directly or indirectly under Ghormley's control.

Also in March, John Gilbert Winant, twice governor of New Hampshire and former chairman of the Social Security Board, had replaced Joseph P. Kennedy as U.S. ambassador to Great Britain. Apparently, Winant was not overly impressed with the U.S. naval representation in London at the time of his arrival. In early April, he cabled the president that he should consider sending a ranking naval officer, such as Admiral Stark or Admiral Pratt, "over here for a brief period in order to bring you first hand the total picture of high naval policy as it has been developed so far in this war." Winant felt that there was "some hesitation" in giving the military attachés complete information but that "the Prime Minister and all others concerned would gladly give . . . a man, known to be in immediate personal contact with you, the whole story."[58] Winant may have felt more confident that "high naval policy" was being adequately reported after Ghormley's return to his post. A few months later, he cabled the president about the difficulties in synchronizing actions in London with developing military policies in Washington but stated that "Ghormley has been most helpful in keeping me informed."[59]

While the United States was making substitutions in its team in London following ABC-1, the British were working to improve intelligence liaison with the U.S. Navy by relaxing some of the restraints previously imposed on intelligence sharing. American observers had been assigned to certain Royal Navy ships and shore stations since September 1940, but observers' access to operational and intelligence information had been strictly limited. The Admiralty had directed that the Americans were not to be shown certain recognition manuals, aircraft recognition signals, certain intelligence reports, and "information and intelligence from Most Secret sources."[60]

The post-ABC-1 change in attitude was reflected in the instructions issued in April 1941 by the Admiralty to commander in chief, western approaches. American observers were to be "granted every facility to study the organization and working of your Headquarters." The observers were to be afforded access to all types of information but were to be asked "in the interests of security, to confine this information to as few persons as possible and to limit its intercommunication as narrowly as practicable for efficiency."[61]

Anglo-American initiatives to develop a common attack on German and Japanese codes were indicative of the new spirit of cooperation engendered by ABC-1. Information derived from communications intercepts had been exchanged previously. However, little had been accomplished in the area of sharing the methods and equipment by which the codes were broken. The first major Anglo-American cooperative efforts in the field of code breaking, as opposed to merely exchanging decoded information, occurred in the spring of 1941. When HMS *King George V* returned to England in February 1941, following delivery of the new British ambassador to the United States, it carried as passengers four American officers, two army and two navy. They were to remain in the United Kingdom for a ten-week period "to confer with the British Code and Cipher Section on general problems of cryptography and cryptanalysis."[62]

The navy report of this mission has either disappeared or is still being withheld from the public. However, the army officers' report, made in April 1941 to the assistant chief of staff G-2 (Intelligence), War Department, is held by the National Archives in Washington. The visiting Americans found the British both "cooperative" and "open-handed" in sharing information. "We were invited to ask questions about anything we saw, no doors were closed to us and copies were furnished of any material which we considered of possible assistance to the United States."[63] In addition to receiving detailed information on the work being carried on at Bletchley Park, the visitors were shown the British direction finding network, nearby communication intercept sites, the Admiralty's communications center, and the Operational Intelligence Centre.[64] Probably the extent of British cooperation that so impressed the visitors was overstated, but it certainly was much greater than at any previous time, due in no small part to a last-minute decision by the prime minister to let slip at least some of the wraps surrounding British code-breaking activities. During the latter part of the American team's visit, Sir Stewart Menzies, with overall responsibility for Bletchley Park because of his position as director of the Secret Intelligence Service, informed Churchill that the British chiefs of staff favored revealing the progress made in "probing German Armed Force cryptography" to the visitors. In asking for permission to make the revelations Menzies assured the prime minister that disclosures would "be confined to the mechanized devices which we utilize and not to showing the results."[65] Churchill's assent, given the next day, opened the door.

A likely reason for the warm reception given this low-ranking military delegation was that the Americans brought with them two copies of the "Purple" machine,[66] created by U.S. Army personnel to decrypt high-level Japanese diplomatic traffic. The nickname "purple" was used to denote the cryptographic system as well as the machine, which duplicated those in actual use by the Japanese. For security reasons, all American work on Japanese military and diplomatic crypto-systems had been hidden behind the term "Magic." Supposedly President Roosevelt was the first to use the term when he was introduced to the results of the American attacks on Japanese codes.[67] Similarly, the British used the term "Enigma" to refer to their machine used to decrypt German military traffic, and the term "ULTRA" as a general cover word for "high grade cypher intelligence."[68] The Government Code and Cypher School retained one American Purple machine at Bletchley Park and sent the second on to Singapore to assist in British code-breaking efforts against the Japanese. It was moved to New Delhi following the fall of Malaya to the Japanese in 1942.[69]

The Americans spent much of their time at Bletchley Park explaining the workings of the Purple machine to their British counterparts. In return, the visitors received detailed information on British success to date against the German Enigma, including word of Bletchley Park's largely unsuccessful attempts to date to break into the variant system used by the German Navy. They were shown and instructed in the operation of the machine, called the "bombe" by the British, used in breaking German ciphers and were told of British success against Italian codes. No offer of a reciprocal gift of an Enigma machine for the United States was made,[70] probably because the British wished American cryptographers to continue their concentration on Japanese codes and to leave German naval Enigma to them. This attitude would change reluctantly by 1943 when the U.S. Navy's newly developed cryptanalytical equipment proved superior to that of the British.[71]

The army report indicated that "the Naval officers spent a good deal of their time on technical matters such as intercept and radio-direction finding (D.F.). They have brought back a complete D.F. installation which represents Britain's furthest advances along these lines." This acquisition must have been well received by the U.S. Navy's technical experts, since U.S direction finding equipment in use at the time was in much need of modernization.[72]

Events of the summer of 1941 gave further evidence of the shift in Anglo-American intelligence relationships from generalized cooperation to specific coordination. In May, Admiral John Godfrey, the British director of naval intelligence, traveled to Washington for a series of meetings with American and British intelligence officials. Godfrey had several reasons for making a trip to the United States and Canada at this critical moment. Since he had become director of naval intelligence, most of Godfrey's experience with the

workings of American intelligence had been gained not from personal observation but from his relationships with Americans in London and from reports
by the British naval attaché in Washington. The product of this experience
was both encouraging and frustrating. Much had been accomplished, but
much more remained to be done if full partnership in naval intelligence was
to be realized. The time for personal diplomacy seemed at hand, especially
since his "old friend"[73] and colleague in London during the 1940 blitz, Alan
Kirk, was now the American director of naval intelligence. One can imagine
that only the most serious considerations would have caused the British DNI
to leave his post for an extended journey to a neutral country at a moment
when the Royal Navy was fighting for its life in both the Atlantic and the
Mediterranean.

By the spring of 1941, Godfrey had become increasingly concerned over
the problem of coordinating American, British, and Canadian intelligence
on German U-boat activities in the Atlantic. In March 1941, Germany had
expanded the zone in which its submarines were allowed to operate without
restriction to include the area around Iceland. The following month, the
United States expanded its security zone eastward to include Greenland and
Iceland, overlapping that of Germany and increasing the likelihood of hostile encounters between U.S. Navy units and German U-boats.[74] At that
time neither Ottawa nor Washington possessed a focal point for antisubmarine intelligence similar to that of the Admiralty's Operational Intelligence
Centre, which brought together in a single location all the various types of
information necessary to provide a comprehensive picture of enemy U-boat
operations Atlantic-wide. Godfrey hoped to set in motion the machinery to
develop similar centers in Canada and in the United States.

Godfrey had heard from the British naval attaché in Washington of the interagency rivalries among American intelligence organizations, of the attaché's problems in obtaining desired intelligence from American sources,
and of his perception that American intelligence reporting was of a lower
quality than that of similar British products.[75] Godfrey determined that the
way to remedy American shortcomings in intelligence was to share British
methods and experience through a "complete fusion of the British and American intelligence services."[76] Godfrey was backed in this ambitious plan by
his colleagues on the Joint Intelligence Committee and by their superiors, the
British chiefs of staff, who lent Godfrey their authority to pursue his intelligence integration goals while in Washington.[77] In addition, Godfrey was concerned about the lack of a single organization to coordinate the secret
intelligence activities of the various American government agencies. He
wished the United States to profit from what he perceived as a British error

in having four separate organizations, all involved in clandestine operations and secret intelligence activities, and to adopt a single, unified American structure.[78]

Godfrey departed for New York on 24 May 1941, stopping en route to meet with British naval intelligence representatives in Lisbon. Because of Portugal's position as a neutral, it had become a key listening post for both the Allies and the Axis and was, therefore, of particular interest to the British DNI. Godfrey was accompanied by his personal assistant, Lieutenant Commander Ian Fleming, RNVR. Fleming's presence on the trip was no accident of protocol. In the spring of 1939, Godfrey had selected Fleming, then a rising young stockbroker, as his personal assistant on the advice of highly placed persons in the British financial community, and he had done so both for Fleming's contacts in the British establishment and for his ability to get along with people. Fleming's role was greater than his title "personal assistant" would imply. He became Godfrey's personal troubleshooter within the Naval Intelligence Division, as well as the DNI's representative to numerous interdepartmental government committees and conferences. Admiral Sir Norman Denning, one of Godfrey's senior assistants throughout his time as DNI, who subsequently became DNI himself after the war, commented of Fleming that "he could fix anyone or anything if it was really necessary."[79] Godfrey planned to use Fleming's skill with people and his ability as a negotiator to help smooth the path in the forthcoming Anglo-American discussions on intelligence cooperation, which Godfrey expected would be difficult.

Godfrey's visit to the United States has been described as "a friendly, intelligent conspiracy [among British intelligence officials in America and Godfrey] to hurry on the process of change."[80] Viewed in this light, his success was spotty at best. On their arrival in New York, Godfrey and Fleming met with "Little Bill" Stephenson, head of British Security Coordination and the leading British Secret Intelligence Service representative in the United States, who also pursued the Admiralty's specialized intelligence interests, particularly those concerned with port security for shipment of war materials to England. Encouraged perhaps by Stephenson, Godfrey was prompt to pay a call on J. Edgar Hoover, director of the FBI. Fleming later described the visit, saying that Hoover "received us graciously, listened with close attention . . . to our exposé of certain security problems, and expressed himself firmly but politely as being uninterested in our mission."[81]

Kirk and the Office of Naval Intelligence proved more forthcoming. Commander Arthur H. McCollum, who in 1941 headed ONI's Far Eastern Section, recalled that Godfrey and Fleming "were shown the works—taken around to anything in ONI and down into the Communications Intelligence set-ups and so on and so forth."[82] Despite his warm reception in ONI, God-frey soon realized that inter- and intradepartmental resistance to any type of joint organization was too strong to overcome without assistance from the highest levels of the American government. According to Godfrey's biogra-pher,[83] Godfrey approached Stephenson and Sir William Wiseman for assis-tance. During the First World War Sir William had headed the British secret service organization in New York and was still resident there. Both men agreed that Godfrey should attempt to bring the intelligence coordination problem to President Roosevelt's attention. An invitation to the White House, arranged by Arthur H. Sulzberger, publisher of the *New York Times*, gave the British DNI the opportunity to state his case for a unified American intelligence organization to the president. After he left the White House, Godfrey was concerned that his arguments had made little impact on Roo-sevelt. However, shortly after his meeting with Godfrey, on 18 June 1941, the president directed the establishment of the Office of Coordinator of Infor-mation, with William J. Donovan as its first director.[84]

Stephenson and others in the British intelligence establishment were de-lighted that the president had selected "Wild Bill" Donovan, who had served the British cause so well in the dark days of 1940, to lead the new in-telligence agency. In his memoirs, Godfrey admitted that he had "discussed" the appointment of a single American intelligence coordinator with Roo-sevelt but stated that it was Ambassador Winant, not he, "who advocated Donovan's appointment."[85] The idea of a single coordinator of U.S. intelli-gence did not originate with Godfrey, nor was the concept new to the pres-ident. All that can be claimed for Godfrey's intervention was that it may have helped crystallize Roosevelt's thinking on the subject. Godfrey's initia-tive had one unfortunate, if only temporary, result. "Old friend" Kirk, who felt that Godfrey had gone over his head in approaching Roosevelt, became distinctly cool to Godfrey and "could not disguise his suspicions of my pres-idential activities."[86]

Godfrey's trip to the United States and to Canada had its positive aspects, despite its lack of success in achieving instant integration of American and British intelligence activities. Godfrey left America with a far better grasp of the capabilities and weaknesses of Kirk's organization, which, within a few months, would be officially allied with his own in the war against Germany and Japan. The British DNI's initiative was later called the precursor to "for-mal alliance and the first stage in the process towards Allied integrated in-telligence that would reach its zenith in [General Dwight D.] Eisenhower's Supreme Headquarters Intelligence Staff."[87]

During his visit to ONI, Godfrey had pressed Kirk to send some of his key staff to London to meet their counterparts in the Admiralty's Naval Intelligence Division and to study British intelligence techniques. The invitation was accepted, but with tragic consequences. Four officers were selected for the trip: Captain Sherwood Picking, assistant director of naval intelligence for foreign intelligence; Commander Arthur McCollum, head of ONI's Far Eastern desk; Lieutenant Commander Walter Chappell, assistant head of the British desk; and Lieutenant Colonel A. Wrangham, Royal Marines, who had been serving as a British liaison officer with ONI. The visit was scheduled for late August 1941. The party was split into two groups, with Picking and Wrangham going on ahead, and McCollum and Chappell following on a later plane. The aircraft carrying Picking and Wrangham crashed while approaching Prestwick, Scotland, killing all on board.[88] McCollum and Chappell received the bad news upon their arrival in London on 1 September 1941. A message from ONI directed McCollum to head the delegation and to "carry out [his] instructions."[89] Since the "instructions" had been given to Picking, not McCollum, the visit was put on hold until Washington could provide additional information.

ONI subsequently directed McCollum to study the British naval intelligence system in detail and to "obtain full info [information on] Joint Intelligence Committee organization, procedure and output."[90] McCollum found Godfrey and his staff in the Naval Intelligence Division to be cordial and forthcoming on all subjects except communications intelligence. McCollum reminded Godfrey that while in Washington he had been shown American progress against Japanese codes. Godfrey was reluctant to reciprocate until Admiral Pound, the first sea lord and chief of the naval staff, instructed Godfrey "'to take his hair down and get off this secretive kick and give you [the American visitors] the works'—or words to that effect."[91] When McCollum was finally made privy to British code-breaking activities, he found that the American navy was "very much ahead" of the British "in relation to Japanese things," and he was not impressed with the validity of British information on the Japanese Navy—his specialty.[92]

In the fall of 1941, at the same time that McCollum was studying British efforts against Japanese codes in England, the head of the British code breakers was visiting those engaged is similar efforts in the United States. Commander Alastair Denniston, a cryptographer in the Admiralty's famous "Room 40" during the First World War and in 1941 head of the Government Code and Cypher School at Bletchley Park, was in Washington to urge America to concentrate its efforts on Japanese military codes and to leave German military and other diplomatic ciphers to the British.[93] This suggested division of cryptographic labor was one that the British continued to urge well into 1943 and one that the United States was never willing to accept.

Visits such as those of Godfrey, McCollum, and Denniston, while not critical to the development of Anglo-American high policy, did serve several useful purposes. The intelligence professionals on both sides of the Atlantic came to know their opposite numbers and to recognize the strengths and weaknesses of their respective organizations. Despite British concern that the U.S. Navy was unwilling to learn from British wartime experience and would insist on "reinventing the wheel," American naval intelligence was profiting from exposure to the Royal Navy's methods of operation. As McCollum pointed out, the Admiralty was much more involved than was the U.S. Navy Department in the tactical direction of warships at sea.[94] Therefore, the Admiralty's Intelligence Division was much more concerned with providing tactical or current intelligence to the commander in chief, Home Fleet, than was its counterpart in Washington to the commander in chief of the U.S. Atlantic Fleet. The significant differences in mission of the two intelligence organizations mandated differences in methods of operation, but as their knowledge of the British system improved, the Americans were coming—albeit slowly—to appreciate the responsiveness of the British naval intelligence system to the needs of the forces it supported and to adopt similar procedures.

The dramatic growth in the number of British military liaison personnel in the United States in the summer immediately preceding America's formal entry into the war prompted Admiral Sir Charles Little, head of the British Admiralty Delegation to Washington, to comment that "Sir William Douglas of the Treasury is pursuing his difficult task here and before he leaves I hope he will be able to reduce the number of British in Washington to below the numbers that were here in 1814 when we burned the capitol."[95] Naval intelligence shared in the population explosion.

At the conclusion of the ABC-1 meetings in March 1941, Admiral Victor H. Danckwerts, a senior member of the British Delegation, was directed by his government to remain in Washington and to form the nucleus of the British Admiralty Delegation. The Admiralty Delegation would, in turn, provide the naval portion of the British Joint Services Mission, the liaison group called for under the terms of ABC-1. The senior Royal Navy, Royal Air Force, and Army officers of the Joint Services Mission were to constitute an overseas extension of the London-based British Chiefs of Staff, itself a joint organization, to present its views to the individual American chiefs of staff, who were at the time still operating as separate entities. Captain Clarke, already in Washington as British attaché for matters of naval cooperation, as well as Danckwerts's assistant on the British delegation to ABC-1, became his chief of staff. Danckwerts was replaced in June 1941 by Admiral Charles Little, who since 1937 had been second sea lord at the Admiralty in charge of all naval personnel matters.[96] By June, some one hundred British naval personnel had arrived in Washington to staff the new organization.[97] Despite its increased visibility through sheer numbers in Washington, the British military presence remained, until after Pearl Harbor, hidden under the umbrella designation of "advisors to the British Supply Council in the United States."[98]

Shortly before leaving Washington, Admiral Danckwerts wrote a letter to the American chief of naval operations, Admiral Stark, in which he outlined his dual role: first, as the representative of the first sea lord to the U.S. Navy, and second, as the senior naval member of the British joint military mission to the United States. At that time, he provided the CNO with a description of the British Admiralty Delegation's organization, which included an intelligence section of four officers, headed by a captain.[99] These officers were to be drawn in part from the British naval attaché's staff in Washington and in part from the Admiralty's Naval Intelligence Division. As time went on, the naval attaché offices in both London and Washington were to play a smaller and smaller role in intelligence exchange as that function was assumed by the Anglo-American military missions to their respective governments.

In time, the mission staffs grew to include specialists in such matters as communications intelligence and secret agent operations. By the late summer of 1941, the naval intelligence organization within the British Admiralty Delegation in Washington was reconstituted as an integral part of the Admiralty's Naval Intelligence Division in London and given the staff designation NID 18. Led by Captain E.G.G. Hastings, RN, NID 18 continued to function as the major channel for the Admiralty's requests for intelligence from the U.S. Navy Department throughout the war.[100]

Hastings's stature increased as the war progressed. In his role as senior representative of the British DNI in the Americas, he was responsible for all general matters of naval intelligence cooperation in the United States and, in June 1942, was additionally charged with coordination of Anglo-American naval intelligence activities in the Caribbean and Latin America, liaison to the New Zealand and Australian DNIs "in respect of intelligence in the U.S.A. operational areas in the Western Pacific," and—if these tasks were not enough—"avoiding overlapping in the promulgation of intelligence."[101]

While the American and British military were developing and installing the machinery of cooperation, a new combatant entered the war. On 22 June

1941, Germany attacked the Soviet Union. The German invasion of Russia significantly altered the political and military relationships between the United States, Great Britain, and the Soviet Union but had less effect on intelligence cooperation. In 1941, the British government began to provide the Russians with bits of information derived from German communications, carefully selected and "sanitized" to hide their source. Naval material was chosen and disguised by analysts in the Admiralty's Naval Intelligence Directorate, then passed for approval to "C"—the director of the Secret Intelligence Service—who had ultimate responsibility for the British signals intelligence program. Under the prefix "EXTINGUISH," which identified its source, the message was then transmitted to the head of the British naval mission in Moscow to use as a bargaining chip with the Russians.[102]

Early in the Russo-German portion of the war, the British established a naval presence at Polyarnoe, the Soviet naval base near Murmansk, and by mid-August 1941, local-level intelligence was being exchanged. In the spring of 1942, the Soviets agreed to permit the Royal Navy to operate a "Y" intercept station at Polyarnoe. The commander of the British operation exchanged raw intercepted German traffic with the Russians and, to encourage them to be more forthcoming, taught them some of the fundamentals of traffic analysis but kept secret the fact that the British were reading German Enigma messages.[103]

Although not a party to the war against Japan in 1942–1943, the Russians were extremely interested in intelligence on the Imperial Japanese Navy. Weekly intelligence meetings were held in London between representatives of the Naval Intelligence Division and members of the Soviet naval mission, paralleling similar gatherings in Moscow. Strict quid pro quo was the order of the day, and the Russians asked much but offered little. When the Red Army closed down Japanese Order of Battle meetings in Moscow, the War Office did the same in London, hoping to force the Russians into a more cooperative mood. The Admiralty threatened a similar shutoff of naval information but did not do so, even though the Soviet navy had "pulled up the ladder" on Japanese intelligence exchange in Moscow.[104] With an unprecedented burst of generosity in the summer of 1943, NID went so far as to give a captured German Enigma machine and instructions for its use to a representative of the Soviet naval mission.[105]

Like Anglo-Soviet intelligence relationships, American and Soviet naval intelligence cooperation proceeded by fits and starts. According to Admiral Harold C. Train, director of naval intelligence in 1942 and 1943, "during his entire directorship, the Russians never sent ONI one shred of valuable information about Japan, the Far East, or the Pacific Ocean, denying even meteorological data necessary to U.S. Fleet operations." More recent evidence, however, indicates that beginning in the spring of 1942, meaningful Soviet-American naval intelligence exchanges took place in both Washington and Moscow.[106]

Between September 1940 and December 1941, the British government worked to overcome its concern about America's ability to protect British secrets while the United States strove to assure itself of England's ability to continue the war. The U.S. Navy Department's reactions to the Admiralty's initiatives in the field of intelligence cooperation were colored by domestic political considerations that precluded overt alliance and by vague feelings of disquiet that opening the cooperative door too far at this stage of the war might lead to a less than equal partnership later. Despite American misgivings, intelligence cooperation did increase and was characterized by exchange of information through the good offices of the Joint Bailey Committee, by British relaxation of restrictions on sharing of information with American liaison personnel, and by increasing numbers of reciprocal visits by American and British intelligence officers to observe and to learn from each other.

By the late fall of 1941, all the major Anglo-American agreements affecting naval intelligence sharing on a nation-to-nation basis had been implemented, and the machinery for cooperation was in place and operating. What had started informally and in great secrecy with the reciprocal visits of Captain Ingersoll to London in 1938 and Commander Hampton to Washington in 1939 had grown and—albeit still in secret—had become formalized through a series of increasingly binding commitments: the Standardization of Arms understandings, the Bailey Committee agreements, and finally the specific provisions of ABC-1. America's entry into the war would have little effect on the terms of these agreements but would increase the volume and perhaps the sensitivity of the information exchanged.

The role of the attaché in naval intelligence decreased markedly as military missions on both sides of the Atlantic began to perform the liaison and intelligence duties traditionally carried on by the naval attaché. Intelligence exchange moved from the realm of diplomacy to that of the military staff. This shift in locus heralded a much more significant change in cooperative intelligence activity. Beginning in mid-1942 with planning for Torch, the Allied invasion of North Africa, intelligence needs of commanders in the field (or at sea) would more often be met directly by their own Allied staffs than by their individual service intelligence resources.

The dominant theme of the period from the late summer of 1940 until the fall of 1941 was one of ever-expanding intelligence cooperation. However, contrapuntal themes of interservice rivalries, especially between the American army and navy intelligence organizations; traditional Anglo-American mutual distrust of motives; and xenophobic postwar considerations continued to impede progress toward complete sharing. Cautious Anglo-American feelers toward increased exchange of information had expanded into a major cooperative effort, despite the adverse undercurrents. The products of the intelligence process were being shared, and the methods by which these results were attained were being traded. All that was lacking was the United States' formal entry into the war to bring about the complete integration of both nations' intelligence resources—or so it seemed.

4.
Growth of Wartime Cooperation

On the morning of 7 December 1941, Japan launched a surprise attack on Pearl Harbor, Hawaii, the principal U.S. naval base in the Pacific, and on U.S Army and Army Air Corps installations nearby. Concurrently the Japanese attacked American forces in the Philippines and British outposts in Malaya and Hong Kong. "It was a bad day all around," presidential adviser Adolf Berle noted in his diary, "and if there is anyone I would not like to be, it is the Chief of Naval Intelligence."[1]

By the end of 1941, the Second World War had become a world war in fact as well as name. The entry of the United States into the war against Germany and Japan removed a major bar to Anglo-American naval intelligence cooperation. However, achieving full sharing was not to be that easy. Personal antipathy on the part of the commander in chief, U.S. Fleet, to "mixing" U.S. and British naval forces often frustrated British efforts to establish jointly manned intelligence centers, while the advent of the combined Anglo-American staff system worked against navy-to-navy intelligence relationships. Despite these setbacks, intelligence cooperation between the two navies continued to expand in the year after Pearl Harbor.

The United States and Great Britain both declared war on Japan on 8 December 1941. However, the United States did not issue a simultaneous declaration of hostilities with Germany. Germany declared war on the United States on 11 December 1941, in what Martin Gilbert described as "perhaps the greatest error, and certainly the single most decisive act of the Second World War."[2] In so doing, Hitler closed the door on the remote possibility that America would choose to devote its exclusive attention to Japan and leave Europe to its fate.

Following America's entry into the war, the British renewed pressure for the closest possible cooperation in intelligence matters. The first opportunity to address the intelligence question, post–Pearl Harbor, occurred in a series of conferences between the American and British chiefs of staff held in Washington from 24 December 1941 to 14 January 1942. The impetus for the meetings, cover-named "Arcadia," came from the prime minister. Churchill had decided as early as 8 December 1941 that he and his top military leaders needed an immediate conference with their now-official American allies to "review the whole war plan in the light of reality and new facts."[3] Churchill and his advisers departed for the United States aboard HMS *Duke of York* on 14 December.

In the military discussions that followed the British delegation's arrival in Washington on 22 December, the U.S. Navy was represented by, among others, Admiral Harold R. Stark, the chief of naval operations and administrative head of the navy; Admiral Ernest J. King, former commander in chief of the Atlantic Fleet, who only a few days earlier had been named commander in chief of the whole of the U.S. Fleet and was thus the head of the operating forces of the navy; and Admiral Richmond K. Turner, the Navy Department's director of plans, who spoke for his own organization and often for naval intelligence as well.[4] The Royal Navy delegation was headed by Admiral Sir Dudley Pound, the first sea lord, and included Admirals R. M. Bellairs and Victor H. Danckwerts, who were old hands at Anglo-American negotiations. Both had held responsible wartime positions in the plans directorate of the British naval staff, and both had participated in the U.S.-U.K. staff conversations (ABC-1) in Washington earlier in 1941. In addition, both were "in close touch" with the British director of naval intelligence; they were his friends and could be counted on to protect the Naval Intelligence Division's interests in talks with the Americans.[5]

The British must have looked with misgiving upon Admiral King's elevation to high office in the U.S. Navy and on his presence at the Arcadia consultations. King had been present at the Anglo-American military staff meetings in Argentia the previous August, but in a subordinate role. By January 1942, King had become America's leading naval officer and would remain so throughout the war. King was approached in influence only by Admiral William D. Leahy, a former chief of naval operations, wartime ambassador to Vichy, France, and, as first chairman of the U.S. Joint Chiefs, the president's personal chief of staff. In British eyes, King was "if not actually anti-British . . . certainly not over-receptive to ideas and suggestions from the Admiralty."[6]

The British had good cause for concern. In August 1941, while he was commander in chief of the U.S. Atlantic Fleet, King had written to the chief of naval operations, "All in all, I think—as usual—that the British are much too intent on managing *our* affairs." Again, shortly before his December assignment to Washington, King had grumbled in a letter to one of his subordinate commanders that "the Admiralty in London appears to insist on knowing where each and every one of our ships are at every hour of the day and night, and the Navy Department seems to acquiesce in this 'curiosity.'"[7] King, once described by his daughter as "the most even-tempered man in the Navy . . . always in a rage,"[8] was to have a profound influence on Anglo-American wartime naval relationships and on the course of Anglo-American naval intelligence cooperation.

So too would the joint/combined intelligence staff system that emerged from the Arcadia conferences. In an early session, the British demonstrated their strong commitment to close intelligence ties by initiating a proposal for post-Arcadia collaboration that went considerably farther than the U.S. side was willing to go. Internal papers of the British delegation reiterated the position expressed by Admiral Godfrey in his 1941 visit to the United States that a single controlling body for American intelligence was badly needed. "It is hoped," one such paper stated, "that the activities of the various Intelligence organizations in the United States (Naval Intelligence, Military Intelligence, Colonel DONOVAN'S organization and the State Department) will become more closely co-ordinated in the future."[9] To this end, the British chiefs of staff agreed "to press the United States Chiefs of Staff to set up a joint intelligence organization for the co-ordination of United States intelligence with which the Joint Intelligence Committee of the British Staff Mission should have contacts."[10]

The United States was reluctant to accept the British position on the intelligence question, probably because of objections by Admirals King and Turner, who were known to be wary of joint action—what King would later call "mixed Forces"—whether with other U.S. non-navy organizations or with foreigners. The original British proposal was submitted on 10 January 1942 and stated in part that "the arrangements for production of complete intelligence to serve the Planning Staffs are of great importance and we suggest that this matter should either be referred to the Combined Planning Staffs for report or considered by the Combined Chiefs of Staff at their next meeting."[11] Three days later, the draft was modified to delete any consideration of the intelligence question by the combined chiefs. Apparently, the United States was unwilling to afford intelligence this prominent a position in the hierarchy of problems confronting the combined chiefs. In its final agreed form, the Arcadia conference's statement on intelligence read: "The question of the production and dissemination of complete Military Intelligence to serve the Combined Chiefs of Staff and the Combined Staff Planners has been referred to the latter body for a report. Here also, it is contemplated that existing machinery will be largely continued."[12] It is clear that this wording, emphasizing "existing machinery" instead of a joint organization, represented a victory for the more cautious American approach to Anglo-American intelligence cooperation.

The British may have lost this skirmish, but they eventually won the organizational war. The following month, the joint planners recommended and the combined chiefs approved the establishment of a U.S. Joint Intelligence Committee, similar in function to the British JIC. The combined chiefs also directed that a Combined Intelligence Committee be formed to meet its own and its planners' requirements for intelligence.[13] The sources of intelligence for grand strategy were gradually changing from estimates prepared by individual military organizations, whose conclusions often varied widely from service to service, to joint estimates and conclusions that were a product of interservice effort.

As has been suggested, America's entry into the war and its close alliance with Great Britain mandated a form of coalition warfare that affected every level of cooperation, from long-range strategy down through tactical planning. The "combined" approach to what became known as "total war" extended well beyond the fields of military planning and strategy, embracing such diverse areas as logistics and supply, economic and political warfare, propaganda, and—of course—intelligence. The changes in the procedures by which the Admiralty and the U.S. Department of the Navy had traditionally furnished intelligence to those who required it came about as a result of an organizational structure imposed on the two navies from the highest levels of their respective governments and one not necessarily of their own choosing. The saving grace of the system, from the viewpoints of both navies, was that it provided a reasonably clear demarcation between intelligence required for current naval operations, which was to be provided directly from the operational headquarters to the forces involved, and intelligence for planning, which was to be provided via the joint/combined staff system.

The joint/combined staff system[14]—joint committees whose members were all from the same nation and represented individual military or government departments, and combined committees whose members represented their countries in a multinational organization—was a creature of wartime necessity and was not looked on initially with great favor by the U.S. Navy. The Arcadia conference of late 1941 and early 1942, in addition to fixing Allied strategic objectives for the coming months, developed an agreed framework for the American-British combined staff system, described in the U.S. Army's official history of World War II as "a unique accomplishment in cooperative effort by the military staffs of two great sovereign powers."[15] Another, almost accidental result of the adoption of the combined staff organization was the creation of the American Joint Chiefs of Staff (JCS) system.[16]

To grasp the way in which Anglo-American intelligence cooperation functioned in the post-Arcadia world, one must first understand the system for determining the strategic direction of the war that developed from the decisions made at Arcadia. The combined staff system that eventuated was essentially three tiered. At the top were the president, as commander in chief of the United States' armed forces, and the prime minister of Great Britain, who was also minister of defence.[17] Field Marshal Sir John Dill, until October 1941 chief of the British Imperial General Staff and senior member of the British chiefs of staff, remained in Washington following the Arcadia conferences to represent the defence minister on the highest organizational plane.

On the next level were the Combined Chiefs of Staff. At Arcadia it had been agreed that this body should be resident in Washington and should consist of the American chiefs of staff and their British counterparts. The senior members of the British Joint Services Mission (Washington) were to represent their service chiefs whenever the British chiefs of staff were not present to meet directly with the U.S. joint chiefs.

The third tier consisted of the various specialized committees created to support the Combined Chiefs of Staff. The most important of these, the Combined Planning Committee, was supported in turn by the Combined Intelligence Committee, which received both its representatives and its intelligence from the individual British and American Joint Intelligence Committees. These national Joint Intelligence Committees were staffed and provided intelligence by the several individual service intelligence agencies: army, navy, and air (Royal Air Force and U.S. Army Air Corps, respectively). In addition, the American Joint Intelligence Committee had a subgroup to represent its interests in London, as did the British Joint Intelligence Committee in Washington. Despite its complicated structure the system worked.

In the combined staff system, the Combined Chiefs of Staff or its planners generated intelligence requirements that were then passed to the Combined Intelligence Committee. Since this committee had no "in-house" capability to provide the desired information, the request was sent to the American and British Joint Intelligence Committees. They, in turn, called on the resources of their national naval and military intelligence organizations to provide the required information and to do the preliminary analysis.

The intelligence "product" then started back up the line. Individual service intelligence organizations provided responses to their staff members on the Joint Intelligence Committees, who attempted to reconcile any differences in analysis and to produce a document that would represent the coordinated position of the United States or the British government on the given question. These national position papers would then be furnished to the Combined Intelligence Committee for resolution of any differences, and an agreed estimate would be sent to the Combined Planning Staff or the Combined Chiefs, as appropriate.

From an intelligence standpoint, the great danger of such a system was that, in an effort to achieve consensus at all the various staff levels, the final product might become so "watered down" as to be of little concrete use to the recipients. This undesirable result was avoided in some measure by permitting the views of the individual intelligence chiefs, such as the directors of naval intelligence, to percolate up through the system as a result of the multiple roles—service, joint, and combined—played by many of the participants in the process.

While the structure for providing intelligence for grand strategy was being created in Washington and London, the mechanism already in place for intelligence cooperation in wartime fleet operations was being sorely tested in the waters of the western Atlantic.

Operation *Paukenschlag* (drumbeat), better known to the German submariners who participated as the "Happy Time," began off the East Coast of the United States in January 1942 and continued until June of that year. During this six-month period, approximately 2 million tons of Allied merchant shipping—over 360 vessels—were sunk by German submarines operating in the western Atlantic within 300 miles of the North and South American coasts. Churchill summed up the magnitude of the submarine assault by saying that "for six or seven months the U-boats ravaged American waters almost uncontrolled, and, in fact, almost brought us to the disaster of an indefinite prolongation of the war."[18]

The U.S. Navy was both ill equipped and ill prepared for antisubmarine warfare on the scale necessary to defeat the German threat. The disaster at Pearl Harbor had caused the navy to withdraw almost all its escort ships from the Atlantic, placing an even greater burden on the already strained British and Canadian resources. It took several months to muster sufficient air and surface escorts to institute a convoy system along the East Coast, and even longer to develop a unified command structure to control all aspects of antisubmarine warfare.[19] As a result of these shortcomings in equipment and doctrine, individual German submarines were able to choose lucrative targets at will. It was only after the introduction of the convoy system that Admiral Karl Dönitz, German commander of U-boats, found the operation of single boats in such a distant area to be "uneconomic" and, in July 1942, shifted his forces to resume attacks on the North Atlantic convoy routes.[20]

Intelligence shortcomings also added to Allied problems in defending against the German U-boat attacks. On 1 February 1942, the Germans introduced a change to the coding machines used by the long-range boats operating in the Atlantic. The modification caused a "blackout" of Bletchley Park's ability to decrypt this type of traffic that lasted until the end of the year.[21] While the British were losing their ability to read German long-range U-boat communications, German cryptographers were improving their capability against British naval codes. Although the time required for decryption remained a problem, by the end of 1942, German code breakers were able to read almost 80 percent of intercepted communications sent in British Naval Cypher No. 3, which was introduced in June 1941 and was used extensively in the Allied North Atlantic convoy system.[22]

When German codes became unreadable, British intelligence officers usually fell back on traffic analysis and direction finding to follow German activities at sea. Direction finding was at its most effective in the central and eastern Atlantic, particularly in detecting German submarine wolf-pack operations, which required a good deal of message traffic back and forth between the U-boats and their coordinating authority in the German-occupied Atlantic port of Lorient. However, the German submarines that were wreaking havoc in the western Atlantic were operating independently, and although they could send and receive radio traffic to and from U-boat headquarters, even while off the U.S. East Coast, they usually kept transmissions to a minimum while in their preassigned operating areas. They were, therefore, relatively immune from detection through their communications.

The Royal Navy looked with dismay upon the mainly ineffective efforts of their American colleagues to find and attack German submarines operating in American waters. British naval intelligence was particularly concerned that the U.S. Navy had failed to develop any type of centralized organization to collect and analyze the countless bits of information needed to determine the numbers and locations of enemy U-boats.[23] Antisubmarine intelligence was fragmented; it was developed at several levels of command, with little exchange of information among intelligence officers at each echelon. The Office of Naval Intelligence "was far too static to play an important role in as dynamic an activity as the U-boat hunt."[24] Relations between Intelligence and Operations were not particularly close, exacerbating the problem of providing timely and believable intelligence to those who needed to act on it.

The Admiralty was also concerned that the degree of cooperation anticipated after the exchange of cryptographic visitors in 1941 had not come to pass. In an attempt to improve the situation, the British code-breaking organization at Bletchley Park initiated a plan for a small British "Y" mission to visit the United States and Canada to exchange information on new developments and to "arrange for the exchange of raw material for the mutual benefit of all the cryptographic organizations."

Captain Humphry Sandwith, RN, the head of NID/DSD 9, the Admiralty's joint Intelligence/Signals Section in the Operational Intelligence Centre, was selected to lead the "Y" mission. Sandwith was an excellent choice, since he could speak with experience and authority on matters affecting both intelligence and communications. His underlying purpose was as much educational as cooperative, as he indicated in a letter to the Canadian DNI: "The proposal [for the meeting] was put up some weeks ago by the GC&CS because it was their impression that Washington knew nothing of W/T intelligence."[25]

The opening session of the Joint U.S.-British-Canadian Discussions, as the conference was called, took place at the Navy Department in Washington on 6 April 1942. In his opening remarks, Sandwith began his educational mission with a detailed presentation of the British organization for radio intelligence, beginning at the top with descriptions of the five members of the governing "Y" committee, then giving particulars of the Royal Navy's organization, and following with a detailed review of the responsibilities of the Operational Intelligence Centre. He stressed the multiplicity of intelligence sources feeding into the center and the extremely close liaison between the OIC and both the Operations staff and the Trade Division, the organization responsible for safe routing of the convoys. His not-too-subliminal message was that the U.S. and Canadian navies would be far better off with operational intelligence centers of their own.[26]

The major work of the conference entailed an exchange of technical information among the American, British, and Canadian "Y" organizations and an attempt to reduce duplication in the promulgation of D/F "fixes" by assigning specific geographic areas of reporting responsibility in the western Atlantic to the USN and RCN. Since the U.S. Navy had started issuing its own D/F information in early 1942, tension had been growing between the two navies over the problems of duplicate U-boat positioning and often conflicting estimates. The conference agreed on the establishment of two independent plotting centers—one in Washington and one in Ottawa—each with its own area of responsibility. These plotting rooms were to become the nucleus of the American and Canadian operational intelligence centers to come.[27]

The U.S. Navy was not as unwilling to profit from British experience in intelligence as the Royal Navy might have imagined. When Admiral Alan Kirk departed London and his assignment as U.S. naval attaché for his new post as director of naval intelligence in Washington he brought with him an awareness of the value of the Admiralty's Operational Intelligence Centre and an enthusiasm for establishing a similar organization somewhere within the U.S. Navy Department. As a result of an early January 1941 meeting presided over by the assistant chief of naval operations, a "chart room" was established in which operational and intelligence information on U.S. and foreign ship movements was brought together and plotted.[28] While this rudimentary effort was a far cry from the Admiralty's Operational Intelligence Centre, it was a start.

President Roosevelt's executive order of 18 December 1941 placed all the U.S. Navy's operating forces under one organization, the United States Fleet, and under one man, Admiral Ernest J. King. At the same time, the president separated King's responsibilities as commander in chief, U.S. Fleet, from those of Admiral Harold R. Stark, who remained, at least temporarily, the chief of naval operations. The CNO retained responsibility for the administration of the Navy Department, for long-range planning, and for personnel and material support.[29] In intelligence matters, the CNO retained direction of the ONI, "which office furnishes information to the Commander in Chief [King]." For his part, the commander in chief "maintains a fleet intelligence section in close contact with the Office of Naval Intelligence and other sources of information."[30]

Admiral King's fleet operational intelligence section included a rudimentary plotting room for U-boat movements, but nothing that could compare with the tracking room headed by Commander Roger Winn, RNVR, in the Operational Intelligence Centre in London. Winn, a rising young barrister in London before the war, came into the OIC in August 1939 as a civilian assistant to the head of the submarine tracking room, a Royal Navy captain. Because of his uncanny success in predicting German U-boat movements, in late 1940, the Admiralty took the unprecedented step of appointing Winn to the key position of head of the tracking room and giving him a direct commission as a commander in the Royal Navy Volunteer Reserve. Patrick Beesly, foremost biographer of British naval intelligence during World War II and Winn's deputy from 1942 on, commented that "it was a stroke of singular good fortune that someone so ideally suited to the job in hand was available and was selected." Beesly wrote of Winn that he used his legal training to bring often skeptical senior officers in the Admiralty to his point of view by treating them with respect, "much as I imagine as a barrister he behaved towards a judge in court." He had the moral courage to present unpopular advice, but he did so in such a way that "the A.C.N.S. [assistant chief of the naval staff], or whoever it was, came to believe that he, and not Winn, had first stumbled on the truth of the matter."[31]

Under Winn's leadership, the tracking room established an extremely close working relationship with the Admiralty's Operations and Antisubmarine Divisions, and with the Movements Section of its Trade Division—the organization that routed convoys passing through the submarine-infested waters of the North Atlantic. So great became Winn's personal reputation and that of his tracking room for predicting enemy ship movements that the Admiralty adopted what Winn called his "working fiction" for the evaluation of German submarine activities. "What could only be an estimate and a guess," Winn said, "was to be taken as a fact and acted upon."[32]

Winn's singular ability in U-boat intelligence analysis was not lost on those few Americans in London who were privy to the secrets of the Tracking Room. Admiral Robert Ghormley, the U.S. special naval observer in England and one of three U.S. naval officers admitted to the tracking room, encouraged the Navy Department to invite Winn to the United States, so the U.S. Fleet's intelligence staff could benefit from his experience. In April 1942, at the height of the German submarine attacks off the U.S. East Coast, Ghormley sent King a letter that enthusiastically supported Winn's prospective visit, told the commander in chief of the tracking room's accomplishments, and commented that "the work they do here is really remarkable."[33]

Admiral John Godfrey, the British director of naval intelligence, was as anxious as Ghormley for Winn's visit to take place. The Admiralty's concern over Anglo-American merchant ship losses in the western Atlantic had been growing, and Godfrey had selected Winn for the delicate task of "selling" the U.S. Navy on adopting British methods of antisubmarine intelligence. Winn was chosen not only for his expertise in U-boat analysis but also for his background as a skilled advocate. And it was thought that his prewar experience as an exchange scholar at both Yale and Harvard might improve his chances of "getting on" with the Americans.[34]

Winn arrived in Washington on 19 April 1942 and the next day met with the American director of naval intelligence and his deputy. It was immediately obvious to Winn, as it was to the director, that Winn was talking to the wrong people. The division of responsibility between the chief of naval operations and the commander in chief, U.S. Fleet, had placed operational intelligence matters clearly within the latter's scope of responsibility. Winn was, therefore, taken to the fleet operational intelligence officer, Commander George Dyer. Winn soon formed the opinion that Dyer, "an able and forceful officer," occupied "a key position in relation to my objective."[35] It took Winn three days to overcome Dyer's "initially skeptical and critical attitude" toward the idea of a submarine tracking organization that was the focal point of all intelligence on U-boat activities, and one that worked in close harmony with the fleet operations staff. Even with Dyer on board, Winn subsequently reported to the Admiralty, it took another four days to "win over and convince" Dyer's superior, Admiral Richard S. Edwards, deputy chief of staff. Finally, after Edwards and Winn returned "mellow" from "an alcoholic luncheon," Winn found that he had won. Once Edwards had agreed and had given the orders to "get the right room and the right men and get going," matters progressed rapidly. Before Winn left for home on 11 May, the American U-boat tracking room "was a going concern."[36]

As an inducement to Edwards to organize a U-boat tracking facility, Winn had "hinted" that should this be done, the British might have "better information to impart." The exigent U-boat situation in the western Atlantic had caused the British to rethink the question of whether greater cryptographic intelligence support to the U.S. Navy was worth the security risk—a move that both Menzies and Godfrey had opposed in the latter part of 1941. The veiled reference to communications intelligence was not lost on Edwards, who agreed to the inauguration of a special communications channel between the British and American submarine tracking rooms by which informal messages containing highly sensitive material might be exchanged. On 3 June 1942, the first of some two thousand such signals passed between the American submarine tracking room in Washington and the Admiralty Operational Intelligence Centre in London, a flow that was not to end until June 1945.[37]

Following his visit to Washington, Winn continued his missionary work in Ottawa, where he was successful in encouraging the establishment of a U-boat tracking room in what was to become the Canadian Operational Intelligence Center. Winn's activities built on those of Captain Sandwith, who had preceded his April conference in Washington with a trip to Canada and an extensive review of the Canadian naval "Y" organization. Like Sandwith, Winn urged the RCN to centralize the reception and promulgation of all information on enemy submarines in a single location. Winn also made arrangements for the Canadian sub tracking room to receive information derived from British code-breaking activities in the form of a daily report of submarine activity sent to Royal Navy commands and to the U.S. Navy. There was, however, one significant difference in the Admiralty's treatment of the

two tracking rooms. The U.S. Navy received raw traffic directly from Bletchley Park in addition to Winn's daily reports, whereas the Canadians did not.
Ottawa began sending regular submarine disposition reports to Washington
in May 1942, and by October, radio teletype circuits had been placed in operation among the three tracking rooms.[38]

The establishment of the American and Canadian submarine tracking
rooms and their close tie-in with the Admiralty's Operational Intelligence
Centre represented particularly significant steps in the development of
Anglo-American naval intelligence cooperation. For the first time, the products of this effort—particularly the contribution of intelligence to the evasive
routing of convoys away from threatening U-boats—had a visibly beneficial
effect on the course of the Battle of the Atlantic. By the spring of 1941, the
Admiralty had determined that defense was the primary mission of naval
convoy escorts, to ensure "the safe and timely arrival of the convoy." Evasive
routing, based on intelligence of wolf-pack locations, became a key ingredient in convoy safety, since the pursuit and killing of U-boats was now a secondary mission. Monthly Allied shipping losses in the North Atlantic
dropped from a June 1942 high of 124 ships, totaling 623,545 tons, to the December low of 46 ships, totaling 262,135 tons.[39] While intelligence could not
claim credit for all this improvement, there was no doubt that intelligence
sharing was beginning to pay off.

Locating the tracking room in the U.S. Fleet's operations staff instead of
within the Office of Naval Intelligence was of significance to the future development of American naval intelligence. Heretofore the U.S. Navy had
followed the British model, combining long-range or strategic intelligence
and short-range or operational intelligence analysis and production in a single organization. With the advent of the U.S. Fleet structure, a sharp demarcation was drawn between these two types of activity, with strategic
intelligence—including intelligence requirements for combined planning—
remaining with ONI, and intelligence needed for operational purposes—for
example, antisubmarine warfare—becoming the responsibility of the fleet
staff. This division of authority did much to define ONI's wartime role as a
producer of intelligence to support the combined intelligence staffs' planning
operations, such as the Allied landings in North Africa in 1942 and in Western Europe in 1944. As will be seen later, Admiral Chester W. Nimitz followed the opposite course in the Pacific theater and established a single
intelligence center, separate from but serving both his single-service fleet staff
and his Pacific theater joint staff. Even though other Allied nations, such as
Australia and New Zealand, were involved, there was never a combined planning organization in Nimitz's Pacific theater.

By mid-1942, with the roles of the producers of strategic and operational intelligence determined, the Americans at last convinced of the value of an all-source current intelligence center to support antisubmarine warfare, and the tracking rooms on both sides of the Atlantic closely tied together, the scene was set for the definitive battle to come against the German U-boats in the Atlantic and for the closest Anglo-American intelligence cooperation that was to be achieved during the Second World War.

As the war expanded to include more belligerents and more areas of the world, intelligence expanded into new sources of information and new methods of analysis. One of the first of the new sources of intelligence to have an impact on wartime planning and operations was aerial photographic reconnaissance and the subsequent interpretation, or "readout," of the photographs.

Military aerial photographic reconnaissance had first been used in the nineteenth century when, during the Franco-Prussian War, the French took photographs from a balloon to aid in identifying German positions during the siege of Paris.[40] It was not until 1937, however, that the Admiralty began to show interest in aerial reconnaissance and aerial photo interpretation as a valuable source of information about the movements of German warships.[41] Immediately prior to the start of the war the British Secret Intelligence Service, not the Royal Navy, flew photographic reconnaissance flights in August and September 1939 over the port of Wilhelmshaven to locate the major units of the German fleet.[42] With the fall of France in 1940, British photographic reconnaissance concentrated on those occupied western European ports where the Germans were massing their forces for the invasion of England.

All photographic interpretation took place at a single location staffed by the Royal Air Force and called the Central Interpretation Unit. The Admiralty did no original photographic interpretation itself but maintained a small staff in the Naval Intelligence Division to coordinate requirements for photographic coverage of naval targets for immediate use by the Operational Intelligence Centre and others of the naval staff.[43]

Prior to the start of the Second World War, the U.S. Navy had no photographic intelligence organization, and its aerial photographic activities were limited to experiments in aerial mapping and charting.[44] Shortly after he arrived in London in the spring of 1941, Admiral Ghormley was made aware of British activities in the field of photographic reconnaissance for intelligence purposes and became interested in its potential for use by the U.S. Navy. He asked that a "competent officer" be sent over from Washington to study British methods.[45]

The officer selected, Lieutenant Commander Robert S. Quackenbush Jr., was the head of photography at the U.S. Navy's Bureau of Aeronautics. After reporting to Ghormley in London, he was posted to the Central Interpretation Unit for a three-month course, from which he emerged greatly enthused about the prospects for the U.S. Navy's gathering intelligence from aerial photographs. Apparently, he communicated his enthusiasm to Admiral Ghormley, who cabled the Navy Department in June 1941 requesting that four additional aviation officers be sent immediately for training in England and recommending that specially selected navy and marine officers, not necessarily aviators, be ordered over for training as soon as possible.[46] Throughout the month of June, Ghormley continued to badger the Navy Department for additional personnel to train in photographic interpretation, strengthening his arguments with the fact that the "British [are] employing in excess [of] two hundred officers and four hundred rates [specialized enlisted personnel] in this work alone."[47]

Commander Quackenbush returned to Washington in the summer of 1941 and began the task of planning a U.S. Navy Photographic Interpretation School. The chief of naval operations directed the establishment of the school in September 1941, and, with impetus provided by the events of 7 December 1941, the school opened its doors in January 1942. The first instructors were those American navy and marine officers who had followed Quackenbush at the Central Interpretation Unit in England. Teaching procedures, texts, and photographic examples were borrowed from the British, since there was neither time nor local expertise available to develop a homegrown product.[48] British wartime experience, once again shared freely with the U.S. Navy, allowed American naval intelligence to enter the war much better prepared than it might otherwise have been to utilize new techniques of photographic intelligence against new techniques of warfare.

A traditional but nonetheless valuable source of intelligence was interrogation—the questioning of "those who had been there," both friend and foe. The first British interrogations of the Second World War were performed not on captured Germans but on the great numbers of European refugees who had fled to England in the 1930s to escape Nazi and Fascist totalitarianism. The object of the questioning was not so much to elicit information (although the Secret Intelligence Service did participate in the interrogations for that purpose) as to determine who should be interned as undesirable enemy aliens.[49] With the fall of France, this flow of refugees was swollen by Polish, French, Belgian, Dutch, and Scandinavian military personnel, all coming to England to join their nations' armed forces in exile. Even after the French defeat, a constant stream of military "escapers and evaders" continued to reach England, all of whom had to be questioned to determine their bona fides, as well as to gain the latest information on the situation in occupied Europe.[50]

British interrogation of prisoners of war began in 1939. As in the case of aerial photographic interpretation, prisoner of war interrogation was carried out at a single location. Under the management of the War Office, the Combined Services Detailed Interrogation Centre developed and practiced the "art" of extracting information from usually reluctant prisoners.[51] Each military service provided its own interrogators, many of whom possessed specialized backgrounds that were of great value in eliciting technical information.

As early as October 1939, British naval intelligence began to receive reports from interrogations of German crewmen captured after successful attacks on their U-boats.[52] It was not until 1942, however, that the British naval staff began to give any great credence to information derived from prisoner of war interrogations. Until the information had been confirmed from other sources, the Admiralty refused to believe early interrogation reports that the Germans had developed supply U-boats and that enemy U-boats could dive as deep as 600 feet.[53]

In mid-1941, the British director of naval intelligence warned his American opposite number "on the dangers of premature questioning by enthusiastic amateurs," citing as an example a case in the early days of the war in which cigarettes, thought to be Irish, were found on a German submarine prisoner, "from which it was wrongly deduced that the submarine had visited a port on the West Coast of Eire."[54] From 1942 on, due in part to improvements in interrogation techniques, more and better information was furnished and more attention was paid to that provided. As the war progressed, the Royal Navy developed a "healthy respect" for prisoner of war intelligence. As evidence of the increased value placed on information from this source, to support the Normandy invasion in 1944, the Admiralty created the Royal Navy Forward Intelligence Unit, whose responsibility it was to conduct immediate prisoner interrogations to gain perishable intelligence on such things as locations of German submarines, E-boats, and other units that might threaten resupply of the troops ashore in France.[55]

An administrative history of the U.S. Office of Naval Intelligence was prepared at the war's end but was never published. In the section dealing with prisoner of war activities, the comment was made that, "prior to World War II, no organized procedure for the interrogation of naval prisoners of war existed within the United States Navy."[56] However, early in the war, the U.S. Navy began to show great interest in the results of British interrogations. In September 1940, the U.S. naval attaché in London used the good offices of the Bailey Committee to obtain copies of British interrogations of captured German submarine crew members conducted in late 1939 and 1940.[57] By the summer of 1941, the U.S. Navy Department felt the need to establish a capability separate from that of the British for the systematic interrogation of "prisoners of Oriental nations" and began to look for persons with the special qualifications required. In addition, the Navy Department made plans to send Americans to the United Kingdom for training in "the handling of European prisoners."[58]

British and American naval intelligence organizations maintained "full and complete liaison" in matters concerning prisoner interrogation from mid-1941 until the war's end. A U.S. naval officer was attached to the staff of the Combined Services Detailed Interrogation Centre in England before Pearl Harbor, and following America's entry into the war, a British naval officer from the center was sent to Washington for nine months to help develop the U.S. naval interrogation capability.[59]

Despite these close initial ties, American and British methods of conducting and reporting interrogations began to vary as time passed. In British eyes, this nonparallel development was unfortunate. An Admiralty postwar internal paper on wartime prisoner interrogation stated that "it would be ingenuous to maintain that the United States naval interrogation section was as successful as we were ourselves." Reasons given for the American shortcomings included overstaffing and retention of less able personnel who allegedly took less interest in their work than did their British counterparts. The insulation of the American Office of Naval Intelligence from the producers of operational intelligence and from those directing U.S. naval operations was also cited as a weakness. "This reflection [on the relative lack of success of the American naval interrogation effort] is not made in the spirit of idle criticism," the writer commented, "but rather to reinforce the lesson which we learned that naval interrogation can never be successful unless it is closely correlated not only with all other sources of intelligence but also with the day to day work of those responsible for formulating technical and tactical strategy."[60]

While British naval interrogation mentors may not have been entirely satisfied with the results produced by their American pupils, a mutually profitable cooperative effort was maintained throughout the war. Naval prisoners were interrogated in the country in which they were first landed, irrespective of which country had sunk their ships, and the resulting interrogation reports were provided to both countries by American and British naval liaison officers stationed in London and Washington respectively, for that purpose.

It is an unfortunate fact of intelligence life that basic information on friendly territory is seldom collected when it is readily available. Only after the once-friendly area is in enemy hands does the need for detailed data on its ports, roads, terrain, beaches, and climate become apparent and pressing. Lack of what is now known as "topographical intelligence" contributed to the British defeat at Gallipoli in 1915—a lesson either ignored or overlooked until after the fall of Norway in 1940.[61] Fully aware of the Admiralty's short-comings in basic intelligence, the British director of naval intelligence called upon three men: "a Royal Marine officer with considerable intelligence experience, one captain, Royal Navy, with considerable hydrographic experience, and one Oxford Don with knowledge of the resources of the academic world"—to attack the problem.[62] They were charged with the extraction, collation, and production of topographical intelligence to meet the needs of the naval staff planners. They produced two types of reports: topographical studies in what came to be known as the Inter-Service Information Series, or ISIS, and short-term "spot" reports on specific areas of immediate interest to the planners. Much of the information from which these studies were prepared was found in what are today called "open source" materials. Public and private libraries, trade and technical journals, foreign and domestic government publications were culled for vital bits of information. Travelers to foreign lands, whether for business or pleasure, were sought out and their brains picked.

In 1941, following his own dictum that "somewhere in or near London can be found *the* great authority on *any* subject—the problem is to find him,"[63] Godfrey organized a Contact Register Section within his intelligence staff specifically to ferret out those in the civil population with specialized information of potential military value. "By 1943 there was hardly an area in the world or a likely subject without the name of some specialist recorded on the 10,000 cards of its index."[64]

At their inception, the topographical studies were prepared in-house by the naval staff solely for its own use. However, it was not long before War, Air, and other ministries were calling on the section to assist them in obtaining topographical information. The topographical section soon outgrew its space in the Admiralty and moved to Oxford, where it could command not only the vast resources of the university but also those of Oxford University Press, a production facility of the highest quality. To accommodate the needs of the other services, the organization was enlarged to include army and Royal Air Force officers and was renamed the Inter-Service Topographical Department (ISTD). Nevertheless, the Admiralty retained overall supervision of the program.[65]

Although the U.S. Navy developed a topographical department in the Office of Naval Intelligence that shared its products with ISTD and received

ISTD products in return, the American organization most resembling ISTD was located in Colonel "Wild Bill" Donovan's Office of Strategic Services (OSS). President Roosevelt had given Donovan a vague and all-encompassing charter "to collect and analyze all information and data which may bear on national security."[66] To carry out this portion of his mission, Donovan formed a Research and Analysis Branch (R&A) in OSS that produced political and economic studies as well as basic intelligence handbooks. From 1942 until its dissolution at the war's end, William L. Langer, former holder of the Coolidge chair of diplomatic history at Harvard, headed R&A. Langer assembled a team of distinguished scholars whose academic credentials fully equaled those of the Oxbridge dons of ISTD. Some forty professional historians served in R&A during the war, "including no less than seven future presidents of the American Historical Association."[67] Gordon Craig, Felix Gilbert, Walt Rostow, Arthur M. Schlesinger, and Carl E. Schorske were all alumni of the R&A Branch of OSS.

According to Admiral Godfrey, Donovan visited ISTD at Oxford on one of his early trips to Britain and was "immensely impressed." Donovan returned to Washington determined to give "whole-hearted support" to ISTD. "This [support]," Godfrey commented, "took the form of lending us just the sort of staff we [at Oxford] needed and could no longer obtain in the U.K."[68] Most of these reinforcements came from the ranks of R&A, although the U.S. Office of Naval Intelligence also provided officers to ISTD, both from its own staff and from the Intelligence Division of Commander U.S. Naval Forces, Europe.[69]

In addition to assisting ISTD with naval personnel, the American Office of Naval Intelligence, in partnership with army G-2, commenced in early 1943 to produce its own topographical reports known as JANIS, joint army-navy intelligence studies, in response to the needs of the U.S. joint chiefs. Later in the war, OSS played an important part in the production of these studies, which were then issued by the Joint Intelligence Study Publishing Board.[70] R&A liaison officers at OSS headquarters in London worked to obtain topographical materials from Britain for American use, as British Naval Intelligence Directorate officers in Washington did for ISTD.

As had been the case with aerial reconnaissance and photographic interpretation, British initiatives in the development of topographical intelligence materials had preceded similar efforts in the United States, and again, America profited from British trailblazing. Other types of intelligence sharing, especially in the fields of counterintelligence and deception, grew as the war progressed and U.S. participation increased. However, for the most part, these disciplines developed later and thus did not share in the lineage of early war cooperation enjoyed by photographic interpretation and prisoner of war interrogation.

The split leadership in the U.S. Navy, which resulted shortly after Pearl Harbor when the duties of chief of naval operations and commander in chief, U.S. Fleet, were separated, persisted until March 1942 and proved, at best, an "awkward arrangement."[71] On 8 March, Roosevelt accepted Stark's resignation as chief of naval operations and appointed King to the post. The operational and administrative responsibilities for direction of the navy were now combined under King. Rather than go into retirement, Stark chose to accept the president's offer of assignment as commander in chief of U.S. naval forces in Europe. In keeping with the president's desire that Stark's departure from Washington not be seen as a demotion or as punishment for indirect culpability in the Pearl Harbor disaster, the London command was upgraded to that of a four-star, or full admiral's, position, as it had been during World War I under Admiral Sims. Stark took a month's leave before departing for London, where he replaced Vice Admiral Ghormley as both commander, U.S. naval forces Europe, and special naval observer on 30 April 1942.[72]

Stark was a particularly felicitous choice for the British assignment. As a young officer, he had served on Admiral Sims's staff in London during the First World War and therefore had background knowledge of the types of problems he might face in his new command.[73] In his former position as CNO, Stark had attended all the major Anglo-American military conferences in 1940 and 1941 and was fully up to speed on cooperative ventures currently under way between the two navies. He was well thought of by the lords of the Admiralty, who professed to admire Stark "both for his sympathy in their darkest hour and for the manner in which he implemented the generous policy of his Government."[74] Stark, in turn, was impressed by the warmth of his reception. Shortly after his arrival in England, Stark wrote to Dudley Knox, his shipmate from World War I London days, that "everyone in Government circles has been more than frank and more than hospitable. My relationships could hardly be closer, or more friendly, or better in any way than they are with all the leaders over here."[75]

During the course of the Anglo-American military conferences of 1941–1942, Stark had become a personal friend of First Sea Lord, Admiral Sir Dudley Pound. They realized that it was in the mutual interest of their naval services that the closest possible working relationship be established between the Admiralty staff in Whitehall and the American naval staff in Grosvenor Square. Both men used their personal friendship as an informal avenue of approach to difficult problems. Their relationship strongly resembled that of General George C. Marshall, U.S. Army chief of staff, and Field Marshal Sir John Dill, head of the British Joint Staff Mission in Washington. Like Stark, Dill had been "turfed out" of the top post in his military service—in Dill's case, chief of the imperial general staff—and moved to a key liaison post in the capital of a wartime ally. Also like Stark, Dill used his personal friendship with Marshall to deal with ticklish questions. Both men found themselves in posts where they had, in Dill's words, "plenty of influence but no power."[76]

The Bailey Committee, heretofore the chief pipeline for the exchange of information between the U.S. Navy in London and the Admiralty, had ceased operations in September 1941, and no formal organization had as yet replaced it. Although Stark's command was primarily administrative in nature, Pound wished to keep Stark fully acquainted with the operational picture and offered Stark the services of a close friend and colleague, Vice Admiral Sir Geoffrey Blake, RN, as personal liaison officer between the two men. Blake had enjoyed a distinguished career at sea in the interwar years, had served as naval attaché to the British embassy in Washington, and was currently assistant chief of the naval staff for foreign operations. Stark accepted, and Blake took up his new duties as FOLUS—flag officer liaison U.S. Navy—in the early summer of 1942.[77]

Blake's appointment was of significance to intelligence cooperation, because it increased both the volume and the quality of British information furnished to American naval authorities. The increase was achieved, ironically, because FOLUS supplanted the Admiralty's Intelligence Division as the chief arbiter of what should be released. With the concurrence of First Sea Lord Pound, Blake made arrangements for very sensitive message traffic, carrying the highest British security classification, "Hush Most Secret" (roughly corresponding to the U.S. Navy's "Top Secret"), to be passed to him personally at Stark's headquarters. Previously, this category of traffic had been rigidly controlled by the Admiralty's Naval Intelligence Division and only a very small percentage had been made available to the Americans. Other types of traffic of a lower security classification that had been screened for release by Intelligence were now passed in greater numbers and without restriction directly to Blake for his use with Stark and his staff.

In addition to messages, Blake was able to gain the prime minister's permission to show Stark and one or two of his principal staff officers two reports of extremely limited distribution within the British government. The first of these, the Cabinet War Room Record, summarized in no more than two pages the military events of the previous twenty-four hours. The second, the

First Lord's Report, was prepared by the captain on duty in the Admiralty operations room and covered naval activities of the previous twenty-four-hour watch period. This latter record was prepared specifically for the eyes of His Majesty and for the first lord, and its distribution had been limited to thirty-nine persons until the exception was made for Admiral Stark.[78]

The great increase in the flow of British information into the American naval headquarters made it impossible for Stark to read each document, no matter how sensitive or interesting it might be. Blake, therefore, performed the additional service of screening the mass of incoming British material and preparing for Stark's attention a daily summary of the most important items. Should Stark wish to go deeper into any subject, Blake would provide him with the original report or message. The following spring, Stark was to become privy to even more sensitive British information when, at the request of the first sea lord, the prime minister invited Stark to attend meetings of the top-level Anti-U-Boat Warfare Committee.[79] Stark was one of only two Americans so selected. The other, W. Averell Harriman, attended because of his status as President Roosevelt's special representative "in regard to all matters relating to the facilitation of material aid to the British Empire."[80]

Stark considered the information he received from these highly restricted British sources to be so valuable that in June 1942 he requested and obtained permission to send the Cabinet War Room Record and the First Lord's Report to Washington for the personal attention of Admiral King. The following month, King visited London and was shown copies of Blake's daily summary. On his return to the United States, King asked the British Admiralty Delegation "if something of the same sort could be supplied to him in Washington."[81]

While the Admiralty and the American naval staff in London were drawing closer together, the same could not be said of their counterparts in Washington. In April 1942, shortly after Admiral King had assumed the additional responsibilities of chief of naval operations, the prime minister felt it necessary to cable President Roosevelt that relations between the two navies were not as close as might be hoped. "We have established the most intimate contacts with the United States Army and Air Force, but as Harry [Hopkins] will tell you we are not nearly so closely linked up on the Navy side."[82]

King may have welcomed British intelligence information, but he was less receptive to other British cooperative initiatives, particularly those suggesting that American naval personnel or naval units be assigned to operate under British (or other foreign) military authority. King expressed himself forcefully on this point in remarks to American, British, and Canadian naval and air officers attending an antisubmarine warfare conference. "A point upon which I have a very strong personal opinion," King said, "is the avoidance of mixed forces. It is always a great pleasure to work with our Allies, and we can always learn something from each other, but, nevertheless, I have had to me what is conclusive proof that these advantages are more than nullified by the handicap of effort that is inherent when forces of different nations, with different customs and systems of command, are brigaded together."[83]

King's dislike of mixed forces apparently extended even to the exchange of liaison officers. In response to a feeler from the British Admiralty Delegation in Washington concerning closer relationships between the American and British naval forces operating in the South Atlantic, one of King's aides wrote on 25 February 1942, "Admiral King directs me to tell you 'the answer is no. These people are too busy to be exchanging visits; I do not desire that liaison officers be exchanged.'" "I am leaving out of the [previous] quotation," King's aide commented, "the appropriate adjectives and modifiers."[84]

Admiral King found the exchange of officers for intelligence liaison purposes equally distasteful. The British Chiefs of Staff informed the U.S. Joint Chiefs of Staff on 28 July 1942 about the British organization for strategic deception and suggested that, should the United States be considering the formation of a similar body, "collaboration should begin immediately with an exchange of liaison officers." Saying that "he had decided objections towards the interchange of liaison officers for this purpose, particularly since liaison officers appointed by the British usually lack the authority to make any decisions," King was able to get the British proposal shunted off to committee.[85]

Assignment of liaison officers was not always to British liking either, but for somewhat different reasons. The British naval staff would have preferred to see American naval officers appointed directly to the Admiralty, as opposed to having them there in a liaison status. Shortly before his departure for Washington in June 1942 to head the British Admiralty Delegation, Admiral Sir Andrew Cunningham was briefed by Godfrey on Anglo-American naval intelligence relationships. At that time, Cunningham expressed the view that "liaison and collaboration were not enough, and that the time had come when British officers should work actually in the Navy Department in Washington . . . not as liaison officers and observers, but as actual working members."[86] A proposal to assign U.S. officers directly to Admiralty was circulated among the British naval staff for comment, to which the director of naval intelligence responded on 10 August 1942 that he had already asked for the assignment of one American naval officer to the Operational Intelligence Centre and for three others, to become "an integral part of N.I.D."[87] Although Godfrey at the same time expressed his hope "that they [the four officers] will be shortly appointed," no such assignments were made until much later in the war and then not to the Operational Intelligence Centre. Nor were Royal Navy officers ever offered posts in the OIC's sister organization, the U.S. Navy submarine tracking room.

While the failure of the British proposal to put American naval officers to work in the Admiralty cannot be traced directly to Admiral King, it is reasonable to think that his strong antipathy to mixed forces and to liaison officers was well known to his subordinates in the office of the chief of naval operations and was a significant consideration in their personnel decisions. It is equally probable that King's negative attitude toward intelligence personnel exchanges impeded progress toward the more fully integrated intelligence program desired by the Admiralty. Later, policies driven by postwar political and economic considerations would have an adverse effect on Anglo-American intelligence cooperation, but in 1942, a major impediment to a closer integration of the British and American intelligence organizations was the unfavorable attitude of the leader of the U.S. Navy.

In the summer of 1942, Allied planning shifted from preparation for an early invasion of France to that for an attack on North Africa. This significant strategic change was prompted in great part by the desire of both President Roosevelt and Prime Minister Churchill to commence a major campaign in 1942, as well as by their military planners' realization that Allied forces in England could not be made ready for a large-scale attack on France prior to 1943.[88]

General Dwight D. Eisenhower, who had arrived in London on 24 June 1942 to take command of U.S. Army forces in Europe, was charged with planning the North African operation, now code-named "Torch." On 27 July he prepared a memorandum outlining his staff requirements for Torch, in which he suggested that the chief intelligence planner be British.[89] His recommendation was accepted, and a British army brigadier was chosen to head the G-2 (Intelligence) section of the Allied Forces Headquarters staff. In addition, most of the key positions in the intelligence section were filled by British officers.[90]

In response to a query from General George C. Marshall, chief of staff of the U.S. Army, asking for Eisenhower's views on how intelligence needs for Torch should be met, Eisenhower replied on 6 August that "all measures of intelligence . . . should be handled by existing agencies after close coordination" by the Joint Intelligence Committees in London and Washington. "It is not repeat not believed that any intelligence group of a separate service either in Great Britain or in the United States can handle this work independently, but that in both countries it must be controlled by the joint bodies established for this purpose." In short, Eisenhower was proposing that the combined staff system for the provision of intelligence, agreed to at the Arcadia conference in early 1942, be put to the test. However, he did recommend that the final decision on all intelligence activities in connection with Torch rest with the supreme commander. Eisenhower was particularly concerned that subversive activities, propaganda, and political warfare should be closely coordinated with the Torch military planners and specifically approved by the supreme commander. "I am convinced," he wrote, "that . . . disaster will inevitably follow mistaken and uncoordinated efforts of agencies not fully informed as to the scope and timing of contemplated operations."[91]

Integral to the Torch concept of operations was the amphibious assault, an ancient form of naval warfare but one little employed in modern times, and never on the scale envisaged for Torch. Final Torch planning called for the Western Naval Task Force, under Admiral Henry K. Hewitt, USN, to land approximately 35,000 Army troops and some 250 tanks at three locations along the Atlantic coast of Morocco. Admiral Hewitt, since April 1942 commander of the Amphibious Force, Atlantic Fleet, was charged with both the planning and the execution of this vast amphibious operation. According to World War II naval historian Samuel Eliot Morison, "Admiral Hewitt, who had seen active service in the Navy for thirty-five years, was admirably adapted for this position by his seagoing experience, his organizing ability, and his tact."[92] This latter virtue was probably put to the test in dealing with his counterpart, General George S. Patton, commander of the Western Landing Force, U.S. Army.

Intelligence planning for the American landings along the Moroccan coast was carried out by Hewitt's staff in Norfolk, Virginia. The planners assembled information from a wide variety of American sources, including the Office of Naval Intelligence, the army's Military Intelligence Service, the Office of Strategic Services, the Department of State, the Hydrographic Office, and various weather bureaus. British contributions were received via Eisenhower's combined planning staff in London, and the British provided "thousands of photographs" taken by reconnaissance aircraft that were used in choosing the "most feasible" landing areas. Despite the multiplicity of sources, gaps in information persisted, and inaccuracies crept in. During the American debarkation in Oran, which began on 9 November 1942, one of the beach approaches, evaluated as "excellent" in the intelligence appreciation, was found to have a sandbar that caused landing craft to ground two hundred yards offshore.[93]

Planning for the Torch landings afforded intelligence a challenge different from any it had faced since the German invasion of Poland in 1939. For the first time, the Allies were on the offensive, and intelligence was being called on to perform the unaccustomed task of predicting enemy reactions.[94] Questions such as the degree of French opposition expected, Spanish reaction, and the likelihood of German intervention were subjects of debate and compromise. Assessments made shortly before the 8 November landing indicated that Allied forces faced their greatest danger at sea en route to their objectives but that once ashore, they should experience no great difficulties[95]—a less than accurate estimate, as things worked out.

Intelligence for the assaults on Oran and Algiers, especially the naval intelligence required by the Eastern Task Force, came primarily from the British. Aside from those American intelligence officers operating under diplomatic cover as consular officials monitoring American food shipments to French North Africa, the United States had almost no intelligence "assets" within the Mediterranean. In contrast, the British, with strategically important locations such as Gibraltar, Malta, and the Suez Canal to defend, were longtime players in the Middle Eastern intelligence game.

The Admiralty's involvement in Middle East intelligence activities dated from 1892, when it first began to receive reports from the Royal Navy's Mediterranean Station.[96] In the summer of 1939, the Admiralty established a scaled-down version of its own Operational Intelligence Centre at Malta, so that "the Commander in Chief, Mediterranean, should have more immediate intelligence of movements of foreign war and merchant ships in the Mediterranean than could be afforded direct from London."[97] The Malta Operational Intelligence Centre obtained much of its information from intercepted communications, especially from Italian naval traffic, and from direction finding analysis. A small team of communications intelligence specialists was embarked in the fleet flagship "to produce 'red hot' deduction for the information of the Commander in Chief." The existence of this operational intelligence group, ashore and afloat, was treated as "most secret," and its activities were kept entirely separate from the "aboveground" worldwide naval intelligence organization, which had offices in Malta, Alexandria, and Cairo.[98]

In countering German U-boats—the greatest potential threat to the Allied convoys bound for Torch—naval intelligence was hampered by its inability throughout most of 1942 to read German submarine communications; however, Italian naval codes had been broken in the summer of 1941, and the use of this source, as well as other types of intercepted German communications and extensive photographic reconnaissance, enabled intelligence to gauge enemy reactions—or, in this case, the lack thereof—to Allied maritime activities. Although the western convoy from the United States and the eastern convoy from the British Isles were detected on occasion during their transits, the enemy was unsuccessful in determining their ultimate destinations, and both convoys reached their objectives without coming under serious attack.[99]

The Admiralty provided the intelligence on landing beaches, ports, and objectives ashore required by the Intelligence Section of the Allied Forces Headquarters staff, much of it coming from the labors of the Inter-Service Topographical Department. The official history of British intelligence in the Second World War noted that "there was little opposition during the landings and this makes it difficult to judge the quality of the intelligence . . . provided by ISTD. But there is little doubt that its reports . . . were of high quality."[100] ISTD was complimented on its contribution to the success of the landings by both Eisenhower and his naval deputy, Admiral Andrew B. Cunningham, RN. Intelligence preparations for Torch proved to be, if nothing else, an excellent practical test of the joint/combined intelligence planning system and an opportunity to work out procedural kinks before the major effort, intelligence planning for Overlord—the Allied invasion of Europe in 1944—got under way in earnest.

In the year from the Japanese attack on Pearl Harbor to the Allied landings in North Africa, significant changes took place in Anglo-American naval intelligence cooperation. Increased German U-boat activity along the east coast of Canada and the United States mandated new countermeasures in antisubmarine warfare. The post-Arcadia conferences between the American and British joint chiefs in early 1942 paved the way for the institution of the joint/combined intelligence system. Provision of single-service, uncoordinated intelligence estimates began to give way to preparation of an integrated, joint and combined intelligence product. The new system received its first test in the planning for Torch and proved workable.

Additional types of intelligence began to come on stream during the year. Information from aerial photography, prisoners of war, and topographical intelligence was combined with that from communications intelligence and from agents to provide the planners with the most comprehensive picture possible of enemy capabilities. The British took the lead in perfecting new techniques of intelligence, and Americans profited from British knowledge.

In 1942, the Admiralty continued its efforts to obtain closer integration of its intelligence activities with those of the U.S. Navy, and Washington continued to resist. The U.S. Navy's reluctance to move more rapidly in the field of intelligence cooperation at least indirectly reflected the attitude of its leader, Admiral Ernest J. King, who continued to look with disfavor upon permitting American ships and sailors to serve under foreign commanders. Post-Arcadia navy-to-navy ties were also weakened by Allied adoption of the joint/combined staff system. As the year 1942 ended and the tide of battle began to turn, the Allies started to look toward an invasion of "Fortress Europe." Intelligence, too, prepared to go on the offensive.

Part Two
Culmination and Turning Point

5·
The Culmination

As the war in Europe entered its fourth year, the tide of battle was beginning to flow in favor of the Allies. The period from the successful Allied invasion of North Africa in November 1942 until the December 1943 selection of General Dwight D. Eisenhower as supreme commander of the Allied Expeditionary Forces preparing to invade Continental Europe marked the high point in Anglo-American naval intelligence cooperation. The carefully orchestrated British campaign to establish close working ties among the Royal, Royal Canadian, and U.S. Navies' submarine tracking rooms was beginning to pay major dividends in the anti-U-boat war. Intelligence activities in all theaters were driven by the strategic decisions made by Roosevelt, Churchill, and their advisers at Casablanca in January 1943. The combined American and British intelligence structure that had been created to prepare for the North African invasion had proved its effectiveness under actual combat conditions and would serve as the model in planning for subsequent campaigns in the Mediterranean and, more important, for the invasion of continental Europe.

By the spring of 1943, while Allied naval fortunes in the Mediterranean were improving, the same could not be said of the situation in the Atlantic. After a lull in January, Allied shipping losses, especially on the convoy routes in the Atlantic, increased alarmingly, peaking in March when U-boats destroyed over 625,000 tons of Allied merchant shipping.[1] Following the strategic line agreed on at Casablanca in January 1943, the highest Allied naval priority became, if had ever ceased to be, defeat of the German U-boat fleet. Allied leaders saw clearly that the Battle of the Atlantic must be won before an invasion of northwest Europe or major offensives in other theaters could be undertaken. Not only were shipping losses unacceptably high, but as American naval historian Samuel Eliot Morison pointed out, "Hitler was still building 'em [U-boats] faster than we could sink 'em."[2]

Adding to the problems presented by the Germans were inter-Allied tensions that hindered effective measures to counter the U-boat threat. As has been noted, duplication in providing directional fixes on U-boats to American and Canadian antisubmarine forces had been settled to some extent by the April 1942 radio intelligence discussions in Washington. D/F duplication was, however, a small part of a much larger problem. In the fight to bring Allied convoys safely across the Atlantic, the Canadian navy's growth in size and responsibility had not been matched by an increase in authority in Allied naval councils. Decisions about areas of responsibility in the western Atlantic affecting the RCN, but made without Canadian approval at the ABC-1 and Placentia Bay conferences in 1941, continued to rankle. Even more painful to Canadian sensibilities was the impression that, instead of championing its push for greater recognition, the British seemed as firm as the Americans about keeping Canada in a subordinate position.

Although the American and Canadian military had been planning together since 1938, Canada had not felt a need to send military attachés to the United States until the summer of 1940. As the wartime role of the Canadian navy grew, attaché representation seemed inadequate, and Canada sought the establishment of a military presence in Washington nearer in stature to that of the British Joint Services Mission. This idea met with disfavor from both the British, who did not want to lose the control over Canadian military policy that such a move would precipitate, and the Americans, who much preferred to deal with a single entity and not with each member of the British Empire on an individual basis. It took a year of importuning and bargaining before the United States agreed to the establishment of a Canadian Joint Staff Mission in Washington in July 1942.

Unfortunately for Canadian naval concerns, the Admiralty and the U.S. Navy were no more interested in dealing with the Joint Staff Mission than they had been in dealing with the attachés. In frustration, Admiral Brodeur, the senior naval member of the Canadian mission in Washington, wrote to Admiral Nelles, chief of the naval staff in Ottawa, that it was his "firm conviction that the U.S.N. policy has been to avoid consulting the R.C.N. representative [Brodeur] on any important matters affecting the two services." To consult, Brodeur felt, "would put the R.C.N. on the same footing as the Admiralty who deal entirely through B.A.D. [British Admiralty Delegation] on policy matters."[3]

In intelligence, the sticking point continued to be U.S. Navy insistence that it alone should promulgate intelligence to Allied naval units—American, British, or Canadian—under its operational control. The RCN felt that it could provide more timely and accurate information than the USN on the northern portion of the western Atlantic and should be allowed to do so. Naval headquarters in Ottawa complained to the British Admiralty Delegation in Washington that limiting Canada's provision of intelligence to units within its coastal waters was at variance with previous Admiralty instructions, and if the Canadian navy were to continue so confined, "there is not much point in keeping up an organization with the high communication expenses entailed." BAD replied that although the work done by the RCN "is of utmost value . . . the situation has altered considerably" since the Admiralty instructions relied on by the Canadians had been issued, that the new U.S. tracking room was now "capable of originating warnings to escorts as quickly as Ottawa," and that "the most efficient arrangement would be for [U.S.] Navy Dept to be the originating authority in the U.S. strategic area except in Canadian coastal zone."[4]

The continuing problem of promulgation of intelligence to the naval escorts, coupled with Canadian concern that the U.S. operational commander in the western Atlantic was transferring RCN ships from one command to another without the concurrence of—or even informing—Canadian naval headquarters, prompted Admiral Nelles to approach Admiral King directly. On 1 December, Nelles proposed to King that a high-level conference be convened to establish a clear division of intelligence duties regarding promulgation of fixes and to discuss the greater issue of operational control. King agreed reluctantly on 17 December, but the conference, which took place in the first two weeks of March 1943, did not come about without additional prodding from Nelles.[5]

From the start, the conference participants realized that the matter of operational authority could not be solved until they were all comfortable with the RCN's ability to provide the quality of operational intelligence support required for convoy control, so they convened a major subcommittee on intelligence. Canadian naval staff headquarters, which had refused to place a member of its "Y" staff on the delegation to Washington, was forced to recall deMarbois from a long-anticipated holiday with his family and get him and Lieutenant Commander D.R.H. Macdonald, RCNVR, the officer in charge of the RCN's Operational Intelligence Centre, on a night plane to Washington. Once a full Canadian team had been assembled, recommendations for the necessary intelligence improvements followed rapidly.

The conference smoothed out the last of the remaining large bumps on the road to American-Canadian naval cooperation in the western Atlantic. It was agreed that Canada would have "general charge (as distinct from strategic control)" of trade convoys while they were in the northwest Atlantic. This word game soothed the amour propre of all concerned and allowed the parties to return to the greater battle against the Germans.[6]

To meet the continuing U-boat threat in the Atlantic, the U.S. Navy formed the Tenth Fleet on 1 May 1943. With no ships to call its own, the Tenth Fleet staff, including its intelligence component, waged war from an office in downtown Washington, D.C., where staff members worked hand in glove with their counterparts at the Admiralty in London. Commander, Tenth Fleet, and commander in chief, U.S. Fleet, were one and the same— Admiral Ernest J. King. King's expert on German U-boat intelligence, Commander Kenneth A. Knowles, was also "double-hatted," with duties on both fleet staffs. Coincident with the creation of the Tenth Fleet, King, acting in his capacity as chief of naval operations, realigned the activities of his naval intelligence organization to provide closer support to the U.S. Navy's operating forces.

At the war's end, Captain Kenneth Knowles, USN (retired), responded to a query from the director of naval history on points that should be covered in a planned command history of the Battle of the Atlantic. Knowles commented that, among other things, the Atlantic was "unique among the campaigns of the war in respect to Allied command relations. There was no supreme commander in the Battle of the Atlantic."[7]

Although Knowles's observation was accurate, during the dark days of 1942 and 1943, British and American leaders considered establishing a unified antisubmarine command for the Atlantic, and Parliament even debated the question. Air Chief Marshal Sir Philip Joubert of RAF Coastal Command and several officers on the staff of Admiral Harold R. Stark, commander in chief, U.S. naval forces in Europe, favored the idea of a single controlling staff for the U-boat war.[8] The Admiralty, however, remained firmly opposed. The first sea lord wrote to the prime minister that if a British officer were chosen as supreme commander, there would be friction with the Americans, and that selection of an American was "unthinkable,"[9] because Americans lacked the necessary knowledge and experience.

Knowles also reminded the director of naval history that "the Atlantic was divided for purposes of administrative and command requirements, but the Battle of the Atlantic was a single operation."[10] Nowhere was this better illustrated than in the provision of intelligence to the forces engaged in the anti-U-boat war. The U-boat tracking centers of the American, British, and Canadian navies kept their own national identities; no "combined" center was ever seriously contemplated, nor were personnel exchanged—except for short visits. Yet the three centers thought and acted as though they were one, in what was probably the most complete and most effective naval intelligence cooperative effort during the Second World War.

By January 1943, the submarine tracking room, the section of British naval intelligence designed specifically to counter the U-boat menace, was operating at peak efficiency. Its American counterpart, the commander in chief, U.S. Fleet's U-boat tracking room, better known as the "Secret Room" because of its exclusive use of communications intelligence, had come into being in late December 1942 and was playing catch-up. "The teamwork between us [U.S./U.K.] was superb," Knowles later said, "and we were ever grateful for their more experienced counsel and advice."[11]

The British and American U-boat tracking rooms were remarkably similar in their physical characteristics and—except that the British room worked around the clock and the U.S. room did not—in their methods of operation. This was perhaps not too surprising, since Winn had been instrumental in organizing the U.S. tracking room during his visit to Washington in April 1942,[12] and Knowles had visited the Admiralty's tracking room on several occasions during the war, including a two-week indoctrination tour in May 1942. Both tracking rooms were small adjuncts to larger plot rooms. In the Admiralty, the larger of the two rooms was the main trade and operations plot, where Allied and enemy naval and merchant shipping information not directly attributable to communications intelligence was displayed. In Washington, the U.S. Navy's main operational plot room was located in the Commander in Chief, U.S. Fleet (COMINCH), Combat Intelligence Division's Atlantic section. Here, as in London, all-source information (disguised or "sanitized" as necessary) was maintained on Allied and neutral naval ships and merchant convoys, as well as estimates of the locations of enemy surface and subsurface forces.[13]

The missions of the small tracking rooms were essentially the same. Both were to receive intercepted and decoded enemy communications and display the information they contained. In addition, data from other sources, such as traffic analysis, direction finding, and sighting reports from ships and aircraft, were presented, along with information derived from TINA, a "rather intricate process" of identifying individual radio operators (and, by extension, the ships in which they were embarked) by their "fists"—"the inherent characteristics of their hand-sending of the radio code."[14] Knowles and Winn would then use the sum of all this information to estimate the locations, movements, and—when possible—intentions of enemy U-boats.

Because it contained information almost exclusively derived from intercepted enemy communications, the American "Secret Room" was off-limits to most of the U.S. Navy Department. Knowles; his assistant, Lieutenant John E. Parsons, USNR; and two others were the only persons to enter the room on a regular basis. Knowles has indicated that "perhaps a half dozen senior officers within the combined [COMINCH/Tenth Fleet] staffs had knowledge that 'Ultra' existed."[15] Entry to the British submarine tracking room was also restricted to those who were permitted to see Ultra material, but despite Churchill's concern for the security of his communications intelligence "eggs,"[16] many more in the Admiralty had access to this "Most Secret" intelligence source than was the case in the U.S. Navy Department. According to Patrick Beesly, Churchill was a regular visitor to the OIC in the early months of the war when he was first lord, but not after he became prime minister. Beesly notes the surprise felt by the head of the OIC that the Admiralty messenger was so prompt in cleaning up after the first lord's visits, until he learned that the messenger was doing a brisk business in the sale of Churchillian cigar butts.[17]

The relative anonymity of those assigned to the two tracking rooms also worked to their advantage in producing intelligence estimates unbiased by political or other extraneous considerations. Both rooms were headed by men with the rank of commander—considered the bottom grade in the "senior officer" category. Their assistants held even lower navy ranks and worked behind closed doors, doing their jobs in a superb manner while remaining virtually unremarked in their respective naval headquarters.

The daily routines of the two tracking rooms differed only slightly.[18] Because of its limited access and the time delays inherent in intercepting, decrypting, translating, and analyzing intelligence derived from enemy communications, the American "Secret Room" did not operate on an around-the-clock basis. Collateral information, such as sighting reports and direction finding positions, went to the main plot next door. The British tracking room, which by the beginning of 1943 had a staff of fourteen, maintained a twenty-four-hour watch that brought together in one place all operational information on the U-boat picture.

The real work of the day began with the early morning arrivals of the senior analysts: Winn and his assistant Patrick Beesly in London, Knowles and his assistant John Parsons in Washington. Information that had arrived during the night was reexamined and correlated with data previously received and held in the voluminous files on individual U-boats that both tracking rooms maintained. Plots of current U-boat positions were updated, and both Winn and Knowles began to order their thoughts for the daily briefing on the submarine picture that each of them presented to the senior officers of the British Naval Staff and the U.S. Navy Department, respectively.

Winn and Knowles exchanged daily analytical summaries of U-boat operations and, in addition, less formal analytical comments and questions. To encourage the most frank and unconstrained exchange of ideas, these messages were treated as personal notes and no regular dissemination of their contents was made outside of the two tracking rooms, although on occasion the commander in chief, U.S. Fleet, and the first sea lord used this "back-channel" to exchange views on submarine matters.[19] By the war's end, over 2,000 serials had passed back and forth between the two tracking rooms. Knowles sent a final message to Winn on 5 June 1945 in which he announced the dissolution of his organization and paid tribute to Winn's accomplishments. "May I express to you my deepest appreciation for your most helpful cooperation during the momentous three years our tracking rooms have worked together. Yours has been the greater burden and responsibility and you have completed your task magnificently."[20]

The Admiralty's naval intelligence organization, including the Operational Intelligence Centre and within it the submarine tracking room, had changed little since 1938, nor had its relationship to the other divisions of the British Naval Staff. The same could not be said for American naval intelligence and its relationship to the rest of the Navy Department. Ever since Admiral Ernest J. King had become commander in chief of the U.S. Fleet in December 1941 and chief of naval operations in March 1942, the organizational structure of the U.S. Navy's shore establishment had been in an almost constant state of change. Finally, in August 1943, an exasperated President Roosevelt directed his secretary of the navy to "tell Ernie [King] *once more:* No reorganizing of the Navy Dept. set-up during the war. Let's win it first."[21]

The establishment on 1 May 1943 of the Tenth Fleet further complicated the intelligence picture.[22] Tenth Fleet was homeported in "Main Navy"—as the headquarters building in downtown Washington was called—and commanded by Admiral King. The fleet was formed so that all the antisubmarine forces in the Atlantic would be responsible to a single commander who could issue orders directly to operating forces without going through the slow and cumbersome chain of command.[23] Convoy and routing became responsibilities of the new organization, and much of its small staff was drawn from the larger COMINCH structure. Many officers were "double-hatted," with responsibilities on both staffs. This was the case in intelligence, where Commander Knowles was both head of the Atlantic section, COMINCH, and chief of the intelligence staff, Tenth Fleet. In a later move, the assistant chief of staff (Combat Intelligence), COMINCH, was double-hatted as director of naval intelligence in the CNO organizational chain.[24] Thus the intelligence responsibilities of the CNO, COMINCH, and Tenth Fleet staffs were intertwined under a single ultimate authority, Admiral Ernest J. King.

Formation of the Tenth Fleet permitted the "Secret Room's" intelligence analysis to be employed in much the same direct manner as that of the British submarine tracking room. Prior to the consolidation brought about by the establishment of the Tenth Fleet, the U.S. Navy's decentralized command structure had made it impossible to adopt British operational intelligence methods. As commander of the Tenth Fleet, King could now exercise the same amount of control over his portion of the U-boat war as his counterpart, the first sea lord, had been doing since the start of the war. Knowles, like Winn, now had immediate access to those who were routing the convoys and to those who were directing the protective forces. U.S. naval intelligence was now in a position to exert greater influence than ever before on the Battle of the Atlantic.

Fortunately, coincident with U.S naval intelligence's opportunity to have greater influence on operations came improvement in the quality of intelligence, which made it of much greater value to the operators. It will be remembered that in December 1942, British code breakers were able once again to break the German codes used to transmit orders to U-boats. Generally, German U-boats did not receive assignments to patrol areas until they had put to sea. From that time until they transmitted the mandatory signal requesting permission to return home, the submarines were under the constant control of U-boat command. To effect this close supervision required a large volume of message traffic. This traffic "presented the Allies with an unprecedentedly rich flow of operational intelligence."[25]

Even though the cryptographers in Bletchley Park had achieved success in breaking the German U-boat code, doing so fast enough for the information to be used effectively in antisubmarine warfare was a continuing problem. To increase security, the Germans had introduced an additional rotor wheel in the coding machines carried by the Atlantic U-boats. As a result, the "bombes," an early form of data processor that the British had constructed to test likely rotor positions of German Enigma machines, were of little value in finding correct solutions to the daily settings on the modified German machines.[26]

As early as the spring of 1942, Washington had seen the need for an independent U.S. code-breaking capability against German U-boat communications and had ordered the U.S. Navy to take appropriate measures, which later included the construction of an American bombe for use against the German navy's four-wheel machines. Despite Bletchley Park's difficulties with existing technology in exploiting the modified German machines, the British seemed reluctant to share what progress had been made with the U.S. Navy and appeared more interested in forcing the code breakers of OP-20-G to concentrate on Japanese naval traffic by denying them access to German U-boat Enigma material. When it became evident that the U.S. Navy intended to attack German Enigma with or without British help, the code breakers at Bletchley became more forthcoming, and a series of cooperative agreements were negotiated.

In the summer of 1943, American-built, high-speed bombes, specially designed to defeat the German navy's four-rotor encryption system, came into use. Each of these new bombes had an output equivalent to six of the older British models.[27] These machines were located in Washington and were operated by the U.S. Navy to produce the solutions, called "cribs," used to decrypt German Atlantic U-boat traffic throughout the remainder of the war. An agreement between Edward W. Travis, head of the British Government Code and Cypher School at Bletchley Park, and Commander Joseph H. Wenger, USN, head of OP-20-G in the U.S. Navy Department, gave American code breakers access to German naval messages to and from German naval units operating out of range of U.S. intercept stations. In return, the Americans provided successful cribs produced by the bombes to assist in the British attack on German naval codes. By August 1943, German naval traffic encrypted on the Enigma machine was read "regularly and rapidly without significant interruption."[28]

In addition to the Anglo-American failure to break the German U-boat cipher before December 1942, another factor contributing to the German navy's success in the Atlantic was its ability to read the Allied convoy code. The German Naval Cryptographic Service (B-Dienst) had been able to break British Naval Cypher No. 3 through most of 1942. Improvements made in late 1942 interrupted the German success until February 1943, when B-Dienst again mastered the British code and continued to read it until its use was discontinued in June 1943.[29]

As British success against the German U-boat codes was determined in great measure by the large volume of traffic intercepted, so German success against the British convoy cipher "was made possible by the many routine signals necessary to direct the complicated convoy routing system."[30] According to the British government's official history of intelligence, "between February and June 1943 the battle of the Atlantic hinged to no small extent on the changing fortunes of a continuing trial of cryptographic and cryptanalytic resourcefulness between the B-Dienst and the Allies."[31] While the German navy, in the face of evidence to the contrary, continued to consider its codes impenetrable, the Royal Navy realized that its codes had been compromised and changed them.

May 1943 is generally accepted as the month that the battle against the U-boats turned in favor of the Allies.[32] The initiative never again passed to the German Navy. In the first twenty-two days of May, thirty-one U-boats were destroyed. Admiral Dönitz, by this time head of the German navy, ordered his submarines withdrawn from the North Atlantic convoy routes. Success in the North Atlantic, however, did not mean the end of the U-boat threat. Subsequent U-boat deployments to the central Atlantic remained of great concern to the Allied planners moving vast quantities of men and supplies to the Mediterranean and England in preparation for the Italian campaign and the cross-channel invasion of 1944. U-boats were seen as an even greater potential threat in the last year of the European war, which became a race against time to end the conflict before Germany could bring its new type of submarine into operation.[33]

There is little question that intelligence played a major role in winning the Battle of the Atlantic, but so many other factors contributed as well that it is impossible to single out any one as *the* key ingredient. Greater air cover from land-based aircraft and from the new escort carriers was important, as were advances in airborne radar and in antisubmarine weaponry, expansion of the high-frequency direction finding system both ashore and at sea, and growing numbers of surface escort ships. Historians have argued that the value of ULTRA in winning the Battle of the Atlantic may have been overrated and that superior American maritime production would have achieved the same outcome eventually.[34] While the relative value of ULTRA to the contest may be open to question, there is little doubt that Ultra, "Y" analysis, D/F, photographic reconnaissance, and all the other types of data that came together in the three operational intelligence centers were fundamental in defeating the U-boats. Working in harmony, these centers provided rapid analysis of all the sources of information and timely promulgation of intelligence. It was the cooperative effort—not the input of any single source—that was vital.

In the early years of the war, the Allies tended to use information on U-boat positions derived from communications intelligence in a defensive sense, routing convoys away from known German wolf-pack positions. Limiting the use of ULTRA in this manner served the twofold purpose of protecting the convoy and protecting the source of the information that caused the convoy route to be shifted. With the arrival of new antisubmarine weapons in the latter stages of the Battle of the Atlantic, intelligence switched to a more positive role by helping to pinpoint locations of U-boats so that they might be attacked and destroyed. The quality of intelligence furnished by the Allied submarine tracking rooms is documented in a U.S. Navy task group commander's after-action report of operations conducted in the central Atlantic in August 1943. The intelligence provided proved "accurate and invaluable in our offensive search. No subs were sighted except in locations given."[35] Had the European war lasted longer, the intelligence–U-boat equation might well have changed again, since the new, snorkel-equipped German boats were harder to detect and faster underwater, rendering most of the Allied antisubmarine weapons systems obsolete.[36]

Jürgen Rohwer, a leading authority on German naval operations in World War II, placed exploitation of ULTRA at the top of his list of factors contributing to the Allied success in the Battle of the Atlantic. Without ULTRA, he concluded, "many more ships, aircraft and support groups would have been necessary . . . and they became available only from the late summer of 1943."[37] Many more tons of Allied shipping would have been lost in the summer of 1943, and in all probability, the Allied timetable for the invasion of Normandy would have been upset. Conversely, we might ask ourselves, what happened when ULTRA wasn't there? It cannot be entirely coincidental that from February to mid-December 1942 and during ten days in mid-March 1943, periods when the British were unable to recover German U-boat codes, the Allies suffered their greatest shipping losses of the war in the North Atlantic.

Historian F. H. Hinsley, who has been asked to deal with the question of ULTRA's importance many times and in many aspects over the years, wrote that "whereas Ultra had been solely responsible for the success of evasive routeing, it was only one of the factors underlying the success of the Allied offensive. . . . But the influence of Ultra on the offensive was enormous. By maximizing the effect of these technical and operational developments which came to fruition in 1943, and by enabling the Allies to pin-point their attacks in a huge theater of operations, it ensured that the Allied victory was complete and decisive."[38]

There is no question that the synergetic efforts of the American, British, and Canadian naval intelligence organizations were key to Allied intelligence success in the Battle of the Atlantic, providing more and better information on U-boat operations than any one of them could have done alone. Patrick Beesly summed up the situation accurately when he wrote that in the three years of their joint existence, the cooperation between the American Combat Intelligence Division and the British Operational Intelligence Centre "was probably closer than between any other British and American organizations in any Service and in any other theatre."[39] The product of this unprecedented association made a major contribution to the winning of the war.

Shortly after the successful Allied landings in North Africa in November 1942 (Torch), Sir John Dill, head of the British Joint Services Mission to the United States, wrote to his countryman and former colleague in Washington, Admiral Andrew B. Cunningham, who was then serving as Eisenhower's naval deputy for Torch. In the course of the letter, Dill commented that Cunningham's previous experience in Washington as head of the British Admiralty Delegation must be "of great value" in getting along with Americans in his current assignment. "In that short time [in Washington] you got to know a great deal about the Americans—their methods and their points of view. We go on fighting our endless battles and I fancy that the closer our operations become interwoven the more difficult those battles will be."[40]

The year 1943 had opened with evidence, if such were needed, of the correctness of Dill's observation. President Franklin Roosevelt, Prime Minister Winston Churchill, and their key political and military staff members met in Casablanca from 11 to 25 January to hammer out details of the Allied military strategy to be followed once victory in Tunisia had been achieved. As was generally the case, the British came to this conference well prepared— even sending to Morocco, in advance of the meeting, a 6,000-ton ocean liner to serve as a floating staff headquarters and communications center.[41] They also came prepared to speak with one voice against any major cross-channel attack on Germany and in support of a Mediterranean strategy that had as its objective defeating Italy, commencing with an assault on Sicily.[42] General Albert C. Wedemeyer, then a planning officer in the Operations Division of the War Department, accompanied Army Chief of Staff George C. Marshall to Casablanca and noted that the British military at the conference "always knew in advance what they wanted. They had aims. Usually their aims could be related to Empire or to their postwar position in the world of commerce."[43] Wedemeyer's comments reflected an increasing awareness among American negotiators of the influence of postwar considerations on current strategic decisions and a growing recognition on their part that Allied postwar agendas were potentially divergent.

American military leaders, marginally accepting a strategy urged by Marshall, favored an attack somewhere in northwestern Europe in 1943. In addition, Admiral Ernest J. King wished to commit more American resources to the fight against Japan. Both King and Marshall concurred with their British colleagues that the paramount Allied problem was to answer the German

U-boat challenge but agreed with the British on little else. After a series of sometimes emotional exchanges of views, which today would be characterized as "full and frank," Allied military leaders agreed to both an invasion of Sicily and the formation of a staff to proceed with detailed planning of a cross-channel invasion of Western Europe.

These decisions, with their underlying perceptions of divergent postwar plans, were to have a significant impact on the course of Allied intelligence cooperation. As will be seen, cooperative ventures after the Casablanca conference came to be measured in terms not only of wartime gains but also of postwar advantage. Eisenhower's selection to command the Sicilian operation and subsequent appointment in December 1943 as supreme Allied commander for the invasion of northwest Europe made it almost inevitable that Allied joint and combined staff agencies, rather than individual service intelligence organizations, would provide the information needed by his planners. Use of a combined Allied staff, supported by joint organizations drawn from individual nations—such as the American and British Joint Intelligence Committees—had proved successful in planning the North African invasion, and Eisenhower saw no reason to change.

As American participation in the war expanded into North Africa and the Mediterranean, new opportunities appeared for intelligence support to the fighting forces involved. On 1 January 1943, Admiral King, in his capacity as commander in chief, U.S. Fleet, approved naval participation in a new American army and navy intelligence organization called the Joint Intelligence Collection Agency, or JICA.[44] The mission of JICA was "to eliminate duplication in the collection, swift transmission and reception of intelligence sent to Washington, and to procure intelligence from Washington and sources within the theater and disseminate it to theater activities."[45] With the blessing of the U.S. Joint Chiefs of Staff, and following approval by General Eisenhower on 23 January 1943, the first unit, JICA North Africa, was established in Algiers at Allied Forces Headquarters and immediately became active in gathering information for use in the Allied invasions of Sicily and Italy. Suboffices soon followed at Casablanca, Port Lyautey, and Tunis. A second JICA covering the Middle East was established in Cairo on 21 June 1943. The agency soon went worldwide, opening offices in India and China and contemplating additional offices in the Pacific and even in London.[46]

The establishment of the JICA system was significant for several reasons. For the first time since the start of the war, American army and navy intelligence organizations had put aside their differences to form a truly joint intelligence agency—something the British had done several years earlier when they created the Middle East Intelligence Centre in Cairo in June 1939.[47]

Also, for the first time, American intelligence attempted to come to grips with the problem of providing from anywhere else but Washington the intelligence needed by American forces operating in the European and Middle Eastern theaters. Additionally, it will be remembered that prior to the Allied invasion of North Africa in November 1942, the American intelligence presence in the Mediterranean area was negligible. Penetration by the United States into that mare nostrum of British intelligence put England on notice that the U.S. intelligence structure was coming of age and in the future could be expected to play an increasingly larger role in shaping Allied decisions. No longer would Eisenhower's combined staff be totally dependent on British sources for the intelligence it required.

"I consider this [the establishment of JICA North Africa] one of the most important projects that ONI has ever undertaken," wrote Captain Ellis M. Zacharias, deputy director of naval intelligence, to Captain Earl Major, USNR, who had been selected to head the naval portion of JICA.[48] Zacharias, who saw himself as father of the JICA concept,[49] had noted that American forces in North Africa had failed to realize the importance of intelligence collected in combat for future operations. "After culling the immediately usable tactical intelligence data from the material to which they [the American forces] obtained access in combat, they discarded the rest."[50] Zacharias's plan called for the establishment of specially trained teams that would operate in combat areas to collect and forward documents and other intelligence materials to Washington for analysis.

Specifically excluded from JICA's reporting charter was what the army called "combat intelligence" and the navy called "operational intelligence," such as order of battle information. The British were particularly insistent that all order of battle information be exchanged through previously established channels in Washington and London.[51] Their concern was not surprising, since in the past, they had been "burned" by unauthorized American reporting of British estimates of enemy order of battle figures. In one case in 1942, the year prior to the establishment of the JICA system, the American naval attaché in Cairo gave a copy of a British naval intelligence estimate on the number of Axis transport aircraft in the Aegean to his colleague, the U.S. Army attaché. The army attaché promptly transmitted it to the War Department, along with a British army estimate on the same subject that contained different figures. Washington helpfully pointed out the discrepancies to the British in London, who apparently "were not amused" and so informed the British naval staff in Cairo, with the result that the U.S. naval attaché was told "unofficially that I might, as a result, be prepared to receive even less information than the limited amount I was then receiving."[52]

At roughly the same time that Captain Zacharias in Washington was working on the problem of timely collection and reporting of combat-derived information, Commander Ian Fleming, RNVR, personal assistant to the British DNI, was tackling the same problem in London. Fleming had studied the operation of German naval assault companies (Marine Einsatz Kommando) in Yugoslavia and Greece. These self-contained units were designed to accompany frontline troops in attacks on naval objectives and had proved successful in capturing intelligence materials and in preventing the destruction of secret documents.[53] Fleming drafted plans for a similar joint service British group and obtained the concurrence of his director, Admiral Godfrey. The DNI proposed the concept to the Joint Intelligence Committee and, after considerable bureaucratic infighting, obtained its approval and that of the British Chiefs of Staff. Many years later, Godfrey wrote that "for such a novel enterprise, it is essential an officer with drive and imagination of the highest order is supervising matters at headquarters and looking after the 'Whitehall front.'" Fleming provided "the driving force . . . [that] ensured rapid transit [of the concept] through the departments with the minimum of red tape."[54] The resulting unit had several names during its life, which extended until the fall of Japan, but was best known as "30 Commando."

The 30 Commando was formed in November 1942 and operated with success in the North African landings. From its inception, one of the unit's chief tasks was the capture of Axis cryptographic materials, especially rotors for the Enigma machine and lists of the daily settings for its wheels.[55] The Government Code and Cypher School at Bletchley Park provided and updated a "black list" of especially wanted enemy signals material and before each Allied invasion held briefings for officers and noncommissioned officers on "urgent current requirements in enemy cypher material" and on the locations of specific signals intelligence targets.[56] Captured material was not examined in the field but returned to Bletchley Park for analysis.

The official history of 30 Commando credits it with doing "good work in Sicily and Italy, capturing a substantial quantity of documents and equipment of operational value."[57] Captured material of interest to American cryptographers was probably provided under terms of previously drawn Anglo-American signals intelligence exchange agreements, rather than through the JICA mechanism. To assist in the activities of 30 Commando and to ensure that American interests in the materials captured were not overlooked, U.S. naval intelligence officers, on loan from the London staff of Commander, U.S. naval forces Europe, were first directly attached to 30 Commando in May 1944, prior to the Allied landings in France, and remained with it until the end of operations in Europe in 1945.

While the JICA system and 30 Commando were not designed as combined Anglo-American cooperative ventures, both contributed to the body of information that was shared at the local and theater levels and at the national level in London and Washington. Both organizations dealt with separate aspects of the same problem, that of timely acquisition and processing of information that became available during the course of battle. Whereas 30 Commando tended to concentrate on rapid acquisition of high-interest materials, JICA's strength lay in its ability to screen large amounts of information and to move that which was truly important quickly from the field to the analysts who needed it.

Allied intelligence cooperation with the official French government, which had ceased at the defeat of France in 1940, did not resume until early 1943. In the interim, intelligence contacts in Europe with the various French resistance groups and the followers of Charles de Gaulle had been maintained at first by the British Special Operations Executive and later expanded by the American embassy in London.

Despite the lack of formal intelligence ties from 1940 to 1943, the Allies were kept well informed of French activities through exploitation of French radio communications. Even before the French were driven out of the war in 1940, the British chief of naval staff "decided that we must obtain access to the French cyphers and were not to be squeamish in our methods."[58] In what British Director of Naval Intelligence John Godfrey described as a "rather picturesque incident," a James Bond–like plan (in all probability originated by James Bond's creator, Ian Fleming) was concocted to steal the codebooks from the safe of the French liaison officer to the Admiralty. When the plan proved infeasible, an alternative scheme was put into effect whereby the officers of a French submarine lying at Malta were duped into leaving the boat. The submarine was then raided, and the required material was seized and flown back to Bletchley Park, where, thanks to the stolen goods, the cryptographers "had difficulty in coping with the [quantity of] French traffic pouring in."[59] The British continued to intercept French naval messages until the 1942 Allied North African invasion,[60] after which the French were—after some controversy—welcomed back into the Allied intelligence camp and Bletchley Park's "reading [of] their mail" ostensibly ceased, although there is evidence that free French diplomatic and naval traffic was read by the Canadians from late 1943 on.[61]

On the heels of the Allied invasion of North Africa, the French Intelligence Service moved its headquarters from Vichy to Algiers. As early as

March 1943, the Intelligence Service approached the newly formed U.S. Joint Intelligence Collection Agency at Allied Forces Headquarters in Algiers for assistance in providing basic information for its files, most of which had been abandoned in metropolitan France, and for help in establishing radio communications with its subordinate units in North Africa.[62]

The following month, the U.S. Navy section of JICA Casablanca called on the local French naval intelligence representative to establish "a free and prompt exchange of information between our organizations."[63] In reply, the French assured JICA Casablanca of their intention to cooperate locally and that their representatives in Oran, Algiers, and Dakar were "being notified of the existence of JICA and ordered to cooperate with this organization to the fullest extent."[64] By July, JICA North Africa was able to assure the American director of naval intelligence that "cooperation with British Security Intelligence and the [French] Deuxieme Bureau is satisfactory, and considerable information of an intelligence nature has been submitted by the latter activity."[65]

Although the French were helpful in providing information to American and British intelligence, France was not considered an "Ally" to the extent that it was represented on Eisenhower's intelligence staff. The combined intelligence organization that had served Eisenhower during the planning phase of the North African landings continued to provide him with the intelligence support he required during the battle for Tunisia. The mostly British-staffed Intelligence Branch moved with the main part of Eisenhower's Allied Forces Headquarters from Gibraltar to Algiers on 24 November 1942.[66] Shortly afterward, a seasoned British intelligence officer from Cairo visited the branch and described it in these unflattering terms: "The British staff were plainly the cream which had been produced by the Intelligence training installations over the past three years. The trouble was that not only did they not know what they ought to be doing, they had learnt a whole lot of wrong things which they ought not to be doing."[67] The same officer's reports of subsequent visits down the line to the intelligence staffs at army and corps headquarters levels proved no more reassuring.

Eisenhower's combined intelligence organization was amply provided with a wide variety of information sources, including high-grade communications intelligence from Bletchley Park, tactical communications intercepts from the local area, photo reconnaissance, prisoner of war interrogation, captured documents, and tactical intelligence derived from battlefield reconnaissance. Among these myriad sources, probably the single most important was the so-called ULTRA material supplied by Bletchley Park, which provided intercepts of messages passing between senior enemy commanders. Valuable as this information was, it contained gaps and still had to be correctly interpreted.

During the Second World War, one of the problems inherent in the use of communications intelligence was that those few persons "in the know" tended to rely on intercepts to the exclusion of other sources of information. Often estimates of future enemy actions were based solely on whether activity indicating a specific move was or was not reflected in enemy communications. Apparently, the intelligence staff at Allied Forces Headquarters was not immune to this type of self-deception.

During 13–14 February 1943, the Germans attacked and soundly trounced Allied forces, primarily American, in the Kasserine Pass–Sidi Bou Zid areas in south-central Tunisia. While communications intelligence contained indications of an impending German thrust, according to the British official intelligence history, "the Enigma provided evidence about them [German intentions] that was so incomplete as to be wholly misleading."[68] British Brigadier Kenneth Strong, who was soon to become Eisenhower's chief intelligence officer and would remain so throughout the war, commented in his memoirs that "accurate reports of the strength and direction of the impending attack had been sent from the front but it appears that they had been discounted both at First Army Headquarters and Allied Forces Headquarters, as being an exaggeration on the part of green and untried troops."[69]

Today there is some question whether these field reports were available in time to affect the intelligence assessment, but in 1943, there was no doubt that the inability to predict the strength and direction of the German attack was looked upon by Eisenhower[70] and Roosevelt,[71] among others, as an intelligence failure. As a result, on 20 February 1943, Eisenhower sent a personal, "eyes only" telegram to General Alan Brooke, chief of the imperial general staff in London, requesting that Brigadier Mockler-Ferryman, Eisenhower's intelligence officer at Allied Forces Headquarters since August 1942, be relieved and replaced "with an officer who has a broader insight into German mentality and method" and also one who possessed "a little more inquisitiveness and greater attention to checking and cross-checking reports from various sources."[72] This latter comment about cross-checking various sources, plus a veiled remark to General Marshall that he was "provoked that there was such reliance placed on particular types of intelligence,"[73] indicated that Eisenhower was well aware of his intelligence staff's propensity to overestimate the importance of communications intelligence.

What could have resulted in a setback to Anglo-American intelligence relationships was avoided when Eisenhower specifically requested a British officer to replace Mockler-Ferryman. Brigadier Kenneth Strong was nominated. Strong, who arrived in North Africa less than a week later to assume his new duties, came with the type of credentials Eisenhower had requested. In 1935, he had served in the German Intelligence Section at the British War Office and two years later had become British assistant military attaché in Berlin, returning to the War Office in August 1939. After a tour as battalion commander, Strong became chief of intelligence for Home Forces, a command originally formed to repel the expected German invasion in 1940 but by 1942 thought of as the spearhead for Allied forces in any invasion of Europe. Strong's posting to Allied Forces Headquarters as chief of intelligence was, in his words, "the start of long and happy associations."[74] Eisenhower, who later in the war referred to Strong as one of "my most trusted staff officers,"[75] must have agreed.

In Tunisia, all organized enemy resistance ceased by May 1943, leaving Allied forces unopposed along the whole North African littoral. Allied convoys were again able to cross the Mediterranean and transit the Suez Canal in relative safety. In the words of Admiral Henry Hewitt, commander of American naval forces in the Mediterranean, "the severed life line of the Empire was spliced."[76]

Planning for the Allied conquest of Sicily (code-named "Husky") began long before the final victory in Tunisia in May 1943. By the date of the invasion, 10 July, the German navy was a negligible factor in the Mediterranean; only six U-boats operated against Husky, and two of those were sunk during the operation.[77] However, the Italian navy, although it had already suffered significant losses in 1943, was still a force to be reckoned with.[78] For that reason, the chief role assigned the Allied navies in Husky was to protect the troop transports while they were en route to their objectives; and, as Allied naval commander Admiral Andrew B. Cunningham, RN, put it in his message to his forces on the eve of the Sicilian invasion, "our primary duty is to place this vast expedition ashore in the minimum time and subsequently to maintain our military and air forces as they drive relentlessly forward into enemy territory."[79]

As was the case in the intelligence planning for Torch, Eisenhower's staff sought the information necessary to prepare the invasion of Sicily primarily from the British, with lesser inputs from Washington and from the recently established JICA offices in Casablanca and Cairo. As before, a primary source of information on Axis military plans came from enemy communications intercepts. Eisenhower's biographer, Stephen E. Ambrose, credited ULTRA with giving the supreme Allied commander "well before Husky was launched . . . a complete picture of the enemy's order of battle on Sicily and in Italy. Equally valuable," Ambrose argued, "Ultra allowed him [Eisenhower] to penetrate the German mind and judge how successful Allied deception measures had been."[80]

In addition to communications intelligence, photographic reconnaissance and interrogation of German and Italian prisoners of war taken during the Tunisian campaign provided major sources of preinvasion intelligence. As the official history of British World War II intelligence indicates, the quality of the intelligence used for planning Husky was difficult to determine. Planners complained that beach intelligence derived from photographic reconnaissance was inadequate and that the most recent maps and charts were often prewar.[81] However, Samuel Eliot Morison wrote that American naval commanders were provided with "excellent" Admiralty Hydrographic Office maps "giving complete land and hydrographic data, with a grid for artillery and naval gunfire." For the most part, this type of intelligence was the product of painstaking work by the Admiralty's Naval Intelligence Directorate and the Inter-Service Topographic Department at Oxford. Morison concluded that "the Western (American) Task Force was unusually well supplied with information."[82]

There was little possibility of disguising the next major Allied objective— capture of Naples and all the Italian mainland south of a line from Naples to Bari on the Adriatic. An intercepted German message reported on 14 August that the head of Italian intelligence was forecasting an attack in the Naples-Salerno area, and German intelligence messages in the next few days predicted landings in the Gulf of Salerno and in Calabria, across the Strait of Messina between Sicily and Italy.[83]

Planning for the attack on Naples ("Avalanche"), which the Combined Chiefs of Staff had ordered on 26 July, began on 1 August with the selection of Eisenhower and his team to command the operation. Planning, in the words of Samuel Eliot Morison, was "even more dispersed, hectic, and exasperating than for 'Husky,'"[84] Time was short, since the actual attack on Naples took place during the night of 8–9 September 1943. Intelligence apparently did not play a great role in the selection of the attack objective or in the planning of the attack, but it gave warning of the spirited German land and air defense that was to follow the landings. Intercepted German army and air force messages indicated that the Germans planned to throw all forces in the Naples-Salerno area into an all-out battle to drive the invaders back into the sea.[85] But after sharp fighting around Salerno, German forces began to withdraw to defensive positions in the north on 17 September, and on 2 October, Allied forces entered Naples. By 9 November, the first anniversary of the Anglo-American landings in North Africa, Eisenhower could tell the forces under his command in all sincerity that they "had written a memorable chapter in the history of . . . arms."[86]

Even as the fight for Italy was just starting, the Allies began to focus their attention on planning for the cross-channel invasion ("Overlord") and on preparations for the battle for northwest Europe that was to follow. The year 1943 closed with President Roosevelt's announcement on 24 December that General Dwight D. Eisenhower had been selected to lead Allied forces in the battle for Europe. Intelligence began to reorient much of its now vast resources, except for those committed only to the Pacific, to support the massive planning effort required to surmount Eisenhower's next and greatest challenge.

At the end of 1943, the naval intelligence structure that had been carefully crafted in the immediate prewar and early wartime years was in place and functioning smoothly. Nowhere was this more apparent than in the successful battle against German U-boats in the Atlantic, in which the efforts of the mutually supportive submarine tracking rooms in London, Washington, and Ottawa marked the culmination of Anglo-American cooperation in naval intelligence.

In the European and Mediterranean theaters, no matter how effective, navy-to-navy intelligence collaboration was less important to the conduct of the war than was the development of the joint/combined intelligence organizations. With the liberation of French North Africa in early 1943, valuable information from French sources began to flow into Allied Forces Mediterranean headquarters, and, beginning in North Africa and spreading eventually to the rest of the Middle East and the China-Burma-India theaters, joint U.S. Army and Navy intelligence collection agencies were established to rationalize the collection of the mass of foreign information required by the American military. With victory in the Mediterranean all but assured, the Anglo-American intelligence structure was approaching the eve of its most severe test—the Allied invasion of Western Europe.

6.

Cracks in the Structure

A turning point in Anglo-American strategic relationships had been reached at Casablanca. Before the Allied victory in North Africa helped decide the issue, and while the question of who would win the war remained moot, Allied military councils reflected an underlying sense of "cooperate or perish." By the spring of 1943, however, the growing realization that the Allies would eventually win caused Anglo-American military relationships to become colored by the idea of national postwar advantage. A result, noted in intelligence as well as in other aspects of the war, was that Great Britain slackened its push for ever-increasing cooperation and became less willing to give way to American desires simply to nourish a cooperative climate.

Despite the signal success of the Allied submarine tracking rooms' alliance in defeating the German U-boat menace in the Atlantic, strains were appearing elsewhere in the Anglo-American intelligence structure. The British director of naval intelligence, long a staunch supporter of stronger intelligence ties with the U.S. Navy, was removed. The Admiralty's Naval Intelligence Division on occasion continued to display a patronizing attitude that rankled its American colleagues, and intelligence cooperation in the neutral countries of Europe was often less than ideal.

On 28 November 1942, as Allied forces in North Africa began the first phase of their drive to capture Tunis, an event took place in London that was to have a profound effect on British naval intelligence. Vice Admiral John H. Godfrey turned over direction of the Admiralty's Naval Intelligence Division to his successor, Captain (later Rear Admiral) Edmund Rushbrooke. Godfrey's dismissal—for this was no routine change of assignments—and the manner in which it was carried out are significant.

Godfrey was promoted to the rank of vice admiral on 15 September 1942. The following day he received a memorandum from the first sea lord, Admiral Dudley Pound, which stated that the vice chief of the naval staff had conducted an investigation into Godfrey's relationship with the other members of the Joint Intelligence Committee and had concluded "that co-operation amongst the Members of the J.I.C., which is important for its proper functioning was not possible as long as you [Godfrey] were a member. . . . I endorse his [the vice chief's] opinion," Pound continued, "and it is therefore with the greatest regret that I am informing the First Lord that I consider your relief is necessary."[1]

Despite Pound's terse dismissal of Godfrey, which left no doubt that the first sea lord had lost confidence in Godfrey's ability to function effectively as director of naval intelligence, his relief did not take place for over two months. During the interregnum, the lame-duck DNI visited Washington and Ottawa to meet with top government leaders in an effort to improve the effectiveness of intelligence cooperation between Britain and its allies in the Western Hemisphere—a somewhat surprising assignment for one who had just been fired for his inability to cooperate.

As Pound's memoranda to Godfrey and to the first lord made clear, Godfrey was being replaced because of his inability to get along with the other members of the Joint Intelligence Committee. However, cooperation is a two-way street. How had Godfrey so angered the other members of the JIC that they felt obliged to demand his recall? Without question, Godfrey was difficult to like. His biographer and admirer Patrick Beesly often used words such as "impatient," "tactless," and "overbearing" to describe his manner.[2] "I have never used the word genius of anyone else," wrote Ewin Montagu, a member of Godfrey's staff during the war who later became judge advocate of the fleet. "This tribute [to Godfrey's skill in intelligence work] is the more sincere as, in most ways, I disliked him as a person."[3] Surely the Admiralty would be reluctant to lose Godfrey's "genius" in intelligence at a critical point in the war merely because of personality clashes with his peers.

Beesly speculated, and subsequent writings by Godfrey have confirmed, that each member of the JIC had hidden reasons for speeding Godfrey's departure. The army director of military intelligence was unhappy because, in addition to purely naval information, Godfrey—at the specific request of Admiral Cunningham—was including matters within the purview of the War Office in the summaries of pertinent communications intelligence intercepts that he regularly furnished to Cunningham, then head of the British Admiralty Delegation in Washington. The root of the problem seemed to be, in Godfrey's words, that "Naval procedure is to give people the truth and let them draw their own conclusions. If comments are needed they are shown separately from the intelligence itself. Military procedure is to give the Commanders what the War Office think Commanders ought to know."[4] Over army protests, Godfrey continued to include such material, but in a reduced amount.

Godfrey had also refused to give in to pressure from the army chief of the Imperial General Staff to agree that the German army had large uncommitted forces that were being held in reserve for either the Eastern or Western Front. Godfrey led the opposition in the JIC to what became known as the "secret army" theory and successfully blocked the JIC from accepting the director of military intelligence's assessment that these forces did, in fact, exist.[5] An agreed JIC paper accepting the army estimate would have bolstered the British strategic position, later expressed with force at the Casablanca conference, against an all-out Allied cross-channel invasion. The British chiefs of staff favored strategic bombing and encouragement of resistance in occupied countries to wear down Germany, coupled with small peripheral incursions against the Continent, rather than a major frontal assault. "Disagreement about the secret army," Godfrey commented, "did not add to the tranquility of the J.I.C. meetings."[6]

The Royal Air Force, too, had reason to wish for a less redoubtable naval member on the Joint Intelligence Committee. A key RAF mission was to destroy German submarine construction and replenishment locations. Godfrey recalled that his analysts had "the painful duty" of examining photographic evidence from RAF bombing of German submarine bases to determine its effectiveness. "The sincerity with which claims were pressed and the heavy casualties among bomber crews created a tense and unhappy atmosphere in which the truth could only too easily become obscured."[7] The RAF, naturally, could not have been pleased to have Godfrey document its lack of success against naval targets.

Beesly has also argued, without offering much corroborative evidence, that Stewart Menzies, chief of the Secret Intelligence Service, may have seen Godfrey as a threat to his own position and therefore may have supported Godfrey's dismissal. Menzies, an army man, had been deputy director of the SIS under Admiral Hugh Sinclair and had succeeded him at Sinclair's death in November 1939. The post of chief of the Secret Intelligence Service was traditionally held by a naval officer, and Sinclair had been director of naval intelligence prior to his appointment as head of SIS.

Sinclair was known to have had cancer well before his death from the disease.[8] In August 1939, Godfrey, then director of naval intelligence, approached Sir Maurice Hankey, a longtime civil servant of great repute and éminence grise of the British intelligence establishment, about the possibility of Godfrey's following Sinclair as chief of SIS. Hankey's biographer indicated that the idea of a naval officer holding the appointment had some support in the Foreign Office, "But nothing came of the approach."[9] Had Menzies known of Godfrey's previous initiatives concerning the SIS job, Menzies might well have wished Godfrey elsewhere.

With the benefit of hindsight, Godfrey acknowledged that he should have been more circumspect and, rather than fight the battles by himself, should have enlisted the aid of the first sea lord. Admiral Pound, however, had become disinterested in intelligence matters, perhaps starting to show signs of the disease that ended his life a year later. The one person who might have saved Godfrey was the prime minister. Churchill had a reputation for intolerance of senior Royal Navy officers who disagreed with him, and Godfrey had achieved this dubious distinction early in the war when he had refused to accept the first lord's overly optimistic estimates of German U-boat losses. No help, then, could be expected from that quarter.[10]

Godfrey's valedictory visit to Washington was more in the nature of an assessment of the progress made since his previous trip in May 1941 than a vehicle for new initiatives. As before, he was accompanied by his personal assistant, Commander Ian Fleming. Fleming remained with Godfrey during the Washington portion of the visit; then, while Godfrey went off to talk to the Canadians, Fleming accompanied Captain "Eddy" G. Hastings, the senior Royal Navy intelligence officer in Washington, to Jamaica to assess the effectiveness of the newly organized combined American-British intelligence center there.

Upon arrival in Washington, Godfrey met with Admiral Cunningham, head of the British Admiralty Delegation, who was to leave that post shortly to become General Eisenhower's naval deputy for Torch. Cunningham and Godfrey examined the process by which the American Office of Naval Intelligence and the British representatives in Washington exchanged intelligence and operational information and found that the chief problem seemed to be obtaining information from the Pacific area, needed both by the Admiralty and by Admiral James F. Somerville, commander in chief of the British Eastern Fleet operating in the Indian Ocean. Following the Royal Navy's withdrawal from the Pacific in the spring of 1942, the U.S. Navy, seeing little to be gained from an exchange of intelligence with British forces no longer directly engaged in the fight with the Japanese, had reduced its intelligence support to the British Eastern Fleet. In his report to the first sea lord following the visit, Godfrey was optimistic: "machinery has been planned which should ensure a very much greater flow of information both on operational matters (such as U.S. submarine patrols) and on tactical and technical lessons learnt in the Pacific, to the Admiralty or to Admiral Somerville direct."[11]

After completing his *tour d'horizon* with Cunningham, Godfrey called on the American director of naval intelligence, at that moment, Admiral Harold C. Train. During Godfrey's tenure as British DNI from 1939 until 1942, no less than six American naval officers held the post of DNI in the U.S. Navy Department. The rapid changes in the U.S Navy's intelligence chiefs were a distinct detriment to effective Anglo-American naval intelligence cooperation. Just as Godfrey would start to know his American opposite number and to work comfortably with him, he was gone, and the mutual learning process had to begin all over again. Godfrey could not be expected to be equally impressed with them all. Of his visit to Admiral Train, Godfrey commented, "Relations with O.N.I. continue most cordial. Admiral Train (the U.S. D.N.I.) and Captain Zacharias (the Assistant Director) are both extremely co-operative, and the latter, at any rate, is very competent and knowledgeable."[12]

In his report, Godfrey put his finger directly on a major impediment to continued improvement in relations between the British Naval Intelligence Directorate and the American Office of Naval Intelligence. While NID was closely involved in direct intelligence support to the Royal Navy's operating forces, "the O.N.I. is firmly wedded to 'security' as opposed to 'operational intelligence,' and large staffs of able-bodied naval officers in Washington and in every naval district are devoting their energies to keeping track of aliens and checking up on reports of suspicious lights, etc., . . . the waste of personnel and effort can be imagined."[13] American naval historian Jeffery M. Dorwart wrote of ONI's late 1941 mission, "unfortunately, while focusing on security aspects, naval intelligence's traditional information-gathering work was reduced to what . . . was a decidedly 'secondary concern.'"[14] Little seemed to have changed in a year.

"Looking back on my visit in July 1941," Godfrey commented, "I think we may regard progress [in intelligence cooperation] as satisfactory." Echoing an unfortunately all-too-common British view, Godfrey concluded, "In assessing their [American] efficiency and receptivity [to British methods] we must be patient and bear in mind that mature officers in the British Navy have, since 1914, been at war for seven years whereas their American colleagues have had barely three years' experience."[15]

This patronizing attitude toward cooperation with the American intelligence community became a continuing stumbling block to closer integration of American and British naval intelligence efforts, especially as the war progressed and the U.S. Navy gained confidence in its own intelligence abilities. With Godfrey's departure from NID, much of the impetus for closer ties with the U.S. Navy disappeared. While in Washington, Godfrey received an unexpected message from the first lord offering an appointment as flag officer commanding, Royal Indian Navy, a vice admiral's post. As he knew that his only alternative would be forced retirement, Godfrey accepted with alacrity.

Godfrey's dismissal came at the zenith of Anglo-American navy-to-navy intelligence cooperation and also at the height of his Naval Intelligence Division's influence, both in the Admiralty and in the councils of those directing the British war effort. Godfrey's successor, Captain Edmund Rushbrooke, was promoted to commodore shortly after becoming director of naval intelligence, but he was not raised to rear admiral, the traditional rank of the incumbent DNI, until the war's end. The practical result of this lowered grade was that Rushbrooke found himself outranked by his peers on the naval staff and on the Joint Intelligence Committee, with a concomitant loss of influence. When Churchill asked the Admiralty's opinion on the changes in the German high command that had taken place in the spring of 1943, the question was referred to the director of plans for a response. Nowhere in the file was there any indication that the Naval Intelligence Directorate was ever asked for its analysis or that the draft reply was ever sent to NID for comment.[16] This bypassing of NID would not have happened in Godfrey's day.

Rushbrooke was a talented naval officer and had been assigned as DNI after a series of commands at sea. He was not without intelligence experience, having been chief of the intelligence staff, China Station, in 1937–1938. However, he does not seem to have felt completely comfortable in the role of DNI. "No, I don't think I got much of a kick out of being DNI," Rushbrooke wrote after the war. "I found it a tremendous strain and often wondered whether I was the right person for the job." Rushbrooke had inherited a smoothly running machine and seldom tried to interfere with its operation by inserting any original thinking.[17]

Rushbrooke was a competent DNI, but his stature as an intelligence officer never approached that of John Godfrey, his predecessor, nor that of DNI "Blinker" Hall in the First World War. That was probably just the way the British intelligence establishment—burned by Hall and therefore twice shy of Godfrey—wanted it. "Godfrey," noted Stephen Roskill, author of the official history of the Royal Navy in World War II, "was the only British admiral to receive no recognition at all for his war service."[18]

Intelligence cooperation with the French government had, as we have seen, been resumed in North Africa in early 1943 following the German occupation of the portion of metropolitan France that had been ruled by Vichy.

Colonel "Wild Bill" Donovan's Office of Strategic Services, however, had been the first American organization to establish intelligence contacts with the French resistance. The first OSS agents arrived in London in November 1941 to be trained in what author and wartime member of the British Secret Intelligence Service Malcolm Muggeridge termed "our frowsty old intelligence brothel."[19] Soon the trainees, showing what the British saw as a lamentable degree of independence, began to establish direct information exchanges with the various foreign intelligence services represented in London, including the French.[20]

The U.S. Navy, too, had not been slow in developing its own contacts in London's foreign intelligence community. In January 1942, the Intelligence Division of Admiral Robert L. Ghormley's Commander U.S. Naval Forces Europe staff first established liaison with the governments in exile. In June, Admiral Harold R. Stark, who had replaced Ghormley two months previously, recommended to Washington that a naval attaché be assigned jointly to his staff and to that of Anthony J. Drexel Biddle, the American ambassador to the governments in exile. The naval attaché was to be accredited to the governments in exile in London, all of which were thought to have "exceptionally good sources of military and political information" and many of which had naval attachés in Washington. State and Navy approved, and Captain John C. Callan, USNR, was appointed to the new post.[21]

Prior to Callan's arrival, Admiral Stark's personal representative to the governments in exile had been Commander Tracy B. Kittredge, USNR. Kittredge, who, with Stark, had been a member of Admiral Sims's staff in London during the First World War, had lived abroad for much of the interwar period, was fluent in French and German, and was well versed in European politics. According to Stark's biographer, "Kittredge became indispensable to Stark in the discharge of his political and diplomatic duties."[22]

Kittredge turned most of his representational responsibilities to the foreign intelligence community in exile over to Callan upon the latter's arrival in London in September 1942 but remained as Stark's personal representative to the French. Kittredge was particularly useful in keeping his commander informed on the resistance movement in France, receiving information directly from de Gaulle's organization in London and from the British Special Operations Executive via the London office of OSS.[23]

Captain Callan soon realized that the road to meaningful intelligence exchange with the governments in exile had been booby-trapped, apparently intentionally, by the British. He reported to the American director of naval intelligence that the governments in exile received their information in two ways: directly from their sources in occupied Europe and through communication channels controlled by the British. In the first case, the information was coming to him "without hindrance." Callan alleged that in the case of information sent by British channels, "much of the material . . . is not made available to the officials of the governments concerned in London." In those cases in which the British did deliver the information, the countries "are, in many cases, specifically instructed not to pass it to American authorities here." Instead, the British gave the exile governments "'handouts' of intelligence items, generally old and of indifferent value," to be used to "placate American demands for information." Callan concluded by saying that in view of the numerous instances of "whole-hearted" cooperation, "it may be unfair to intimate that the British are following a deliberate policy of keeping all intelligence of real value concerning the occupied countries to themselves. This, however, seems to be the case."24

When Callan's letter reached the Navy Department, the Foreign Intelligence Branch of the Office of Naval Intelligence admitted that "the situation outlined by Captain Callan undoubtedly exists." However, far from expressing outrage at the British undercutting the effectiveness of its man in London, ONI's Foreign Intelligence Branch suggested that Callan be directed to limit his contacts with governments in exile to operational matters, since "the procurement and transmission of ordinary intelligence items . . . appear to be beyond the scope of the Naval Attaché's duties"25—strange words from an organization whose chief reason for existence was to process and disseminate information received in great part from U.S. naval attachés, who were its agents in the field.

In addition to hindering the U.S. naval attaché's efforts to obtain information from the governments in exile, the British were less than totally open with the Americans in other intelligence matters. In the original liaison agreement between the U.S. War Department and the British cryptographic authorities, made in the spring of 1943, the British reserved the right to withhold from the Americans messages they considered "too hot" for general dissemination. This type of intercept traffic was placed in a special system called "Res" (Reserved) and given limited distribution.

After a year of intermittent agitation by the Americans, the agreement was renegotiated. Messages in the "Res" series were to be screened and divided into four categories: those that could be released for general circulation; those that could be sent to Washington on a "limited distribution" basis; those that could be read by the American liaison officer but not retransmitted, even in substance; and "items that would continue to be unqualifiedly withheld." Since the U.S. Army and Navy Signals Intelligence agreements with the British were negotiated individually and the navy document has not been released to the public, it is not possible to say if similar restrictions were imposed on traffic of naval interest, but it is reasonable to believe that this would have been the case. Another class of reports contained material that "C" did not wish the Allies to become aware of; these were flagged by him before being released to the Naval Intelligence Directorate. Such messages were circulated by hand and never allowed in files to which Allied personnel had access.[26]

Another crack in the structure of Anglo-American intelligence cooperation was revealed when the OSS and other American intelligence agencies attempted to stage their own operations from the British Isles into occupied Europe. The U.S. Joint Chiefs of Staff were asked to consider a British paper that would, if approved, give the British what was in effect veto power over all such operations. Commenting that "we are not a refugee government," the OSS pointed out that JCS approval would "reduce the OSS Secret Intelligence Service to a subordinate and subservient status" and would "ultimately not only do harm to the good relations between the two countries but will hamper the united war effort by destroying any effective American intelligence service in that [the European] theater." The OSS objection concluded with the thought that the British recommendations did not disclose "the fact that all raw material intelligence, no matter how obtained, is processed and evaluated through British machinery." Therefore, the supreme Allied commander "will have only that intelligence which has met the British test."[27]

The less than complete intelligence cooperation that began to surface in the spring of 1943 appeared traceable to the growing realization on the part of the Allies that the issue of which side would win the war was no longer in doubt. Both American and British politico-military strategists began to look beyond victory toward postwar relationships. Secretary of the Navy Knox reflected this type of thinking in a 5 May 1943 letter to Admiral Nimitz in the Pacific. "The British have always been very intelligently aware of their own interests in world affairs," Knox wrote. "In fact, their international policy has been a pretty concrete demonstration from the British point of view of an enlightened self interest. Consequently, in the pursuit of such a policy, there are many things now transpiring which seem to us to indicate at least as great a concern about postwar conditions as it does concerning the winning of the war."[28]

Mention has been made previously of the Contact Section of the British Naval Intelligence Directorate, whose job it was to dig up experts and sources of information on any conceivable subject that might be of interest to naval intelligence. As American intelligence became more active in providing for its own needs by establishing its own sources, it ran afoul of the British policy that any such approaches in London must be made through the Contact

Section of the naval intelligence staff. In the Admiralty's postwar history of NID 21, the Contact Section, it was stated that "by forcing the American outposts in London to deal through the Admiralty section, British firms were protected from being directly approached in London. This not only saved further duplication, but enabled us to keep an eye on what the Americans were seeking; for there was a strong reciprocal mistrust on the part of Britain that these requests might supply material for post-war economic penetration."[29]

British naval intelligence was not the only body to harbor suspicions of postwar motives. In a 13 January 1943 conference of U.S. Navy counterintelligence officials at the Office of Naval Intelligence in Washington, a question was asked concerning policy on cooperation with the British. "What we would like to do, of course," the responder stated, "and what we should always try to do, is to have a one-way pipeline coming this way, but you have to trade. You have to give them something. You have to cooperate wholeheartedly on the war effort, but we don't propose to give them anything that will prejudice the interest of the United States after the war."[30]

The cooperation between the submarine tracking rooms in the Admiralty and the Navy Department during the Battle of the Atlantic demonstrated how close operational intelligence ties could become. This unity of effort was not, unfortunately, always found in other parts of the American and British naval intelligence organizations. In the spring of 1943, NID 17-Zed, the section of the British Naval Intelligence Directorate charged with psychological warfare and "black" (unattributable) propaganda against the German navy, invited the head of Op-16-W, the section of the American Office of Naval Intelligence assigned a similar mission, to London. The object of the visit was, once again, to study British operations and work out methods of cooperation. The American officer returned to Washington confident that his trip would produce "extremely satisfactory" results.[31]

However, according to the administrative history of the American Office of Naval Intelligence, misunderstandings arose during the summer of 1943, "since 17-Zed tended to restrict Op-16-W to purely theoretical discussions of the naval war and, in fact, seemed to regard our branch as an auxiliary of their own." The hoped-for cooperation was not realized, and "contacts with 17-Zed were reduced to a minimum." When scripts were forwarded to 17-Zed for clearance, they either "brought forth a 'no comment' or some acrimonious remarks on their [the British] part." In 1944, "for all practical purposes, liaison was discontinued."[32]

Intelligence had begun to regain some of its traditional paranoia concerning the motives of others—even close friends. Without doubt, the shift in focus from the immediate problem of self-preservation to the longer-range questions of national interest in the postwar world retarded the growth of Anglo-American intelligence cooperation but did not by any means destroy it. Those actions on both sides that were detrimental to intelligence cooperation should be examined within the context of the closest intelligence relationship that had ever been achieved between two sovereign nations. The course of true cooperation was never completely smooth, nor should it have been expected to be.

During 1943, the Allied intelligence war in the West was not confined to the major combat zones of the Atlantic and North Africa; it continued with varying degrees of success in the neutral peripheries of Sweden and the Iberian Peninsula. Sweden was of particular importance, because it offered the Admiralty a window on the Baltic from which to observe German naval activities and to gain advance warning of any German attempt to break out into the North Sea through the narrow waters of the Kattegat between Denmark and Sweden.

Germany was as aware of Sweden's strategic location as the British were and kept pressure on the Swedish government to observe the strictest neutrality in its dealings with both sides. Strict neutrality did not make the Allied naval attachés' job any easier. Captain Henry Denham, who held the post of British naval attaché in Stockholm throughout the war, commented ruefully that "reticence was brought to a fine art in the conversation of every Swedish officer or Foreign Office official. They were unwilling to discuss any subject which might have some professional savour. . . . It was most disheartening to find that all doors expected to lead to sources of intelligence were literally slammed in one's face."[33] Despite these handicaps, Stockholm became one of the most valuable Allied listening posts for naval information during the war.

Unfortunately, Denham's relationship with the U.S. naval attaché was not as productive as might have been anticipated. In the postwar narrative of his activities in Sweden, Denham indicated that "the American Attaché . . . whom we had hoped might be helpful, turned out to be if anything a slight hindrance. The first embarrassment arose after one of Colonel Björnstierna's [chief of Swedish Combined Intelligence and one of Denham's sources] reports on German military 'leaked' from the American Legation to the German Legation." The report had been sent to Washington in the U.S. naval attaché's code; however, "it was never actually proved whether this message was intercepted in its cyphered form or whether a copy of the message was stolen from the American Legation in Stockholm and handed to the Germans, but probably the latter."[34] Although Denham thought that his contacts with the U.S. naval attaché in Stockholm were "of no value at all," at Gothenburg "an excellent US Consul-General helped us all through the war."[35]

"A high proportion of German intelligence operations against Britain [during the Second World War] were mounted from the Iberian Peninsula."[36] We have this assessment from no less an authority than "Kim" Philby, "one of the most remarkable [British-Soviet] double-agents who have been exposed in our time."[37] In 1941, Philby had become head of the British Secret Intelligence Service's section dealing with counterintelligence activities in the Iberian Peninsula and was, therefore, in a unique position to assess Allied and Axis espionage and counterespionage operations in that part of the world. The United States and Great Britain carried on extensive intelligence activities in both Spain and Portugal—not, however, without considerable inter- and intramural infighting.

Unlike in Sweden, where the chief object of Anglo-American intelligence was to gather information on the Germans, in Spain the Allied goal was essentially one of counterintelligence: to deny the Germans access to the information available in Spain by reason of its proximity to the Straits of Gibraltar and to ensure that Spanish territory was not used by the Axis for purposes hostile to Allied interests. As early as November 1941, the U.S. naval attaché in Singapore had informed Washington of indications, probably received from British sources, "that the Jap embassy Madrid is obtaining [the] sense of our diplomatic traffic to that capital."[38]

British naval historian Stephen Roskill wrote that in the early days of the war Spain had repeatedly violated neutrality by helping German navy raiders and U-boats, as had occurred in the summer of 1940 when the Spanish government permitted "the tanker *Winnetou* to use the Canary Islands as a base from which to fuel U-boats."[39] The German intelligence network in Spain enjoyed a virtually unstoppable flow of information on Allied ship movements in and out of the British naval base at Gibraltar and through the straits from a variety of official and unofficial Spanish sources. "On one occasion, when the Germans thought that a convoy might have slipped through in bad visibility one night, they got the Spaniards to lay on a special air reconnaissance flight for their benefit."[40]

Anglo-American naval intelligence cooperation in Spain dated from the early days of 1941, when the U.S. Navy wished to place a naval observer in the strategically important Balearic Islands, a Spanish province in the western Mediterranean off the east coast of Spain. The Spanish government refused to permit a U.S. naval officer to be stationed anywhere except Madrid. The U.S. Department of State refused to approve a navy plan to assign a consular officer to the Balearics to provide the necessary reporting.[41] Fortunately, Alan Hillgarth, a retired Royal Navy officer, was British vice-consul in Palma, Mallorca, the capital city of the Balearics. Through his good offices, the American Office of Naval Intelligence was able to receive the information it desired.[42]

Hillgarth was subsequently recalled to active duty and assigned, at the behest of Director of Naval Intelligence John Godfrey, to Madrid as the first British naval attaché to Spain. Hillgarth, who spoke excellent Spanish and had good contacts in high Spanish political and social circles, did much to counteract German influence within the Franco government. His colleague, the American naval attaché in Madrid, was able to return the favor done the U.S. Navy in the Balearics by sharing—quite unofficially—with Hillgarth reports made by the U.S. naval attaché in Berlin.[43]

In its efforts to monitor German activities in Spain, the U.S. Office of Naval Intelligence was willing to consider any source of information, no matter how unusual. In November 1942, Sidney Franklin, "a U.S. citizen and well known professional bullfighter," approached the American naval attaché in Mexico City and stated that he had learned from Spaniards in Mexico that the Germans were refueling and repairing submarines in Spain. Franklin indicated that, because he was well known in the bullfighting world, he had "access to many circles not ordinarily open to most persons" and offered to go to Spain at his own expense to gather information that might be of value to the U.S. Navy. The archives reveal that the U.S. Navy gave serious consideration to Franklin's offer, but they do not indicate whether his initiative was ever acted upon.[44]

While Allied intelligence in Spain performed well in its attempts to frustrate German efforts to gain information on Allied activities in the Mediterranean, in Portugal the situation was not all that clear, and results were harder to judge. Portugal's international position was, in Kim Philby's estimation, "horribly complicated and fuzzy," and its leaders were more cautious and therefore more neutral than those of Spain. In the field of intelligence, "neutrality" translated into willingness on the part of some senior Portuguese government officials to accept money from both the British and the Germans. Philby commented that "it was usually impossible to assess which side derived most advantage, if indeed any, from this tangle."[45]

The Germans used Portugal as an outpost for dispatching and controlling agents destined for assignments in Great Britain, Africa, and the Western Hemisphere, as well as for collecting information on Allied shipping and on the flow of American arms and equipment to England and the Mediterranean.[46] British attempts to counter German espionage efforts were carried on mainly by agents of the Security Service (MI-5) and the Secret Intelligence Service (MI-6), assisted by the military and naval attachés. In addition, there was a contingent from the Special Operations Executive (SOE), the British group charged with sabotage and other nonintelligence missions against the Germans. The SOE Lisbon group, according to a knowledgeable insider, seemed "to spend as much time fighting the other secret British organizations as it spent in dealing with the enemy's."[47]

American contributions to the Lisbon intelligence community included the military and naval attachés and the representatives of the Office of Strategic Services. Another American player, U.S. naval liaison officer, Lisbon, joined the game when the U.S. Navy formed the Commander U.S. Naval Forces Northwest African Waters (COMNAVNAW) staff shortly after the Allied invasion of North Africa. Whatever his primary mission, the U.S. naval liaison officer also had intelligence responsibilities, having been directed by COMNAVNAW to collect information on such espionage "targets" as the activities of the Japanese embassy staff in Lisbon.[48]

American naval intelligence in Portugal suffered from a twofold coordination problem. At the local level, meaningful coordination of intelligence reporting to reduce duplication or false confirmation was almost totally lacking. In addition, information from Lisbon reached the U.S. Navy Department via a large number of overlapping and confusing paths. Information developed by the British Secret Intelligence Service in Lisbon on activities of the Portuguese Ministry of Marine came to the American Office of Naval Intelligence from the Washington representative of British Security Coordination, New York. Information developed by the British embassy in Lisbon reached ONI not from the U.S. Department of State or from the U.S. naval attachés in Lisbon or London but from the U.S. military attaché, Lisbon, via the War Department in Washington. The Federal Bureau of Investigation provided ONI with information of naval interest intercepted on a German clandestine radio circuit from Hamburg to Lisbon. Where the FBI got the information in the first place is not known, but it may well have come from a British source via British Security Coordination, New York. In one instance, ONI learned of the arrival in Washington of an OSS shipment of papers taken from the office of the Japanese naval attaché, Lisbon. ONI found out about the papers not from the OSS but from the U.S. naval liaison officer, Lisbon, via COMNAVNAW.[49]

The intelligence problems in Portugal were not attacked seriously until the fall of 1942, when American diplomat and Soviet specialist George F. Kennan was assigned to the American Embassy in Lisbon. Kennan wrote in his *Memoirs* that, in addition to his normal duties as counselor of the embassy, he was asked, "privately and informally, to take the lead in trying to straighten out the dreadful confusions which our various intelligence people had created, among themselves and with the British, in their efforts to insert themselves into the already seething cauldron of espionage and counterespionage that wartime Lisbon constituted."[50] There is no indication that he was successful.

In 1943, Allied naval intelligence followed dichotomous paths. At the same time that Anglo-American naval intelligence reached its closest and most effective levels of cooperation in the mutually supportive submarine tracking rooms during the Battle of the Atlantic, it was also entering into gradual decline as the influence of joint and combined intelligence grew to overshadow navy-to-navy relationships. Admiral John Godfrey's dismissal from his post as British director of naval intelligence had stilled a strong voice for increased intelligence exchange between the Admiralty and the U.S. Navy Department, and wartime proliferation of competing Allied intelligence agencies added to the confusion without enhancing cooperation.

By the end of 1943, American intelligence was feeling increasingly restive in its perception that the British were attempting to perpetuate a teacher-pupil relationship. Cracks in the structure of cooperative intelligence, as in other Anglo-American wartime relationships, were beginning to appear as both sides recognized that the tide of battle had turned and competition for postwar hegemony began to supplant cooperation born of wartime necessity.

Part Three
The Pacific

7·
Interwar Faltering Steps

Anglo-American involvement with the Pacific began long before the events of the 1930s that led to the tragedy of Pearl Harbor. The drive—particularly in the nineteenth century—to "open" China and Japan to the blessings of Western religion and commerce took place under the protection of British and American warships as well as those of France, Germany, and Russia.

In the latter half of the nineteenth century, it would have been difficult to see Japan as a potential threat to Anglo-American interests in the Pacific. From the arrival of Commodore Matthew Perry's small U.S. Navy squadron in Tokyo Bay in July 1853 until the end of World War I, Americans watched, often patronizingly but without apprehension, Japan's progress from feudal empire to modern nation. The Imperial Japanese Navy offered so little threat to American interests in the Pacific that until 1907 the U.S. Navy had not even contemplated drawing up a War Plan Orange (orange was the color assigned to Japan for war gaming purposes, just as blue always denoted U.S. forces and red, British). In that year, attacks on Asian immigrants in California triggered a "war scare" in the sensationalist American press and aroused sufficient concern in the U.S. government to cause the Naval War College to consider for the first time a blue-orange war contingency.[1]

Naval intelligence cooperation in the Far East between the United States and Great Britain had its roots in the shared experience of the First World War and in mutually supportive actions in China during the interwar years. Growing concerns on the part of both navies over Japanese expansionist activities in the mid-1930s notwithstanding, intelligence cooperation was mainly low-level and informal. Both navies were working independently to break into the numerous Japanese naval codes, with varying degrees of success, and the results were unshared. Naval intelligence organizations of Britain's Far Eastern dominions, Australia and New Zealand, were small, their efforts were uncoordinated, and they were heavily dependent on the Admiralty rather than on their own resources for necessary intelligence.

American and British maritime interest in the Far East long predated Perry's arrival in Japan. In 1579, Sir Francis Drake crossed the Pacific in his ship the *Golden Hind*—visiting the Palau Islands, the Philippines, and the Spice Islands of the Malay Peninsula—and returned to England the following year laden with a cargo of the riches of the Orient. Word of fortunes to be made in trade with the East spread rapidly in Elizabethan England, and in 1599, the East India Company was founded to exploit this new source of potential wealth. One hundred years later, the company began trading operations in Canton and by the mid-eighteenth century was deeply involved in the China trade.

By 1900, British influence in the Far East was at its zenith. Protected by the ships of the Royal Navy operating from Hong Kong, Shanghai, and Weihaiwei, British merchants controlled almost three-quarters of the China trade.[2] However, in this golden age of colonialism, Britain's position in East Asia was challenged not only by France, its usual opponent, but also by Russia and Germany.

Unlike its rapid involvement in the China trade, Britain's interest in Japan, which dated from the early nineteenth century, was slower to develop. As early as 1808, a Royal Navy frigate successfully obtained supplies from the reluctant Japanese in Nagasaki harbor by threatening bombardment. Thus began a period of British "gunboat diplomacy" with Japan that culminated, in 1863, with the ships of the Royal Navy flattening much of the city of Kagoshima on the southern island of Kyushu. This successful shelling convinced Japanese leaders of the superiority of Western naval doctrine over their own and led—ironically, in the light of Japanese naval victories in 1941 and 1942—to a Japanese decision to seek British aid in training the future Imperial Japanese Navy in the image of the Royal Navy.[3]

While Britain and the other European Great Powers vied for wealth and influence in Asia, the United States, too, was looking toward the Pacific. American interest had been piqued by publication in 1890 of Admiral Alfred T. Mahan's *The Influence of Sea Power upon History*. Motivated by Mahan's "strong-navy" argument; by the need to defend Hawaii, Guam, and the Philippines (new American outposts in the Pacific acquired in 1898); and by the idealistic and economic appeals of the American "open-door" policy of free trade with China, the U.S. Navy sharply increased its attention on the Far East.

The United States had long operated in Asian waters with an impunity gained from sharing the protective umbrella created by the Royal Navy on the China Station. U.S. and Royal Navy ships in the Far East aided each other on occasion, including one incident in 1859 in which Commodore Josiah Tattnall violated American neutrality and went to the assistance of a British admiral wounded in a skirmish with the Chinese, coining the phrase "Blood is thicker than water!"[4] The U.S. Navy had decided as early as 1908 that Pearl Harbor would be its chief naval base in the Pacific, but it was not until 1921 that the British Committee of Imperial Defence elected to turn Singapore into the "Gibraltar of the Far East."[5] In the 1920s, informal cooperation between the men and ships of the U.S. and Royal Navies on the China Station "probably was," according to author and former Yangtze "River Rat" Admiral Kemp Tolley, USN, "at an all time high. This was due partly to camaraderie built up during World War I and partly to the pure practicality of cooperative enterprise."[6]

The rise of militarism in Japan during the 1930s, which led to the Japanese takeover of Manchuria in 1931 and to full-scale war with China in 1937, further increased Anglo-American concern over the course of events in Asia. On 12 December 1937, the American gunboat USS *Panay*, at the time engaged in evacuating Americans—including State Department officials—from war-torn Nanking, was bombed and sunk in the Yangtze River by Japanese naval aircraft that subsequently machine-gunned the survivors. In Tokyo, U.S. Ambassador Joseph C. Grew, fearing that this affront to American sovereignty might lead to an immediate break in diplomatic relations, "began to plan the details of hurried packing in case we might have to leave."[7] However, Japan's prompt admission of responsibility and tendering of an apology with the promise of compensation defused the immediate crisis.

The British government, whose gunboats on the Yangtze were attacked by the Japanese at the same time as the *Panay*, had, since November 1937, been trying without much success to encourage the United States to a combined show of naval force in the Far East. President Roosevelt, with the *Panay* incident fresh in mind, rekindled British interest in cooperative action by sending the U.S. Navy's director of plans on a secret mission to the Admiralty in London in January 1938 to explore the possibility of "parallel actions" in Asia. Although little came of the ensuing discussions, at least the first faltering steps toward Anglo-American cooperation in the Pacific had been taken.[8]

One of the greatest American pre–world War II cryptographic successes was the breaking of the Japanese diplomatic code, which allowed American negotiators at the 1922 Washington conference full access to the secret instructions being cabled from Tokyo to the Japanese delegation—a success that the Americans chose not to share with the British.[9] Great Britain fully reciprocated this lack of cooperative spirit. Not only had the British broken the Japanese diplomatic codes themselves but they were also reading some American diplomatic traffic.[10] One British cryptanalyst recalled that at the end of the First World War, as the flow of foreign military traffic declined, diplomatic traffic grew in importance, and "in the early days of 1920 the strongest section of the G.C.& C.S. [Government Code and Cypher School—the code breakers] was the United States Section."[11]

Since the war against Japan was primarily a maritime struggle, "it is not surprising," as British military historian Ronald Lewin pointed out, "that almost from the beginning the richest and, at times, the decisive source of information was the system of codes used by the Japanese Navy."[12] Recognizing that this might be the case, both the Admiralty and the U.S. Navy Department began independent attacks on Japanese codes well before World War II. Following the formation of a Naval Section at the British GC&CS in 1924, work on breaking Japanese naval codes began, and despite the difficulties involved in training intercept operators in the special Morse code symbols used for the Japanese language, "a number of Japanese cyphers were duly broken."[13] In the same year, the Royal Navy established a listening post afloat on the flagship of the China Station and local collection of Japanese navy radio traffic and its decipherment commenced. By 1935, cryptographers at the Far East Combined Bureau (FECB) in Hong Kong, the chief British intelligence organization in Asia, had made significant progress in breaking several Japanese naval codes, and work was progressing on Japanese merchant shipping and consular codes. Unknown ciphers were sent back to England for exploitation.[14]

Unlike the U.S. Army, whose "Black Chamber" was established in 1917, the U.S. Navy apparently did not engage in code-breaking activities during the First World War.[15] The navy created its first communications intelligence staff positions in 1924 in the Code and Signal Section of the Navy Department's Office of Naval Communications under the cover name "Research Desk." That same year, the navy's first shore-based intercept station was officially established in Shanghai. Prior to Shanghai, the only station charged with intercepting foreign communications had been on board the USS *Huron* in Far Eastern waters.[16]

Lieutenant Laurence L. Safford, an Annapolis graduate, became the first head of the Research Desk. Safford soon realized and was able to convince his superiors that without a constant flow of traffic for analysis, little could be accomplished in breaking the Japanese naval codes. "A single code message is worthless except as a curiosity," Safford wrote. "We must have all the traffic to and from a given station and messages by the hundreds and by the thousands to have any chance of solving foreign codes."[17] To fill the need for a large volume of coded Japanese messages, in addition to Shanghai, intercept stations were positioned in Peking, Guam, Hawaii, and Manila.[18]

The navy was prompt in putting its newly established Far Eastern eavesdropping capabilities to good use. Intelligence reports from the U.S. naval attaché in Tokyo, among others, indicated that the Imperial Japanese Navy was planning a major fleet exercise in October 1927. Ellis Zacharias, one of the few U.S. naval officers trained in the Japanese language in prewar years, was sent to the staff of Commander in Chief, U.S. Asiatic Fleet, under "cover." His true assignment was to lead the team of navy personnel who were copying and studying Japanese naval communications. Realizing that his nominal home port of Shanghai was too far away from the anticipated Japanese maneuver area to intercept tactical communications, Zacharias and a small contingent of radiomen and equipment moved aboard the USS *Marblehead*, which was about to depart for a series of well-publicized courtesy visits to various Japanese ports.

Zacharias's report to the commander in chief, U.S. Asiatic Fleet (later forwarded to the director of naval communications in Washington), analyzing the results of his successful mission has been preserved in the National Archives.[19] The efforts of Zacharias and his team, the first such directed against Japanese fleet maneuvers, proved remarkably fruitful, both in quantity of coded information obtained and in quality of tactical data, such as individual Japanese ship call signs, recovered. Zacharias's small detachment was the forerunner of the mobile radio intelligence units (RIUs) that were first embarked in 1942 to give commanders at sea rapid access to information derived from on-board analysis of Japanese tactical communications that bore on their current operations. By the latter days of the Pacific war, these RIUs had proved their worth to the extent that one carrier admiral wrote, "No Task Group Commander in the Fleet can now afford to be without an RI unit."[20]

The main bastion of British intelligence in Asia during the 1930s remained the Far East Combined Bureau. Unfortunately, the bulk of its records were destroyed in the days before Singapore fell to the Japanese, and it is therefore difficult to be precise in answering questions such as when first contact was made between the British at FECB and the U.S. Navy's code breakers in the Philippines. Established in Hong Kong in 1935 and moved to Singapore in 1939, the FECB grew out of the Royal Navy's intelligence organization on the China Station. Since 1927, the British army had maintained its chief intelligence office in Shanghai and wished the FECB to be located there; however, the Royal Navy wanted Singapore. Hong Kong was the compromise. FECB was organized into two sections: one dealing with "Y" matters and direction finding, the other concerned with decryption of Japanese radio traffic. Both were directly under the chief of intelligence staff.[21] All three British services were represented by the heads of their local intelligence organizations, but the Royal Navy's chief of intelligence staff, China Station, was primus inter pares. With a Royal Navy man at its head and with its administrative control vested in the Admiralty, it is not surprising that Air Chief Marshal Sir Robert Brooke-Popham, RAF, commander in chief of British forces in the Far East at the time of the Japanese attacks in 1941, found the combined bureau "somewhat unbalanced in that attention was mostly concentrated on Naval intelligence, while Army and Air intelligence took a minor place, the latter especially being quite inadequate."[22]

In addition to the service intelligence organizations and the Government Code and Cypher School, the British Secret Intelligence Service was active in the Far East during the interwar period, apparently with mixed success. Brooke-Popham commented in a draft copy of a July 1942 report that he submitted on the history of his then-defunct Far East Command that "the weakest part of the intelligence system was the Secret Intelligence Service."[23] It is of interest to note that these and other unflattering remarks by Brooke-Popham concerning the performance of the Secret Intelligence Service in the Far East were deleted from the final version of his report.

By the late 1930s, it seemed increasingly likely that the United States would become involved in war with Japan and would join in the world conflict then spreading from Europe to the Middle East and Asia. American and British naval intelligence had long been active in the Far East, but they had been acting independently. Working in their own watertight compartments, British and American code breakers had achieved varying degrees of success against many different Japanese codes at different times, but the solution to the cipher of chief concern to both navies, the major Japanese navy operational code—called JN-25 by the American code breakers—remained elusive. There were other players in the Far Eastern cryptographic game—the Dutch, Australians, and New Zealanders—but their cooperative contributions would have to await the commencement of hostilities.

Although the Spanish and Portuguese were both active during the sixteenth century in seeking wealth and knowledge in the far reaches of the Pacific, it probably fell to the Dutch early in the next century to make the first landfall on the continent we now call Australia. By the middle of the eighteenth century, the British were beginning to see commercial possibilities in the land-mass then known as New Holland, and the Admiralty sent Captain James Cook on his famous three voyages to explore and lay claim to the lands of the Southwest Pacific. British colonization of the area of southeastern Australia began in 1788, motivated either by the government's need to find an alternative dumping ground for its convicts—the American colonies no longer being available for this purpose—or by the desire to establish a bastion for British commerce in the Southwest Pacific. Although British colonization did not end, transportation of convicts to Australia virtually ceased in 1840, and after a struggle for control between imperial rule and self-government, the Commonwealth of Australia came into being on 1 January 1901.

The development of an independent army and navy followed close on the heels of commonwealth status; however, loyalty to the Empire remained, and over 300,000 Australians served the Allied cause in the First World War. The Royal Australian Navy (RAN) was founded in 1911, and shortly thereafter, the bulk of the Royal Navy installations and equipment in Australia passed into the hands of the fledgling RAN. As might be expected, ties between the two navies were extremely close; RAN officers and ratings received advanced training in England in RN schools and served on RN ships, and RN officers filled many key positions in the RAN hierarchy. Although an independent navy, in time of war, the RAN was expected by both countries to serve as an extension of the Royal Navy and under its direction.

Australian naval intelligence has a history almost as long as the RAN itself. In 1911, the assistant of the first naval member of the Australian Commonwealth Naval Board (ACNB) was charged with the supervision of intelligence matters, and intelligence was established as a separate branch of the Navy Office in June 1914. Although little was recorded about the activities of Australian naval intelligence during the First World War, its efforts were of sufficient value to prompt a commendatory letter from Admiral of the Fleet and First Sea Lord "Jacky" Fisher to the Australian first naval member, which stated that "the excellence of your Intelligence Service has been our admiration during the war." In response to a query by the Australian prime minister in June 1918, the Navy Office listed the major responsibilities of Australian naval intelligence as twofold: to serve as a node in the Admiralty's worldwide intelligence reporting system, and to provide the ACNB with information on the countries bordering the Pacific to enable the board to make policy decisions.[24]

Australian naval signals intelligence is generally thought to have had its beginnings in the work of Commander Eric Nave, RN, in the late 1930s;

however, in World War I, Frederick William Wheatley, onetime headmaster of the Royal Australian Naval College and a German linguist, was made responsible for RAN code-breaking activities. Fortuitous capture of a German codebook and key list designed to permit communication between German naval vessels and their merchant ships gave Wheatley sufficient information to work out subsequent changes to the key lists and enabled the Australians to read messages from the German Pacific Fleet. The results of these labors were shared with the Admiralty and may have led to Fisher's words of praise for Australian intelligence.[25]

In 1919, Admiral Jellicoe, commander of the British fleet at the Battle of Jutland, was asked by the Australian government to stop off on the way to his new post as governor-general of New Zealand and study the needs of the future RAN. In his report, Jellicoe pointed out that a naval threat to Australia could come from only two nations: the United States, which he discounted as highly unlikely, and Japan, which, although allied to Great Britain in the recent war, had begun to show ill feeling toward Britain and, by association, Australia and New Zealand. Not surprisingly, he urged the closest cooperation between the RAN and the Royal Navy and that, rather than develop an independent naval force, Australia concentrate on procuring ship types that would contribute to the overall strength and balance of the British Pacific Fleet. He commented that the Australian Naval Intelligence Division had not been developed as fully as the Admiralty might have wished and urged that it be expanded, using the Royal Navy's intelligence organization as its model.[26]

Far from expanding, in the interwar years, Australian naval intelligence fell prey to the same shortages of both funds and staff that beset the intelligence services in the United States and Great Britain. By January 1919, the intelligence branch had been reduced to near zero, and in 1921, "Intelligence" ceased to be a branch of the naval staff. Only the Admiralty's offer of an officer, to be paid from imperial funds, kept the RAN intelligence organization from disappearing altogether. For most of the interwar period, naval intelligence was an additional duty of the assistant chief of the naval staff, who had little time to devote to the task. Whatever intelligence work was accomplished was done by a more junior RAN officer designated assistant director and by his civilian clerk. David Horner, an Australian historian specializing in the Second World War, wrote that "with few intelligence gathering facilities of their own the Australian services relied almost exclusively on information received from British sources, and in turn the British passed on what they thought the Australians needed to know."[27]

Coast watching was perhaps the only area in which Australian naval intelligence did not have to play catch-up as the Second World War approached.

The Jellicoe report in 1919 had recommended the formation of some type of coastguard service, but little was done to further that recommendation until 1922. Then, at the invitation of the RAN, the three Australian services met to discuss the idea of coast watching and concluded that Australia needed an organization of patriotic citizens living along its long coastline and in the island territories that, in time of war or emergency, would report unusual events, ship movements, and other types of useful information. Recruitment of coast watchers began in 1923, starting first with government officials such as customs officers, then expanding to nongovernment planters and merchants, many of whom were reserve officers, and even—where the European population was unusually sparse—missionaries. By the war's start in 1939, over seven hundred coast watchers were on the rolls.[28]

Much of the credit for the coast watchers' state of readiness in 1939 must be given to Commander Rupert Long, RAN. "Cockey" Long—the nickname attributed to his days as a naval cadet, when his young voice tended to break and emit roosterlike noises—was certainly the most important officer in Australian naval intelligence throughout the war and one of the most influential Allied naval intelligence specialists serving in the Pacific theater. After an early career in various RN and RAN ships and schools, Long came ashore as district intelligence officer in Sydney in 1934. Long's position gave him access to leaders in the local business community, and, as John Godfrey was to do a few years later in London, he began to develop contacts outside the navy that would serve him well throughout the war. Those interviewed by Long's biographer described him as being "an extraordinary manipulator of people. He was friendly, constantly and professionally cheerful, likeable, helpful, a sympathetic listener, generous with his praise; he made people *want* to do what he intended them to do."[29] During his time in Sydney, Long gained hands-on experience in the tradecraft of naval intelligence—interrogating friendly ship captains who had visited Japanese ports, working with the British network of reporting officers in the Pacific, and becoming familiar with the strengths and weaknesses of the Australian coast-watching organization.

As the international situation became more unsettled, Australian naval headquarters recognized a need for greater emphasis on intelligence than could be provided part-time by the assistant chief of the naval staff. It directed that the position of assistant director of naval intelligence be created and that Long be transferred from Sydney to Melbourne to fill the new job. On 20 April 1936, Long became de facto head of Australian naval intelligence, a position he held until the war's end in 1945.

After assuming his new duties, Long embarked on a campaign to improve the coast watchers' equipment and to expand their coverage in the territories of Papua and New Guinea. In August 1939, his efforts resulted in the establishment of a staff officer (Intelligence) position at Port Moresby, for which Long selected Commander Eric Feldt, RAN, a retired naval officer turned civil servant with wide experience in the Northern Territory. Feldt accepted and immediately started to expand the coast-watcher recruiting program. Once war came, Feldt became head of the coast watchers and was afforded a great deal of autonomy in directing their activities, while remaining dependent on the Australian director of naval intelligence for supplies, personnel, and political support. Although the coast watchers would eventually come under the umbrella of MacArthur's Allied Intelligence Bureau, Feldt, through Long, was able to keep a great measure of control in the hands of the Australian navy.

New Zealand, Australia's neighbor to the southeast, did not have its own navy during the First World War, and it was not until 1920—certainly with the blessing of Governor-General Lord Jellicoe—that New Zealand achieved a measure of naval independence with the formation of the New Zealand Squadron of the Royal Navy. In the interwar years, perhaps because of its isolated location some four thousand miles from the nearest of the Japanese Mandates, New Zealand was not overly concerned with its own security, believing in some vague way that it would be protected by the British Fleet on China Station if required. This left the Admiralty with the ticklish problem of interesting New Zealand in investing in its own protection, thus saving imperial defense funds already thinly spread and badly needed elsewhere. In 1936, the New Zealand Naval Board, consisting of the minister of defense and three Royal Navy officers, was created to administer "all ships, establishments and personnel" of the navy. Just before the start of the war in 1939, the total strength of the New Zealand division of the Royal Navy consisted of two cruisers and one minesweeper and a total of eighty-two officers, eight of whom were New Zealanders and the remainder Royal Navy.[30]

Naval intelligence got its start in New Zealand with the appointment in 1921 of a Royal Marine to Wellington as district intelligence officer, reporting to the chief of intelligence staff, China. Almost immediately, the funding tug-of-war began. The Royal Navy Commodore Commanding New Zealand Station at Wellington suggested that the district intelligence officer be transferred to his staff. The Admiralty responded favorably, but only if the officer were paid from New Zealand funds—whereupon the matter died. To further intelligence reporting in the South Pacific at minimum cost, in 1925 the Admiralty asked the New Zealand government if it would be interested in establishing (and paying for) a naval intelligence regional center, similar to those operated on the Royal Navy's behalf by the Australians and the Canadians.

In reply, the New Zealanders diplomatically informed the Admiralty that they were unwilling to undertake that responsibility at the moment.

Two years later, the Admiralty again raised the question of greater participation by the New Zealand government in local naval intelligence. This time, the commodore commanding the New Zealand Station pointed out to the naval secretary in Wellington that he had little use for an intelligence officer in peacetime but would certainly need one in the case of war. He recommended that the Admiralty assign an officer to his staff who would perform primarily as an operations officer—not in itself a full-time job—but with the additional duty as intelligence officer, which would be enough to keep one person profitably employed. If this were done, the position of district intelligence officer could be abolished, perhaps saving money. The Admiralty agreed, and with the consent and probably the funds of the New Zealand government, the position of staff officer, operations and intelligence, came into being.[31]

As was the case in Australia, New Zealand recognized the need for the establishment of a coast-watching service as early as 1935. The plan adopted called for provision of four district intelligence officers, two on North Island and two on South Island, to coordinate the activities of the fifty-eight coast-watching stations that had been organized by September 1938. These stations were manned by local harbor employees or by lighthouse keepers, despite some misgivings on the Admiralty's part that coast-watching duties might contravene the immunity granted lighthouse keepers under international law. The system was not extended to the outlying islands until after the start of the war in Europe.[32]

In both Australia and New Zealand, the coast-watching organizations were in addition to the network of reporting officers established by the Admiralty as the Pacific Naval Intelligence Organization. This network was controlled by the chief of intelligence staff, Singapore, who was responsible for coordinating the collection of naval intelligence from a vast area that included China, the East Indies, North and South America, Canada, Australia, New Zealand, and the South Atlantic east of Capetown.[33] Following the fall of Singapore and the move of the chief of intelligence staff from the Pacific to the Indian Ocean, reporting officers in the Southwest Pacific were generally folded into the coast-watchers' organization, but the Admiralty's Pacific naval intelligence network continued in operation—reduced in scope to the eastern Pacific and Latin America and coordinated by a member of the British Admiralty Delegation in Washington.

As the world moved closer to war in May 1939, the Admiralty directed the Royal Navy officer serving as staff officer intelligence in Wellington to initiate local liaison with the French navy. Accordingly, a conference was arranged in Papeete in July, which showed the French to be as ill prepared in intelligence as was New Zealand. In its Pacific territories, the French navy had but one reporting officer, who depended on information passed to him sporadically from harbormasters via captains of trading schooners that had called at the island ports. He had no facilities for emergency communications with his sources.[34]

Traditionally, intelligence cooperation in the Southwest Pacific had been triangular in nature, with the British chief of intelligence staff in Hong Kong and later in Singapore at the apex and in control. That liaison in matters of defense between Australia and the British and between New Zealand and the British was better than between the two Dominions became a matter of concern to the New Zealand Chiefs of Staff in 1938. "It should be at least as close as with Great Britain—in fact, in view of the similarity of our problems both in peace and war, it is very easy to make out a case for it being even closer." Intelligence liaison was in better condition than other defense matters, because Australia and New Zealand did exchange intelligence reports, but there was much room for improvement.[35]

In the interwar years, cooperation between the British Dominions in the Far East and the United States on mutual defense or intelligence matters was essentially nonexistent. America had little economic stake in Australia and New Zealand, because restrictive Empire trade policies had made it so. Unwavering British assurances that the base at Singapore and the Royal Navy would always be there to defend them, coupled with the high cost of independent defense, led the Dominions to depend exclusively on the British shield, and no other avenues of defense were explored. It was not until the Second World War revealed the hollowness of British assurances that the Dominions began to look to Washington and the U.S. Navy as a potential alternative avenue for protection.[36]

During the immediate prewar period in the Pacific, despite the strains caused by political issues, Anglo-American naval intelligence cooperation seemed to have a life of its own that did not necessarily depend on or replicate the ups and downs of what one historian termed the "bargaining for supremacy"[37] that went on in the late 1930s between British and American military leaders.

American and British naval commanders in Far Eastern waters had been working together since the late 1920s and exchanging information that might help counter Japan's expansionist plans. In November 1933, Admiral F. C. Dreyer, RN, commander in chief, China Station, on his own initiative concluded an informal agreement with Admiral F. B. Upham, USN, commander in chief, Asiatic Fleet, to employ a personal code in communicating with each other. News of this agreement, when it reached London, provoked consternation. The DNI commented that "there seem to be serious objections to this arrangement, and no apparent overriding advantages." He saw the code as being potentially insecure and, should the Japanese get wind of it, "would, very naturally, give rise to disquiet and suspicion." Furthermore, he argued, "it is difficult to see under what circumstances in normal times the necessity arises for exchanging secret messages with the U.S. Navy, or any other Navy for that matter." The Admiralty agreed with its DNI and directed Admiral Dreyer to cancel the arrangement forthwith—which he did, saying in a letter to Admiral Upham, "The knowledge that our personal co-operation is so frank and complete renders it so much the easier to make this suggestion [to cancel]." As would happen with increasing frequency during the Pacific war, an initiative for cooperation in the field was blocked by headquarters.[38]

During the late 1930s, British forces and American marines in Shanghai shared tactical intelligence. Captain Ingersoll's mission to the Admiralty in 1938 and the subsequent return visit of Commander Hampton, RN, to the American chief of naval operations in 1939 dealt primarily with operational cooperation in the Pacific. However, the discussions did disclose the existence of an ongoing, if informal, program to exchange intelligence concerning Japanese military activities. During the Ingersoll visit, "it was agreed that a wider exchange of intelligence on all subjects connected with Japan was desirable."[39]

On 25 July 1939, Admiral Thomas C. Hart broke his flag in the cruiser USS *Augusta*, anchored in Shanghai harbor, and assumed command of the U.S. Asiatic Fleet, relieving Admiral Harry E. Yarnell as commander in chief. The fleet's impressive title belied its small size and its complete inadequacy to defend American interests in the Far East. Since Hart was one of the few four-star admirals in the prewar U.S. Navy, he might have been expected to command a larger and more powerful force—one more in keeping with his high rank. However, in the case of the Asiatic Fleet, both the title and the commander's rank were matters of "face," determined more by the representational aspects of the assignment than by the strength of the fleet. Four stars made Hart equal or senior to the foreign naval officers—British, French, or Japanese—with whom he would have to deal.[40]

Hart had previously been stationed in Washington in the post of chairman of the General Board of the Navy, the body that served as chief adviser to the secretary of the navy on matters of policy. After his assignment to the Asiatic Fleet was announced in early March 1939, Hart, with characteristic thoroughness, began to prepare for his new duties, visiting both the Department of State and the Office of Naval Intelligence. At State, Hart found that "the top two men in the Far Eastern Division either had the situation summarized in notes or had it in their heads so that I could be given the picture as they saw it concretely and completely. In our own Office of Naval Intelligence," Hart added gently, "the situation was not quite the same."[41]

After several months on station in the Far East, Hart complained in a memorandum that he "produced in June 1940 [but] never sent to anyone" that information flowed from China and Japan to ONI, but "the Comman- der in Chief [Asiatic Fleet] gets nothing *from* ONI."[42] Three months previ- ously, Hart had asked the chief of naval operations to have ONI send him information on any significant changes in merchant ship traffic patterns in the Pacific. "I can't think of any better barometer," Hart wrote.[43] There is no indication that his request was ever honored.

Since, according to Hart's biographer, "a major part of Hart's mission was to find out what the Japanese were up to," he was forced to become his own intelligence analyst, using funds specially provided for the purpose to collect information and to produce his own evaluations of the situation in Asia, which he dutifully shared with the Navy Department.[44] When these reports produced no reaction from ONI, he wrote acerbically to the chief of naval operations, "I do at least directly request that we be informed of those respects in which our own estimates [similar to the one going forward in this mail] are disagreed with by your own people."[45]

Admiral Hart's efforts to promote Anglo-American naval cooperation began early in his tour of duty. Shortly after his change of command, Hart paid a courtesy call on Vice Admiral Percy Noble, commander of British naval forces in Chinese waters, who, later in the war, became head of the British Admiralty Delegation in Washington. During the course of what had been arranged as a visit of protocol, as opposed to a discussion of substantive issues, Hart nevertheless planned on having a "very confidential" talk with Noble about what might be done in the case of "actual hostilities with the Japs."[46] The call took place on 25 August 1939, but the hoped-for private dis- cussion did not. The increasingly volatile situation in Europe forced Noble to cut the visit short, collect his ships, and depart suddenly for Hong Kong.

While the Far Eastern history of the United States and Great Britain demon- strated that, should the necessity arise, their navies could work together, there is little evidence to indicate that this cooperation—be it in intelligence or in operations—was anything more than local in nature and unsanctioned in other than vague principle by either Washington or London. British interests in the Pacific centered around protection of trade and defense of Empire, neither of which goals loomed large in the American agenda for Asia. Whereas in the Atlantic, in the months before the war and after its outbreak in 1939, there was general Anglo-American agreement that the sea lanes between England and America were vital to the survival of Great Britain, there was no such meeting of the minds in the Pacific. United States' strategic planning for the Pacific in the late 1930s called for stopping any Japanese naval excursion in the central Pacific and then moving back into the western Pacific to regain lost ground, tacitly admitting that the Philippines could not be defended. British strategy, in contrast, centered on the defense of Singapore and, through it, protection of Australia, New Zealand, and the various British colonial holdings in Asia. Variant strategic concepts, coupled with a U.S. unwillingness (for domestic political reasons) to undertake overt military planning with the British, doomed Anglo-American naval cooperation in the Far East to slow and spasmodic progress. The coming of the Second World War found the naval intelligence organizations of the British Dominions in the Far East even less ready to cope with the Japanese threat than were those of the mother country or her American friends.

8.
Too Little, Too Late

Earlier tentative approaches to cooperation that had been taken in London and Washington had yet to exert much influence on actions in Singapore or Manila. Such local initiatives in exchanging operational and intelligence information as were sanctioned were carefully monitored and limited. Despite this, as war came to Europe and threatened to spread to the Pacific, the navies of Australia and New Zealand, as well as the American and British Pacific forces, began both separately and collectively to organize for war. The time between the German invasion of Poland and the Japanese attack on Pearl Harbor produced a heightened awareness of the interwar shortcomings in intelligence organization, collection, and exchange, and measures were started to correct these deficiencies.

The American and Royal Navies had been involved in the Far East for a longer time and to a greater extent than had their land and air services. They therefore had more to gain (or lose) should cooperative measures succeed (or fail). By the fall of 1941, when the soon-to-be-Allied navies had begun to look seriously at increased intelligence cooperation, it was too late.

As the outbreak of war in Europe drew closer, the concern voiced by the New Zealand Chiefs of Staff in 1938 over the lack of cooperation among the Commonwealth nations in the Pacific intensified. By September 1939, New Zealand's Organization for National Security had established a close liaison with the Australian government and had commenced a weekly exchange of information between the two prime ministers' offices. To further this effort, the New Zealand naval secretary was asked to provide material for these weekly summaries, and "if it is considered at any time that certain information is of such importance that it should be communicated without delay . . . the necessary action will be taken."[1]

In late December 1940, the Admiralty instructed Captain F. J. Wylie, RN, recently relieved as commander of the Far East Combined Bureau (FECB), to make a liaison visit to Australia and New Zealand for the twofold purpose of acquainting their intelligence staffs with the work being done by the combined bureau and of improving the Royal Navy's overall intelligence operation in the Pacific. In this instance, both the reports of the visitor (albeit highly censored) and, at least in the case of Australia, the visited have survived in Australian records. Both reports speak of the interest shown in the activities and organization of the FECB and discuss the practicality of forming combined operational intelligence centers patterned on the combined bureau in the two Dominions. Wylie indicated privately that the intelligence officers of both countries were overloaded and voiced concern about finding additional suitable staff to assist them. Australia's desire to start a cryptographic organization, which had received lukewarm support from Wylie, was not mentioned in the censored version of the British report.[2]

The Australian naval staff also raised the question of the status of intelligence cooperation with the Dutch naval forces, a matter of considerable concern to Commander Long and his intelligence department. Wylie indicated that intelligence liaison had been arranged between Batavia and Singapore, but that nothing had been received to date of great interest, and the little offered by the Dutch pertained almost exclusively to the Netherlands East Indies. What was unstated, or not in the public record, was cooperation with the Dutch in signals intelligence. The Dutch had placed an army cryptographic team in Bandung in 1933 and a navy team in Batavia the following year, achieving significant results against a limited number of Japanese naval codes. At some time prior to the Japanese attacks in 1941, the Dutch had started to share their cryptographic results with the FECB and with Australia and New Zealand.[3]

Apparently, the Royal Australian Navy felt that its interest in intelligence relating to those parts of the Netherlands East Indies closest to northern Australia would be better served by direct access to the Dutch than by use of the FECB as an intermediary. Accordingly, the Dutch naval liaison officer stationed with the Australian Navy Office in Melbourne was pressed into service as an intelligence communication channel. In April 1941, the Australians offered use of this channel to the New Zealand Navy to send and receive information to and from the Dutch, and the offer was accepted. In June, the New Zealand navy liaison officer in Singapore was able to reassure the chief of naval staff, Wellington, that "co-operation with the Dutch is good and improving." By September, an Australian naval officer had been posted to Batavia for liaison duties, including intelligence exchange, with the Royal Netherlands Navy. In that month, his duties were broadened to include representing the New Zealand Naval Board in the Dutch East Indies, specifically "acting as a link for the exchange of Intelligence between the [New Zealand] Naval Board and CZM [Dutch Naval Forces]." Notwithstanding all the intelligence liaison activity that took place in the months immediately preceding the Japanese attacks, as late as October 1941, Commander Long wrote to his liaison officer in Batavia that "I have an uneasy feeling that we, here in Australia, do not receive all the information that Singapore has to give us, and that Singapore does not provide all the information they should to CZM."[4]

Prior to Captain Wylie's visit to Wellington in January 1941, Lieutenant Commander E.K.H. St. Aubyn, RN, the New Zealand navy's staff officer, operations and intelligence (the two staff positions were still combined at the time), had visited Melbourne to arrange for greater intelligence exchange, particularly of coast-watching reports and of direction finding bearings. Liaison with the French was also discussed, and St. Aubyn's report noted that New Zealand's relations with Tahiti were more satisfactory than those between Australia and Noumea.[5]

Encouraged by Captain Wylie's visit, the Dominion naval intelligence organizations continued to press for better and faster intelligence from the FECB. In March 1941, Lieutenant Commander St. Aubyn, who had been transferred to Singapore as New Zealand naval liaison officer, received a letter from the chief of naval staff, Wellington, in which he pointed out the delays previously experienced in receiving current political intelligence by air mail from the FECB and expressed his gratitude for the weekly message now being sent. But he asked St. Aubyn to impress on Captain K. L. Harkness, RN, chief of the combined bureau, that New Zealand needed "hot" operational intelligence as soon as it became available. The chief of naval staff indicated that his prodding of the FECB was not prompted by the navy's needs alone. "I find that the War Cabinet always show the very liveliest interest in this subject. Consequently they are gradually learning the value of Naval Intelligence." In a personal letter to a colleague the following month, St. Aubyn indicated that he was doing what he could to get "adequate information" to the Naval Board but that New Zealand suffered from an identity problem. "It would surprise you to know how many people, otherwise well informed, think that when they have told D.N.I. Melbourne something, they have told N.Z. and all the Pacific as well."[6]

Coincident with the stepped-up intelligence exchange program, Australia and New Zealand both began to examine ways in which intelligence could be made more useful to the consumer—in this case, the respective military staff organizations of both countries. As a first step, Australia organized an Area Combined Headquarters (ACH) in Melbourne in 1939 to deal with "trade defence measures." In essence, the ACH was designed to provide local operational control of joint naval and air operations. To support its mission, and with the British FECB in Singapore as a model, the ACH structure was modified in August 1940 to provide authority for a Combined Operational Intelligence Centre (COIC), in which operational intelligence from all three services could be collated, analyzed, and submitted to the three service chiefs of staff. The COIC first met on 16 October 1940. As the war drew closer to Australia, satellite COICs were opened in Townsville in the northeast, Darwin in the north, and Perth in the west to support the regional ACH. All were staffed by experienced RAN intelligence officers from the parent COIC in Melbourne.[7]

The establishment of the COIC did not meet with universal approval. In October, Australian DNI Long grumbled, in a personal note to his trusted subordinate, Eric Feldt, that the only way that the COIC came into being was through "extreme Air Force pressure," because it had no intelligence organization of its own and wanted the COIC to fill that need.[8] Long's reluctance to go "joint" was understandable when one recalls that at this stage of the war the only threat to Australia was from the sea, in the form of German raiders. Trade defense, the rationale for establishment of the COIC, was a navy responsibility involving the protection and routing of merchant shipping. Intelligence to support trade defense came to Long's operational intelligence watch team from a number of sources, some of them sensitive, including the Royal Navy's intelligence reporting network. Long feared that channeling this flow of intelligence through a combined organization that had little "need to know" would subject the material to misinterpretation by army and air force watch officers unfamiliar with naval operations and to possible source compromise through the greatly increased number of people who would become privy to the information. Australian army intelligence—at this point in the war, concerned chiefly with domestic security—also had little interest in forming a joint intelligence center.[9]

Immediately following the first German raider attacks on shipping in the South Pacific in November 1940, the Australian chief of naval staff directed Long to detail a team of officers who were to have no duties other than operational intelligence and were to report directly to the DNI. Long thereupon dropped his objection to the COIC and decided to control that organization, using the mandated operational intelligence team as its nucleus. In January

1941, with the concurrence of the other two directors of intelligence, Long became both DNI and director of the COIC. Beginning on 1 February 1941, the COIC commenced publication of a weekly summary of events and actions taken and a daily report of Japanese military activities.

The German raider sinkings in the vicinity of Nauru, which was jointly administered by Great Britain, Australia, and New Zealand, produced the same galvanic response in Wellington as it had in Melbourne. New Zealand had formed a Combined Intelligence Committee in March 1938, designed to deal more with matters of intelligence policy than with operational intelligence. As recommended by the Combined Intelligence Committee, in September 1940, the Chiefs of Staff ordered the formation of a Central War Room and Combined Intelligence Bureau. At the request of the New Zealand chief of naval staff, his counterpart in Melbourne provided detailed information on the mission and progress in building the Australian Central War Room and COIC, with the result that the two intelligence organizations were almost identical in structure. As they had in Australia, German raider attacks caused a reorganization and rapid increase of the naval staff in New Zealand's Combined Intelligence Bureau and gave rise to greater liaison and exchange of information with COIC Melbourne and with the FECB in Singapore. In October 1941, the Combined Intelligence Bureau was replaced by a COIC. As was the case in Australia, the New Zealand director of naval intelligence, Commander F. M. Beasley, RN, became director of the COIC and was specifically charged with responsibility for liaison with overseas intelligence authorities. A postwar Admiralty study of intelligence during the Pacific war comments, without further explanation, "It was from this centre [New Zealand COIC] that British Naval Intelligence in the South Pacific was directed."[10]

Radio intelligence, generally called "Y" information, was one of the sources of intelligence feeding into the newly formed COICs. At this juncture, radio intelligence was limited to the products of direction finding and traffic analysis, since the results of the U.S. and the Royal Navies code-breaking activities in the Far East were not shared with Australia and New Zealand, and the two nations had no cryptographic capability of their own. Both, however, were making significant contributions to the British Far Eastern direction finding organization.

In February 1940, Commander Eric Nave, RN, who specialized in Japanese navy codes, returned to Australia on sick leave from his previous posting to the FECB, Singapore. Nave subsequently joined the Australian navy's first "Y" organization, then being formed by Commander Jack B. Newman, RAN. Intercept of foreign coded traffic had been carried out in Melbourne prior to this time, but that was a British combined bureau operation, and Australia was only marginally involved. Using materials supplied by Singapore, Nave continued his cryptographic work with an attack on a low-level code sometimes used by the Japanese consul general in Sydney. As tensions increased in the summer of 1941, Nave made arrangements for two of his staff to receive additional cryptographic training in Singapore and for them to bring back some of the solutions to high-grade diplomatic ciphers that the FECB had obtained. By October 1941, the RAN signals organization had completed training the first group of Royal Australian Air Force operators in Japanese Morse code, preparing them for duty in the newly formed RAAF "Y" station in Darwin, where they would intercept communications from the Japanese Mandated Islands that could not be obtained in the south.[11]

New Zealand made a small start in signals intelligence in 1940 and soon became a member of the Far East direction finding net, sharing results with both Australia and Singapore. The New Zealand Chiefs of Staff recognized the value of the new organization at the time they created the COIC in Wellington and made arrangements to place the naval "Y" staff close by, so direction finding information could pass rapidly to the combined intelligence staff. Lieutenant H. Philpott, RNZN, a warrant telegraphist in 1939, became the linchpin in the New Zealand navy's "Y" organization. After a spring 1941 trip to visit signals intelligence organizations in Melbourne, Batavia, and Singapore, Philpott reported with pride that "it was satisfactory to know that Singapore puts a good deal of faith in our interpretation of what is wanted of us and in general chooses New Zealand stations for special duties." Philpott also noted in the same report that the Australians indicated that they had had great success in using women as telegraphists engaged in "Y" work. He would have liked to do so in Wellington but was precluded by a regulation forbidding women to be assigned to night watches. Recognizing that it would soon be essential for women to replace men needed for combat service, Philpott offered to start evening classes for women in Morse code, "as a voluntary organisation unconnected with the Naval Service."[12] By December 1941, the British-controlled signals intelligence network in the Pacific was operating smoothly, lacking only U.S. participation to complete its coverage of Japanese communications. As will be seen, remedy of this defect would be slow to come, and when it did, it would mark a shift in signal intelligence primacy in the Pacific from the Royal to the U.S. Navy.

Other tentative steps toward multinational naval cooperation in the Far East took place in Singapore in November 1940 and Batavia in January 1941. These conferences were, however, more Anglo-Dutch than Anglo-American in composition, although Captain William R. Purnell, USN, Admiral Hart's chief of staff, attended both as an observer.[13] Apparently little of substance was accomplished at either of the meetings, but they helped set the scene for an April 1941 Singapore conference. This was the only prewar conference held in the Far East of the then and future Allies in which the United States was a full participant. Again, Captain Purnell was the lead U.S. military representative and was the sole American to sign the meeting report.

The American-Dutch-British (ADB) conversations that began on 21 April 1941 in Singapore included delegates from Australia, New Zealand, and India, as well as the three principals, and were called to plan for concerted action against the Japanese should they resort to military force against any of the attending nations.[14] The meeting was an outgrowth of the American-British conversations (ABC-1) that had been held in Washington in March 1941, after which the American and British chiefs of staff had agreed that a subsequent meeting should be held in Singapore "as soon as practicable" to draw up a "practical operating plan" to implement the agreements—a goal that was to prove elusive.[15]

Following the March 1941 ABC-1 meeting, Rear Admiral V. H. Danckwerts and his chief of staff, Captain A. W. Clarke, both of whom had been members of the British delegation to the ABC-1 conversations and had remained in Washington with the British Admiralty Delegation, visited Hawaii to confer with Admirals H. E. Kimmel, commander in chief, Pacific Fleet, and C. C. Bloch, commandant of the Fourteenth Naval District. The purpose of their visit was to further Anglo-American naval planning efforts in the Pacific and, in Clarke's case, to see his daughter, who was in Hawaii "for the duration."[16] If the British officers had hoped to forge an agreed Pacific strategy to present at the forthcoming Singapore conference, they were disappointed, for their Hawaiian interlude was unproductive.[17]

In the spring of 1941, although the possibility of Japanese attacks on American and British possessions in the Pacific was real and was recognized as such by both countries, the threat in Asia did not appear as imminent as that posed by the Germans in Europe. Therefore, both parties approached the problem of cooperation in the Far East with less selflessness of political purpose than they had shown by moving in concert to counter the German juggernaut in the west. During the March 1941 ABC-1 conversations, the British representatives had insisted that the agreed outline of defense policies include the statement that "a cardinal feature of British strategic policy is the retention of a position in the Far East such as will ensure the cohesion and security of the British Commonwealth and the maintenance of its war effort."[18] The ensuing ADB conversations in Singapore were in great measure an unsuccessful British attempt to translate the policy of defense of its Far Eastern empire into practical military plans.

Both U.S. Army Chief of Staff General George C. Marshall and Chief of Naval Operations Admiral Harold R. Stark rejected the agreement reached in Singapore. They found the plan too "political" in nature and therefore beyond the scope of their authority as military leaders; it was also at variance with parts of the ABC-1 agreement and, at least on the naval side, too much concerned with defensive measures, such as convoy and escort duties, rather than with potential offensive actions.[19]

The Americans took exception to the fact that the proposed plan called for U.S. naval forces to defend British possessions in the Far East without any significant help from the Royal Navy. The American army and navy chiefs therefore advised their British counterparts that "until such time as a plan is evolved whereby British naval forces take a predominant part in the defense of the British position in the Far East Area, they [the U.S. military leaders] will be constrained to withdraw their agreement to permit the United States Asiatic Fleet to operate under British strategic direction in that area."[20]

Putting the best possible face on the refusal, the British chiefs of staff became convinced that most of the American objections were "due more to misinterpretation of the report than to any fundamental differences in strategic thought" and began a redraft of the document. In its altered form, ADB-1 was no longer an operational plan drafted by commanders in the field but had grown to be a multinational agreement at the highest military level in each of the countries concerned. All political matters were excised and exiled to an appendix containing "recommendations," and the plan became little more than an agreement to cooperate, with operational decisions to be made later. Even in its watered-down state, ADB-2, as it was now called, did not please the U.S. Navy. The U.S. chief of naval operations found that "an effective combined operating plan appears impossible," and he planned to take no action on ADB-2.

By late November, the Admiralty was able to inform Admiral Phillips, then en route to the Far East with the Royal Navy's Force G, that the American military chiefs had agreed to combined operational planning, which was to be delayed until he had arrived and assumed command of the Eastern Fleet. A preliminary conference of British Empire participants, called for Singapore during the first week in December, was actually in session when the first Japanese attacks occurred.[21] Needless to say, Washington's reluctance to accept the strategies proposed in ADB-1 did little to improve the local climate of cooperation among the Americans, Dutch, and British in the Far East, nor did it do anything to promote the growth of combined intelligence planning.

The next link in the chain of Anglo-American intelligence cooperation in the Pacific was actually forged in England in the fall of 1940. It will be recalled that in the summer of 1940, just prior to Special Naval Observer Admiral Robert L. Ghormley's arrival in London, the Admiralty created the Bailey Committee to study potential areas for Anglo-American naval cooperation. The Bailey Committee's recommendations became the basis for British discussions with Ghormley and the other American observers at the series of meetings cover-named "Standardization of Arms." To implement the mutually agreed measures, including intelligence cooperation, the Joint U.S./U.K. Bailey Committee was formed in London and met at regular intervals until the eve of the U.S. entry into the Second World War.[22]

The fourteenth meeting of the Joint Bailey Committee, held on 16 October 1940, dealt specifically with the exchange of intelligence between U.S. and British naval authorities in the Far East. "In particular the desirability of the exchange of information regarding the movement of Japanese forces was stressed."[23] In addition, provision of secure communication channels for the exchange of intelligence between the British commander in chief, China, and the U.S. commander in chief, Asiatic Fleet, was explored, as was the possibility of exchanging liaison officers between the two fleets. As a result of the Joint U.S./U.K. Bailey Committee meeting, or of a local initiative between Admiral Hart and his British opposite number, Vice Admiral Sir Geoffrey Layton (who had taken Vice Admiral Sir Percy Noble's place as commander in chief, China Station), liaison officers were exchanged in November 1940.[24]

During 1941, the last year of relative "peace" for Anglo-American forces in the Pacific, concern increased in both Washington and London over the slow growth of naval intelligence cooperation in the Far East. Both governments realized that intelligence cooperation in Asia did not approach the closeness that was being achieved in the Atlantic/European area, but neither the Office of Naval Intelligence nor the Admiralty's Naval Intelligence Division seemed able to do much to improve the situation.

Admiral Godfrey, the British director of naval intelligence, shared the general uneasiness over the state of intelligence cooperation in the Pacific. He was concerned that the British and American intelligence organizations in the Far East might not have the "big picture" as seen in London and Washington and that they might be overly occupied with local problems. Despite assurances from the British commander in chief, China, that "the present liaison with Manila is excellent," Godfrey thought that an Anglo-American intelligence conference in Hawaii "would be a good opportunity to resolve any doubts which may exist as to the efficiency of our intelligence organizations in the Pacific."[25] Godfrey saw the proposed conference as an opportunity "to examine intelligence resources open to the British and U.S. authorities in the Far East, to enquire into deficiencies in the existing organizations, and to propose immediate remedies, where necessary." The British DNI toyed with the idea of attending himself, but he had already visited Washington in June and was scheduled to go to Canada, and it was time for him to get home.[26] Captain E. G. Hastings, RN, Godfrey's representative in Washington, suggested that in view of the reluctance of the commander in chief, China, to send his intelligence officer to Hawaii, "the incentive must therefore come from here [i.e., the U.S. Navy Department]."[27] There is no indication that the U.S. Navy showed any desire to pursue the idea, and the meeting never took place.

By the summer of 1941, the machinery for Allied naval cooperation in the Far East had been discussed and, at least in the case of naval intelligence, had in some measure been put into place. However, concrete results from these efforts were slight. Naval historian Samuel Eliot Morison commented that "in contrast to the Atlantic war, where the United States and Royal Navies cooperated as virtual allies before the German declaration . . . the three future allies in the Pacific failed to cooperate before 8 December 1941, and did 'too little and too late' thereafter."[28]

Failing to interest the U.S. Navy in a combined conference the Admiralty attempted a unilateral approach. To urge the U.S. Pacific Fleet staff to provide more information, Captain Hastings, the Admiralty's jack-of-all-intelligence-trades in Washington, scheduled a trip to Hawaii in late December 1941 that was postponed sine die by the Japanese attack on Pearl Harbor. Once again, as had often been the case from the fall of France in 1940 until America's entry into the war in December 1941, the British took the initiative in attempting to enlist the U.S. Navy in a cooperative intelligence program. That they were less successful in the Far East than in Europe was in part because of a U.S. perception that the threat to American interests was less serious in Asia than in Europe, and in part because of the feeling that a closer alliance with the British in the Far East might lead to Americans being forced to support imperialism by defending British colonial possessions in the area.

There is no question that the American and British cryptographic organizations in the Far East were in contact with each other prior to December 1941.[29] However, because of the loss of prewar records when both CAST (named after the third letter of the phonetic alphabet then in use) in the Philippines and the FECB in Singapore were evacuated to safer locations in early 1942, it is difficult to measure with any degree of certainty the extent of cooperation between the two entities. Whatever cryptographic collaboration might have taken place, there is no indication that it bore fruit in the form of greater success in penetrating Japanese navy codes.

As has been noted, in the 1920s, both the British and the Americans established cryptological organizations in Asia. Because the Admiralty had assumed overall responsibility for British cryptographic activities in the Far East, the code breakers, drawn from the Royal Navy and from the Government Code and Cypher School, were first assigned to the chief of intelligence staff, commander in chief, China, in Hong Kong.[30] In 1935, when British intelligence activities in Asia were centralized with the establishment of the FECB in Hong Kong, the cryptographic unit was included, and when the combined bureau moved to Singapore in 1939, the cryptographers moved also.[31]

The U.S. Navy's cryptographic efforts in the Far East, which had started originally in Shanghai and aboard ship, soon expanded to include locations in Guam and in the Philippines. The Radio Security Station of the Marine Detachment, Peking, was established in 1927 and for a time replaced Shanghai as the major U.S. Navy intercept location on the Asian mainland; but in 1935 Peking was disestablished, in part because of the threat to its security posed by Japanese military activities in northern China, and its personnel were sent back to Shanghai.[32] Shanghai, in turn, was closed in December 1940 and its staff transferred to the Philippines, ultimately to staff Monkey Point on Corregidor, which was then under construction in a tunnel and had been authorized because the navy felt the need for "a secure COMINT post in the Ultimate Defense Area of the Philippines."[33]

Cryptographic cooperation in the Far East probably dates from the historic spring 1941 visit of four American army and navy code breakers to the British Government Code and Cypher School outside London.[34] At that time American-made copies of the Japanese coding machine (called the Purple machine by the United States) were given to the British, and technical details of American success in breaking the Japanese diplomatic codes were provided. One of the American party, Captain Abraham Sinkov, U.S. Army, who later in the war headed the U.S. Army's contingent of code breakers at MacArthur's headquarters in Australia,[35] reported that the British "were enthusiastic about future cooperation along cryptographic lines" and that "one important point in the program [of proposed cooperation] was a request for cooperation in the Far East."[36]

Shortly after the American trip to Bletchley Park, a U.S. naval officer stationed at CAST, the U.S. Navy's code-breaking site in the Philippines, visited the combined bureau in Singapore to establish liaison and to plan a concerted attack on the Japanese codes.[37] Following this conference, Commander Malcolm Burnett, RN, traveled to Station CAST, on Corregidor, to study its work against Japanese naval codes. The story is told that because

Burnett's visit was secret and was not disclosed to the U.S. Army, which administered the island, he had to be smuggled aboard disguised as a U.S. Navy ensign. "Kinder old for an Ensign," commented the U.S Army security officer who passed him.[38]

Burnett and his close friend Commander Eric Nave, RN, were the Royal Navy's two leading experts on Japanese cryptographic matters. Both had worked in GC&CS in London in the interwar years, and in the late 1930s, both were stationed at the FECB in Singapore. With the start of the Pacific war, their paths diverged: Burnett to the British Eastern Fleet and eventual duty as liaison to the American cryptographers in Hawaii, and Nave to Australia and the combined bureau that was to become MacArthur's main code-breaking organization.

According to an American source, then a member of Station CAST, Burnett's visit did little to bring the American and British code breakers in the Far East closer together and did not result in any cryptographic breakthroughs in solving the key Japanese navy operational code. British sources, however, credit Burnett with inaugurating a method in which JN-25 messages intercepted by one organization but missed by the other were exchanged regularly, by means of the weekly Pan American Airways clipper, employing a "safe-hand" bag system designed with elaborate built-in precautions to protect the secret nature of the exchange.[39]

Throughout 1941, second only to information on Japanese intentions, the key questions plaguing Great Britain and its Dominions in the Pacific concerned United States' capabilities and plans in the western Pacific and the intelligence on which these unknowns were based. The desired information was potentially available in several locations, and attempts were made in all of them. Obviously, Washington, seat of the federal government and headquarters of the U.S. Navy, was prime. Here the members of the British Admiralty Delegation carried on the quest. Next in importance as a source of information was Hawaii, home port of the U.S. Pacific Fleet. Finally, local liaison with the U.S. Asiatic Fleet and U.S. naval observers stationed in the Far East was attempted, whenever and wherever possible.

In November 1940, three Royal Navy officers left England bound for the United States. They were officially attached to the British embassy in Washington, but their primary duties were to be naval observers to the U.S. Pacific Fleet. The senior officer among them, Commander C.R.L. Parry, was nominally assigned to the battleship USS *West Virginia*, but his assignment was much broader than that of "observer" to a single ship, for he carried with him special British naval ciphers "to enable Commander in Chief United States Fleet [to be renamed U.S. Pacific Fleet in February 1941] to communicate direct with British authorities in emergency." In all probability the Anglo-American agreement that brought Parry to Hawaii was the same one that sent Lieutenant Commander Joseph H. Wellings, USN, to England and to the British Home Fleet, also with the status of observer.[40]

The Dominions were as anxious as the mother country for information from the U.S. Navy—especially intelligence. Australia sent Commander H. M Burrell, RAN, former director of plans on the naval staff, to Washington on a semisecret mission in November 1940. In keeping with President Roosevelt's desire that all contacts with Allied governments be low-key, Burrell traveled as a civilian, ostensibly attached to the Australian legation to expedite the purchase of naval supplies. Burrell brought with him a considerable amount of intelligence on the South Pacific area, which gave him entrée to Admiral Walter Anderson, then director of naval intelligence; Brigadier General Sherman Miles, Army G-2; and Adolf Berle, who followed intelligence matters for the Department of State. On his return, Burrell stopped in Hawaii to share intelligence with the Pacific Fleet staff, continued on to Melbourne to report the results of his trip, then returned promptly to Washington—this time as Australian naval attaché.[41]

New Zealand no less than Australia was interested in establishing closer intelligence ties with the U.S. Navy. Lieutenant Commander R. J. Bailey, RN, on loan to the New Zealand navy, was sent to Washington in July 1941, his appointment thinly disguised as that of naval supply liaison officer, to represent the New Zealand chief of naval staff. Bailey's instructions stated that "exchange of intelligence with the U.S.A. and Canada is most important and you should look into the question of improving our liaison with both countries." The naval staff in Wellington had contributed to the well-received Australian information package that Commander Burrell had taken to Washington and Hawaii in November 1940. Later, the New Zealand chief of the naval staff followed up this information with a reminder to the British naval observer at Pearl Harbor that New Zealand had a resident naval officer stationed in Suva, Fiji, engaged in intelligence duties. "We have a good deal of information both from the Naval and Air aspect about our area," he wrote, "but naturally I do not know whether the United States authorities are more or less up to date than we are. It is obvious that we could each learn a good deal from the other."[42]

As Anglo-American ties drew closer in the summer of 1941, Commander Parry's assignment with the U.S. Pacific Fleet was changed from naval observer to that of liaison officer. Earlier, in response to a request for assistance from the New Zealand chief of naval staff, Parry had protested that his status was "strictly that of 'Observer'" and that he could not become involved in matters of policy. Once designated a liaison officer, Parry immediately became involved in questions of intelligence exchange. On a familiarization visit to Singapore, Melbourne, and Wellington in August 1941, Parry carried with him a request for intelligence assistance from the U.S. Pacific Fleet commander that included questions on Japanese and German naval activity in the South Pacific, as well as requests for hydrographic information and charts of the Gilbert, Caroline, and Marshall Islands. In responding, Lieutenant Commander F. M. Beasley, RN, staff officer (Intelligence), Wellington, wrote to Parry that he was delighted to provide all the information in his files concerning CINCPAC's questions, but commented, "I think you will agree that we have now made a pretty good start as regards exchange of information from our end, and feel you should seize this opportunity to press for a quid pro quo."[43]

By the summer of 1941, with the realization that war with Japan was impending, both Washington and London became acutely conscious that intelligence cooperation in the Far East was not all that it should be. In mid-July, the U.S. naval attaché in London cabled the Navy Department that the "British War Council composed of representatives Navy Army and Air Force is desirous of obtaining full exchange of information on Far East" and listed more than half a dozen locations in East and Southeast Asia where the British were especially interested in trading intelligence.[44]

The Navy Department replied promptly, agreeing to the proposed exchange and stating that "instructions to effect full and continuous interchange of information on matters concerning Far East have been issued to [U.S.] Naval Attachés and Observers" at the locations specified by the British. Washington requested that the Admiralty issue similar instructions and that the United States be informed when this had been done. The message concluded by indicating that the U.S. Army was taking similar steps.[45]

Early in August 1941, the U.S. naval attaché, London, was able to assure the Navy Department that appropriate British intelligence organs had been instructed to undertake the exchanges and that the "Admiralty suggests contact with Far East Combined Bureau Singapore with view to maintaining touch with Sail Item Sail [SIS in the phonetic alphabet then in use, referring to British Secret Intelligence Service representatives operating in the Far East]."[46]

The Anglo-American agreement on full exchange of intelligence was not binding on the Dominions, which had not been a party to the messages between the U.S. Navy Department and the Admiralty that preceded the agreement. In September, implying that the initiative for cooperation had come from the United States, the British government informed Australia and New Zealand of its acceptance of the agreement and suggested that they might wish to consider similar steps. "Full" exchange, they were reminded, still carried the caveat that information from "most secret sources" could not be passed directly to local American intelligence officers but must be exchanged through the FECB in Singapore.[47]

Five days before the Japanese attack on Pearl Harbor, the chief of naval operations, Admiral Harold R. Stark, radioed his Asiatic Fleet commander, Admiral Thomas C. Hart, that "in view of existing situation CNO considered [sic] it very important that you exchange full military information with the British and Dutch naval Commanders in Chief except in cases where you consider it definitely inadvisable." Stark suggested that the information exchanges be channeled through the U.S. naval observers in Batavia and Singapore.[48] This advice, however sound, came too late to do much good.

In the waning weeks of relative peace in the Far East, two top British military officials made visits to Manila that contributed to the climate of cooperation, even if the visitors did little to offer practical steps to achieve the desired result. Air Chief Marshal Sir Robert Brooke-Popham, commander in chief of all British forces in the Far East, visited General MacArthur in early October and wrote to him warmly after the trip, "I know you agree with me that these personal meetings develop cooperation far more effectively than any amount of writing."[49]

Following Brooke-Popham's visit to Manila, U.S. Army implementation of the Anglo-American information-sharing program was subsequently confirmed in a late October message from the U.S. Army observer in Singapore to General MacArthur in Manila, which stated, "this Office has received instructions from War Department that there will be free exchange of information except cryptography between intelligence agencies of British and United States" and that "British are complying fully."[50]

Despite British willingness to share, MacArthur was to prove a difficult partner. In responding to a request for information from Brooke-Popham's staff, MacArthur sent nothing and equivocated: "I am completely in accord with an interchange of information but do not wish to let it degenerate into stereotyped form which so frequently characterizes the intelligence activities of military and naval officers."[51] In the latter part of November, MacArthur replied curtly to a personal request from Brooke-Popham for information on current Japanese naval activities in Camranh Bay, Indochina: "this Headquarters has no information not known by British intelligence."[52]

The final British visit before the outbreak of the war with Japan took place on 5 December 1941. Vice Admiral Sir Tom Phillips, RN, called by Samuel Eliot Morison "one of the youngest and most able flag officers in the Royal Navy,"[53] arrived in Manila with key staff members to confer secretly with Hart and MacArthur. Phillips had been detached from his duties as vice chief of the naval staff in London the previous month and directed to proceed to the Far East with the modern battleship HMS *Prince of Wales* and the battle cruiser HMS *Repulse*. The transfer of additional ships to the Far East served a twofold purpose. It fulfilled Prime Minister Churchill's promise made to President Roosevelt at the Atlantic Charter conference to provide visible deterrence to Japanese aggression in Asia by strengthening British naval forces in the area. In addition, it provided an opportunity to exile Phillips, once thought to be a favorite of Churchill's, who had too often disagreed with the prime ministers's views.[54] The ships Phillips brought were to form the nucleus of a new Eastern Fleet, which Phillips was to command and for which he had been promoted to full admiral—thus avoiding a precedence problem with the more senior Vice Admiral Layton, who remained commander in chief, China Station.[55] As he prepared to meet Hart, Phillips must have felt a rueful sense of déjà vu, since it had been he and Captain Ingersoll of the U.S. Navy who had met with equal secrecy in London in 1938 to discuss cooperation in the Pacific— the first milestone on the road to prewar, Anglo-American planning for concerted action in the Far East. To date, however, the road had led nowhere.

Hart was impressed with Phillips. He found Phillips to be made of "good stuff . . . decidedly the intellectual type with a first-rate brain."[56] During their brief and occasionally heated discussions, the admirals examined potential joint measures to counter the imminent Japanese attack anticipated by both. In the end, Hart agreed to send four U.S. destroyers to participate in the defense of Singapore and to operate under Phillips's command, requiring only that Phillips augment his forces by recalling three Royal Navy destroyers from Hong Kong to join the Eastern Fleet.[57]

Phillips's stay in Manila was cut short by receipt of intelligence indicating that a large Japanese convoy had been sighted steaming westward through the Gulf of Siam, destination unknown. Hart relayed the information to Washington, as did American officials in Singapore—presumably from British sources. The American embassy in London also sent Washington reports on the convoy it had received from the British.[58] Sighting of the convoy was one of the few concrete bits of warning intelligence on impending Japanese activities to reach the policy makers in Washington before the actual Japanese attacks. On 6 December, Phillips returned to Singapore to resume command of his small "fleet." Within a week, both the admiral and his fleet had ceased to exist.

War came as promptly and destructively to the Far East as it had to Hawaii. In Manila, Admiral Hart was awakened at 3 A.M. with an unofficial but accurate report that the Japanese had struck Pearl Harbor. In advance of official confirmation, Hart immediately notified the Asiatic Fleet of the start of hostilities, thus alerting his striking force of cruisers and destroyers, which he had prudently deployed to the south of Luzon in late November. Some seven hours later, he received orders to execute the war plan against Japan.[59]

At noon on 8 December, a strong force of Japanese aircraft attacked U.S. Army airfields in the Manila area. As in Hawaii, the bulk of the American aircraft were caught on the ground, and the resulting losses were so severe that the U.S. Army's Far East air force was never able to offer any serious challenge to Japanese superiority in the air.

Without air cover, Manila became open to attack at will by the Japanese. On 10 December, Japanese bombers struck the U.S. naval base at Cavite for over two hours, destroying the yard and crippling several ships and submarines that had been in overhaul there. The Asiatic Fleet's patrol aircraft were similarly attacked from the air, and many were destroyed at their moorings. "By 11 December," Samuel Eliot Morison wrote, "it was unpleasantly clear that the Navy, without shore based aircraft, could not control the seas around the Philippines."[60]

The British in the Far East were faring no better than the Americans. Hong Kong was bombed almost immediately. Japanese troops entered Thailand and began a simultaneous attack on British forces in Malaya. British authorities' lack of foresight was clear to Lieutenant Commander E.P.G. Sandwith,[61] who left England to join the Far East Combined Bureau in August 1941. Although he was convinced that the Japanese intended war, "I found no appreciation of this in Naval circles in Singapore." He also noted that the direction finding equipment operators in his charge were poor, and their results useless. Sandwith's concern that his and others' warnings of the impending Japanese attack had fallen on deaf ears was later confirmed by British code breaker Malcolm Burnett, who had been in Singapore at the war's start.[62]

Upon hearing that the Japanese were making amphibious landings in Malaya, Admiral Tom Phillips put to sea from Singapore on the evening of 8 December with the bulk of the Eastern Fleet's combatants, now code-named Force Z, hoping to engage the Japanese invasion armada in the Gulf of Siam. On 10 December, caught in the open with no air cover of its own, Force Z was no match for the attacking Japanese aircraft. *Prince of Wales* and *Repulse*, so recently arrived in Far Eastern waters, were sunk, and Admiral Tom Phillips was lost, along with the ships that were the pride of his fleet.[63]

The speed and force of the Japanese attacks disrupted intelligence, much as it had military operations. Lieutenant Commander Bailey, the New Zealand navy liaison officer in Washington, informed the chief of naval staff, Wellington, on 18 December 1941, "Am endeavouring ensure you get all information from British and U.S. sources which in any way concerns you. ABC-1 arrangements for direct interchange between British and U.S. authorities failed under initial strain and recovery will be slow." In those confused days of late December, rumors abounded and wild schemes proliferated. Dutch intelligence officers in Batavia toyed with the idea of retransmitting intercepted Japanese messages, the contents of which they were unable to determine, to Japanese naval commands other than those to which the original messages had been sent, in the hope that so doing "may lead to confusion and uneasiness amongst the enemy." When told of the plan, New Zealand Signals Intelligence Chief Philpott commented that he would be "horrified" if the Dutch went through with it, and both the Australian and New Zealand DNIs opposed the idea, fearing that it would be more likely to confuse their own "Y" organizations than the enemy's.[64]

Historian James Leutze, in his epitaph for Western colonialism in the Far East, said, "Perhaps nothing could have saved it, but there can be no question that the lack of unified goals, the absence of coordinated plans, and the inability of commanders to subordinate narrow national interests to the common good contributed to the disarray and ultimately to the disaster."[65] The same underlying explanation applies equally well to Allied cooperation in Far Eastern naval intelligence.

It is difficult to determine why Anglo-American naval cooperation flourished in the Atlantic and foundered in the Pacific. One reason may have been that intelligence cooperation in the Atlantic was based on a series of navy-to-navy agreements between Washington and London, crafted and implemented by skilled, high-ranking liaison officers in both capitals whose major assignment it was to smooth the cooperative path. In the Far East, the Allied fleet commanders, half a world away from Europe and North America, were powerless to conclude all but the most minor agreements without referral to their respective seats of government. The abortive American-Dutch-British agreements reached in Singapore in 1941, only to be torpedoed later by the War and Navy Departments in Washington, exemplify this problem.

Progress in breaking Japanese naval codes, key to intelligence success in the Pacific, remained largely unshared between the U.S. Navy's analysts at CAST and those of the Royal Navy at the Far East Combined Bureau, nor had any structure been created for rapid dissemination of the fruits of the code breakers' efforts—that "most secret" operational intelligence—vital to the several Allied naval staffs responsible for countering the Japanese at sea.

Anglo-American planning for structured intelligence exchange in Europe was not replicated in the Far East, and local initiatives to improve the situation met with resistance in Washington and indifference in Hawaii. Last-minute attempts on the parts of both London and Washington to encourage intelligence sharing before the Japanese attacks were futile.

9.
Organizing for Cooperation

After a spurt in growth immediately following the Japanese attack on Pearl Harbor, Anglo-American naval intelligence cooperation in the Pacific entered a period of decline that started with the departure of the British fleet from East Asia in 1942 and ended only with its return in 1945. Hardening American attitudes—especially that of Admiral Ernest King, leader of the U.S. Navy—toward Royal Navy participation in the largely American Pacific war impeded intelligence cooperation. The intelligence organizations supporting the South and Southwest Pacific commands, with the exception of the Australian and New Zealand coast watchers, were largely American controlled and offered little scope for British influence.

British efforts to gain tactical information on enemy activities in the Pacific, thwarted by American roadblocks, moved underground and were conducted mainly through Dominion surrogates privy to American military and naval intelligence secrets.

In early January 1942 at the Arcadia conference in Washington, the American and British chiefs of staff decided to form the first of what would grow to be a number of supreme commands—combined Allied staffs—each charged with management of the war in its own area of responsibility. On 10 January 1942, the ABDA (American, British, Dutch, Australian) combined command came into being in Java under the leadership of British General Sir Archibald Wavell, who, when informed of the appointment, reportedly said, "I've heard of [being left] holding the baby—but this is twins!"[1] The next day, the Japanese commenced their attack on the Dutch East Indies. On 15 February 1942, Singapore surrendered to the Japanese, and on 21 February, Wavell informed Churchill that "the defence of the ABDA area has broken down," and "I see little further usefulness for these headquarters."[2] The command was dissolved four days later.

In this time of confusion, Anglo-American intelligence in the Far East was plagued more by dispersal than by disunity. By 1 February 1942, the British intelligence personnel at FECB Singapore had been withdrawn. Some went to Java to form the nucleus of the intelligence staff in the ABDA command.[3] The bulk of the combined bureau's navy cryptographers were relocated to Colombo, Ceylon, and subsequently to Kilindini in East Africa, leaving the Americans at Station CAST on Corregidor as the chief Allied code-breaking facility in the Far East. The demise of the FECB and its replacement by chief of intelligence staff, Eastern Fleet, was not made official until 7 August 1942.[4]

The men of Station CAST were of vital importance to the U.S. Navy and to the war effort, not so much for their current contribution as for their potential. The official history of the Naval Security Group noted, "the fact that these 61 persons [of Station CAST] formed a significant proportion of the small number of experienced COMINT personnel available to the Navy made the possibility of losing them a matter of extreme concern." Should these men be captured and subjected to torture, "the possibility of losing the intelligence advantage gained by seventeen years of study and solution of Japanese codes and ciphers would be real and dangerous."[5]

On 1 February, Admiral King, commander in chief, U.S. Fleet, instructed Admiral Hart to evacuate his codebreaking personnel by submarine. The CAST staff was divided into four teams, officer and enlisted, each one containing the nucleus of a code-breaking organization: that is, each team had its share of technical and language officers, cryptographic trained yeomen,[6] and intercept radiomen. The first team of seventeen, including CAST's commanding officer, was removed by the submarine USS *Seadragon* on 5 February. They were off-loaded in Surabaya, then traveled overland to Bandung, where they joined forces with the Dutch radio intelligence team already established there. This bit of Allied cooperation was short-lived, since U.S. naval forces in the Dutch East Indies were ordered to withdraw to Australia, and once again the CAST team packed up its codebooks and machines and departed by submarine. Two teams left Corregidor on board the submarine USS *Permit* on 15 March, and the final team left in *Seadragon* on 6 April 1942.[7] All the teams eventually found their way to Melbourne, Australia, where, in cooperation with the Royal Australian Navy, they organized the Fleet Radio Unit, Melbourne (FRUMEL), which was to play a significant role in intelligence activities throughout the war in the Pacific.[8]

CAST's arrival in Australia was not entirely unexpected. The Australian naval attaché in Washington told his chief of naval staff on 19 February that the U.S. Navy had a number of cryptographers and wireless telegraph (W/T) operators specially trained to read Japanese transmissions departing the Philippines, some of whom were already en route to Java and the rest due to leave soon. He suggested that, should the U.S. Navy elect to send them to Australia, the Royal Australian Navy undertake arrangements with Admiral Glassford, commander of U.S. naval forces in the area, to fold these new-comers into the RAN's code-breaking organization. Melbourne's response was enthusiastic, noting that such a group would be "a valuable addition" to the RAN code breakers and commenting, "we should be glad of services of any who can be made available."⁹

It will be remembered that Captain E. G. Hastings, RN, the senior British naval intelligence representative in the United States, had aborted a late-December 1941 trip to Hawaii whose purpose had been to further Anglo-American intelligence cooperation in the Pacific. He was to have been accompanied by Lieutenant Commander F. M. Beasley, RN, New Zealand di-rector of naval intelligence, who was interested in obtaining greater and quicker intelligence support from the Commander in Chief, Pacific Fleet (CINCPAC) staff. Beasley felt this need to be even more pressing once the U.S. and Royal New Zealand Navies¹⁰ were united in common cause against the Japanese. He wrote to his Australian counterpart, Long, on 8 January 1942 that "intelligence arrangements between us and the U.S. are lamenta-ble" and that he planned to make his postponed trip to Hawaii to "have a shot at breaking the ice." That Beasley's concern was echoed by the higher echelons of the RNZN was evidenced by a minute from the naval secretary to the New Zealand minister of defence in which he termed intelligence re-ceived from the United States as "dangerously scanty." Prior to Beasley's de-parture, the New Zealand chief of naval staff sent a message to his opposite number in Melbourne explaining the need for the visit and requesting input. The Australian CNS responded promptly, fully endorsing the need for per-sonal contact and reiterating, "As you are well aware, we receive practically no information whatever [from CINCPAC]."¹¹

Beasley departed for Hawaii by air on 18 January, stopping en route at Fiji, Canton, and Palmyra Island, and arriving on the evening of 21 January Hono-lulu time. The following morning, accompanied by Captain Parry, the British naval liaison officer, Beasley called on the commander in chief, Pacific Fleet. Their conference lasted two and a half hours. Beasley was unimpressed by the American admiral. "I was disappointed with Admiral Nimitz, who struck me as being an old man, slow and perhaps slightly deaf." Admiral Nimitz's opinion of Beasley is unrecorded. Perhaps the admiral was preoccupied with concerns greater than those of entertaining a relatively junior foreign naval officer.

Following his interview with Admiral Nimitz, Beasley began discussions with the CINCPAC intelligence staff, in particular Commander Joseph Rochefort, head of the fleet cryptographic organization, and Commander Edwin Layton, the fleet intelligence officer. These conversations were more to Beasley's liking, and "a number of things were fixed up very satisfactorily—particularly as regards W/T and D/F and Y intelligence." Talks with the CINCPAC operations, communications, and intelligence staff members continued the next day, followed by an "extremely depressing" tour of the damage at Pearl Harbor and an early-morning departure for New Zealand. After a brief stop in Wellington to report, Beasley flew on to Melbourne to share his information with the RAN.[12]

Perhaps anticipating the demise of the ABDA command, in early February, the Combined Chiefs of Staff recommended the formation of Allied naval elements into an adjoining command to the southeast to be called the ANZAC Force. Commanded by Vice Admiral Herbert F. Leary, USN, the ANZAC Force was given the task of defending the eastern approaches to Australia and New Zealand. Admiral Leary set up his headquarters ashore in Melbourne, where he operated separately from but in close cooperation with the Australian and New Zealand Naval Boards, which retained administrative control of their forces. At the insistence of Admiral King, who had been assigned immediate strategic direction of the force, operational control was vested solely with Admiral Leary.

Intelligence support for the ANZAC command became the de facto responsibility of the Australian director of naval intelligence. As usual, current intelligence was in short supply. In late February, DNI Long wrote to his liaison officer in Batavia asking if he could arrange to have the Australian Naval Board, and through it COMANZAC, supplied with intelligence concerning the ABDA area that could be used as a basis for "sound appreciations or forecasts." He was being questioned by COMANZAC about the situation in the ABDA command but had no information on which to base a reply.

With the concurrence of Admiral Leary, the New Zealand chief of naval staff had recommended that Lieutenant Commander Beasley be the RNZN liaison officer to the ANZAC staff, and Beasley took up his new post in Melbourne shortly after his return from Hawaii. But since the ANZAC command was dissolved at the end of April, his stay was brief. In early April, he sent the New Zealand chief of naval staff details of the proposed South Pacific Command (COMSOPAC) structure that would replace COMANZAC and would place Australia and New Zealand into different strategic areas. He noted correctly that, upon the plan's implementation, "the importance of having a N.Z.N.L.O. [New Zealand naval liaison officer] here [in Melbourne] is obviously greatly reduced."[13]

Beasley's role did not disappear, but its emphasis was shifted from general liaison to intelligence planning for the coming COMSOPAC organization. In mid-April, he informed his superiors in Wellington that it appeared that the new command would be headquartered in Auckland and that its intelligence center would be located there. "I understand that COMANZAC is suggesting that I should form the nucleus for this organization," Beasley wrote. "If you concur in this proposal it looks as if I shall be leaving here at the end of the month." Never one to pass up the opportunity for travel, Beasley concluded, "I have suggested to COMANZAC that I should return via Noumea, Fiji and Tonga so to come primed with the latest first-hand knowledge of the development of these places."[14]

Following the fall of Singapore, the dissolution of the ABDA command, and Allied losses at sea (including the British, Australian, and American cruisers *Exeter, Perth,* and *Houston,* respectively), those Royal Navy ships that were able to do so withdrew to Ceylon (now Sri Lanka) to join a reconstituted British Eastern Fleet being formed by Admiral Sir James Somerville. In essence, the Royal Navy disappeared from the Pacific, not to return until early 1945.

The Pacific war that the Royal Navy missed was largely American and predominantly naval. Following the late February 1942 demise of the ABDA command in Java, the American and British Combined Chiefs of Staff—with the blessing of Churchill and Roosevelt—agreed to parcel out the war into three strategic areas. The Pacific was to be the primary concern of the United States. The Middle East, India, and parts of Africa and Southeast Asia were to be regions of primary British concern. Western Europe, the third major strategic area, was to be treated as a matter of common Anglo-American concern. Only the Russian front and China were excluded. In March 1942, the United States agreed to carry out its responsibilities for strategic direction in the Pacific through the Joint Chiefs of Staff, who would retain overall responsibility for conduct of military operations in the area.

"Against all common sense," one American historian commented, and "against the dictates of military doctrine . . . the Pacific was divided into two theaters."[15] The lion's share of the region went to Admiral Chester W. Nimitz, who became commander in chief, Pacific Ocean Area (CINCPOA), under the JCS structure, in addition to his purely naval responsibilities as commander in chief, Pacific Fleet. What remained of the Pacific (which included Australia, large segments of Japanese-occupied territory in the Dutch East Indies, Malaya, and the Philippines, as well as the intervening waters) was designated the Southwest Pacific Area and was to be commanded by General Douglas MacArthur.[16] The U.S. Navy assumed executive agency for the Pacific Ocean Area and the U.S. Army for the Southwest Pacific Area. This division of authority along service lines led to the growth of two dissimilar intelligence organizations to serve the two equally dissimilar commanders in chief.

Admiral Nimitz subdivided his territory into three regional commands: the North Pacific Area, centered around the Aleutian Island chain; the Central Pacific Area, which included Hawaii, the Gilberts, the Marshalls, and Japan; and the South Pacific Area, whose waters extended from the equator southward and whose western boundary abutted that of MacArthur's Southwest Pacific Command. Nimitz and his staff in Hawaii retained direct control of operations in the North and Central Pacific Areas but created a subordinate organization, Commander South Pacific Area (COMSOPAC), to direct all naval and military activities in that region.

The first COMSOPAC-designate, Admiral Robert L. Ghormley, left London in April 1942 and was replaced by the ex–chief of naval operations, Admiral Harold R. Stark, as commander of U.S. naval forces in Europe. While Ghormley was en route to his new command, with stopovers in Washington and Hawaii, planning for his headquarters and its intelligence component continued. The U.S. Navy Department instructed COMANZAC to form a nucleus intelligence group, "in anticipation of the establishment of a naval base in New Zealand . . . for the U.S. Southern Pacific Force." Personnel for the group were to be obtained from local resources, including intelligence personnel recently sent to the area and those withdrawn from the Netherlands East Indies upon the dissolution of the ABDA command. The first order of business for the nucleus group was to identify individuals who had in-depth knowledge of the islands in the new SOPAC area and to begin "to collect all available data concerning these islands."

Planning to expand the nucleus group once it had been established in Auckland was also undertaken. COMANZAC recommended that the already existing facilities of the New Zealand Combined Operational Intelligence Centre (COIC) in Wellington be utilized, "including [the] extensive coastwatching system throughout [the] South Pacific Islands." So doing would offer the twofold advantage of access to all New Zealand–held information as well as to that available to COIC Melbourne, "since the C.O.I.C.'s of Australia and New Zealand exchange complete information at present." In addition, the U.S. naval attaché in Wellington was directed to approach New Zealand Naval Headquarters for assistance in determining how the proposed intelligence center should be organized and staffed. In their reply, the New

Zealanders suggested a small staff of ten officers and the necessary administrative personnel, with one officer to be assigned as liaison between New Zealand naval intelligence in Wellington and the center in Auckland. Once again, Lieutenant Commander Beasley's name cropped up for posting to Auckland, where he would have been a likely candidate for the proposed liaison position.[17]

By the time Admiral Ghormley arrived in New Zealand on 21 May 1942, preliminary planning was under way for what was to be known as the Guadalcanal campaign – the first operation in the Pacific war, according to naval historian Samuel Eliot Morison "in which the United States took the strategic offensive." Resisting urging from the New Zealand navy to establish his headquarters in Wellington, Ghormley broke his flag in the tender USS *Rigel* in Auckland harbor and commenced around-the-clock preparations for Guadalcanal.[18]

The same directive that brought COMSOPAC into existence also established COMSOWESPAC, under General Douglas MacArthur. MacArthur, too, had a navy. Briefly commanded by Vice Admiral Herbert F. Leary, USN, the former COMANZAC, and subsequently by Vice Admiral Arthur S. Carpender, USN, Commander Allied Naval Forces Southwest Pacific was a small force composed of what remained of the former U.S. Asiatic Fleet—mostly submarines—and units of the Royal Australian Navy, including the cruisers HMAS *Australia, Canberra,* and *Hobart*.[19] A force of this size was obviously incapable of providing the support required for any major move to retake lost ground in the Southwest Pacific, leaving MacArthur the unappetizing prospect of having to go cap in hand to Nimitz and Halsey for naval forces to transport and protect his troops.

When MacArthur arrived in Australia in mid-March 1942, he brought with him the "Bataan Gang"—U.S. Army officers who had been with him in the Philippines—to form the nucleus of his new staff. One member of the gang, Colonel (later Major General) Charles A. Willoughby, became head of G-2 (Intelligence), from which position he would spend the better part of the war trying to gain or maintain control over the numerous and disparate Allied intelligence organizations operating in and out of Australia. Some of these units, such as the Australian coast watchers and the COIC, were in existence when MacArthur arrived; others grew up later. All played a role in Allied intelligence cooperation that will be explored later.

While the United States was assuming primary responsibility for the war in the Pacific, Anglo-American naval intelligence cooperation in the Pacific theater was deteriorating. Intelligence cooperation among the Allied forces in the Far East had started on a high note after the Japanese attacks in Hawaii and Asia and then slowly faded. Despite constant, quiet pressure by Admiralty representatives in Washington and London, there was little improvement in the flow of U.S. Navy intelligence to Admiral Somerville's British Eastern Fleet until early 1945, when the Royal Navy reentered the Pacific.

There were several reasons for this lessening of naval intelligence cooperation. Once the British Eastern Fleet had withdrawn to the Indian Ocean in March 1942, its need for detailed operational intelligence on Japanese naval activity in the Pacific became much harder to justify. More or less concurrently with the British fleet's departure from the Pacific war, Admiral King, who was not overly fond either of the British or of intelligence liaison with their forces, became commander in chief of the U.S. Fleet and chief of naval operations. Finally, in March 1942, shortly before the battles of the Coral Sea and Midway, a power struggle began to develop between the navy in Washington and in Hawaii for primacy in analysis of naval intelligence on the Pacific. This struggle was waged on two fronts: one, to determine which organization—the Office of Naval Intelligence or the Director of Naval Communications—would control the code breakers; the other, to establish whether Pearl Harbor or Washington would be recognized as the authority on naval intelligence in the Pacific. This intramural warfare was to affect both the amount of Pacific intelligence provided the Allies and the choice of who would do the providing.

Intelligence sharing with newfound Allies began soon after Pearl Harbor. Combat Intelligence Bulletin No. 1, produced by Commander Joseph Rochefort's code-breaking team on 16 January 1942, was sent "To the Britishers in Another [cryptographic] System," according to its distribution list. Shortly thereafter, the British Eastern Fleet; the chief of the naval staff, Melbourne; and the New Zealand Naval Board appeared in the bulletin's distribution list as individual recipients.[20] Intelligence sharing was not limited to the top command levels alone. On 20 January 1942, the commander in chief, U.S. Fleet, authorized exchange of "information considered essential for others to know" between commands "of approximately equivalent echelons operating in adjacent areas."[21] Now navy task force commanders in the South and Southwest Pacific Areas could exchange information directly with each other and with their counterparts in the Australian and New Zealand navies without routing everything through their respective national military and naval headquarters. The Navy Department followed this general permission with specific direction on 11 February to include COMANZAC "for all intelligence concerning enemy."[22]

Once the Royal Navy had been withdrawn from the Pacific in the spring of 1942, the importance to the British of liaison officers with the Pacific Fleet increased dramatically. The unknown author of a recently released postwar history of their activities stated, "Upon them & them alone the Admiralty & the War Cabinet relied for information as to how far the war in the Pacific was keeping step with American official reports on its progress, & the truth about the methods & the efficiency of the U.S. Navy. They were also advance envoys of the British Pacific Fleet."[23]

After Japanese navy attacks on Ceylon in May 1942, it was decided to move Eastern Fleet Headquarters to Kilindini in East Africa, and half of the signals intelligence (SIGINT) staff went with it. This permitted the Eastern Fleet to be supplied with enemy communications intercepts without interruption; however, the arrangement proved unsatisfactory. Communications reception was poor, there was no chance for liaison with the other British services, and morale suffered. The SIGINT team moved back to Colombo in September 1942, where it rejoined the expanded group of code breakers resident there in an organization known as HMS *Anderson*.[24]

When Admiral Sir James Somerville became commander in chief of the Eastern Fleet in February 1942, he immediately asked the Admiralty to approach the U.S. Navy for assignment of a liaison officer to his staff. The request was apparently granted, since a later note in the first sea lord's files discussed details of the American officer's passage to the Far East.[25]

Around 26 March 1942, when Admiral King became chief of naval operations, intelligence liaison with the British in the Far East became more restrictive. Sharing of information also began to suffer. In early April, COMINCH directed the U.S. naval observer in Colombo to inform Admiral Sir Geoffrey Layton, former British commander in chief, China, and now commander in chief, Ceylon, that the scope of information exchange envisaged by him was "unnecessary and undesirable" because the "Indian Ocean and Pacific Theaters are entirely separate strategic entities."[26]

The British were not slow to take umbrage. The next month, the U.S. naval observer, Colombo, informed the American director of naval intelligence that "on two occasions when I wanted to send some dope on the [British] fleet," local naval authorities indicated that if the U.S. Navy Department required the information, "it should be released by the Admiralty through B.A.D. [the British Admiralty Delegation] Washington."[27]

In the spring of 1942, Japanese military leaders agreed to a two-pronged strategy. To strengthen its newly established defensive perimeter in the Southwest Pacific and Indian Oceans, Japan would mount an offensive to capture Port Moresby in New Guinea. To gain the decisive victory over the U.S. Pacific Fleet, seen by Admiral Isoroku Yamamoto, commander in chief of the Japanese Combined Fleet, as key to defeating the United States, the

Imperial Japanese Navy would attack Midway and the Aleutians and force the U.S. Navy to fight.[28] Japanese attempts to carry out this strategy resulted in the naval battles of the Coral Sea in May and Midway in June 1942, which together marked a turning point in the war against Japan. Japanese territorial expansion was halted, and the United States prepared to go on the offensive.

Samuel Eliot Morison termed the Battle of the Coral Sea "a tactical victory for the Japanese, but a strategic victory for the United States."[29] Although the Japanese inflicted the greater damage, the invasion of Port Moresby was thwarted, and the two Japanese aircraft carriers that took part could not be made ready in time to participate in the Battle of Midway. During the course of the battle, Nimitz, in Hawaii, found himself in the unique situation of receiving reports of damage to his own forces faster through the intercept of Japanese communications than from American reporting.[30]

For the first time in the Pacific war, American intelligence had been able to give adequate warning of enemy plans. According to the author of the Imperial Japanese Navy's postwar battle history, "if the Japanese had any great disadvantage . . . it was the relative inferiority of their intelligence about the size and numbers of U.S. and Australian ships in the area."[31] This disparity in intelligence would continue and would grow wider as the Pacific war progressed.

If the Japanese attack on Pearl Harbor was the greatest intelligence failure of the Pacific war, Midway was its greatest intelligence success. On 4 May 1942, just as the Battle of the Coral Sea was about to begin, Commander Rochefort and his band of code breakers in Hawaii began to receive hints in intercepted communications that another major Japanese naval operation was in the offing and that it might be aimed at a location in the central Pacific.[32] By 8 May, analysts in Hawaii were beginning to describe the Japanese units involved as the "Midway Strike Force." The invasion date was first projected to be around the end of May, but as evidence in Japanese communications grew, Rochefort became more precise, and on 27 May he estimated that the attack on the Aleutians would begin on 3 June and on Midway on the fourth.[33] On 3 June, Japanese carrier aircraft bombed Dutch Harbor, Alaska, and on the following day the Battle of Midway commenced.[34]

Japanese losses at Midway were so severe that Imperial Naval Headquarters attempted to keep the truth not only from the general public but also from the Japanese navy itself. An intercepted 14 June message in the files of Fleet Radio Unit Melbourne from the commander in chief, Combined Fleet, states, "This is to be handled carefully by all subordinates to ensure there will be no leakage within or without departments. Our losses were 1 carrier sunk and 1 badly damaged and one cruiser badly damaged." FRUMEL commented that Japanese losses "unquestionably" were four aircraft carriers and one cruiser, and that the commander in chief, Combined Fleet, "is apparently feeding false information to his own subordinates, presumably for purposes of morale or propaganda."[35]

British authorities continued to be concerned by the delays in receiving what little naval intelligence they did get from the Pacific. According to Samuel Eliot Morison, when Nimitz asked the British to lend one of their three carriers then in the Indian Ocean to assist in defending Midway, "he received the discouraging reply on 19 May that none could be spared" and that British intelligence indicated no threat to the Aleutians or the Hawaiian Islands.[36] British naval historian Stephen Roskill, in defending the refusal, stated that "it was clear from Admiralty's records that neither the nature nor the quality of the American Navy's intelligence regarding Japanese movements reached London until the 19th or 20th May." Roskill blamed any "misunderstanding" that might have occurred "partly on American slowness in giving the Admiralty the full intelligence of which they were possessed by the middle of May."[37] The official Australian naval history supported the British position by adding that "records disclose no inkling" of Rochefort's early May analysis of Japanese intentions as ever "having reached Australia."[38] These assertions of lack of timely information are difficult to accept when one examines the few records of FRUMEL that are now on file in the Australian archives. The FRUMEL entry for 15 May 1942 reads:

> Association in message headings of the 3rd Carrier Division with C-in-C [commander in chief] 5th Fleet, C-in-C 1st Fleet, 7th Cruiser Division plus MAYA and ATAGO, 17th and 21st Destroyer Divisions and additional unidentified units, which could compose a useful striking force. Their association with 1st and 5th Fleets suggests they may proceed north.
>
> Another network associates C-in-C 2nd Fleet with 1st and 2nd Carrier Division.
>
> *It is suggested the first force may operate in the Aleutians, and the second force may make another attempt on Hawaii or attack other islands in the Central Pacific.*[39]

Since this report was available to the Australians in FRUMEL on the fifteenth, it is highly unlikely that it was not immediately forwarded to Australian naval intelligence in Melbourne and, through it, to the British Eastern Fleet commander in the Indian Ocean and to London.

In the preface to his history of the G-2 (Intelligence) section of the Southwest Pacific staff, General Charles A. Willoughby, MacArthur's G-2, commented sourly that agencies such as FRUMEL "were integrated into the general structure of theater intelligence but from their faltering infancy all possessed an incurable trend toward independence."[40] Despite, or perhaps because of, Willoughby's desire for tight control of intelligence, a structure of Allied intelligence agencies—those of the "incurable trend toward independence"—grew up outside of Willoughby's direct authority.

In April 1942, only a month after his arrival in Australia, General MacArthur co-opted the COIC in Melbourne into his headquarters organization (GHQ). When the general shifted his headquarters to Brisbane in July, COIC went with it. Coming under GHQ took the center out of the intelligence chain of command and put it directly under the MacArthur's chief of staff, General Richard K. Sutherland, which ensured COIC's prompt access to new information—not always the case when it had been limited to information chosen by the operators to be furnished to intelligence. Along with Fleet Radio Melbourne and MacArthur's code breakers in the Central Bureau, COIC was one of the few intelligence organizations in the theater to escape the grasp of General Willoughby. He saw its output, "a sort of daily situation report," as giving rise to "the suggestion of competition" with his own daily product and thus "proving a constant source of embarrassment."

At the time COIC left Australian control, Commander Long, who had been serving as both its director and the director of naval intelligence, relinquished the COIC post, and the directorship passed to the Royal Australian Air Force. Despite a later influx of U.S. Army and Navy personnel, command of the organization remained in Australian hands throughout the war. Although Long was no longer directly involved in the operation of COIC, those loyal to him were, and it is likely that sensitive information, not otherwise available to the British, made its way from COIC to Long and subsequently to the Admiralty.

Since FRUMEL was under the direct command of the Navy Department's code breakers in Washington, it, too, remained outside of that group of intelligence agencies under the operational control of G-2—a situation that caused General Willoughby considerable distress. What disturbed Willoughby most about FRUMEL was that he was not on the very short list of MacArthur's staff officers cleared to see navy "Magic" communications intercepts. Willoughby's displeasure over FRUMEL and its activities could only have been exacerbated by reported instances of navy officer-couriers showing the Magic intercepts to MacArthur alone, then ostentatiously burning them in Willoughby's presence.[41] In the early days, FRUMEL had been MacArthur's chief source of naval intelligence support and his major source of all types of information derived from intercepted Japanese communications. FRUMEL grew into a "combined" intelligence unit, with Royal Navy,

Australian, and New Zealand naval personnel, in addition to those from the United States assigned to it. Through a series of British and American liaison officers, FRUMEL kept in touch with British code-breaking activities in the Eastern Fleet area and, indirectly, with Bletchley Park.[42] In addition to its direct access to MacArthur, FRUMEL provided immediate intelligence support to MacArthur's navy. As was the case with COIC, information not passed directly to the British was available to them through Long's Australian naval intelligence organization, which was in regular contact with both FRUMEL and the U.S. naval intelligence staff of COMSOWESPAC. FRUMEL was involved in both traffic analysis and code breaking, the latter effort directed principally against the Japanese navy's operational code, JN-25.

The Central Bureau (CB), like COIC, was another GHQ staff agency producing intelligence that escaped Willoughby's control. In early April, MacArthur informed Washington of his pressing need for additional U.S. Army cryptographic personnel to supplement the few who had been evacuated from the Philippines. On 15 April, the CB was activated in Melbourne under the command of Brigadier General Spencer B. Akin, MacArthur's chief signal officer both in the Philippines and in Australia, and one of the few staff officers to have direct access to the commander in chief, with Major Abraham Sinkov, a member of the U.S. Army-Navy team that visited Bletchley Park in 1941, as commander of the American army detachment. In addition to the U.S. Army personnel, the CB consisted of contingents of veteran Australian army code breakers who had seen service in North Africa; experienced British intercept operators, some of whom had come out of Java and some from Singapore; and a Royal Australian Air Force component.[43]

At the outset, there was no naval representation in the Central Bureau, although this soon changed when Commander Eric Nave, the Royal Navy's Japanese language expert, was added to the staff. Nave had been sent from Singapore to Melbourne in 1940 to convalesce from a tropical illness. There he helped form the Royal Australian Navy's signals intelligence organization and later was assigned to the Australian portion of FRUMEL. A mid-1942 British report indicated that cooperation among the three FRUMEL leaders— Fabian in charge of the U.S. section; Nave, the Australian section; and Newman, Australian traffic analysis—was unsatisfactory, "mainly owing to the inability of Nave to 'hit it off' with either Fabian or Newman." Perhaps with this personality conflict in mind and with the need for his services elsewhere, the Royal Navy ordered Nave to return to the United Kingdom. At the request of the Australian army chief of staff, the chief of naval staff asked the Admiralty that Nave be retained and assigned to the CB. When no favorable response was forthcoming from the Admiralty, the matter was pushed up the military command chain to Akin. Whether or not Akin had any influence on the Admiralty's final decision is not clear, but Nave remained with the CB for the duration of the war, where he was primarily responsible for work against Japanese ground-based naval air communications. Relations with FRUMEL were never close, despite the fact that much of the CB's effort was against Japanese naval air codes.[44]

As MacArthur's intelligence structure for the Southwest Pacific Area was beginning to take shape in Brisbane, similar activity was taking place in Admiral Ghormley's South Pacific Area. In July 1942, Admiral Ghormley received CINCPAC's operation order to move against Guadalcanal. Ghormley transferred his headquarters from Auckland to Noumea, New Caledonia, a French possession whose defense had been assumed by the United States in March 1942 with the landing of some 17,000 U.S. Army troops sent from Australia. Intelligence planning for the forthcoming assault moved into high gear, and "a rapid and elaborate build-up" of COMSOPAC's intelligence organization began.

Planning was hampered by a lack of current information about the area. The only charts of the Solomons available to Ghormley and his staff dated from 1897 and 1908. Intelligence officers from both the Royal Australian and New Zealand Navies were sent to Noumea to expedite the flow of intelligence needed for the Guadalcanal assault, especially information from the coast watchers. A U.S. Navy intelligence team was flown to Australia to obtain information from planters and others who had been evacuated from the area, and some of the former residents actually accompanied the invading U.S. Marines to identify landmarks. Aerial reconnaissance was undertaken and some photography achieved, but Japanese aircraft often drove off the intelligence collectors before they were able to complete their mission. The amphibious attack, based on what little information could be assembled on such short notice, began on 7 August 1942 and met with initial success.[45] It took almost six months of bitter combat ashore and four major naval battles in the surrounding waters to complete the task.

One of the casualties of the drawn-out Guadalcanal campaign was Admiral Ghormley. In an unexpected and rapid move that surprised even his chief of staff, Nimitz replaced Ghormley with Admiral William F. ("Bull") Halsey on 18 October 1942.[46] Admiral Halsey brought with him a number of officers who had been on his staff when he had commanded Task Force 16 on the USS *Enterprise*. Among them was Major (soon to be Colonel) Julian Brown, USMC, who had been Halsey's intelligence officer on the *Enterprise* and was to become head of his COMSOPAC intelligence organization. After a burst of cooperative effort in planning for the COMSOPAC intelligence center, once the center moved from Auckland to Noumea, provision of information to New Zealand and Australia began to suffer. The change was first noted in Washington. Messages from COMSOPAC to COMINCH that had previously been made available to the New Zealand naval liaison officer were withheld, and the New Zealander was told that such information must be obtained by local liaison within the SOPAC area.[47]

From Wellington's standpoint the liaison situation was not much better. In late October, J. G Coates, a member of Parliament in New Zealand and spokesman for the government, wrote to Admiral Halsey that the New Zealand government was anxious to discuss the intelligence liaison matter with the admiral. "Though the New Zealand Government are situated in, and supplying both bases and forces for, the South Pacific Area they receive literally and actually no information from the Headquarters of the area." Coates pointed out that a previous request to send a liaison officer to the COMSOPAC staff had been refused, and "it is desired to provide some practicable and reasonable method of liaison acceptable to the Commander of the South Pacific Area." The desired intelligence post was not established until January 1943.

Captain K. L. Harkness, RN, former commander of the defunct Far East Combined Bureau and now representative of the British director of naval intelligence, visited Noumea in December 1942. "Admiral Halsey was friendly, but extremely reticent about his intelligence service. Colonel J. Brown, U.S. Marine Corps, Head of the Intelligence Staff, ComSoPac was hardly less evasive." The Admiralty in its postwar study of intelligence in the South Pacific area summed up the situation thus: "At the end of 1942 . . . there was very little liaison between British forces & the American South Pacific Command. Admiral Halsey's Headquarters were at Noumea, in New Caledonia, & liaison with C-in-C India and C-in-C Eastern Fleet was non-existent, except through Washington."[48]

The one bright spot in an otherwise dismal record of Allied intelligence cooperation during 1942 was provided by the services of the Australian and New Zealand coast watchers. As previously noted, the Australian Coast-watching Service had been organized by the Royal Australian Navy after World War I and came under the jurisdiction of the director of naval intelligence in Melbourne.[49] The coast watchers were volunteers, drawn mainly from the planters and government officials who in the years prior to World War II had worked in the Australian and British protectorates that made up the Solomon Islands chain, located off the northwest coast of Australia— lands unknown to most Americans in 1941 but soon to become a part of their history: Bougainville, New Georgia, and, above all, Guadalcanal.

As the Japanese extended their conquests in early 1942 to include the Dutch East Indies and the Bismarck Archipelago to the northeast of the Solomons, the coast watchers stayed behind, as their code name "Ferdinand"[50] implied, not to fight but to provide warning of Japanese movements at a time when other methods, such as Australian radar or reconnaissance aircraft, were either in short supply or nonexistent. To afford its members the dubious protection of status as combatants, the coast watchers were integrated into the Royal Australian Navy in March 1942, where they subsequently performed with great success in the Battle of the Coral Sea and the Battle for Guadalcanal.[51] Using clandestine radios, the coast watchers sent reports on Japanese defenses as well as troop and aircraft locations to Australian naval intelligence, which then relayed the information to the U.S. Marines in the South Pacific Force. Immediate warning messages were sent in the clear on radio frequencies that the U.S. Navy could monitor. In return, Allied forces supported the coast watchers with airdrops of food and supplies.[52]

At the request of COMSOPAC, in October 1942, Australian and New Zealand naval intelligence combined resources to expand the coast-watching organizations in the Solomons area. During the negotiations, Australian DNI Long took care to see that the new posts remained under naval control. He wrote to his representative Eric Feldt, "I consider it is essential that the Number One man of each post should be Naval. The Americans have learnt to respect Australian Naval Intelligence, but I am doubtful of their reception of posts with R.A.A.F. or Army personnel in charge."[53]

As the war progressed, the coast watchers were integrated into MacArthur's Allied Intelligence Bureau, where they were responsible for providing information to both Halsey in the South Pacific Area and to Carpender in the Southwest Pacific Area.[54] Willoughby's history of his G-2 organization called the coast watchers "by far the best organized and most productive of all intelligence agencies operating in the Southwest Pacific area" and one that "continued to render increasingly spectacular service." According to Admiral Halsey, "the coastwatchers saved Guadalcanal and Guadalcanal saved the Pacific."[55]

As Torch, the Allied invasion of North Africa, marked a turning point in the war in the West, so did Midway and Guadalcanal in the Pacific. Slowly at first, but with increasing momentum, American and Allied forces in the South and Southwest Pacific would go on the offensive, carrying the battle to Japan, island by island. As was the case in North Africa, the switch from defense to offense called for a change in sources and types of intelligence to meet the needs of the advancing forces.

In the Pacific, naval warfare was itself undergoing dramatic change. The U.S. Marine Corps, whose troops would spearhead so many of the amphibious assaults to come, recognized early in the war that the evolution of amphibious warfare demanded changes in the traditional methods of intelligence support. In March 1942, the commandant of the Marine Corps recommended that the Navy Department establish a series of advanced intelligence centers in various parts of the Pacific to support future offensive operations.[56] The chief of naval operations agreed and asked the commandant to develop a plan for such centers.[57] The resulting study was then sent to commander in chief, Pacific, for his comments.

At the time that the marines raised the question of advanced intelligence centers, Admiral Nimitz in Hawaii had the U.S. Navy's only functioning intelligence organization in the Pacific. It had received some unexpected personnel augmentations in the form of officer linguists when the overseas Japanese language program ended in November 1941, as well as enlisted band members from the crew of the battleship USS *California*, who had become "technologically unemployed" when their ship was sunk at Pearl Harbor with all their instruments aboard. However, the intelligence unit remained entirely too small to support operations of the size contemplated to fight the Pacific war.[58]

The Pacific Fleet intelligence organization consisted of two parts. Rochefort's code breakers worked directly for Admiral Nimitz but were controlled administratively by the commandant of the Fourteenth Naval District at Pearl Harbor, a small unit called Combat Intelligence that provided reference support to the code-breaking team and served as liaison between the team and the Pacific Fleet staff. Nimitz's tiny headquarters intelligence division, led by Commander Edwin T. Layton, was charged with keeping the commander in chief, Pacific, and certain of his key subordinate commanders informed of current operational intelligence, drawn principally from radio intercepts.[59]

With the inadequacies of his own intelligence organization clearly in mind, Admiral Nimitz informed Washington that, while he agreed in principle with the concept of intelligence centers scattered around the Pacific, his own needs would have to come first. "In view of the nature of the war in the Pacific, it is essential that combat and other intelligence be made constantly available to the Commander in Chief, U.S. Pacific Fleet, in a form which will permit its ready use for his own purposes and for his dissemination to proper commanders in time for effective action."[60] To meet his needs, Nimitz proposed immediate establishment of a Joint Intelligence Center at Pearl Harbor, with follow-on centers at Dutch Harbor for the North Pacific Area and at Auckland and Melbourne for the South and Southwest Pacific

Areas, respectively. Admiral King agreed and ordered the director of naval intelligence to get on with the task.[61]

The Intelligence Center, Pacific Ocean Areas, was officially established in June 1942 and began to function as a unit some two months later.[62] Its structure was to provide a pattern for the ensuing advanced centers elsewhere in the Pacific. In its basic form, the center consisted of an intelligence situation plot, which displayed all known or suspected locations of enemy forces, and major sections dealing with radio intelligence, air intelligence, and photo interpretation. The center also contained counterintelligence and security sections, as well as units specialized in exploitation of prisoner of war interrogation reports and of captured enemy equipment.[63] The organization continued to expand in size and responsibility throughout the war and, in the spring of 1945, was to play a major role in the provision of basic intelligence to the Royal Navy as it returned to the Pacific.

The year 1942 marked the turn of battle in the Pacific and a period of organization and growing pains for Allied naval intelligence. Spurred by Japanese military successes, ad hoc efforts to cooperate showed promise but soon faded as highly organized units came into being that were tailored more to satisfying the specific intelligence requirements of individual commanders than to creating a structure that would meet the needs of all. Formation of two separate and often hostile Allied commands in the South and Southwest Pacific had a centrifugal effect on the individual intelligence organizations in the area.

The story of Anglo-American naval intelligence in the Pacific was not inspiring. Cooperation grew more slowly and was less extensive than that in the Atlantic. Measures agreed on in the months just before the Japanese attacks were too little and too late to affect the events of 7 and 8 December 1941. Nor could those agreements have been implemented in time to have much impact on the Anglo-American defeats in early 1942 that forced the Royal Navy's withdrawal from the Pacific.

The Royal Navy, with no visible presence in the Pacific, was hard put to convince the U.S. Navy of its need for intelligence on a war in which it was only marginally involved. As the Pacific war progressed and the American position on intelligence exchange hardened, the Admiralty was increasingly dependent on the Dominions to fulfill—second hand—its intelligence requirements.

10.

"Support" Vice "Cooperation"

"I do not need Paul Revere (with three lanterns) to tell me that the British are coming," Pacific theater commander Chester W. Nimitz wryly informed the Navy Department in December 1944. "The attached paraphrase of six Top Secret dispatches reads like an operation order for an occupation force. Perhaps it is intended to be an occupation force."[1] Thus did the U.S. Navy welcome the idea of the Royal Navy's return to the Pacific and to the war at sea with Japan.

In the words of one British naval historian, "After the destruction of Force Z [whose two capital ships, the battleship, HMS *Prince of Wales* and the battle cruiser HMS *Repulse*, were both sunk off the coast of Malaya in December 1941] it was more than three years before major British units again operated east of Singapore. By that time, a whole war had gone by."[2]

As the fortunes of war turned against Japan and U.S. forces continued their island-by-island advance toward the Japanese home islands, the intelligence resources necessary for these successes became increasingly centralized in U.S. or U.S.-dominated organizations. In part because of internecine warfare between Hawaii and Washington for primacy in Pacific intelligence analysis, and in part as a reaction to Anglo-American signals intelligence agreements between Bletchley Park and the U.S. Navy Department, U.S. military leaders became increasingly unwilling to exchange information with the British except through Washington and London, and intelligence liaison between the U.S. Pacific and British Eastern Fleets suffered accordingly.

Not until the return of the Royal Navy to the Pacific had been offered and accepted in late 1944 did this downhill trend reverse and intelligence cooperation undergo a sudden and dramatic improvement.

*   *   *

As was noted in the previous chapter, the first major Royal Navy unit to feel the effects of the reduction in the flow of naval intelligence from the South Pacific was the British Eastern Fleet. As early as August 1942, Admiral Sir James Somerville, sensitive to his lack of Japanese signals intelligence and to the inadequacies of Kilindini and Colombo, sent his chief Japanese code breaker Commander Malcolm Burnett, to London to explore the possibility of linking British cryptographic facilities in the Indian Ocean to the U.S. Navy's net that included Washington, Hawaii, and Melbourne. Burnett had excellent credentials for the assignment, since he was thoroughly familiar with British code-breaking efforts through his service at the Far East Combined Bureau and with American progress against Japanese navy codes through his liaison activities in 1941 with the U.S. Navy's cryptographic unit, Station CAST, in the Philippines.

When he arrived in London, Burnett was told that it was impossible to link the Eastern Fleet to the U.S. Navy net, "owing to the U.S. refusal to give us the required type of cypher machine." He was also informed that at an October meeting in Washington between Commander Joseph Wenger, USN, head of OP-20-G, and Commander Edward Travis, RN, head of Bletchley Park, it had been agreed that Washington would be the main center for the Japanese operational code JN-25 exploitation, with recoveries to be sent to Bletchley Park for further transmission to the Eastern Fleet. Burnett subsequently received permission to visit Washington to share his technical expertise on Japanese naval codes with his American colleagues. While there, Burnett was asked by Wenger to explore ways in which Japanese traffic intercepted by the Eastern Fleet could be passed directly to Washington. "Commander Travis replied that Washington and Kilindini were to communicate only through the existing B.P. [Bletchley Park] link."

Burnett returned to England in early 1943 and used the time awaiting transportation to the Eastern Fleet to work at Bletchley Park. There he found that the Japanese naval section was "snowed under with raw material supplied to them by Washington, and could only raise enough staff to sort it and file it away," and that "B.P only forwards to Kilindini those records which arrive from Washington in duplicate." Burnett concluded his report to Admiral Somerville, "I cannot but look on the B.P. effort as anything but a brake of our primary objective, which is the supply with the least possible delay to C. in C. E.F. [commander in chief, Eastern Fleet] of all information available from Japanese Special Intelligence sources." It is clear from the tenor of Burnett's report that in this instance the British, more so than the Americans, were at fault in impeding direct intelligence cooperation between local commands in the Pacific area.[3]

Admiral Somerville visited Washington in mid-1943, in his capacity as commander in chief, British Eastern Fleet. At that time he indicated to Admiral King the "desirability" of an American naval intelligence officer being assigned to the intelligence organization of the Eastern Fleet, as well as British naval intelligence officers being assigned to the staff of CINCPAC and COMSOWESPAC (MacArthur's navy). The Admiralty concurred and went so far as to nominate one of its most experienced intelligence officers, Captain D.N.C. Tufnell, former British naval attaché to Japan (1939–1941) and currently head of the Eastern Fleet's intelligence staff, for the CINCPAC position.[4] In response to Somerville's overtures, King commented that, "inasmuch as the results of intelligence are furnished in finished form for digest by operations officers, the assignment of additional officers as intelligence liaison officers does not seem warranted." King must have had a change of heart, because by December 1944, Tufnell was assigned to Pearl Harbor, although not as Admiral Somerville's representative.[5]

Throughout 1942, the feeling had persisted among British leaders in both London and Washington that "we are not obtaining all we should from the Pacific."[6] When British Director of Naval Intelligence Admiral John Godfrey visited Washington in October 1942, as much of his time was consumed in addressing the problem of information flow from the Pacific as was devoted to intelligence collaboration, the stated reason for the trip. Fortuitously, at the same time as Godfrey's trip, the American naval liaison officer to Admiral Somerville was in Washington on much the same mission—to increase the amount of U.S. Navy operational and intelligence information passing from the Pacific to the commander in chief, Eastern Fleet. Godfrey reported that as a result of their combined efforts, "machinery had been planned which should ensure a much better flow of information," but he was realist enough to add the caveat, "time will tell how the machinery works in practice."[7]

Because of the difficulty in obtaining permission for the assignment of liaison officers to the various U.S. naval intelligence organizations in the South and Southwest Pacific, the Admiralty resorted to the technique of repeated visits by Royal Navy officers of various ranks and degrees of expertise to Australia and New Zealand, where there was no problem in obtaining the assistance of RAN and RNZN intelligence officers, many of whom were RN officers lent to the Dominion navies for the duration. Through these contacts, the visitors were able to receive a warmer reception from Allied intelligence organizations than would have been the case had the visits been made "cold," without local support. Previously noted visits of this nature included that of a British visitor whose unsigned report detailed his findings concerning "Y" activities in New Zealand, FRUMEL, and the Central Bureau in Australia in the summer of 1942, and that of Captain Harkness, RN, representing the British director of naval intelligence, to Noumea during the course of "his extended visit to the Eastern and Pacific theatres of war" in December 1942. Malcolm Burnett's lengthy visit to Washington in November and December 1942 would also fall in this category.

Commander R. Laird, staff officer (Intelligence) to the commander in chief, Eastern Fleet, visited Noumea, New Zealand, Hawaii, and Australia in March and April 1943, after which he reported in detail on the New Zealand "Y" and "SI" (special intelligence, i.e., cryptographic) organization and on the changes taking place in the naval intelligence structure in the Pacific. In April 1943, Captain Tufnell, soon to be British intelligence liaison officer to CINCPAC, visited New Zealand and reported his findings to the chief of intelligence staff of the Eastern Fleet. Finally, in March 1944, Captain Alan Hillgarth, RN, chief of intelligence staff (designate) to the British Pacific Fleet, visited Australia and reported on its various intelligence organizations. Hillgarth's fulsome praise of Long following the visit was indicative of the esteem in which the Royal Navy held its surrogates in the South and Southwest Pacific. "It is difficult," wrote Hillgarth in the fall of 1944, "to speak of any intelligence entity in Australia or the S.W.P.A. without learning that Commander Long [the Australian DNI] either started it or is still influencing it in the best interests of everybody. Nothing much can happen in Australia without his knowledge." Perhaps the best summary of the value of the surrogates was furnished by the Admiralty's postwar evaluation of naval intelligence in the Pacific: "The essential lesson is that in spite of its token forces & staff the British Navy was strongly represented . . . [by] Cdr. Long, the Australian D.N.I. & New Zealand's long succession of D.N.I.S. These men . . . evaded absorption by the U.S. forces & they kept the D.N.I. London fully appraised of the situation, never exaggerating & never losing sense of proportion & of honour. They played for time & prepared the way for the coming of the British Pacific Fleet."[8]

Commander Malcolm Burnett's failure to gain permission for local intelligence exchange demonstrated one type of roadblock to Pacific intelligence cooperation. The battle between the code breakers in Hawaii and Washington for leadership in Pacific intelligence analysis was another. Both had the effect, intended or not, of reducing or at least delaying the provision of Pacific intelligence to the Royal Navy. As Washington moved to limit distribution of Hawaii-produced intelligence to the Pacific Command area, Royal Navy subscribers elsewhere, such as the British Eastern Fleet in the Indian Ocean, were forced to depend on intelligence from the Pacific that had been filtered through Washington and London, with a concomitant loss in timeliness and therefore usefulness. As Lord Curzon, fighting for increased funds for the Government Code and Cypher School in the 1920s, put it, "the practical use to which the information can be put is proportionate to the rapidity with which it can be made available. The minimizing of delay is a matter of supreme importance."[9]

The struggle between Washington and Hawaii arose because, as Admiral Nimitz's intelligence officer Edwin Layton emphasized often after the war, radio intelligence was not an exact science. Layton indicated in his memoirs that in examining the intelligence available before the battles of both the Coral Sea and Midway, the analysts in Washington reached erroneous conclusions, whereas those of the Pacific Fleet analysts were correct.[10] In both cases, Washington was forced to issue hasty revisions to its original estimates as evidence mounted that it had guessed wrong.

No matter how diplomatically handled, being right when your boss is wrong—especially if your boss is the chief of naval operations—is bound to draw a reaction. In mid-March 1943, a staff officer in the Department of Naval Communications in Washington recommended to his superiors that the CINCPAC intelligence bulletin not be sent to the British, Australians, or New Zealanders. He suggested instead that the bulletin be prepared in the Navy Department, "because COMINCH [commander in chief, U.S. Fleet] would want to pass on what was being sent to these [foreign] addressees," and that the Navy Department's bulletin be given only to the Admiralty, which could then "take care of their own people."[11]

After a series of messages between Washington, Hawaii, and London, COMINCH determined that his organization would control distribution of the CINCPAC Bulletin. Nimitz's intelligence staff was permitted to send the bulletin only to those U.S. Navy subscribers within his command area. OP-20-G, the code breakers in the Department of Naval Communications, not the Office of Naval Intelligence, would pass the bulletin to their counterparts at Bletchley Park for further transmission to the Admiralty and to the commander in chief, Eastern Fleet. The U.S. Navy's Fleet Radio Unit, Melbourne, would provide the bulletin to the Australian and New Zealand Naval Boards.[12]

While the change in who controlled the bulletin's distribution was a clear-cut political victory for Washington over Pearl, it was, on a more subtle plane, a defeat for naval intelligence, because distribution of information derived from intercepted communications was now vested in the Communications as opposed to the Intelligence Directorates of the Navy Department. Once again, ONI's stature was diminished in eyes of the Anglo-American intelligence community as a whole.

There the matter of distribution of the bulletin rested until 8 July 1944, when COMINCH notified the British that publication of the CINCPAC bulletin was to be discontinued immediately.[13] A similar message sent to Pacific Fleet commands stated that "as the strategic or tactical situation develops CINCPAC will address bulletins to appropriate commands."[14] In effect, this move cut the Australians and New Zealanders as well as the British off from formal, automatic distribution of U.S. Navy intelligence originated by the commander in chief, Pacific Fleet. Considering the close working relationships that had been established between the U.S. and Royal Australian Navy code breakers in Melbourne and their colleagues on the intelligence staffs of both COMSOPAC and COMSOWESPAC, it is highly probable that an informal exchange of information continued, with the information once again channeled to the Admiralty through its surrogates in Australia and New Zealand. The cooperative door was closed even further on 2 August, when Washington directed Hawaii to limit information passed to the British on communications channels specifically designed for transmission of radio intelligence "to that which has a bearing upon areas in which the British have strategic responsibility."[15] It will be remembered that the United States had sole strategic responsibility for the Pacific, and the British for the Middle East, Africa, and India.

Thus did the U.S. Navy gradually but inexorably cut off the Admiralty and the British Eastern Fleet from direct intelligence support by U.S. naval forces in the Pacific. The situation would improve dramatically in early 1945 as the Royal Navy returned to the Pacific but would never reach the high plateau of sustained, shared intelligence achieved by the two navies during the Battle of the Atlantic.

During 1943, the intelligence organizations of the commander in chief, Pacific, and commander in chief, Southwest Pacific, and their subordinate commands evolved into a structure that would remain essentially unchanged until the war's end.

When Admiral Nimitz's headquarters staff became truly "joint" in September 1943, with the addition of army and marine officers in all major divisions, its intelligence organization was modified to reflect the changes. On 7 September, the intelligence center was reconstituted as the Joint Intelligence Center Pacific Ocean Area (JICPOA) under the command of an army officer who was also the assistant chief of staff for intelligence on the Pacific joint staff.[16] Captain Layton continued as fleet intelligence officer on Nimitz's purely naval staff. Thus, there were two separate but closely tied staffs to fulfill the commander in chief, Pacific's dual responsibilities as theater commander under the JCS and as a naval commander under the commander in chief, U.S. Fleet.

Paralleling those naval intelligence organizations in the South and Southwest Pacific, in the Northern Pacific Area an advanced radio intelligence unit consisting of one linguist and three radiomen was established in January 1943.[17] Although it remained small in comparison to its sister organizations, by November 1943, the unit had grown to the status of an advanced intelligence center and was reporting intelligence to Hawaii and Washington.[18]

It was a complicated but effective intelligence structure. When an operation was approved by the JCS in Washington and passed to CINCPAC for planning, the Joint Intelligence Center would begin preparation of an "intelligence book" that listed information either on hand or needed to carry out the operation successfully. The center then began compiling the required data, tasking its subordinate commands and the Office of Naval Intelligence to provide pertinent information. When the headquarters staff was in agreement on the major aspects of the operation, the plan and its intelligence book were passed down the line to the operational commander for detailed planning and implementation. Because of time pressures, general and specific planning often took place simultaneously at different command levels.[19]

While there was no question that Nimitz needed comprehensive intelligence support in Hawaii to fulfill his overall responsibilities, the need for operational intelligence was as pressing in the South and Southwest Pacific areas as it was in Pearl Harbor. Admiral Halsey's South Pacific Force, redesignated the Third Fleet in March 1943, had created its own intelligence organization in Noumea, subsequently commanded by a series of U.S. Marine Corps and Army officers but, oddly, no naval officer. As it evolved, the intelligence staff included sections concerned with operational, photographic, and communications intelligence. There was a small prisoner of war interrogation section in Noumea, but the bulk of POW interrogation information was received from the Allied Translator and Interpreter Service of MacArthur's GHQ in Brisbane. In addition, COMSOPAC provided close support intelligence teams to units in combat.

Admiral Halsey did not keep a separate organization in Noumea for communications intelligence but relied on Australia and New Zealand for his support. Since late June 1942, a small U.S. Fleet Radio Unit had been in operation in Auckland, New Zealand. Later the U.S. unit moved to Melbourne, Australia, where it was joined with Fleet Radio Unit, Melbourne (FRUMEL). The austere but well-regarded New Zealand Navy Special Intelligence Centre continued to operate in Wellington, receiving its code-breaking assignments from Melbourne and serving as COMSOPAC's communications link for transmission of "Special" between FRUMEL (and through it, the navy cryptographers in Hawaii and Washington) and Noumea. Admiral Halsey subsequently assigned a liaison officer to Melbourne to screen the large volume of "Special" available there and to pass messages of interest to COMSOPAC in Noumea. The Wellington center intercepted Japanese communications unavailable to other listening posts and passed the traffic to Melbourne for analysis, and the center also became SOPAC's direction finding link in the U.S. Navy's Pacific D/F organization, passing its information directly to COMSOPAC. As the war moved west and the threat to New Zealand itself diminished, intelligence staffs created for the emergency became redundant. In September 1943, the New Zealand naval secretary recommended to the chiefs of staff that "in view of the general improvement in the strategic situation," a watch was no longer required in the Central War Room, "except during working hours." By May of the following year, the Ministry of Works was casting covetous eyes on the space occupied by the Central War Room, in the hope of converting it to other uses.[20]

COMSOPAC's intelligence cooperation with the Allies, never great, improved only marginally as the war progressed. In the course of a "fact-finding" mission in April 1943, one of the Eastern Fleet's senior intelligence officers paid a call on Admiral Halsey. Using the admiral's polite interest in the activities of the Royal Navy in the Indian Ocean as a wedge, the visitor made arrangements "that a Southern Pacific daily bulletin should be passed to C-in-C Eastern Fleet every day. Admiral Halsey's C. of S. [chief of staff] asked if they could be similarly informed when we had something worth telling."[21]

MacArthur's intelligence organization differed from that of Nimitz in several significant respects. The staff itself was not "combined" in any real sense of Allied participation, nor was it "joint," as was Nimitz's. With the exception of Australian General Sir Thomas A. Blamey, commander of Allied land forces, MacArthur's key staff officers were drawn from the U.S. Army. Most of them, like Willoughby, were members of the "Bataan Gang" that had come with MacArthur from the Philippines.[22] Nimitz's intelligence organization consisted of a small nucleus on the Pacific Fleet staff, with decentralized supporting agencies such as the Fleet Radio Unit, Pacific, and JICPOA feeding information to the central headquarters. On MacArthur's staff, the G-2 (Willoughby) "made strenuous efforts to maintain and defend basic staff principles, particularly the absolute centralization of intelligence and the operational control of all GHQ [General Headquarters] intelligence agencies."[23]

The organ of centralization created by Willoughby, the Allied Intelligence Bureau (AIB), was in fact a loosely administered collection of predominantly

Anglo-Australian organizations with little in common except the secrecy of their operations. After a series of organizational fits and starts, ably documented by Alan Powell in *War by Stealth*,[24] by 1943 AIB had evolved into five sections. The first of these, the Philippine Regional Section, was involved in support to Philippine guerrillas. Although under an Allied bureau commanded by an Australian, this unit was basically American controlled and, because of MacArthur's emotional ties to the area, well supported by his GHQ. Less well supplied with men or equipment was the Netherlands East Indies Regional Section, which was commanded by a Royal Netherlands Navy officer and conducted clandestine operations in former Dutch territories. Since there had been little love lost between the Dutch and the native population prior to the arrival of the Japanese, the infiltration teams received little local support, were often betrayed to the Japanese, and were generally unsuccessful.

The Northeast Regional Section was, in effect, the coast watchers. Commander Long, the Australian DNI, had been proposed to head this section and at one time had even been considered for the post of controller of AIB, but both of these appointments fell through, and the Northeast Region command went to Commander J.C.B. McManus, RAN, Long's assistant in Melbourne. McManus's skill in striking a balance among the contending egos of the AIB controller, the DNI, and Willoughby contributed to the continued success of the coast watchers.[25]

The fourth section, the Services Reconnaissance Department (SRD), had developed from a small detachment of the British Special Operations Executive (SOE) that had become active in the Far East in the last few weeks of 1941. Those to whom Churchill had given the mission to "set Europe ablaze" had only enough time to set a few small bonfires before being driven out of Malaya by the Japanese. The follow-on organization for unconventional warfare, Special Operations Australia, operating under the cover name Inter-Allied Services Department (commonly shortened to ISD), was set up in part using SOE funds by Lieutenant Colonel G. E. Mott, a British Army officer who had come to the Far East with SOE and escaped to Java and later to Australia. In the ensuing protracted struggle for control between SOE in London and GHQ in Brisbane, SRD's mission gradually changed to intelligence collection and its charter to engage in clandestine warfare became limited to activities outside the Southwest Pacific Theater.

The last section, Secret Intelligence Australia (SIA), was a direct offshoot of SIS (MI-6) in London. SIS was active in the Far East before the war, and following the fall of Singapore, one of its agents, Captain Roy Kendal, RNR, appeared in Brisbane to continue SIS work from Australia. SIS continued to pay the bills, and because of this direct linkage to London, SIA's activities were looked on with some suspicion by both the Australians and MacArthur's headquarters.

The Far Eastern Liaison Office (FELO) was an organization devoted to "black" propaganda designed to strengthen native morale in Japanese-occupied territories, to lower Japanese morale, and to mislead the enemy—with results that AIB historian Powell described as "problematic." FELO had started under the wing of AIB but was later transferred first to the Political Warfare Division of the Australian Ministry of External Affairs and finally to the Australian army. In addition to its propaganda duties, FELO had a secondary mission of intelligence collection.[26]

All these clandestine organizations, however different their modi operandi, had one thing in common: to carry out their missions, they needed transportation from their staging areas in Australia to whatever enemy-occupied territory was their target. In this respect, the Dutch were more fortunate than the others because they had two Royal Netherlands Navy submarines that, although in poor material condition, could be used to carry raiding parties to their objectives. The other groups had to obtain transportation from the forces assigned to COMSOWESPAC, which usually meant submarines. As Admiral Kinkaid, commander of naval forces, SWPA, informed General MacArthur, he was willing "to make every effort to support the AIB projects outlined within the limits of the forces available to him not committed to operations of a higher priority." A British postwar analysis, which was probably correct, revealed that COMSOWESPAC's intelligence officer, Captain McCollum, who had to pass on all requests for transportation assistance, soon began to feel that "Special Operations Organisations were the bane of his life." With some justification, McCollum felt that "combat submarines were much better employed on the task for which they were designed—torpedoing enemy ships."[27]

Although U.S. Navy submarines were adept at getting the SRD patrols to their destination, they were often less successful in their recovery, primarily through a lack of training and equipment for clandestine work—both possessed in full measure by the SRD teams. After initial resistance by Admiral Ralph W. Christie, commander of U.S. submarines, Southwest Pacific, it was decided to experiment with putting an SRD detachment aboard a U.S. submarine to help bring out a patrol. The results were classic. Lieutenant Commander Sam Dealey, skipper of the submarine USS *Harder*, with an experienced SRD team led by Major Bill Jinkins, Australian imperial forces, aboard, left Freemantle on 26 May 1944 to retrieve a party from British North Borneo. En route to his objective, Dealey encountered and sank two Japanese destroyers. After the SRD detachment had effected a successful rescue of its people, Dealey returned to the battle and sank another Japanese destroyer— the only captain of a U.S. submarine to sink three enemy destroyers in a single patrol. The combined success of the submarine and its SRD party, according to Alan Powell, ensured that there would be more SRD/USN operations. In all, some eight joint SRD/USN war patrols were conducted between June 1944 and March 1945, collecting intelligence, rescuing Allied personnel, and dealing with "targets of opportunity"—such as searching fishing boats suspected of harboring Japanese radio transmitters that were reporting U.S. Navy ship positions.[28]

In addition to those organizations under the AIB umbrella, there were others that were more directly controlled by Willoughby and GHQ. These included the Allied Geographical Section, which produced terrain and hydrographic studies of the largely unmapped and uncharted Southwest Pacific area, and the Allied Translator and Interpreter Section, which performed valuable services in the fields of enemy document translation and prisoner of war interrogation. All these Allied intelligence organizations contained Australians and New Zealanders who were in touch with their national intelligence headquarters, which in turn were in regular contact with British intelligence organizations in England, the Indian Ocean, and India; therefore, British intelligence had indirect access to U.S. naval intelligence from the South and Southwest Pacific, even though no purely British naval intelligence organizations remained in the area.[29]

At the same time that the South Pacific Force became the Third Fleet, the Southwest Pacific Force became the Seventh Fleet. To review, at the time of the dissolution of COMANZAC in the summer of 1942, COMSOWESPAC had come into being as the naval component of the commander in chief, Southwest Pacific Area. To provide for its intelligence needs other than in the field of communications intelligence (provided by FRUMEL), a small intelligence organization had been created in Brisbane, which, by the fall of 1942, consisted of seven U.S. naval officers directed by Captain Hudson, the staff combat intelligence officer.[30]

MacArthur's navy component drew on all the Allied and combined intelligence activities in the theater for its support, especially on the Combined Operational Intelligence Centre, the Allied Air Intelligence Center, and the Allied Intelligence Bureau, which directed the activities of the coast watchers. Despite the magnitude of this support, Admiral A. S. Carpender, USN, the force commander in late 1942, felt the need for an advanced intelligence center directly responsive to his needs and requested that Washington provide the required personnel "as soon as they do become available."[31] Admiral

Carpender's initiative led to the formation of what was later to be known as the Seventh Fleet Intelligence Center (SEFIC).

Although in existence since spring 1943, SEFIC was not officially established as a separate command under Seventh Fleet until 18 May 1944. At that time, Arthur McCollum, now promoted to captain and in charge of Seventh Fleet intelligence, was assigned additional duty as commanding officer of the new center.[32] McCollum was one of the U.S. Navy's leading specialists on Japan, having been assistant naval attaché in Tokyo in the 1930s and subsequently head of the Far Eastern Desk in the Office of Naval Intelligence. While with ONI, McCollum had been instrumental in developing the concept for the U.S. Navy's advanced intelligence centers, which he patterned after the British Operational Intelligence Centres in London and the Far East.[33] By the time of its constitution as a separate command, SEFIC had become a major producer of tactical, strategic, and technical intelligence in support of U.S. operations in the Southwest Pacific Area.[34]

Since his arrival in Australia, McCollum's relations with Australian DNI Long had been extremely cordial. Both Long and the various Royal Navy visitors who came to Australia in 1943–1944 spoke highly of the job McCollum was doing personally but voiced the opinion that his staff was not as well versed in intelligence as he and that an unnecessarily large amount of intelligence duplication existed between the intelligence activities of COMSOPAC and COMSOWESPAC. Considering the state of relations between MacArthur and the U.S. Navy, they were probably correct in this latter analysis.[35] Despite Long's ability to work with McCollum and other U.S. Navy intelligence officers, Royal Navy visitors' reports also reveal an undercurrent of cooperative tension. In commenting on special intelligence in Australia in 1943, Captain Laird, RN, reported, "Cdr Long has to obtain all this Special Intelligence [by inference, U.S. Navy's Magic intercepts] by underhand means which must make it very difficult for him." In 1944, Captain Hillgarth, RN, commented that "the nature of the U.S. Naval Intelligence organization, with its sharp cleavage between Combat Intelligence and O.N.I., coupled with an increasing reserve where the R.A.N. is concerned, handicap him [Long] considerably and he is forced to have recourse to underground methods to obtain some of the information he must have in order to discharge his job adequately."[36]

As MacArthur's war moved closer to Japan, the Seventh Fleet intelligence organization moved with it—from Brisbane to Hollandia, on New Guinea, and eventually to Leyte. The Australian Combined Operational Intelligence Centre, which had become a part of MacArthur's Headquarters Staff in 1942, followed the same route, eventually arriving in Leyte in November 1944.[37]

As the year 1944 began, it seemed for a time as though the British Pacific Fleet might never be formed and that the Pacific war might be left entirely in the hands of the United States. In London, the prime minister and his military advisers were at odds over strategy, and in Washington, Admiral King worked to make sure that the Royal Navy's return to the Pacific would be, if at all, on his terms.

As the Admiralty prepared for Sextant, the November 1943 Allied conference in Cairo, a small British planning staff in Washington was already at work with their U.S. Navy counterparts exploring potential British contributions to the naval war in the Pacific. At Sextant, it was agreed that the main thrust against Japan should be made in the Pacific, as opposed to Southeast Asia. The Royal Navy was to implement this strategy by reducing the size of its Eastern Fleet in the Indian Ocean and, drawing units from the Eastern and Mediterranean Fleets, making a new force, the British Pacific Fleet. This fleet would be based in Australia and would operate either with MacArthur's forces in the Southwest Pacific or with those of Nimitz in the Central Pacific Area, as the military situation at the time dictated.[38]

When the Cairo report was submitted, the prime minister initialed it, signifying its acceptance. However, when the British chiefs of staff followed with their implementing plans, the prime minister took exception to the whole idea. Churchill wished to see British strategy centered on the Indian Ocean and on an effort to liberate former outposts of the Empire in Southeast Asia, particularly the Malay Peninsula. The prime minister was concerned that the Royal Navy would play second fiddle to the U.S. Navy in the Pacific, and there was no assurance, he felt, that the United States would welcome the British back.[39]

British misgivings about the Royal Navy's potential reception had been fueled by a March 1944 letter from President Roosevelt to the prime minister that stated in part that "there will be no specific operation in the Pacific during 1944 that would be adversely affected by the absence of a British Fleet detachment"[40]—hardly a pressing request for help. In addition, Admiral King's objection to combined operations with the Royal Navy in Pacific waters gave rise to concerns.

The degree of King's personal animosity toward the British has been a topic of debate by naval historians on both sides of the Atlantic for years; however, in the case of the British Pacific Fleet, there were sound operational reasons for his uncompromising attitude. King's objections were echoed by the senior U.S. naval liaison officer to the British Eastern Fleet, who, in November 1944, would inform Nimitz that "the British Fleet is not sufficiently trained to keep up with the standard of performance maintained in our own fleet, either in combat operations or in refuelling at sea." The liaison officer concluded that "the obvious solution, as Admiral King has already stated, is to assign them [the British] a specific objective where they can operate more or less independently of our principal naval force."[41]

Since the Royal Navy's supply system had been built around a string of naval bases scattered throughout the world that were now nonexistent, King was also concerned about the Admiralty's ability to provide logistic support to a major fleet far away from home waters. In a more personal vein, King saw the British return as an "intrusion" and objected to having a fleet arrive at the end of the fight to share in the victory.[42] The British were keenly aware of King's misgivings but saw them as arising more from political than from operational considerations. "I have a feeling," wrote the head of the British Admiralty Delegation in Washington to the first sea lord, "that King does not want to see too powerful a British Fleet in being when peace eventually comes."[43]

The Admiralty's reasons for wishing to return to the Pacific were as strong as King's objections. First, there was the matter of pride. The British naval staff history of the war with Japan put it that "no opportunity must be given for critics to say that England, having taken all she could from America to help her to beat Hitler, stood out of the war against Japan and left the U.S.A. to fight alone."[44] The British felt that it was critical for their fleet to join Nimitz's forces in the main move against Japan rather than allow it to be relegated to a sideshow in the Southwest Pacific under MacArthur. Admiral Sir Bruce Fraser, commander in chief–designate of the British Pacific Fleet, realized that the Royal Navy must learn to perform in the modern environment of the fast carrier task force or be willing to accept a postwar status as a second-class navy. Operating in a back area—no matter how well suited the task was to British capabilities—would be, Fraser felt, "nothing less than disastrous to our national prestige."[45] Although unstated in any official British naval history, a compelling reason for choosing Admiral Bruce Fraser to lead the Royal Navy back into the Pacific must have been his potential for establishing friendly working relations with Nimitz, Halsey, and their staffs. A recent biographical evaluation of the leading British admirals of the Second World War found Fraser to be charming and intelligent, technically aware, with great personal and staff officer skills. "It is difficult not to see Fraser as a symbol of all that the Royal Navy had been working towards throughout the war."[46]

By the time of the Second Quebec Conference in September 1944, Churchill and his chiefs of staff had resolved their differences, and all were agreed that the British Pacific Fleet should be formed and that it should play

a significant role in the defeat of Japan. During the conference, Churchill offered the services of the fleet to Roosevelt, who interrupted him to say, "no
sooner offered than accepted." Following the president's decision, King, according to First Sea Lord Cunningham, "gave way, but with a very bad
grace. . . . [He] made it quite clear that it [the British Pacific Fleet] must expect no assistance from the Americans. From this rather unhelpful attitude
he never budged." With or without Admiral King's blessing, the Royal Navy
was returning to the Pacific.[47]

Intelligence impacted the December 1944 Fraser-Nimitz discussions in
Hawaii both early and indirectly. In late November 1944, Commander
Rudolph J. Fabian, USN, who was described as having "been on intelligence
duty with the [British] Eastern Fleet," appeared in Hawaii bearing a message
from Admiral Fraser that discussed the reasons for his impending visit.[48]
Fabian was U.S. naval intelligence's own will-o'-the-wisp in the Pacific. As a
lieutenant, Fabian had been the leader of the CAST code breakers evacuated
from the Philippines to Australia in early 1942. He subsequently commanded
the U.S. Navy portion of Fleet Radio Unit, Melbourne, leaving there for
Colombo in January 1944, where he worked with the British cryptographic
organization. By then promoted to commander, Fabian served as acting senior
U.S. naval liaison officer to the Royal Navy's East Indies Station, in addition
to his radio intelligence duties.[49]

Admiral Fraser and several British Pacific Fleet staff officers arrived in
Hawaii on 16 December. The visitors included Lieutenant Commander
Charles S. Sheppard, RN, who had been selected by Captain Alan Hillgarth,
chief of naval intelligence for both the Eastern theater and the British Pacific
Fleet, for the delicate task of winkling out as much intelligence support as
possible from CINCPAC. Sheppard, who had previously been Hillgarth's
choice to plan the structure of the British Pacific Fleet's intelligence organization, was therefore well acquainted with what was available from British
sources and what would be needed from the U.S. Navy.

The operational role to be played by the British Pacific Fleet in the overall scheme of the naval war had to be defined before the type and amount of
intelligence support could be determined. Discussions on this problem occupied the senior staffs of both fleets for the first two days, during which time
Sheppard met with Captain Tufnell, RN, who by then had become senior
British naval liaison officer to CINCPAC, and with Commander Malcolm
Burnett, RN, once again assigned to a liaison role with a U.S. Navy cryptographic unit—in this case, Fleet Radio Pacific at Pearl Harbor. By the evening
of 19 December, it had been decided that the British Pacific Fleet (BP) would
operate as the equivalent of a U.S. fast carrier task force under either the U.S.

Third or Fifth Fleets. That having been determined, the intelligence negotiations could begin.

At the outset, it was clear that there would be no problem as far as non-ULTRA material was concerned. JICPOA was prepared to meet and even exceed British expectations for support. The sticking point was ULTRA. The British position, propounded with force and skill by Sheppard, was that the BP status was somewhere between that of an area naval commander (e.g., CINCPACFLT or COMSEVENTHFLT) and that of the numbered (e.g., Third and Fifth) fleets and, therefore, should receive intelligence support commensurate with this status. In the American view, expressed by the deputy U.S. Fleet intelligence officer (Captain Layton being away), the BP was nothing more than a fast carrier task force and should be treated accordingly regarding the provision of ULTRA. The preliminary intelligence meeting held on the morning of 20 December was unable to resolve several key questions on who would get what, and at the insistence of Commander Sheppard, the conflicting views were passed up the line for the respective commanders in chief to decide. At the formal intelligence conference that afternoon, attended by Admirals Nimitz and Fraser and their senior staffs, CINCPAC determined that the BP should get a level of ULTRA support equal to but no greater than that given the commanders of the Third and Fifth Fleets. Although it provided only about two-thirds of the loaf desired by Sheppard, the decision was a clear-cut victory for the British position. Following his return to Australia Sheppard wrote in a personal letter to Hillgarth that once the status of the BP had been decided, "I do not think that more could be obtained. . . . It was just as well that Captain Layton was away, as I doubt we would have got the few extra 'concessions' that we did." Later, in commenting on the results of the conference to the British DNI, Captain Hillgarth said, "I consider Lt Cdr Sheppard did extremely well under great difficulties. He is an outstanding intelligence officer on whom great reliance can be placed." Arrangements were made to supply ULTRA intelligence to the BP commencing 1 January 1945.[50]

Intelligence started flowing promptly. In early January, a Royal Navy intelligence officer visited JICPOA to arrange support for the British Pacific Fleet. Distribution lists for current Pacific Fleet intelligence publications were changed to add appropriate British commands, and the British were offered basic intelligence publications, charts, and aerial photographs from the large inventory maintained by JICPOA for issue to U.S. Fleet units on their way to the war zone. "We took the British intelligence officer into our stockroom to select what he wanted," the senior U.S. naval officer at JICPOA recalled. "He wanted nearly everything. When it was added up . . . there were two plane-loads of intelligence material to be transported to Sydney."[51]

On 15 March 1945, the British Pacific Fleet reported to Admiral Nimitz for duty as Task Force 57 and received U.S. Navy teams to assist in adjusting to American tactical and communications procedures.[52] In addition to the material being furnished by Hawaii, British access to American intelligence derived from intercepted Japanese communications had been assured a few days earlier when Admiral King had agreed to provide the needed information. In thanking King for his assistance, Admiral Somerville, former commander of the Eastern Fleet and now head of the British Admiralty Delegation in Washington, wrote on 8 March that "I am most grateful to you for responding so generously and so promptly to my request to be given Japanese naval intelligence obtained from most secret sources."[53] Provision of intelligence on Japanese aviation had previously been assured in an agreement worked out by the Joint Intelligence Committee in Washington and agreed to by the American army and navy chiefs and the British Air Ministry, whereby the exploitation of Japanese aviation-related materials would be done by various American military agencies, including the Office of Naval Intelligence, and the results furnished to Great Britain.[54]

Tactical or operational intelligence support was also provided the British task force. In preparation for operation "Iceberg," the invasion of Okinawa, Royal Navy units that were to take part were given results of American photographic reconnaissance of the islands, which was, as British naval historian S. W. Roskill pointed out, the chief source of intelligence available to the invading forces. British "Y" units were embarked in HMS *Indefatigable* and HMS *King George V*, but their effectiveness was limited by a number of factors, including inadequate equipment and lack of trained personnel. An after-action report from HMS *King George V* indicated that "the material from CINCPAC assumed a greater knowledge of the area than the 'Y' party possessed & it was difficult to separate the relevant material from the masses of information supplied.[55]

Despite an increase in the flow of intelligence once the British Pacific Fleet had become a part of Nimitz's armada, American operational intelligence support to the British force remained less direct, and therefore less timely, than that provided the U.S. Navy. In December 1944, as the war moved closer to the Japanese home islands and farther from Hawaii, Admiral Nimitz chose to move to an advanced headquarters on Guam, taking with him a small intelligence staff to provide direct operational intelligence support to the Central Pacific force. One of the officers chosen to serve in the advanced intelligence unit recalled that, in general, the Royal Navy provided intelligence directly to its forces through use of its own embarked radio intelligence support teams, similar to those assigned to U.S. carriers,[56] and that "from our headquarters on Guam, we were not giving intelligence support directly to the British Pacific Fleet." Non-naval ULTRA was to be supplied to the commander in chief, BP, through British and Australian sources. But as Sheppard pointed out, since under the terms of the Pearl Harbor intelligence agreement there would be a knowledgeable American liaison officer with access to the British intelligence organization in Colombo, "great care will have to be taken in doing this [providing non-naval ULTRA]," so as "not to give cause for cutting us off from what we will receive under the agreement."[57]

Since no good deed is entirely appreciated, the British response to American largesse in intelligence support was not always enthusiastic. Sheppard was "afraid that they [CINCPAC staff] are not going to help us more than necessary, though I do not question their ability." In Hillgarth's opinion, American ability to assess information correctly was suspect. He wrote to the British DNI in February that "while the Americans were giving us everything from 'the most secret stuff all down to terrain handbooks' we have no say in the matter. 'This is a bad thing and I do not trust their interpretation of operational intelligence, & as regards basic books, etc., they swamp everyone with paper.'" Hillgarth's final, resigned, and somewhat bitter evaluation of the U.S. Navy's intelligence support of the British Pacific Fleet epitomized the role reversal that had taken place in Anglo-American cooperation in naval intelligence during the war years. "We are apparently in the position of having to rely entirely on Pearl Harbour for all our Intelligence, & on American Intelligence officers for all interpretation of it. In other words we are in their hands."[58]

Having dealt in some detail with the vicissitudes of Anglo-American naval intelligence cooperation in the Pacific, it seems only fitting to take at least a glance in passing at the Axis partners' naval intelligence cooperation—especially that between Germany and Japan. It will be remembered that Great Britain had provided intelligence to the United States in the early years of the war with little expectation of quid pro quo, but in the hope of binding America closer to the Allied cause. In the same way, Germany furnished intelligence and technical and operational information to the Japanese in the hope of stimulating greater naval activity in the Indian Ocean that might take some of the pressure off German forces in the Mediterranean–Near East area. Like the Americans of 1939–1941, the Japanese of 1942–1944 offered little in return.

Axis-Japanese collaboration in intelligence has been traced as far back as 1939 in the Far East. Decrypts of Japanese messages indicate that, at the time, the Italian consul general in Hong Kong was passing information on local British defenses to his Japanese colleague. In Europe, postwar decryptions of messages from Japanese naval attachés in Berlin and Rome detail contacts in 1940 between the attachés and the Abwehr and Servizio Informazione Segrete, respectively.[59] In his study of General Hiroshi Oshima, Japanese prewar military attaché and wartime ambassador in Berlin, Carl Boyd fixes December 1941 as the high point in German-Japanese military cooperation. Certainly by 1942, Tokyo was showing little inclination to follow up on German initiatives for the exchange of information on British and American ciphers. By 1943, it had become apparent to the Germans that they would receive little from the Japanese in return for the cryptographic material previously furnished, and despite the best efforts of the Japanese naval attaché in Berlin, German sources began to dry up.[60]

Following the Allied landings in Normandy in 1944, as the outlook for Germany became progressively gloomier, the Germans seemed more inclined to cooperate with the Japanese code breakers, reportedly agreeing to give them access to the German signals intelligence organization. There is no evidence that Tokyo ever attempted to implement these plans. In an assessment dated 17 July 1944, Bletchley Park concluded that, while at the lower level there appeared to be a genuine desire to cooperate on signals intelligence methods and results, "the Japanese General Staff had not been convinced and was politely obstructive: the German General Staff while willing to collaborate had no positive desire of the kind that destroys barriers." In the field of scientific information, the British concluded that "the Japanese are clearly gaining far more than their ally from their mutual technical liaison."[61]

On occasion, the little cooperation that did exist tended to work against the German navy. The few German U-boats that made it to the Pacific in the latter months of the war operated from shared bases in Penang, Singapore, and Surabaya and were protected by Japanese Guard Forces while entering or leaving port. Guard Force messages giving detailed information on courses, speeds, and arrival and departure times were intercepted by Allied cryptographers in Colombo and FRUMEL and the information passed to MacArthur's antisubmarine forces. Thus alerted, Allied submarines were prepositioned along U-boat transit lanes and achieved significant success.[62]

The Japanese ambassador, the military attachés, the naval attaché, and the chief of the Japanese Inter-Service Mission in Europe constituted the main channels for passing German information to Tokyo. A British study on the value of information derived from intercepted diplomatic traffic commented that the Japanese ambassador reported just what the German Foreign Office wanted him to and that "where he comments he usually appears gullible." In a similar vein, the British noted that "the Japanese Military Attachés everywhere report almost any rumours and seem to believe almost anything although, very occasionally, they cannot help getting accurate information." The Japanese navy received better marks. The naval attaché, Berlin, and chief of the Inter-Service Mission "appear highly intelligent and critical of information given to them when they comment."[63]

Less than nine months after the Royal Navy had reentered the Pacific, and five months after Task Force 57 had taken part in its first major amphibious assault—the invasion of Okinawa—Japan surrendered. Shortly before the war's end, Admiral Nimitz ordered Admiral "Bull" Halsey, commander, Third Fleet, to destroy what remained of the Japanese navy through aerial attacks. In a deliberately political move, Halsey assigned only minor targets to the British aviators of Task Force 37 (as the British forces operating with Halsey were now designated) and reserved the major naval base at Kure and the port of Kobe for the Americans. " 'I hated to admit a political factor into a military equation,' Halsey recalled. 'My respect for Bert Rawlings [Admiral Sir Bernard Rawlings, at-sea commander of the British Pacific Fleet] and his fine men made me hate it doubly, but Mick [Rear Admiral Robert B. Carney, chief of staff to Admiral Halsey and a postwar chief of naval operations] forced me to recognize that statesmen's objectives sometimes differ widely from combat objectives, and that an exclusively American attack was therefore in American interests.' "[64] In the formal surrender on the deck of the USS *Missouri*, Admiral Sir Bruce Fraser, representing His Majesty's government, signed in third position following the representatives of the United States and China. Delegates from the Soviet Union, which had been in the war against Japan for less than thirty days, and those from the remaining British Commonwealth and Allied nations then signed, completing the ceremony.

After the surrender, the U.S. Navy's intelligence organization in the Pacific, built painstakingly during the wartime years, was dismantled with great haste. The first to go—even before hostilities ended—was FRUMEL. Field processing of intercepted Japanese communications had dwindled in the final stage of the Pacific war and was supplanted by increased production in Washington and Hawaii. By December 1944, most of the American members of the FRUMEL team had been moved to forward support areas and the station turned over to the Australians.[65]

SEFIC, which had followed MacArthur's advancing forces from Brisbane to Hollandia and finally to Manila, was dissolved shortly after the Japanese surrender.[66] The advance intelligence unit on Guam moved back to Hawaii in September 1945. Within three months of the war's end, JICPOA, which in its heyday employed over eighteen hundred persons, had closed its doors.[67] With the dismantling of the U.S. naval intelligence organization and the gradual fading away of the British Pacific Fleet, Anglo-American intelligence cooperation in the Pacific, driven once again by divergent political agendas, returned to its prewar level of ineffectiveness.

Anglo-American naval intelligence cooperation during the years 1943–1944 in the Pacific essentially did not exist. The breakdown of the intelligence structure that had proved successful in Europe and the Atlantic arose more from distance than from animosity—although some U.S. Navy suspicion of motives certainly carried over from prewar differences. The Royal Navy, too, had its concerns. As expressed in a postwar report "the British view was that attempts were being made to absorb British intelligence into the American organisation, & to use the information gained for purposes other than the prosecution of the war."[68] Infighting between U.S. Navy staffs in Washington and Pearl Harbor for preeminence in Pacific intelligence analysis and reporting did its share to hamper Anglo-American intelligence cooperation by delaying or restricting the distribution of intelligence to the Royal Navy. Admiral Ernest King's uncompromising opposition toward Royal Navy participation in the Pacific war restricted intelligence as well as other forms of Anglo-American naval cooperation.

After a bitter battle between Churchill and his military leaders, a British Pacific Fleet was created to fight alongside the U.S. Navy in the final assault on Japan. Its newly selected commander, Admiral Sir Bruce Fraser, left Ceylon for Hawaii on 4 December 1944, uncertain of the reception that his news of the Royal Navy's impending return to the Pacific would bring. The spigot of intelligence materials turned on by British success at the Pearl Harbor conferences provided for the British Pacific Fleet's immediate needs, but in a reprise of naval intelligence cooperation in 1939–1940, the flow was all one way—only this time from the U.S. to the Royal Navy. Whether closer coordination, undertaken sooner, would have affected either the start or the course of the war with Japan is moot. There was never a good opportunity to find out.

Part Four
Denouement of Wartime Alliances

II.
Twilight of Cooperation

The Allied decision to undertake a cross-channel invasion of Europe was made at Casablanca in January 1943. At Quebec in August, Churchill and Roosevelt accepted the recommendations of their Combined Chiefs of Staff and set D day for the invasion, now named Operation Overlord, as 1 May 1944. In December, General Eisenhower was chosen to lead the Allied forces in the campaign. The final phase of the war in Europe was about to begin.

Anglo-American naval intelligence faced its most severe test in preparing for the Allied invasion of Normandy. Detailed planning for the seaward aspects of the invasion was centered in the intelligence staff of the Allied Naval Commander Expeditionary Force, which, after a period of adjustment, created a smoothly running organization to tap American and British resources for the intelligence it required. Navy-to-navy intelligence sharing became largely a thing of the past, replaced by the corporate system of collection and analysis embodied in the combined staff system. As the end of the European war neared, America and Britain each shared a common suspicion that the other was moving to gain postwar advantage, and their wartime cooperation in intelligence as in other fields suffered as a result.

Throughout 1943, an Anglo-American staff in London had been hard at work planning the myriad details involved in an undertaking of the magnitude of a cross-channel invasion. To head the planning effort, a British army officer, Lieutenant General Sir Frederick E. Morgan, had been selected as COSSAC—chief of staff to the as yet unnamed supreme allied commander. Morgan, who had served under Eisenhower as early as October 1942, was well versed in combined operational planning. From his headquarters in England, Morgan had been in charge of planning contingency landings in connection with Torch in North Africa, had they been required. He was then directed to plan the invasion of Sardinia and, when that idea was shelved, the invasion of Sicily.[1]

Admiral Bertram Home Ramsay, RN, was selected to plan and command the naval side of Overlord (or Neptune, as the actual assault phase was code-named), with the army and air portions led by General Sir Bernard Montgomery and Air Chief Marshal Sir Trafford Leigh-Mallory. Ramsay had been involved in Allied preparations for the invasion of northwest Europe since May 1942, when the Admiralty had appointed him naval commander, Expeditionary Force, with duties that involved planning the naval side of the operation and direction of all naval forces involved.[2] In 1940, Ramsay had commanded Operation Dynamo, the evacuation of British and French soldiers from Dunkirk, and his success in this massive cross-channel operation plus his reputation for attention to detail in complicated planning made him an ideal choice to lead Neptune.

After planning and operational assignments in the Mediterranean, Ramsay returned to London in October 1943 to resume his former post, now titled Allied naval commander, Expeditionary Force, unpronounceably abbreviated ANCXF. In addition to his skills as a planner, Ramsay brought to the assignment a proven ability to work in harmony with Americans and, as his biographer indicated, "a capacity to learn from experience . . . a sense of humour; an uncompromising ability to know when to stick to a point and a wholly unflappable approach that commanded the respect of all of those who came within range of his powers." In the months to come before the invasion, both his sense of humor and his unflappability were to be sorely tried.[3]

The initial joint plan for Overlord-Neptune was issued in February 1944 and called for a two-pronged assault on beaches in the Normandy area. U.S. forces were assigned the western area, and British forces the eastern. Rear Admiral Alan G. Kirk, USN, was designated commander of the Western Task Force and charged with landing the First U.S. Army on "Utah" and "Omaha" beaches. Rear Admiral Sir Phillip Vian, RN, who in 1945 would lead the British carrier task force attached to Nimitz's Pacific Fleet into the final battle with the Japanese, was chosen Eastern Task Force commander.

Admiral Kirk, called by Samuel Eliot Morison "the key American Naval figure in Neptune-Overlord," arrived back in London in mid-October 1943 to participate in the planning that led to his new appointment.[4] Kirk's previous tours in England—first as U.S. naval attaché and subsequently as chief of staff to commander, U.S. Naval Forces Europe, Admiral Harold R. Stark—were excellent preparation for combined planning with the Anglo-American COSSAC staff. In addition, his exposure to naval intelligence matters in his

London assignments, as well as his service as director of naval intelligence in 1941, gave him an insight, rare among American flag officers of his time, into the value of intelligence to operations.

Intelligence planning for Overlord-Neptune was, as one might expect, done on a greater scale and in more detail than had ever before been attempted. Although it is nowhere specifically stated, there was a de facto division of intelligence responsibility, with Admiral Ramsay's staff (ANCXF) mainly concerned with intelligence required to put the Allied forces successfully ashore in Normandy and the supreme commander's staff concentrating on postlanding intelligence needs. This division of responsibility was reflected in the composition of both organizations. Although both staffs were organized in the joint/combined form mandated by Eisenhower, the ANCXF intelligence staff was more combined than joint, since most of its personnel were drawn from either the U.S. or the Royal Navy. The same was essentially true in the case of the Intelligence Division of the supreme commander's headquarters staff, where the Allied army and air personnel far outnumbered those of the navy.

Eisenhower's first choice to head his intelligence staff, and the person eventually given the task, was British Major General Kenneth W. D. Strong, who had been Eisenhower's G-2 at Allied Forces Headquarters in the Mediterranean. However, until May 1944, another British former staff officer of Eisenhower's, Major General John F. M. Whitely, was assigned as G-2.[5] The British War Office had refused Eisenhower's request for Strong on the grounds that the London staff assignments were draining too many experienced senior officers from the Mediterranean Theater. Strong, however, felt that the War Office refusal was at least in part based on its concern that Strong had become "too American" in outlook. After acrimonious discussions between General Walter Bedell Smith, Eisenhower's chief of staff, and General Alan Brooke, chief of the imperial general staff, failed to resolve the problem, Eisenhower successfully appealed to Churchill for Strong's services.[6]

Strong's Intelligence Division had two prime responsibilities: first, to collect and analyze all types of information on the enemy; and second, to deny the enemy information on Allied invasion planning. The division did not collect information directly, nor did it directly task the collectors. Rather, it worked through the already established intelligence organizations of its subordinate commanders, giving them general guidance on collection areas of interest, as well as providing "spot" requirements of special urgency or importance. In addition to information furnished by its subordinates, the Intelligence Division received reports and estimates from the American Office of Strategic Services, from resistance groups in occupied Europe, from the

Political Warfare Executive, and from the Army and Navy Departments in Washington and the British Joint Intelligence Committee in London.[7] The Intelligence Division provided its subordinate commands with intelligence summaries and intelligence annexes to staff reports. It also issued special top-secret digests, which gave, among other things, the Intelligence Division's prognosis of what courses of action the enemy might take.[8]

As early as October 1941, the British army had recognized the need for a specialized organization to concentrate on intelligence requirements that would arise from any plan to regain continental Europe. In response to this need, the army formed a section under General Headquarters, Home Forces, to study German defenses on the coast of France. In early 1942, representatives of the Admiralty's Naval Intelligence Division joined the organization, which was renamed the Combined Intelligence Section (CIS). Since the organization contained no Americans at the time, the word "Combined" in the title was a misnomer under the definitions adopted by the British and American chiefs of staff in February 1942; however, the title had been selected before the Anglo-American definitions were agreed upon.

After COSSAC became Supreme Headquarters, Allied Expeditionary Forces (SHAEF) in early 1944, the Combined Intelligence Section, which had added American personnel and had been renamed the Theater Intelligence Section (TIS), was taken over by the SHAEF Intelligence Division.[9] Since the TIS was essentially a collector and producer of operational intelligence on German defenses and troop dispositions along the French coast, its amalgamation violated at least in part SHAEF's intelligence charter not to become directly involved in collecting intelligence but to leave that task to the subordinate army, navy, and air commanders.

As more and more special agencies were added, the headquarters intelligence staff grew from 35 officers (20 British and 15 American) at the end of 1943 to over 160 by May 1944.[10] Included in this 160 was the TIS staff, which had grown to 50, at least 6 of whom were U.S. naval officers employed primarily in photo interpretation.[11] According to an Admiralty representative attached to TIS, relations between the Royal Navy members of the section and their U.S. Navy colleagues were excellent. "We never had one difficulty or dispute with . . . the U.S. Naval officers [at TIS or on Admiral Ramsay's staff, ANCXF]," perhaps, the writer commented, because of "very careful and considerable lobbying of the American intelligence officers over the luncheon table, or over drinks."[12]

All forms of intelligence cooperation in Overlord were highly structured within the combined staff organization. Overall intelligence policy was set by the supreme commander's staff, then passed down to the component army, navy, and air commanders for specific planning. It was the responsibility of SHAEF's Theater Intelligence Section to collect, analyze, and produce intelligence of interservice interest, such as coastal defenses. Officers skilled in naval intelligence were assigned at all staff levels to formulate requirements and to process and disseminate the intelligence required by both the American and British naval task forces. ONI in Washington was tasked to provide recognition material for ships and aircraft and summaries of naval intelligence from non-Anglo-American sources. The Admiralty's Naval Intelligence Division furnished information on enemy mining, ship dispositions, and landing beach charts and mosaics. Commander, U.S. Naval Forces Europe, provided special studies as requested on topics such as enemy capabilities in chemical warfare.[13]

Unlike the intelligence process used by the Combined Chiefs of Staff, the responses to Overlord requirements went directly from the providing agency to the requester, for example, from the Admiralty's Naval Intelligence Directorate to the Allied naval commander's intelligence planners, without the intervening step of being passed through some type of Joint Intelligence Committee for coordinated response. Except for the informal liaison that had grown up in London between the intelligence staffs of the Admiralty and that of the commander, U.S. Naval Forces Europe, there was no real navy-to-navy cooperation involved. Provision of intelligence had become corporate.

While COSSAC/SHAEF directives made it clear that operational intelligence was to be the concern of the individual subordinate commanders, what was not made clear was the relationship between SHAEF and its subordinate commanders and their parent service headquarters, such as the British naval staff in the case of the Allied naval commander. An Admiralty report made shortly after the successful invasion of France indicated that in the early planning stages, COSSAC had not made proper use of the Naval Intelligence Division's resources. "It is not an exaggeration to say," the report continued, "that the Admiralty had to force their attention on to S.H.A.E.F. to bring about the 100% co-operation required to ensure a successful outcome of such complicated planning."[14]

Gradually, all the strands of the British naval intelligence were gathered together in support of Overlord. In November 1943, the deputy director of naval intelligence began holding a series of informal weekly meetings to discuss Neptune-Overlord support. Attending, in addition to members of the Naval Intelligence Division's staff, were the head of the Naval Section in TIS, SHAEF; the staff officer (Intelligence) of the Allied naval commander, Expeditionary Force; a representative of 30th Assault Unit, the group charged with frontline intelligence collection; and the Royal Navy member of Intelligence Section (Operations), a suborganization of the British Joint Intelligence Committee that served as liaison and point of contact between the intelligence producers and the joint users.

In February 1944, Naval Intelligence Division support to invasion planning became more formalized with the formation of an Overlord committee, which was composed of essentially the same organizations as the informal group that had been meeting since the previous November but with higher-ranking participants. Also in February, the director of naval intelligence upgraded the level of his representation on Admiral Ramsay's Naval Expeditionary Force staff to captain to fill a newly established position of assistant chief of staff (Intelligence). With the formation of the Overlord committee and the assignment of one of their own to Admiral Ramsay's staff, "we in N.I.D. felt that at last we were properly welded on to A.N.C.X.F.'s set-up."[15]

From the naval point of view, the chief threat to the invasion came from German submarines, especially from those that had been fitted with the Snorkel—a breathing tube that allowed the submarine to use its diesel engines while submerged and thus reduce the risk of detection. According to Admiralty estimates, in an admittedly worst-case scenario, upward of 170 U-boats could be available for use in the channel by D day, and Allied planning was predicated on the threat of attack by at least 120. A combination of aggressive Allied patrolling, good intelligence, and German problems in the use of the new Snorkels and in underwater navigation made the actual U-boat threat much less than had been feared. Only thirty of the Snorkel-equipped boats actually sortied against the invasion forces.[16]

Timely provision of communications intelligence to the planners and later to the forces at sea in the invasion armada and ashore in France became a primary concern. "To prevent delays detrimental to the conduct of operations which would result from any attempt to canalise information through the Supreme HQ," the Combined Chiefs of Staff instructed London and Washington to send ULTRA information directly to the major headquarters in the field, as well as to the supreme Allied commander's staff.[17] The first message to reach Eisenhower's headquarters from Bletchley Park without going through one of the service ministries was dispatched on 26 January 1944.[18]

Sending ULTRA information directly to field commands was a relatively new concept, requiring new procedures that had first been developed by the British and later adopted, with one significant variation, by the United States. Special Liaison Units (SLUs) were attached to major American and British commands to receive ULTRA from Bletchley Park and provide it to those who were cleared to see it. In the British system, according to American historian Stephen Ambrose, "the SLUs were only glorified messengers who handed on the complete Ultra intercepts to their superiors."[19] In the case of the American SLUs, "their primary responsibility will be," Army Chief of Staff George C. Marshall wrote to Eisenhower, "to evaluate Ultra intelligence, present it in usable form to the Commanding officer, [and] assist in fusing Ultra with intelligence derived from other sources."[20] Professor F. H. Hinsley indicated that "the system operated without any serious hitch" in providing the necessary communications intelligence support both to the Overlord-Neptune planning staffs and to the forces in France once the invasion was under way.[21]

By the time of the invasion, the American naval staff in London, Admiral Stark's Commander U.S. Naval Forces Europe, was much less involved in cooperative ventures with the Admiralty—including intelligence cooperation—than it was in the immense task of providing logistic support to U.S. naval forces involved in Neptune-Overlord. The Office of Naval Intelligence in Washington also had little direct input into intelligence planning for Overlord, other than to help provide the trained personnel required to fill the various U.S. Navy billets in the intelligence staffs of Supreme Allied Headquarters and of its subordinate naval commander, as well as assignments to combined intelligence organizations—such as those providing topographical, aerial reconnaissance, and prisoner of war interrogation support to the Overlord planners.

Overall, the Allies won the intelligence battle that was a part of the successful invasion of Europe. Had German intelligence on what was taking place in Great Britain been anywhere near as good as Allied information on German activities in France, Overlord might have had a much different outcome.

As D day approached, the problem facing the Allied Naval Expeditionary Force commander's intelligence staff was not so much one of obtaining the necessary intelligence but rather one of dissemination. "The size of the [dissemination] task may be judged," the naval commander in chief wrote in his after-action report, "from the fact that 15,000 Annexes, each one a small book in itself, had to be distributed without the individual recipients being on one hand overburdened or on the other under-informed."[22] The assault forces received last-minute reconnaissance information on underwater obstacles guarding the beaches, enemy strengths and dispositions—especially positions of German naval units expected to oppose the seaward portion of the invasion—and enemy minefields. This type of data was provided on an increasingly frequent basis as D day approached and was updated by means of regular situation reports once the battle had been joined. Items of operational significance were immediately passed by radio to those requiring the information. In return, operational commanders who obtained useful intelligence during the course of the landings were to report it back to the Expeditionary Force commander in chief.[23]

Provision of intelligence prior to D day received good marks both from the naval commander in chief and from his principal subordinate commanders. "On the whole the intelligence provided was accurate, and several references in reports from Force Commanders testify to this fact . . . in general all the defences were accurately foretold, and there were no major surprises."[24]

How well intelligence was able to support the invasion, once it was under way, is illustrated by the bombing of the German naval installations at Le Havre that resulted in the crippling of the German E-boat fleet.[25] In the weeks leading up to the Allied landings, these high-speed torpedo boats had been deadly in their attacks on Allied ships training for Overlord, and since the invasion, they had proved to be the most effective weapon in the German naval arsenal against Allied forces at sea.

Before the time of Neptune, Allied cryptographers had been regularly reading the code, nicknamed "Dolphin," used by the E-boat skippers and their headquarters to communicate with each other. Messages derived from Dolphin were passed from Bletchley Park to the Operational Intelligence Centre in London, where they were combined with other pertinent information and provided to Admiral Ramsay's escort force commanders who were responsible for defending the Allied convoys crossing the Channel. Although Dolphin was seldom broken in time to affect daily operations in the sense of allowing defenders to know in advance where the hit-and-run attacks would occur, it was most helpful in establishing the numbers and locations of the E-boat flotillas.

Although the ports from which the E-boats operated were known through communications intelligence well in advance of D day, action to neutralize them—the subject of heated debate by naval planners—was not taken. To do so would have incurred the double risk of having the Germans suspect that their codes had been broken and—since the main E-boat base was Cherbourg—might also tip the Germans off to the planned invasion landing areas, thus nullifying the carefully orchestrated deception plans for Overlord. Action had to be delayed until after the first landings and until the E-boats were concentrated in one port.

The necessary elements came together on the evening of 14 June 1944. Because of changes in their deployment patterns and bad weather, the bulk of the E-boat fleet was known through signals intelligence to be concentrated in Le Havre. Admiral Ramsay had personally requested that Bomber Command mount this special attack, which would utilize newly developed "Tall-boy" bombs, each weighing twelve thousand pounds, as well as conventional ordnance. Joined with the work of the code breakers was information gained from photographic reconnaissance missions flown on the morning of the fourteenth that pinpointed the moorings of the E-boats. Intelligence reports from French resistance groups, prisoner of war interrogations, and previous photographic missions had established details of the port and the heavily reinforced concrete pens that sheltered the E-boats and their companions the T-boats, the larger and slower torpedo boats.

The bombing attacks, unusual daylight raids designed to catch the boats at dusk just before their departure on patrol, were remarkably accurate and destructive—as was confirmed by intercepted German naval communications reporting the havoc and by poststrike photographic intelligence. In his diary entry for 15 June, Ramsay wrote that "the Bomber Command strike on Havre was highly successful & achieved magnificent results."[26] Much of the success can be attributed to timely collection and interpretation of a variety of intelligence sources and dispatch in getting the required information to the operational commands.

Almost immediately after D day, intelligence began to flow back from the assault areas. The 30th Commando, the highly trained intelligence collection unit described in chapter 5, went into action with the first British forces that landed at H hour on D day. Their targets were German coastal radar locations and missile-launching sites, which intelligence had determined the previous December were targeted against Bristol,[27] and eventually German naval headquarters in Cherbourg. In the course of these operations, "large amounts of documents and equipment of very high grade intelligence value" were seized and returned to the United Kingdom for exploitation.[28]

Once the beachhead had been secured and forces began to move inland, responsibility for naval intelligence processing in U.S.-controlled occupied areas on what was then called "The Far Shore" shifted from the Naval Expeditionary Force commander to Commander U.S. Naval Forces Europe. COMNAVEU's Special Intelligence Units provided intelligence and photographic personnel for reconnaissance parties to accompany the U.S. Army in securing port areas and also furnished translators and prisoner of war interrogators specialized in naval matters. These reconnaissance parties would disseminate time-sensitive information to U.S. Army commands in the immediate area, then return the bulk of the material to London for further processing by appropriate intelligence agencies, both British and American, with the results being fed back into the system to the SHAEF staff and to its field commanders. Cooperation between the COMNAVEU mobile intelligence units and the British 30th Commando was close and resulted in exchanges of liaison officers and in joint operations, such as one involving the search for and exploitation of a major German torpedo arsenal located underground near Versailles, just after the liberation of Paris.[29] As was indicated earlier, intelligence derived from intercept of enemy communications was provided to the operational commanders by Special Liaison Units attached to each major headquarters for that specific purpose.

While victorious Allied forces were in the process of mopping up the Germans on the Contentin Peninsula and securing the vital port of Cherbourg, planners in the Mediterranean were preparing for the invasion of southern France. Operation Anvil, as it was then called, had been tentatively adopted at the Quebec conference in mid-1943 as a diversionary attack in the south to support Overlord in the northwest. Since that time, differences in strategic thinking had surfaced between the American joint chiefs, who wished to continue the operation in support of Eisenhower, and the British chiefs of staff, strongly backed by Churchill, who wished to concentrate available forces for an all-out push to bring the Italian campaign to a successful conclusion and then continue the drive northeast into the Danube valley. Even though it could not be timed to coincide with Overlord, Anvil was still vital to Eisenhower's strategy, because its success would give him a second French port, Marseille, to reduce the pressure on Cherbourg, where supplies were becoming backlogged. Once again, differences in military strategy were manifestations of underlying differences in political postwar agendas and gave warning of the weakening of cooperative ties that would follow victory.[30]

Churchill continued intense pressure on Eisenhower to change his mind on Anvil—now renamed "Dragoon" by Churchill, "perhaps because he felt the new title expressed his resentment over the pressure to which he had been subjected to make him accept an undertaking in which he did not believe."[31] The final decision to proceed was not made until 8 August, one week before the planned invasion date; however, preparations had continued even as the strategists wrangled.

The overall outline of Dragoon had been completed by Christmas 1943, and detailed planning had commenced early in the new year. Unlike Overlord, Dragoon was to be primarily a U.S. operation, with additional participation by the Royal Navy and French forces. Admiral H. Kent Hewitt, commander in chief of the U.S. Eighth Fleet, was in charge of the naval portion of the assault. With a wide variety of beaches along the French Mediterranean coast to choose among, landing site selection became a major problem. Samuel Eliot Morison commented that "Captain Leo A. Bachman,

Admiral Hewitt's Intelligence officer, probably came to know more about the beaches of Provence than anyone in the long and varied history of that region."[32] In the end, areas to the east of Toulon, near Frejus and St. Tropez, were selected because German defenses were thought to be lighter there than around the ports of Toulon and Marseille.

Following the pattern set by Overlord, overall intelligence planning for Anvil-Dragoon was carried out by the combined Anglo-American intelligence staff of General Sir Harry M. Wilson, who had replaced Eisenhower as supreme Allied commander, Mediterranean. Specific intelligence planning was delegated to Admiral Hewitt's staff, which performed its tasks in coordination with the intelligence staffs of the U.S. Army force commanders whose troops would make the landings. Again, the Anglo-American naval intelligence cooperation that did take place was more of the corporate variety than navy-to-navy.

Admiral Hewitt's report of intelligence activities following the landings indicated that U.S. Navy intelligence officers, who had been briefed in detail about the types and possible locations of desired enemy material, made valuable finds. German minefield charts and cryptographic material were recovered, the report stated; "the greatest aid to the operating forces, however, occurred upon capture of Toulon and Marseille when intelligence officers located German harbor-blocking, demolition, and mining plans which greatly facilitated the task of harbor clearance."[33] Captured documents were sent to a joint Royal Navy–U.S. Navy document exploitation center in the Mediterranean theater, and the results were provided both to the Admiralty and to the U.S. Navy Department, as well as to local commanders. Prisoner of war exploitation was also handled cooperatively by teams that included specially trained U.S. Navy officers from the Combined Services Detailed Interrogation Centre's branch in Rome. Captured enemy equipment was sent for joint U.S. and British examination in theater, then forwarded for further analysis "in accordance with agreed policies of the Admiralty and the [U.S.] Navy Department."[34] Cooperation was still taking place, but no new ground was being broken.

Overlord's and Dragoon's success in northwestern and southern France closed a chapter in the U.S. and Royal Navies' battle to defeat Hitler in Europe, but the book was still open. On the basis of estimated building rates of the new types of U-boats and information from intercepted communications that German submarines were planning joint operations with long-range aircraft, the British Operational Intelligence Centre predicted that an "all out U-boat campaign" would take place in the latter weeks of 1944. For that reason, the Admiralty urged the Canadian navy to keep its escorts in readiness to protect Atlantic shipping lanes and advised that "no commitment can be undertaken elsewhere which will impede the fulfillment of this task." Well into 1945, the Canadian submarine tracking room in Naval Headquarters Ottawa remained unwilling to release its watch officers to other duties for fear of a recurrence of U-boat warfare. That the expected battles did not take place at all or were less severe than anticipated was due in no small measure to a reordering of U.S. Army Air Corps and Bomber Command's target lists to strike more harbors in which new construction submarines were fitting out, thus delaying their completion until the war's end. Also, by this stage of the war, the American, British, and Canadian submarine tracking rooms were so seamlessly coordinated in their sharing of information that their intelligence, derived from ULTRA as well as more conventional sources, would usually reach the antisubmarine operational forces within a matter of hours of intercept, thereby greatly increasing its value to the hunters.[35]

Despite the continuing U-boat threat in the Atlantic and Mediterranean, the Allies began a major repositioning of their naval forces, as the British Eastern Fleet and the U.S. Pacific Fleet were beefed up with men and ships less urgently required in Europe. Anglo-American naval cooperation in the war's closing months was marked by an agreement between the two navies to carve out separate spheres of control rather than to act in concert. On 14 November 1944, Admiral Ramsay, who had remained as Eisenhower's principal naval commander, and Admiral Stark, commander of U.S. naval forces in Europe, agreed, "after protracted staff discussions," on a posthostilities plan that called for the Royal Navy to withdraw from all French ports and turn their administration over to U.S. and French authorities. The British would have sole responsibility for those ports lying to the northeast of the French border, except for a small American presence at Bremen and Bremerhaven. As a result of these negotiations, the U.S. Navy assigned two flag officers to Germany. Admiral Ghormley came full circle, returning to Europe to relieve Admiral Kirk as the senior U.S. naval officer on Eisenhower's staff and subsequently as commander, U.S. Naval Forces Germany. Admiral Robert E. Schuirmann, former director of naval intelligence, became commander, U.S. Naval Forces Bremen, where, probably without British knowledge, he had been given an additional task by Admiral King to collect all the information he could on German advances in rocketry, communications, and naval engineering.[36]

The physical separation embodied in the 14 November agreement was symptomatic of a more general divergence in outlook and postwar goals that had been apparent since early 1943 at Casablanca and had since grown, coloring high-level strategy for both Overlord and Dragoon. By early 1944, this divergence had begun to show itself in Anglo-American naval intelligence relationships. On 12 January, Admiral Percy Noble, head of the British Admiralty Delegation in Washington, complained to the first sea lord that he sensed a "tightening up on the part of Americans to our requests" and stated, "there is no doubt that the Americans have stiffened up in their attitudes towards us"—a change, Noble felt, that was at least in part because "the Americans think that the war in Europe may end fairly soon," and because they did not want too strong a Royal Navy when that happened.[37] In the weeks to follow, Noble sent the first sea lord other letters enlarging on his perception of the change in American attitude and speculating on the reasons for it. A 5 February minute from the Admiralty's director of plans to the first sea lord echoed Noble's concerns.[38] Another straw in the wind of lessened cooperation could be seen in a January request from Commodore E. N. Rushbrooke, the British director of naval intelligence, to Admiral Harold Stark at U.S. naval headquarters in London, for his assistance in getting the Navy Department in Washington to send the Admiralty copies of technical documents, particularly those dealing with communications, captured from the Japanese. Stark's reply was supportive, but noncommittal.[39] One would not have expected a matter apparently so routine to receive such high-level attention if the cooperative machinery had been operating smoothly.

Far from wishing to deny their technological advances to the U.S. Navy as they did in 1940–1941, by 1944, scientists with the Royal Navy were actively considering ways to keep technology flowing in an easterly direction. In April, the Admiralty's director of scientific research prepared a paper designed to get key staff members—including the director of naval intelligence—thinking about postwar research and development cooperation. He commented that he did "not consider it any too soon to make a move towards deciding what post-war arrangements we want to work for" and noted that there was "no reason to expect initiative being taken on the U.S. side." Throughout the summer, the Admiralty continued its cautious probing of U.S. naval representatives in London and Washington to determine American receptiveness to continued postwar exchange of technical information.[40]

Elsewhere in the Anglo-American intelligence community, the winds of change were beginning to blow. In his history of the Research and Analysis (R&A) Branch of Donovan's Office Of Strategic Services, Barry Katz pointed out that "at the broadest level, the priorities of R&A London, like those of the Office of Strategic Services generally, began at about that time [March 1944] to experience 'a shift in major emphasis, so far as Europe is concerned, from studies for military plans to those of post-hostilities, primarily military government and civil affairs.'"[41] Historian Felix Gilbert, at the time head of the German Section of R&A London, commented that there was a perception of differences in approach between the United States and Great Britain with regard to postwar civil government in Germany. Gilbert did not find Britain's position on this issue to be "wholly innocent" of desire for postwar political advantage and noted that "the English have a very clear realization of the changes in the power constellation which the war has brought about."[42]

By the spring of 1945, the U.S. Joint Intelligence Committee had become reluctant to share its working papers, especially those dealing with postwar U.S. plans for the Pacific. In recommending refusal of a British request for "all U.S. J.I.C. papers referring to the war against Japan," the U.S. JIC commented that "such a policy would not be at variance with British practice. Although the British J.I.C. has been generous in sending us copies of its papers, we do not receive them all." An appendix to the JIC paper contained a list of JIC studies on the Pacific since October 1944, which indicated that less than 20 percent had been furnished to the British.[43]

In the final months of the European conflict, it became apparent that the U.S. government was making a sharp differentiation between information needed to win the war and that relating to the postwar world. The British naval attaché in Washington noted the "general tightening up in the supply of information from the Navy Department," giving as an example a recent memo from the Joint Aircraft Committee that stated in part, "It is contrary to the policy of the U.S. Government to authorize the disclosure to British of U.S. technical information classified 'Confidential' or higher, which may not fairly be considered useable in the prosecution of the war against Japan." Since his British colleagues had received similar indications from other parts of the American government, the attaché felt that the "closing down on the supply of information from the U.S." was not confined to the Navy Department and probably stemmed from the Department of State.[44]

Perhaps the attaché was aiming too low in blaming the Department of State, since the change in attitude toward cooperation originated at a higher level. In August, the prime minister expressed his concern over the decrease in the cooperative flow in a telegram to the president that elicited the disappointingly noncommittal response that the matter had been referred to proper authorities. Lend-lease, which had been the keystone in the Anglo-American "special relationship," ended as far as the Royal Navy was concerned in a circular instruction from the U.S. Navy Department dated 9 August 1945 that made it clear that "it is the policy of the Navy Department to terminate immediately all lend-lease financed from Navy appropriations

... to all foreign governments, including all material, services or information, whether for emergency, operational or any other purposes." The Admiralty minute sheet that circulated the American directive in the naval staff ended with the comment that "it can only be concluded that the American attitude is that there is no longer any legal sanction for supplying 'defense' information to the United Nations." By this time, the situation with regard to scientific intelligence exchange had deteriorated to the point that Air Chief Marshall Sir John Slessor felt it necessary to write to his superiors that, should continued cooperation in scientific development and intelligence prove impracticable, British intelligence organs should be charged with ferreting out U.S. secrets. "The Americans are an insecure people and I do not believe we should have any serious difficulty in finding out all they are doing if we were prepared to spend the money to do so."[45]

On 6 June 1945, one month after Germany's surrender and one year after the successful Allied landings in France, Admiral Stark announced that not one U.S. Navy ship remained in British waters. On 13 July, General Eisenhower formally disbanded the SHAEF staff.[46] The war in Europe was over. There was very little intelligence structure to dismantle. The war's most successful cooperative effort in naval intelligence, that of the U.S., British, and Canadian submarine tracking rooms, had ended on 21 June 1945 with the disbanding of the current intelligence section of the Commander in Chief, U.S. Fleet, staff. One week earlier, Admiral King's antisubmarine command, the Tenth Fleet, had been similarly disestablished. Royal Navy presence in Washington diminished rapidly, leaving only a small British naval staff to carry on intelligence and other liaison duties with the U.S. Navy Department. In London, under a variety of postwar names, Commander U.S. Naval Forces Europe remained active, carrying out liaison with the Admiralty and its Naval Intelligence Division, but on a much reduced scale. The corporate intelligence structure, formed with SHAEF headquarters at its apex, wound up its affairs and disappeared, as did the Anglo-American intelligence committees that had been created to support the Combined Chiefs of Staff. U.S.-U.K. coordination of communications intelligence matters in the postwar world may have fared somewhat better than did other forms of intelligence cooperation, but records of these activities are still shrouded in secrecy in the archives of both nations. Recent study indicates that even in the field of communications intelligence, the road to cooperation was not smooth. Probably the need to join forces in attacking communist cryptographic systems was the mortar that held cryptographic cooperation in place, while other cooperative efforts, such as Anglo-American atomic research, came to a rapid halt.[47]

As navy-to-navy intelligence cooperation reached its highest point during the Battle of the Atlantic in 1943, corporate naval intelligence cooperation had its finest moments in the successful Allied invasions of Normandy and of southern France in 1944. Anglo-American naval forces and their supporting intelligence organizations played an increasingly less significant role as the final battles against Germany moved inland. Provision of naval intelligence to Allied forces on the European continent and in the Atlantic and Mediterranean continued to function smoothly, but without new initiatives. As Allied planners' thoughts turned toward Japan and the Pacific, leaders in the Royal Navy found an increasing resistance on the part of the U.S. Navy to share strategic intelligence on Japan—especially intelligence that might bear on the future U.S. role in the Far East. Led by Admiral King, whose aversion to mixed forces had not diminished over the years, opposition to the combined staff system ensured its early posthostilities demise, and with it, much of combined intelligence.

Anglo-American cooperation in naval intelligence did not, however, completely disappear at the war's end. After sharp retrenchment, intelligence cooperation rose again, phoenix-like, from the ashes of the immediate postwar period in response to the nascent threat to both nations from the spread of communism. Without the clear and present danger posed by the Soviet Union, it is doubtful that Anglo-American intelligence cooperation could have survived the political and economic strains of a multipolar, postwar world or faced such divisive issues as the creation of the state of Israel and the collapse of colonialism. But cold war cooperation between the intelligence organizations of the U.S. and the Royal Navies would never match in openness or effectiveness the level of mutual support reached during 1942 and 1943 in the winner-take-all battle against the German U-boats in the Atlantic. In the years that followed the Second World War, permanent interests would once again determine the relationship between permanent friends.

12.

In Retrospect

If the course of Anglo-American cooperation in naval intelligence during the period 1939–1945 were displayed in graphic form, one would see a line rising sharply from its inception until late 1942, leveling off in a high plateau from late 1942 until the end of 1943, then gradually declining as the war's end neared. This pattern was unique to Europe (the whole Europe-Atlantic-Mediterranean area). In the Pacific, the line would rise slowly from 1939 until December 1941; show a brief, sharp rise; then, after March 1942, decline and remain flat until the spring of 1945, when the line would again show a dramatic but brief upward turn until the Japanese surrender. The high points on the Pacific graph would be well below those on the European, nor would the Pacific graph show an extended period of fruitful cooperation in 1942–1943, as seen in the European picture.

Although the overall patterns of European and Pacific cooperation were dissimilar, in both cases, the rising line from 1939 into 1942 resulted from the same underlying circumstance—British initiative. With only brief and minor exceptions, the impetus for cooperation in naval intelligence came from the British not the American side. The Admiralty took the lead in relaxing pre-war regulations against information sharing, abandoning its traditional quid pro quo intelligence exchange policy, and stifling its well-founded concerns about the U.S. Navy's ability to keep a secret. In addition, the latent Anglo-phobia of some U.S. Navy leaders had to be overcome, or at least accepted in encouraging cooperation.

The more politically sensitized divisions of the British naval staff, Plans and Intelligence, were in the vanguard of those urging greater cooperation. The Operations and Technical divisions, unable to see any immediate professional advantage to be gained from increased cooperation, were more reluctant. Winston Churchill, both during his tenure as first lord of the

Admiralty and later as prime minister, gave the Admiralty the push required to move it in the direction of Anglo-American naval cooperation. It was he who saw more clearly than others how vital it was to British interests to involve the United States, in whatever ways possible, in the battle to save Europe from Hitler. Considering the American political climate of isolationism in 1939–1940, Britain could not hope for open support of the United States. Therefore, what could more effectively bind America to the British cause than secret agreements to exchange secret information?

Other British leaders, such as Admiral John Godfrey, the director of naval intelligence, had equally pragmatic reasons for encouraging a one-way intelligence sharing, not only of information but also of techniques, with the U.S. Navy. The more the Royal Navy could induce its potential colleagues to adopt British methods, the easier and quicker the transition when the inevitable wartime coalition took place. Long before America's entry into the war, the British government was willing to make room in its schools to train American naval aviators in photographic interpretation and to make badly needed prisoner of war interrogators available to teach their skills to the U.S. Navy. It was, as Secretary of the Navy Frank Knox put it, a matter of "enlightened self-interest" to have Allies-to-be in the U.S. Navy trained as early and as properly as possible. It was a matter of increasing concern to the Royal Navy that during the latter stages of the war the pupil became both more adept and more unruly.

U.S. intelligence relationships with the widely separated British Dominions do not lend themselves readily to graphic portrayal. Canada faced a twofold challenge: first, to get the United States and Great Britain to accept Canada as a full partner in the naval intelligence war, and second, to convince the United States to deal with Canada as a sovereign entity and not as a subset of the British Empire. As the war progressed, it became increasingly apparent that if Canada wished to have a significant role in the postwar intelligence arena, it would have to become more closely allied to the United States, while retaining its historic ties to England.

In the Southwest Pacific, too, the exclusive bonds to Great Britain were slipping, caused in great part by the sense of abandonment felt in 1941–1942 when England was unable to provide heretofore unquestioned protection for its outposts. As the U.S. Navy prepared to fill the void left by the Royal Navy's departure from the Pacific in 1942 and to assume the role of defender of Australia and New Zealand, intelligence relationships with Hawaii and Washington dominated if not supplanted those that had existed with Singapore and London. From early 1942 until the war's end, Anglo-American intelligence cooperation in the Pacific was essentially a one-way street, with information provided reluctantly by the U.S. Navy and repeatedly sought by the British either directly from the Americans or—failing that—through surrogates in those Australian and New Zealand naval intelligence organizations that had grown up during the war in the shadow of American intelligence. It can be argued that, despite the lack of a physical Royal Navy presence in Pacific waters, closer intelligence cooperation between the British Eastern and American Pacific Fleets could have produced an atmosphere in which meaningful combined naval operations might have taken place— the lending of a British carrier during the Battle of Midway being but one example.

Almost every British writer of naval history, when dealing with the havoc created by German submarines along the East Coast of the United States in the early months of 1942, has bemoaned the U.S. Navy's failure to learn from two years of British wartime experience in countering U-boats. What many of these authors failed to realize was that the American concept of decentralized operational command did not readily lend itself to adoption of British methods, which were designed for the Admiralty's more centralized command structure. In the case of intelligence, there was no way of organizing a U.S. Navy counterpart of the Admiralty's Operational Intelligence Centre until an American navy operational staff existed for a center to support. Such an operational staff did not come into being until Admiral Ernest King formed the Commander in Chief, U.S. Fleet (COMINCH), staff after the U.S. entry into the war, then took direct command of operating forces by creating the Tenth Fleet. Nevertheless, from 1939 to the latter part of 1942, to many on both sides of the Atlantic, Anglo-American cooperation meant adoption of British ways—which caused cooperation to be either encouraged or resisted, according to one's point of view.

In the Pacific, the prewar cooperative graph sloped upward at a less sharp angle than in Europe, suggesting that Pacific cooperation was of less importance and harder to develop. The pressures for and against cooperation were essentially the same but differed in degree. In Europe, the British were fully occupied with the problem of survival and tended to see differences with Japan as somewhat less critical. Therefore, the cooperative impetus was less strong. Conversely, many Americans viewed British calls for Far Eastern military cooperation as masking imperial ends, such as use of the U.S. Navy as a British surrogate to protect Singapore, and, for that reason, were resisted all the more firmly.

The golden age of Anglo-American cooperation in naval intelligence was mainly confined to a single threat, in a single theater, and for a single—relatively short—period of the war. While German U-boats remained a matter of concern from 1939 until 1945, the problem was critical in the Atlantic from the beginning of 1942 until mid-1943. Britain's survival could not be assured, nor could the war be taken to Germany, until the Atlantic sea lanes were relatively secure. Anglo-American navy-to-navy intelligence cooperation was at its closest and most successful in the Battle of the Atlantic against the German U-boat threat. Key was the relationship among the three submarine tracking rooms located in London, Washington, and Ottawa. Although widely separated, and without physically exchanging personnel, the three centers thought and acted as one. That they were so successful resulted in great part from their very facelessness. Staffed by relatively junior officers, hidden away from the limelight in the interiors of their respective naval headquarters, the tracking rooms were able to exchange views openly and informally and perform their analysis without constraints of national pride or the pressures of naval policy. Their combined effort—incorporating, when available, the priceless information derived from intercepted German communications—provided the operational commanders with a weapon of inestimable value, both defensively, to move Allied convoys out of harm's way, and offensively, to position Allied antisubmarine forces to best hunt and kill enemy U-boats. If there is one aspect of the Second World War in which the value of cooperative intelligence to victory cannot be questioned, it is in the Battle of the Atlantic.

Yet while Anglo-American naval intelligence was enjoying its greatest success in the Atlantic, there was no comparable cooperation in the Pacific. With the departure of the Royal Navy from Far Eastern waters in the spring of 1942, combined operations against a common enemy became impossible, and the intelligence structure to support Anglo-American naval cooperation in the Pacific died aborning. The naval intelligence cooperation that did take place in the Pacific did so on purely American terms, making full use of Australian and New Zealand intelligence capabilities and leaving the Royal Navy on the margin. Unable to build a convincing case for its need of operational intelligence on the Japanese and with little to offer in return, the Royal Navy was placed in an untenable position in seeking cooperation. American intelligence, in whatever measure provided, was impeded in reaching the British by inter- and intraservice struggles for intelligence primacy in the Pacific. What little information the British could furnish was, in its turn, impeded in reaching American naval forces in the South and Southwest Pacific by filtration through Washington or through British Commonwealth intelligence organizations in Australia and New Zealand.

Even in Europe, close Anglo-American intelligence cooperation was relatively short-lived. The diminished cooperation in navy-to-navy intelligence that was becoming increasingly evident by the spring of 1944 was an outgrowth of organizational and political shifts that had started much earlier.

The Casablanca conference marked a turning point in Anglo-American perceptions of the Second World War. Fears for survival began to give way to confidence in an eventual Allied victory. Concern over postwar political and economic relationships grew apace with confidence in Germany's defeat. The gradual shift in national attention from winning the war to positioning for peace, which was becoming increasingly evident at the highest levels in the Allied strategic direction of the war, was mirrored in Anglo-American naval intelligence relationships. British interest in expanding Anglo-American naval intelligence cooperation was supplanted by fear that increased cooperation would entail unacceptable risk to vital political and economic policies. Constraints on the types and quantities of information exchanged began to appear on both sides of the Atlantic, as information was scrutinized for postwar advantage as well as wartime utility.

At the same time that cracks began to appear in the wall of Anglo-American cooperation, the way in which naval intelligence was exchanged began to change dramatically, at least in Europe. Navy-to-navy intelligence relationships gave way to intelligence by committee—to what might be called the incorporation of intelligence. In many cases—but certainly with the significant exception of the U-boat war—the direct link between the producer of naval intelligence and the operator who used it began to disappear. In the case of American naval intelligence, this change was first seen in early 1942 when naval intelligence, instead of passing directly from the Navy Department to the chief of naval operations/commander in chief, U.S. Fleet, took the longer and less direct path from producer, through a Joint U.S. Army-Navy Intelligence Committee, then through a Combined U.S.-U.K. Intelligence Committee en route to its eventual user, the Combined Chiefs of Staff. The identity of the intelligence was lost in the multilayered staffing, hence its "incorporation." In the case of operational planning, such as that for Torch in North Africa or Overlord in Europe, the path was shorter—from producer to Allied Headquarters' Intelligence Section—but again the navy-to-navy partnership had been superseded by the corporate planning structure. In rationalizing intelligence support, many of the positive aspects of navy-to-navy cooperation disappeared, and this disappearance, coupled with growing concern over postwar influence, caused the cooperative graph to show a downward slope in the final year of the war in Europe.

Two aspects of intelligence provision in the Pacific during the latter part of the war set it apart from the European pattern. First and most obvious was that intelligence was not combined, in the sense that British input was almost nonexistent. Second, at least in the case of the South and Central Pacific areas, the war was not really a joint operation but an all-navy show, and the link between the producers of naval intelligence and the users remained unbroken. The process of intelligence incorporation never really enjoyed a climate in which to develop. The power struggles for intelligence primacy between Washington and Hawaii hurt Anglo-American naval intelligence cooperation by slowing and perhaps reducing the flow of Pacific intelligence to the British, but it was a comparatively minor problem. When the Royal Navy returned to the Pacific in the spring of 1945, American intelligence support to British forces increased dramatically, from both Washington and Hawaii. But while cooperation was great in quantity, it was limited in scope to that required for immediate operations and, since the flow of information was essentially one way, could not be termed a mutual sharing.

Events and politics influenced naval intelligence cooperation, but so did individuals—both positively and negatively. Whatever his motivations, the strongest impetus for greater Anglo-American cooperation in naval intelligence came from the British director of naval intelligence, Admiral John Godfrey. During his tenure as DNI, from early 1939 until late 1942, Godfrey constantly strove to expand Anglo-American naval intelligence relationships, both by using the influence of his position on the naval staff to encourage increased cooperation and by sending his best and brightest from the Naval Intelligence Division to America to preach the gospel of cooperation based on the Royal Navy's experience. The record does not show any significant initiative toward the improvement of naval intelligence cooperation between London and Washington to have been undertaken after November 1942, the date of Godfrey's untimely departure from the Admiralty.

Godfrey had no peer in American naval intelligence. The rapid turnover of directors in the Navy Department and the low esteem in which the director's position was held almost guaranteed that the incumbent would have little influence in U.S. Navy councils. The American naval officer with the most influence, albeit indirectly, on Anglo-American naval intelligence cooperation was the chief of naval operations/commander in chief, U.S. Fleet, Admiral Ernest King. King's often-stated aversion to mixed forces and to foreign liaison officers, while not specifically directed against naval intelligence cooperation, had the effect of limiting it. On a more positive note, President Roosevelt's and Prime Minister Churchill's favorable inclination toward the navy, toward intelligence, and toward cooperation in general created a climate that was particularly helpful in the pre–Pearl Harbor period when the structure of intelligence cooperation was first being crafted. Undoubtedly, the president's prompt and unqualified acceptance of the prime minister's offer of a British fleet for the war against Japan smoothed the way for the Royal Navy's return to the Pacific in 1945 and reassured the

Admiralty that its forces would receive the intelligence support they needed from the U.S. Navy.

Intramural feuding between Hawaii and Washington was detrimental to Anglo-American naval intelligence cooperation in the Pacific, in that it decreased both the quantity of information provided and the timeliness with which it was delivered. Even more detrimental in a larger sense was the inability of the intelligence organizations of the War and Navy Departments to work together, or at the very least to present a united front to the British. These intramural rivalries in Washington were replicated in the Pacific in the bifurcated command structure that pitted Admiral Nimitz against General MacArthur. During his May 1941 trip to Washington, Godfrey was concerned that U.S. Army-Navy intelligence rivalries would block any American move toward a single intelligence service (which they did) and, more important, would preclude formation of an American Joint Intelligence Committee (which they did not) to work in concert with the British Joint Intelligence Committee that had already proved its worth in the previous two years.

Unlike the situation at the end of the First World War, when wartime Allied intelligence organizations virtually disappeared, following World War II, Anglo-American naval intelligence—expanded to include the contributions of Canada, Australia, and New Zealand—survived immediate postwar dichotomous goals to unite once again against the common enemy of worldwide communism. By an agreement drawn up by the American and British directors of naval intelligence shortly after the war's end, American naval intelligence officers stationed in London were "seconded" (released from their primary duties at U.S. Naval Headquarters) to the Naval Intelligence Division in the Admiralty to fill three billets that were fully integrated into the British organization and otherwise would have been filled by Royal Navy officers. These assignments were designed to provide a trained cadre of active-duty naval officers should a rapid expansion of Anglo-American naval intelligence be required in the event that the cold war heated up. Apparently, the program was not reciprocal, and no British officers are known to have been stationed in Washington under this agreement. The Americans' duties in the Admiralty involved study of the Soviet submarine force, and the Anglo-American partnership in Soviet naval analysis grew into an annual Canadian–United Kingdom–United States (CANUKUS) conference to exchange views on Soviet naval developments that continued at least into the 1980s. Later in the cold war ANZUKUS (Australia, New Zealand, United Kingdom, United States) intelligence conferences were held periodically to assess the Sino-Soviet naval threat. Despite the binding ties engendered by a common enemy—the Soviet Union—when postwar political agendas diverged, intelligence cooperation suffered, as was the case during the Suez crisis of 1956.

When all is said and done, what effect, if any, did Anglo-American cooperation in naval intelligence have on the outcome of the war? Was intelligence the key to winning the war? Obviously not. Commanders, armies, navies, and, increasingly, economic factors win wars. Good intelligence can be rejected, and erroneous information accepted. However, lack of good intelligence can place a nation in an inferior position, as the Allies found out in the Atlantic during communication "blackouts" when German naval traffic was unreadable. In the end, it is the commander's decision that counts. Without the high quality of Allied intelligence, the war might well have dragged on for another two years. Without Anglo-American naval intelligence cooperation, the period of delay in winning the war would in all probability have been even longer.

The question then becomes, was the cooperative effort of greater value than the sum of its parts? Nowhere is the worth of this synergism better demonstrated than in the use of communications intelligence during the Battle of the Atlantic. The Americans' sometimes reckless zeal to produce the most helpful product was tempered by well-founded British concern about protecting the source of the information. As Kenneth Knowles put it, "Perhaps it is fair to say that the British were more clever in its [ULTRA's] use, and we, more daring."[1] Combining these talents produced a vastly superior product than could have been achieved individually.

Cooperation did not show a continuous upward movement as the war progressed but varied in pace and degree under the influence of factors external to the naval intelligence organizations involved. If one were to construct a continuum with Churchill's special relationship at one extreme and—as some recent historians have suggested—a struggle of suspicious America against perfidious Albion at the other, Anglo-American cooperation in naval intelligence would fall somewhere near the center. What is important to remember is not the degree of cooperation attained but that the most meaningful and valuable cooperation took place in a field as traditionally unilateral and secret as intelligence. Herein lies the uniqueness of the Anglo-American naval intelligence relationship during the Second World War. Its importance in no way diminished as permanent interests again overshadowed wartime alliances in the postwar world.

Notes

Preface

1. John Baylis, *Anglo-American Defence Relations 1939–1980: The Special Relationship* (New York: St. Martin's Press, 1980), 1.
2. David Reynolds, *The Creation of the Anglo-American Alliance 1937–41: A Study in Competitive Co-operation* (Chapel Hill: University of North Carolina Press, 1982), 1. For additional discussion of the competitive aspects of the cooperation, see James R. Leutze, *Bargaining for Supremacy: Anglo-American Naval Collaboration 1937–1941* (Chapel Hill: University of North Carolina Press, 1977).

Chapter 1. Uneasy Beginnings

1. Num. 13:17, 18, quoted in Allen Dulles, *The Craft of Intelligence* (New York: Harper and Row, 1963), 10.
2. Dulles, *Craft of Intelligence*, 19.
3. Jeffery M. Dorwart, *Office of Naval Intelligence: The Birth of America's First Intelligence Agency 1865–1918* (Annapolis, Md.: U.S. Naval Institute Press, 1979), 10.
4. Department of the Navy, Order #292, 23 March 1882, quoted in [Wyman Packard], "Notes on the Early History of Naval Intelligence in the United States," *ONI Review* 12 (April–May 1957), World War II Command File, box 116, Operational Archives, Naval Historical Center [hereafter NHC], Washington, D.C., 171.
5. Secretary of the Navy to Mason, 25 July 1882, ibid., 185.
6. Christopher Andrew, *Her Majesty's Secret Service: The Making of the British Intelligence Community* (New York: Viking, 1986), 8–9.
7. A. R. Wells, "Studies in British Naval Intelligence, 1880–1945" (Ph.D. diss., University of London, 1972), 22.
8. Patrick Beesly, "British Naval Intelligence in Two World Wars—Some Similarities and Differences," in *Intelligence and International Relations*, ed. Christopher Andrew and Jeremy Noakes, Exeter Studies in History no. 15 (Exeter: University of Exeter, 1987), 255. Andrew, *Her Majesty's Secret Service*, 15.

9. Dorwart, *Office of Naval Intelligence*, 141.

10. According to Beesly, "British Naval Intelligence," 255, the name Department of Naval Intelligence was not changed to the more familiar Naval Intelligence Division (NID) until about 1918. Throughout this book, ONI and NID are used to refer to the American and British departmental intelligence organizations, respectively.

11. Beesly, "British Naval Intelligence," 255.

12. Donald McLachlan, *Room 39: A Study in Naval Intelligence* (New York: Atheneum, 1968), 376.

13. H.M. Ambassador's No. 121, 16 January 1917, Public Record Office [hereafter PRO], Kew, England: Admiralty: War History Cases and Papers (ADM 199): ADM 199/1157, Co-Operation with the United States Navy in Event of U.S. Entry into Present War, 1940, 4. In 1940, the British naval staff prepared a study of the history of Anglo-American naval cooperation during the First World War for use as precedent for similar cooperative efforts in World War II.

14. Ibid.

15. F.O. 37811, 19 February 1917, ibid.

16. Memo for N.A. [naval attaché], Washington, 24 March 1917, ibid., 5.

17. F.O. 35296, 17 February 1917, ibid., 4. For a detailed description of the Admiralty's code-breaking activities in World War I, see Patrick Beesly, *Room 40: British Naval Intelligence 1914–1918* (New York: Harcourt Brace Jovanovich, 1982). For one of its most significant successes, see Barbara W. Tuchman, *The Zimmermann Telegram* (New York: Ballantine Books, 1979).

18. Beesly, *Room 40*, 11.

19. Tuchman, *Zimmermann Telegram*, 157.

20. Beesly, *Room 40*, 216.

21. David Kahn, *The Codebreakers: The Story of Secret Writing* (New York: Macmillan, 1967), 293.

22. Ibid., 297.

23. Dorwart, *Office of Naval Intelligence*, 125.

24. William J. Morgan and Joye L. Leonhart, *A History of the Dudley Knox Center for Naval History* (Washington, D.C.: Dudley Knox Center for Naval History, 1981), 6.

25. Tracy B. Kittredge, "U.S.-British Naval Cooperation, 1940–1945" (microfilm, ca. 1950), vol. 1, chap. 2, app., World War II Command File, box 252, Operational Archives, NHC, Washington, D.C.

26. Dorwart, *Office of Naval Intelligence*, 123–124.

27. O.M. 260, undated, but probably September or October 1917, PRO: ADM 199/1157, 10.

28. Mary Klachko with David F. Trask, *Admiral William Shepherd Benson: First Chief of Naval Operations* (Annapolis, Md.: U.S. Naval Institute Press, 1987), 95.

29. Beesly, "British Naval Intelligence," 260.

30. F. H. Hinsley et al., *British Intelligence in the Second World War: Its Influence on Strategy and Operations* (London: HMSO, 1979), 1:10.

31. Dorwart, *Office of Naval Intelligence*, 107.

32. Wells, "Studies in British Naval Intelligence," 50.

33. Beesly, "British Naval Intelligence," 256.

34. Undated handwritten entry following entry dated 3 June 1917, PRO: ADM 199/1157, 8.

35. Balfour to Cecil, 3 June 1917, PRO: ADM 199/1157, 12.

36. R. A. de Chair (rear admiral, former British naval attaché to Washington 1902–1905 and member of the Balfour delegation in 1917), undated, but received in Admiralty 25 June 1917, PRO: ADM 199/1157, 13.

37. Tuchman, *Zimmermann Telegram*, 70.

38. Leutze, *Bargaining for Supremacy*, 20.

39. Jeffery M. Dorwart, *Conflict of Duty: The U.S. Navy's Intelligence Dilemma, 1919–1945* (Annapolis, Md.: U.S. Naval Institute Press, 1983), 14.

40. [Packard], "Notes on Early History," 179.

41. A. G. Denniston, "An Account of the Origin and Work of the Government Code and Cypher School (GC&CS)," Denniston file, DENN 1/4, Churchill College Archives, Cambridge, 2. Ironically, in view of happenings during the Nixon years in Washington, D.C., GC&CS's first home was Watergate House.

42. The abbreviation SIS is used to denote the organization variously known as the Special or Secret Intelligence Service, MI-6 (a holdover from the days of its control by the War Office), or, more informally, "The Firm." A good general history of the organization and its activities is contained in Andrew, *Her Majesty's Secret Service*.

43. Little material is available in either American or British records that have been made public on the degree of intelligence cooperation between the two countries during the interwar years. The major culprit is British security regulations. In a 25 February 1965 letter to Admiral John Godfrey, Admiral Norman Denning, at that time chief of intelligence, Ministry of Defence, included "co-operation with other intelligence agencies" in his list of materials that "must never be released" to the public (McLachlan-Beesly file, MLBE 1/2, Churchill College Archives, Cambridge). The U.S. Navy has followed the practice of not releasing any information of British origin that has not previously been released by them, even though by American security standards the material is considered declassified.

F. H. Hinsley, the leading official historian of British intelligence during the Second World War, has seen no indication of cooperation between the two naval intelligence organizations before 1937 and has stated that it was not until the winter of 1940–1941 that intelligence provided by the United States "began to make a contribution, if as yet an insignificant one to Whitehall's appreciations" (Hinsley, *British Intelligence*, 1:311).

44. Dorwart, *Conflict of Duty*, 140.

45. Report forwarded by Staff Officer (Intelligence) Shanghai Concerning Japanese Landing Craft and Operations, 26 September 1938, PRO: Admiralty: Admiralty and Secretariat Papers (ADM 1): ADM 1/9589.

46. Bingham to Roosevelt, 5 January 1937, President's Secretary's file [hereafter PSF] 52, Franklin D. Roosevelt Library, Hyde Park, N.Y.

47. Michael I. Handel, "Leaders and Intelligence," in *Leaders and Intelligence*, ed. Michael I. Handel (London: Frank Cass, 1989), 7.

48. Christopher Andrew, "Churchill and Intelligence," in Handel, Leaders and Intelligence, 183.

49. Hugh Dalton, *The Fateful Years: Memoirs 1931–1945* (London: Frederick Muller, 1957), 366. Dalton was Labour member of Parliament and minister of economic warfare in addition to his duties as political head of SOE.

50. Churchill to Kennedy, 10 December 1939; Kennedy to Churchill, 23 December 1939, PRO: ADM 199/1928, Misc. Collection of 1st Lord's Papers Operation "Catherine."

51. Roosevelt to Churchill, 11 September 1939, in Francis L. Loewenheim, Harold D. Langley, and Manfred Jonas, eds., *Roosevelt and Churchill: Their Secret Wartime Correspondence* (New York: Saturday Review Press, 1975), 89.

52. Churchill to First Sea Lord, 16 October 1939, in ibid.

53. Dorwart, *Office of Naval Intelligence*, 109.

54. Arthur M. Schlesinger, Jr., *The Coming of the New Deal*, vol. 2 of *The Age of Roosevelt* (Boston: Houghton Mifflin, 1958), 523.

55. Ibid., 61.

56. Astor to Roosevelt, 18 April 1940, PSF 116 (Astor), Roosevelt Library.

57. James, minute, 4 December 1936, PRO: Admiralty: Naval Intelligence Papers (ADM 223): ADM 223/286, Operational Intelligence Centres, vol 1. James, minute, 8 December 1936, ibid. James, minute, 11 February 1937, ADM 223/84, references cited in Hinsley, *British Intelligence*, chap. 1–10.

58. Patrick Beesly, *Very Special Intelligence: The Story of the Admiralty's Operational Intelligence Centre 1939–1945* (London: Hamish Hamilton, 1977), 11. "All source" in this context refers to information derived from both communications intercepts and nonelectronic or "collateral" sources.

59. Patrick Beesly, "Operational Intelligence Centre, Naval Intelligence Division 1939–1945." *Naval Review* 63 (July 1975), 225.

60. Admiralty, minute, 23 June 1937, PRO: Admiralty: Admiralty and Secretariat Cases (ADM 116): ADM 116/4302, Anglo-American Information Exchange.

61. Troup (DNI), minute, 9 June 1937, quoting H. M. Ambassador at Washington to Foreign Office, 247, 31 March 1937, ibid.

62. Safford (Op-20-G) to Op-20-A, Navy Department, 20 August 1937; SRH-281, United States Navy, File of Correspondence with the Department of State 1919–1950; Record Group 457, Records of the National Security Agency (NSA); National Archives [hereafter NA], Washington, D.C.

63. Wesley K. Wark, "In Search of a Suitable Japan: British Naval Intelligence in the Pacific Before the Second World War," *Intelligence and National Security* 1 (May 1986), 190–191.

64. Davis to the Secretary of State and the President, 29 April 1937, PSF 28 (GB: 8 March 1937–19 September 1938), Roosevelt Library.

65. Leutze, *Bargaining for Supremacy*, 17–18.

66. Lindsay to Foreign Office, 17 September [sic, probably December] 1937,

quoted in a minute on "The Visit of Commander Hampton to the U.S.," PRO: ADM 116/3922, Documents on US Establishment of "Neutrality Patrol" 1939.

67. Lindsay to Foreign Office, 2 January 1938, ibid.

68. Roosevelt to Leahy, 22 December 1937, PSF 78 (Navy Dept. 1936–7), Roosevelt Library.

69. *The Reminiscences of Royal E. Ingersoll* (New York: Oral History Research Office, Columbia University, 1965), 70–72, Operational Archives, NHC, Washington, D.C.

70. Director of Plans, minute, 17 January 1938, PRO: ADM 1/9822, Record of Conversations Between Captain Ingersoll, U.S.N. and the Naval Staff at the Admiralty (1937–38).

71. Ingersoll to CNO, January 1938, PRO: ibid.

72. Early (presidential press secretary) to Roosevelt, 28 January 1938, PSF 146 (Stephen T. Early), Roosevelt Library.

73. Memorandum, undated, initialed "DJC" (Daniel J. Callaghan, presidential naval aide), PSF 82 (D. J. Callaghan), Roosevelt Library.

Chapter 2. Changing Attitudes

1. Tromp minute, 17 February 1938, PRO: ADM 1/9546, Embarkation of Allied Naval Attachés or Observers in HM Ships.

2. United States Naval Administration in World War II, Office of the Chief of Naval Operations, Office of Naval Intelligence [hereafter ONI Administrative History], vol. 2 (Washington, D.C.: Naval History Division, n.d.), World War II Command File, box 115, Operational Archives, NHC, Washington, D.C., 622.

3. PRO: ADM 116/4302.

4. Secretary of the Navy Confidential letter (Op-16-F), to Distribution, 28 September 1940, file 181, "Exchange of Technical Information With the British Government," COMNAVEU Series II, Operational Archives, NHC, Washington, D.C.

5. Cordeaux to McLachlan, 9 April 1966, McLachlan and Beesly File, MLBE 1/1, Churchill College Archives Center, Cambridge.

6. Committee of Imperial Defence, Minutes of the 333d. Meeting, 6 October 1938, PRO: ADM 116/3637, CID Request for Identification of Deficiencies in Military Brought to Light by Czech Crisis.

7. Troup to Rushbrooke, 18 October 1938, PRO: ADM 1/10226, Operational Intelligence Centre, Singapore. PRO: ADM 1/9567, Staff Officer (Intelligence), Capetown. PRO: ADM 1/9679, Provision of Career Path for Officers Involved in Operational Intelligence Duties.

8. Wesley K. Wark, *The Ultimate Enemy: British Intelligence and Nazi Germany, 1933–1939* (Ithaca, N.Y.: Cornell University Press, 1985), 148.

9. Wells, "British Naval Intelligence," 81.

10. Dorwart, *Conflict of Duty,* 99.

11. Stephen W. Roskill, Foreword to John H. Godfrey, *Memoirs* (1965), Godfrey File, GDFY 1/6, Churchill College Archives Center, Cambridge, 5:ix.

Roskill, Foreword to Patrick Beesly, *Very Special Admiral: The Life of Admiral J. H. Godfrey, CB* (London: Hamish Hamilton, 1980), xvi.

12. Beesly, *Very Special Admiral*, chaps. 1–5.

13. Wells, "Studies in British Naval Intelligence," 114.

14. Beesly, *Very Special Admiral*, 104.

15. Miscellaneous notes on John Godfrey by Vice Admiral Ian Campbell, RN. McLachlan Beesly Papers, MLBE 6/2, Churchill College Archives Center, Cambridge.

16. Beesly, "British Naval Intelligence," 260.

17. Godfrey, *Memoirs*, GDFY 1/6, 5:139. Apparently, this opinion of Kirk was widely held in NID. Beesly (*Very Special Admiral*, 173) and McLachlan (*Room 39*, 217), both of whom were assigned to NID during the Kirk/Godfrey era, used this quote in their characterizations of Kirk.

18. *The Reminiscences of Alan G. Kirk* (New York: Oral History Research Office, Columbia University, 1962), Operational Archives, NHC, Washington, D.C., 118.

19. Ibid., 122.

20. Godfrey, *Memoirs*, 5:139.

21. Kirk to Anderson, letter of 20 June 1939, Papers of Alan G. Kirk, box 2, folder, Attaché's Correspondence 1939–1940, Operational Archives, NHC, Washington, D.C.

22. Kirk, *Reminiscences*, 122.

23. Ibid., 133.

24. Godfrey to D.C.N.S., 21 June 1939, PRO: ADM 1/10218, Adapting Naval Intelligence Division to War Conditions.

25. Director of Plans, minute of 24 March 1939, PRO: ADM 116/3922. Lindsay to Foreign Office, 21 March 1939, ibid.

26. Hampton to Director of Plans, 23 June 1939, ibid.

27. Hampton to Director of Plans, 27 June 1939, ibid.

28. Neville Chamberlain, statement, 30 September 1938, quoted in Winston S. Churchill, *The Gathering Storm*, vol. 1 of *The Second World War* (Boston: Houghton Mifflin, 1948), 318.

29. John Colville, *The Fringes of Power: 10 Downing Street Diaries 1939–1945* (New York: W. W. Norton, 1985), 28.

30. United States Naval Administration in World War II, Commander in Chief U.S. Naval Forces in Europe [hereafter COMNAVEU Administrative History], vol. 3 (Washington, D.C.: Naval History Division, n.d.), World War II Command File, box 282, Operational Archives, NHC, Washington, D.C., 13.

31. F. H. Hinsley and C.A.G. Simkins, *Security and Counter-Intelligence*, vol. 4 of *British Intelligence in the Second World War* (London: HMSO, 1990), 33.

32. Colville, *Fringes of Power*, 48.

33. Hinsley, *British Intelligence*, 1:103. "The Polish, French and British Contributions to the Breaking of the Enigma," Appendix I to that volume, 487–495, is a particularly good treatment of the subject.

34. ALUSNA LONDON to OPNAV, message of 31 October 1939; ALUSNA

LONDON to OPNAV, message of 27 November 1939; OPNAV to ALUSNA LONDON, message of 28 November 1939; file 1, ALUSNA and SPENAVO LONDON messages, September 1938–September 1941, COMNAVEU Series I, Operational Archives, NHC, Washington, D.C. ALUSNA, which stands for American Legation, U.S. Naval Attaché, is one of several military acronyms still in common use whose original meaning has all but disappeared.

35. DNI minute, 4 May 1940, PRO: ADM 116/4302.

36. Bloch (CINCUS) to Andrews (Commander Scouting Force, U.S. Fleet), letter of 8 December 1939, Bloch Papers, box 1, folder: Adolphus Andrews, Manuscripts Division, Library of Congress, Washington, D.C. The acronym CINCUS (commander in chief, U.S. Fleet) carried unfortunate connotations subsequent to 7 December 1941 and was changed to COMINCH.

37. DNI minute, 26 February 1940, PRO: ADM 116/4302.

38. Leutze, *Bargaining for Supremacy*, 66.

39. Martin Gilbert, *Second World War* (London: Weidenfeld and Nicolson, 1989), 37.

40. Kittredge, "U.S.-British Naval Cooperation," 117.

41. See note 54, chapter 1.

42. Kennedy to Roosevelt, PSF Diplomatic File 53, folder: G.B. Joseph Kennedy, Roosevelt Library. Leutze, *Bargaining for Supremacy*, 130. JIS Appreciation of Germany's Intentions, No. 230, PSF 5, Roosevelt Library. N. Butler, British Embassy, to Roosevelt, PSF Diplomatic File 47, folder: G.B. Jan–June 1941, Roosevelt Library. British Naval Attaché, Washington to ONI, 10 January 1940, PSF Department File 78, folder: Navy Department, Jan–April 1940, Roosevelt Library.

43. Embassy London to the Secretary of State, telegram of 12 July 1940, in Kittredge, "U.S.-British Naval Cooperation," 77.

44. DNI to VCNS (Vice Chief of the Naval Staff), minute of 2 August 1940, PRO: ADM 223/84.

45. "Program, Colonel Donovan, 22 July–1 August 1940," Papers of Alan G. Kirk, box 3, folder: Correspondence 1939–41, Operational Archives, NHC, Washington, D.C.

46. PRO: ADM 223/84.

47. Kirk to Donovan, letter of 14 August 1940, Papers of Alan G. Kirk, box 3, folder: Correspondence D, Operational Archives, NHC, Washington, D.C. Donovan to Kirk, letter of 27 August 1940, ibid.

48. PRO: ADM 223/84.

49. Kirk to Anderson, letter of 24 June 1940, box 227, General Records of the Department of the Navy, Record Group 80, NA, Washington, D.C.

50. ONI Administrative History, 360–361.

51. Robert Dallek, *Franklin D. Roosevelt and American Foreign Policy 1932–1945* (New York: Oxford University Press, 1979), 244. Winston S. Churchill, *Their Finest Hour*, vol. 2 of *The Second World War* (Boston: Houghton Mifflin, 1949), 227. James MacGregor Burns, *Roosevelt: The Lion and the Fox 1882–1940* (New York: Harcourt Brace Jovanovich, 1956), 441.

52. Stanley W. Dziuban, *Military Relations Between the United States and Canada 1939–1945*, vol. 8, pt. 5, of *The United States Army in World War II* (Washington, D.C.: Historical Division, Department of the Army, 1959), 13.

53. Wesley K. Wark, "Evolution of Military Intelligence in Canada," *Armed Forces and Society* 16 (fall 1989), 82.

54. P. W. Nelles [chief of Canadian Naval Staff, Ottawa] to Dudley Pound [first sea lord], letter of 21 July 1939, PRO: Admiralty: First Sea Lord Papers (ADM 205): ADM 205/3, First Sea Lord's Personal War Records, Private Secret Correspondence, 1939.

55. Deputy Minister of the Canadian Naval Service, Desbarats, to Admiralty, letter of 28 October 1910, file 1023-4-1, RG 24, vol. 3856, Public Archives of Canada, Ottawa, Canada [hereafter PARC]. Admiralty to Desbarats, letter of 14 December 1910 and enclosure thereto, ibid. Desbarats to Admiralty, letter of 3 January 1911, ibid. "Naval Intelligence in Canada," file 81/520/1480, Directorate of History, Department of National Defence [hereafter D.HIST], Ottawa, Canada, 2.

56. "Naval Intelligence Organisation of Canada," memo of September 1919, from Assistant Director, Naval Staff, to Chief of the Naval Staff, File 1023-4-3, RG 24, vol. 3856, PARC.

57. Chief of Staff, Department of Naval Service, to the Director of the Naval Service, memo of 22 October 1917, ibid.

58. James A. Boutilier, Introduction to *The RCN in Retrospect 1910–1968*, ed. James A. Boutilier (Vancouver, B.C.: University of British Columbia Press, 1982), xxi. "Naval Intelligence in Canada," D.HIST 81/520/1480.

59. W.G.D. Lund, "The Royal Canadian Navy's Quest for Autonomy in the North Atlantic: 1941–43," in Boutilier, *RCN in Retrospect*, 139.

60. David Kahn, *Seizing the Enigma: The Race to Break the German U-boat Codes* (Boston: Houghton Mifflin, 1991), 215–216, provides a vivid picture of a direction finding station in action. For British definitions of "Y"-related terms, see E.G.N. Rushbrooke, DNI, to Distribution, letter of 20 March 1943, file 1008-75-44, RG 24, vol. 3807, PARC.

61. C. E. Allan, "Building a Canadian Naval Operational Intelligence Centre 1939–1943" (paper prepared for the Second Naval Historical Conference, Halifax, Nova Scotia, 8–9 October 1993), 2. Peter St. John, "Canada's Accession to the Allied Intelligence Community 1940–1945," *Conflict Quarterly* 4, no. 4 (fall 1984), 5. "Naval Intelligence in Canada," D.HIST 81/520/1480.

62. Biographical Sketches of Captain J.M.P.B. deMarbois, CBE, RCN, file Jock deMarbois, D.HIST 81/520/1480.

63. "Organization of the Canadian Naval Staff, Ottawa, 1 June 1943," file NMCS 9-1, RG 24, vol. 11978, PARC. "Notes on the History of [the] Operational Intelligence Centre in Canada," [hereafter "OIC History"], D.HIST S. 1440-18.

64. Allan, "Building a Canadian Naval OIC," 1. "OIC History," 1941, 6.

65. Memo from deMarbois, DDSD (Y), to Director Signals Division, Naval Staff Headquarters (NSHQ) of 17 May 1943, file NSS 1008-75-19, RG 24, vol. 3806, PARC.

66. Lothian-Hull, Memorandum of Conversation, 11 June 1940, PSF Diplomatic File 46, folder: G.B. 1940 (1), Jan–Jul, Roosevelt Library. Lothian-Hull, Memorandum of Conversation, 24 June 1940, ibid.

67. Mark S. Watson, *Chief of Staff: Prewar Plans and Preparations*, vol. 2 of *The United States Army in World War II: The War Department* (Washington, D.C.: Historical Division, Department of the Army, 1950), 114.

68. Kittredge, "U.S.-British Naval Cooperation," Notes and Appendices, 143. Watson, *Chief of Staff*, 114.

69. Kittredge, "U.S.-British Naval Cooperation," 115.

70. Obituary of Admiral Sir Sidney R. Bailey, *Times*, 30 March 1942, contained in box 12, folder 62, Papers of Charles Lockwood, Manuscripts Division, Library of Congress, Washington, D.C.

71. *The Reminiscences of Vice Admiral Bernard L. Austin, USN (Ret.)* (Annapolis, Md.: U.S. Naval Institute Press, 1971), 99–102.

72. Godfrey, minute of 2 July 1940, PRO: ADM 199/1158, Bailey Committee.

73. Section VII, Bailey Committee Report, 6 August 1940, Bailey Committee Memoranda, file 20, COMNAVEU Series II, Operational Archives, NHC, Washington, D.C.

74. Austin, *Reminiscences*, 119–120.

75. Joint Intelligence Subcommittee, memorandum of 10 August 1940, "Anglo-American Standardization of Arms Committee," PRO: ADM 199/1159, Co-operation with the U.S. Navy in the Event of U.S. Entry into the War, 1.

76. Ibid., 2.

77. Kirk to Donovan, letter of 14 August 1940, box 3, folder: Correspondence D, Kirk Papers, Operational Archives, NHC, Washington, D.C.

78. Kirk, *Reminiscences*, 166–167.

79. Ibid.

80. Ghormley to Knox, letter of 23 August 1940, folder: 1, Ghormley Correspondence, 1940, COMNAVEU Series II, Operational Archives, NHC, Washington, D.C.

81. Beesly, *Very Special Intelligence*, 99.

82. Anglo-American Standardization of Arms Committee, Minutes of Meeting, 31 August 1940, PRO: ADM 199/1159.

83. Gilbert, *Second World War*, 120.

Chapter 3. Forging Ahead

1. Meeting with Captain Kirk, U.S. Naval Attaché on 4th September 1940, PRO: ADM 199/1159.

2. ALUSNA London, 071321 September 1940, Action to OPNAV. ALUSNA and SPENAVO London messages, September 1938–September 1941, file 1, folder 1, COMNAVEU Series l, Operational Archives, NHC, Washington, D.C.

Sometime between September 1939 and September 1940 the Navy Department changed its method of referencing naval radio dispatches. Previously, they were identified by originator, day, month, and year (e.g., ALUSNA London 0027

Nov 1939). When multiple messages began to be transmitted from the same location on the same day, the system broke down. To end the confusion, the transmission hour, using the twenty-four-hour clock, was added in what was later called a date-time group (DTG). The above reference (ALUSNA London 071321 Sep 40) translates to "U.S. Naval Attaché, London, message originated at 1321 (1:21 P.M.) on 7 September 1940." A later refinement was made to use standard Greenwich mean time (GMT) in place of local time in most references. This permitted messages from different locations to be ordered sequentially. GMT is indicated by putting the letter "Z" after the DTG. The complete modern reference would then be: ALUSNA London 071321Z Sep 40.

3. Bailey Committee Report, 11 September 1940, PRO: ADM 199/1159.

4. Kittredge, "U.S.-British Naval Cooperation," 188.

5. Stark to Ghormley, letter of 16 October 1940, file 79, Ghormley Correspondence, COMNAVEU Series II, Operational Archives, NHC, Washington, D.C.

6. B.C.(J) Sixth Meeting, 23 September 1940, PRO: ADM 199/1159. Bailey Committee Report, file 21, COMNAVEU Series II, Operational Archives, NHC, Washington, D.C.

7. Bernard L. Austin, handwritten note, undated, file 19, Austin, Bernard L., LCDR USN, Notes and Correspondence 1940–1941, COMNAVEU Series II, Operational Archives, NHC, Washington, D.C., emphasis Austin's.

8. B.C.(J) Fourteenth Meeting, 16 October 1940, PRO: ADM 199/1159.

9. Director of Naval Intelligence to Director of War Plans, memorandum of 14 November 1940, box 227, General Records of the Department of the Navy, Record Group 80, NA, Washington, D.C.

10. Stark to Ghormley, letter of 13 January 1941, SPENAVO file 39, Communications Procedures & Facilities, COMNAVEU Series II, Operational Archives, NHC, Washington, D.C.

11. Bailey to First Sea Lord, minute of 6 May 1941, PRO: ADM 1/12783, Liaison with the U.S. Mission in London.

12. Memorandum for Admiral Bailey's Committee, No. 16, 19 September 1940. Memorandum for Admiral Bailey's Committee, No. 381, 9 June 1941, file 20, Bailey Committee Memoranda, COMNAVEU Series II, Operational Archives, NHC, Washington, D.C.

13. Bailey, report of 1 January 1941, PRO: 199/1156, Exchange of Secret Technical and Operational Information with U.S.A. 1939–1941.

14. Bailey Committee Report, 11 September 1940, PRO: ADM 199/1159.

15. Pott to Godfrey, letter of 14 January 1941, PRO: ADM 223/84.

16. James Leutze, ed., *The London Journal of General Raymond E. Lee*, 1940–1941 (Boston: Little, Brown, 1971), 207.

17. Ibid., 212.

18. Robert E. Sherwood, *Roosevelt and Hopkins: An Intimate History* (New York: Harper and Brothers, 1948), 230–264. Gilbert, *Second World War*, 150.

19. Minute, undated, initialed T.S.V.P. (Admiral T.S.V. Phillips, Vice Chief of the Naval Staff), PRO: ADM 1/11168, Co-operation with the United States. Discussions with Mr. Hopkins 1940–1941.

20. Godfrey, *Memoirs,* Godfrey file, GDFY 1/6, 5:131, Churchill College Archives, Cambridge.

21. Gilbert, *Second World War,* 107.

22. Stewart Alsop and Thomas Braden, *Sub Rosa: The O.S.S. and American Espionage* (New York: Reynal and Hitchcock, 1946), 80. Additional information on ONI's role in the selection and assignment of control officers is contained in ONI Administrative History, 850.

23. Cordell Hull, *The Memoirs of Cordell Hull* (New York: Macmillan, 1948), 2: 951.

24. Alsop and Braden, *Sub Rosa,* 81.

25. Andrew, *Her Majesty's Secret Service,* 462–463.

26. *Home Waters and the Atlantic,* vol. 2 of *Naval Staff History* (London: Admiralty, 1961), 60–61. British source, box 50, Operational Archives, NHC, Washington, D.C. *Naval Staff History* is the Admiralty's once-classified report of the war at sea.

27. Stephen Roskill, *Hankey: Man of Secrets* (London: Collins, 1974), 3:446–447.

28. Chiefs of Staff, 174th Meeting, 9 June 1940, PRO: Ministry of Defence: Combined Operations and Headquarters Records (DEFE 2): DEFE 2/699, Combined Operations Early History, vol 2.

29. Ibid., 36–37.

30. Edward Thomas, "The Evolution of the JIC System up to and During World War II," in *Intelligence and International Relations,* ed. Christopher Andrew and Jeremy Noakes (Exeter: University of Exeter, 1987), 228. Military Attaché, London, Intelligence Report, BES-175, 4 June 1941, forwarded by Stark to Knox 23 June 1941, box 228, Record Group 80; NA, Washington, D.C.

31. Leutze, *Bargaining for Supremacy,* 163.

32. Dorwart, *Conflict of Duty,* 117.

33. Don Whitehead, *The FBI Story: A Report to the People* (New York: Random House, 1956), 165–166.

34. Astor to Roosevelt, 18 April 1940, Astor to Roosevelt 20 April 1940, PSF 116, Roosevelt Library.

35. Berle to ONI, G-2, FBI, 24 June 1940. Berle to Watson, 25 June 1940, folder: State Department 1939–1940, PSF 12, Roosevelt Library.

36. Edwin T. Layton, *"And I Was There:" Pearl Harbor and Midway—Breaking the Secrets* (New York: William Morrow, 1985), 168. Ronald Lewin, *The American Magic: Codes, Ciphers and the Defeat of Japan* (New York: Farrar Straus Giroux, 1982), 67, indicates that the joint Army-Navy Intelligence Committee was not authorized until 11 October 1941 and did not meet until after 7 December 1941.

37. Leutze, *Lee Journal,* 295.

38. Godfrey, *Memoirs,* 5:133.

39. Leutze, *Bargaining for Supremacy,* 183–196, contains a detailed discussion of the political atmosphere affecting the development of Plan DOG. William L. Langer and S. Everett Gleason, *The Undeclared War 1940–1941* (New York: Harper and Brothers, 1952), 271–272.

40. Stark to Ghormley, 19 November 1940, Ghormley Correspondence, file 79, COMNAVEU Series II, Operational Archives, NHC, Washington, D.C.

41. Kittredge, "U.S.-British Naval Cooperation," 115.

42. Leutze, *Bargaining for Supremacy*, 171.

43. Ibid., 205. Watson, *Chief of Staff*, 118.

44. Joint Committee on the Investigation of the Pearl Harbor Attack [hereafter PHA], *Hearings*. 79th Cong., 1st sess. Pursuant to S. Con. Res. 27 (Washington, D.C.: Government Printing Office, 1946), 3:1052. At the hearings, General George C. Marshall, chief of staff of the U.S. Army in 1940–1941, testified that "Admiral Stark brought up the proposition [for the talks] and I acquiesced. He arranged the meeting."

45. Leutze, *Lee Journal*, 202.

46. Joint Planning Committee, 21 January 1941, Papers of Admiral Richmond K. Turner, USN, box 20, folder: Director Joint War Plans Division, Special File #1, 1937–1941, Operational Archives, NHC, Washington, D.C.

47. Watson, *Chief of Staff*, 384.

48. United States-British Staff Conversations Report (Short Title ABC-1), 27 March 1941, PHA, *Hearings*, 15:1487.

49. Lund, "Royal Canadian Navy's Quest," 143.

50. Joint Canadian–United States Basic Defense Plan No. 2, 12 August 1941, PHA, *Hearings*, 15:1585. Marc Milner, *North Atlantic Run: The Royal Canadian Navy and the Battle for the Convoys* (Annapolis, Md.: U.S. Naval Institute Press, 1985), 28.

51. Annex I to ABC-1, 27 March 1941, PHA *Hearings*, 15:1497.

52. B.U.S.(J)(41)31, 6 March 1941, file 193: U.S.-British Staff Conversations, Papers 1941, COMNAVEU Series II, Operational Archives, NHC, Washington, D.C.

53. ABC-1, 27 March 1941, PHA *Hearings*, 15:1495.

54. Ghormley to Pound, 26 April 1941, PRO: Admiralty: First Sea Lord Papers (ADM 205): ADM 205/9, First Sea Lord's Personal War Records 1939–1945: file 3, U.S. Naval Co-operation April–December 1941.

55. Stark to U.S. Naval Attachés and Naval Observers, 27 November 1941, box 228, General Records of the Department of the Navy, Record Group 80, NA, Washington, D.C.

56. See note 5.

57. Stark to Ghormley, 5 April 1941, Papers of Harold R. Stark, series II, box A1, folder: Stark Correspondence April June 1942 [sic], Operational Archives, NHC, Washington, D.C.

58. Winant to Roosevelt. STATETEL 1309, 3 April 1941, PSF 9 (Winant), Roosevelt Library.

59. Winant to Roosevelt, STATETEL 3338, 31 July 1941, ibid.

60. Admiralty message to all major commands, 18 December 1940, PRO: ADM 199/1156. "Most Secret sources" almost certainly refers to information derived from analysis of enemy communications.

61. Admiralty to C-in-C Western Approaches, 22 April 1941, SPENAVO

London, General File 1940–1941, file 162, COMNAVEU Series II, Operational Archives, NHC, Washington, D.C.

62. A. Sinkov and Leo Rosen to Assistant Chief of Staff, G-2, 11 April 1941, SRH-145, Collection of Memoranda on Operations of SIS [Signal Intelligence Service] Intercept Activities and Dissemination 1942–1945, Record Group 457, NA, Washington, D.C., 002. Sinkov later compiled an admirable war record as head of the U.S. Army's contingent of code breakers attached to General MacArthur's Southwest Pacific Headquarters. See Edward J. Drea, *MacArthur's ULTRA* (Lawrence: University Press of Kansas, 1992).

63. A. Sinkov and Leo Rosen to Assistant Chief of Staff, G-2, 11 April 1941, SRH-145, Collection of Memoranda on Operations of SIS Intercept Activities and Dissemination 1942–1945, Record Group 457, NA, Washington, D.C., 002.

64. Kahn, *Seizing the Enigma*, 237.

65. "C" to Prime Minister, letter of 26 February 1941. PRO: Government Code and Cypher School: Signals Intelligence Passed to the Prime Minister. Messages and Correspondence (HW 1), HW 1/2.

66. There has been considerable speculation over the years as to whether the U.S. delegation brought one or two "Purple" machines for the British. Prescott Currier, who was one of the two naval members of the team, stated in a talk to the National Security Agency, reprinted in *Cryptologia* 20 (July 1996), that the team carried with them two machines.

67. Thomas H. Dyer, review of *The American Magic*, by Ronald Lewin, *Cryptologia* 7 (January 1983), 79.

68. Francis H. Hinsley to T. J. Smith, letter of 26 February 1980, quoted in T. J. Smith, unpublished ms., SRH-143, "ULTRA and the Battle of Britain: The Real Key to Success?" 18 May 1980: RG 457; NA, Washington, D.C., 23.

69. Kahn, *Codebreakers*, 23.

70. Thomas Parrish, *The Ultra Americans: The U.S. Role in Breaking the Nazi Codes* (New York: Stein and Day, 1986), 65. Kahn, *Seizing the Enigma*, 237.

71. Ralph Erskine, "Naval Enigma: A Missing Link," *International Journal of Intelligence and Counterintelligence* 3 (winter 1989), 504. Colin Burke, *Information and Secrecy: Vannevar Bush, Ultra, and the Other Memex* (Lanham, Md.: Scarecrow Press, 1994), chap. 11, details the successful American project to build a high-speed bombe to attack the German submarine cryptographic problem.

72. Sinkov and Rosen to Assistant Chief of Staff, G-2, 11 April 1941, SRH-145, RG 457, NA, Washington, D.C., 004. "OIC History," 1941, 7. Prescott Currier, "My 'Purple' Trip to England in 1941," *Cryptologia* 20(July 1996), 193–201. The development of both land-based and shipboard HF/DF is covered in detail in Kathleen B. Williams, *Secret Weapon: U.S. High-Frequency Direction Finding in the Battle of the Atlantic* (Annapolis, Md.: U.S. Naval Institute Press, 1996).

73. Godfrey, *Memoirs*, Godfrey file, GDFY 1/6, Churchill College Archives Center, Cambridge, 5:134.

74. Paul R. Schratz, *Submarine Commander* (Lexington: University Press of Kentucky, 1988), 11.

75. Beesly, *Very Special Admiral*, 180.

76. McLachlan, *Room 39*, 220, quoting Godfrey.

77. Beesly, *Very Special Admiral*, 181.

78. Ibid.

79. John Pearson, *The Life of Ian Fleming* (New York: McGraw-Hill, 1966), 89, quoting Denning.

80. McLachlan, *Room 39*, 228.

81. Pearson, *Ian Fleming*, 107.

82. *The Reminiscences of Arthur H. McCollum* (Annapolis, Md.: Oral History Program, U.S. Naval Institute, 1973), 1:338.

83. Beesly, *Very Special Admiral*, 181–183. See also: McLachlan, *Room 39*, 229–230, and Godfrey, *Memoirs*, 5:133.

84. Anthony Cave Brown, *The Last Hero: Wild Bill Donovan* (New York: Times Books, 1982), 165.

85. Godfrey, *Memoirs*, 5:132. Bradley F. Smith, "Admiral Godfrey's Mission to America, June/July 1941," *Intelligence and National Security* 1 (September 1986), 441–450, indicates that Admiral Godfrey took a stronger line in advocating Donovan's appointment to the president than Godfrey was later prepared to admit in his memoirs.

86. Godfrey, *Memoirs*, 5:139.

87. Wells, "Studies in British Naval Intelligence," 339.

88. Ghormley to Stark, 2 September 1941. King, FADM, Correspondence, box 1, file: "September 1941," Operational Archives, NHC, Washington, D.C.

89. McCollum, *Reminiscences*, 342.

90. OPNAV 032240 SEPT 41, ACTION ALUSNA LONDON. ALUSNA & SPENAVO London messages, series I, file 1, folder 6: Secret messages August–September 1941, Operational Archives, NHC, Washington, D.C.

91. McCollum, *Reminiscences*, 346.

92. Ibid., 350.

93. Cmdr. Denniston, May 1943, "Informal Memorandum by Cmdr. Denniston Outlining His Original Concept of American Liaison," SRH 153, MIS War Department. Liaison Activities in the U.K., 1943–1945, RG 457, NA, Washington, D.C., 016.

94. McCollum, *Reminiscences*, 354.

95. Little to Pound, 6 November 1941, PRO: ADM 205/9.

96. A. V. Alexander, 1st. Lord to Knox, 15 May 1941, PRO: ADM 1/14994, Correspondence with COL KNOX.

97. Leutze, *Bargaining for Supremacy*, 254.

98. Langer and Gleason, *Undeclared War*, 522.

99. Kittredge, "U.S.-British Naval Cooperation," 332.

100. Captain H.R.M. Laird, RN, "General Report on NID 18," PRO: ADM 223/107, references used in Hinsley, *British Intelligence in the Second World War*.

101. Admiralty, DNI, to distribution, message of 11 May 1942, Navy Department, N-2: 30/68/3, pt 3. War, 1939–41. Exchange of Intelligence, National Archives Head Office, [hereafter NAHO], Wellington. B.A.D. Washington to Distribution 2215Z 19 May 1942, ibid. Admiralty to Distribution 1759B/3 June 1942, ibid.

102. "EXTINGUISH TELEGRAMS," PRO: ADM 223/298, NID 12—Selections From History, 15.

103. Bevan to DNI, letter from Polyarnoe of 13 August 1941, PRO: ADM 223/249, Private Correspondence of the D.N.I., 1941–1945. "U.S.S.R. 'Y' Collaboration: A Solitary Success," PRO: ADM 223/284.

104. Hinsley, *British Intelligence*, 2:61. DNI to Miles (Moscow), letter of 20 January 1943, PRO: ADM 223/249. Miles (Moscow) to DNI, letter of 6 February 1943, ibid.

105. Receipt from the Soviet Naval Mission to Paymaster Lieutenant R. Hutchings for one German Cypher Machine 'Enigma,' 15 July 1943, PRO: ADM 223/289, Weekly Intelligence Meetings 1942–1943.

106. Dorwart, *Conflict of Duty*, 215. Bradley F. Smith, *Sharing Secrets With Stalin: How the Allies Traded Intelligence, 1941–1945* (Lawrence: University Press of Kansas, 1996), 118 ff., provides a detailed and balanced view of U.S.-Soviet intelligence cooperation.

Chapter 4. Growth of Wartime Cooperation

1. Beatrice B. Berle and Travis B. Jacobs, eds., *Navigating the Rapids, 1918–1971: The Papers of Adolf A. Berle* (New York: Harcourt Brace Jovanovich, 1973), 383.

2. Gilbert, *Second World War*, 277.

3. Churchill to Roosevelt, 9 December 1941; Winston S. Churchill, *The Grand Alliance*, vol. 3 of *The Second World War* (Boston: Houghton Mifflin, 1950), 609.

4. Ernest J. King and Walter Muir Whitehill, *Fleet Admiral King: A Naval Record* (New York: W. W. Norton, 1952), 353.

5. McLachlan, *Room 39*, 219.

6. Beesly, *Very Special Intelligence*, 107.

7. King to Stark, 29 August 1941; King to Ingram, 20 September 1941; Papers of FADM Ernest J. King, series I, Correspondence 1918–Feb 1942, box 1, file: September 1941, Operational Archives, NHC, Washington, D.C.

8. W. J. Holmes, *Double-Edged Secrets: U.S. Naval Intelligence Operations in the Pacific During World War II* (Annapolis, Md.: U.S. Naval Institute Press, 1979), 142.

9. Washington War Conference December 1941–January 1942, War Cabinet Chiefs of Staff Committee Papers prepared for and considered by the British Chiefs of Staff, COS(42)78, PRO: War Cabinet: Chiefs of Staff Committee. Memoranda (CAB 80): CAB 80/34, Meetings of the British Chiefs of Staff, Papers on the Arcadia Conference, December 1941–January 1942.

10. Meeting of the British Chiefs of Staff held 13 January 1942, concerning post-Arcadia collaboration, COS(42)79, PRO: CAB 80/34.

11. JCCS-8, 10 January 1942, PSF 1 (Arcadia), Roosevelt Library.

12. U.S. Department of State, *Foreign Relations of the United States, the Conferences at Washington 1941–1942* (Washington, D.C.: Government Printing Office, 1968), 234.

13. Hinsley, *British Intelligence*, 2:42.

14. Post-Arcadia Collaboration, ABC-4, 14 January 1942, Foreign Relations of the United States, *The Conferences at Washington, 1941–1942, and Casablanca 1943* (Washington, D.C.: Government Printing Office, 1968), 233, wherein it was determined that "the word 'joint' should be applied to Inter-Service collaboration [within a single nation] and the word 'combined' to collaboration between two or more United Nations." These definitions were not in effect in mid-1940 when the British chiefs of staff instituted an interservice Combined Intelligence Committee. A subcommittee of the JIC, the Combined Intelligence Committee was organized as a special warning body for the specific purpose of bringing together all sources of information that bore on the German invasion threat. By the time the combined/joint system came into effect in 1942, the Combined Intelligence Committee had outlived the reason for its creation, was for all practical purposes defunct, and therefore caused no definitional problems.

15. Ray S. Cline, *Washington Command Post: The Operations Division*, vol. 2 of *The United States Army in World War II: The War Department* (Washington, D.C.: Office of the Chief of Military History, Department of the Army, 1951), 47.

16. Ibid., 98.

17. J.M.A. Gwyer and J.R.M. Butler, *Grand Strategy*, vol. 3, *June 1941–August 1942* (London: HMSO, 1964), 395. Cline, *Washington Command Post*, 100–104, offers an excellent account of the British-American staff system from an American perspective.

18. Winston S. Churchill, *The Hinge of Fate* (Boston: Houghton Mifflin, 1950), 126 (table), 109.

19. Ladislas Farago, *The Tenth Fleet* (1962; reprint, New York: Drum Books, 1986), 108.

20. Jürgen Rohwer, "Allied and Axis Radio Intelligence in the Battle of the Atlantic: A Comparative Analysis," paper delivered at the Thirteenth Military History Symposium, U.S. Air Force Academy, Colorado Springs, Colo., 12 October 1988, 11.

21. Jürgen Rohwer, "The Operational Use of 'ULTRA' in the Battle of the Atlantic," in *Intelligence and International Relations*, ed. Christopher Andrew and Jeremy Noakes, Exeter Studies in History no. 15 (Exeter: University of Exeter, 1987), 281.

22. Ibid., 279.

23. Beesly, *Very Special Intelligence*, 107.

24. Farago, *Tenth Fleet*, 76.

25. Signals Department, Admiralty, memo of 9 February 1942, file 1008-75-10, RG 24, vol. 3805, PARC. Sandwith to Brand, letter of 19 February 1942, ibid.

26. Captain H. R. Sandwith, RN, "Discussion of British W/T Intelligence Organization," paper presented at the opening meeting of the Joint U.S.-British-Canadian Discussions, Navy Department, Washington, D.C., 6 April 1942, File 1008-75-20, RG 24, vol. 3806, PARC.

27. D.HIST. S. 1440-18, "History of the Operational Intelligence Center," 1942, 5.

28. McCollum, *Reminiscences*, 303.

29. B. Mitchell Simpson III, *Admiral Harold R. Stark: Architect of Victory, 1939–1945* (Columbia: University of South Carolina, 1989), 117.

30. COMINCH (Commander in Chief, U.S. Fleet) War Diary, 7 December 1941–31 December 1942, entries for 15 January 1942 and 18 February 1942, World War II War Diaries, box 1, file 1, Operational Archives, NHC, Washington, D.C.

31. Beesly, *Very Special Intelligence*, 58. Patrick Beesly, "Appreciation of Roger Winn," McLachlan/Beesly file, MLBE 6/1, Churchill College Archives Center, Cambridge.

32. McLachlan, *Room 39*, 115, quoting Winn.

33. SPENAVO (Ghormley) to King, 6 April 1942, Papers of FADM Ernest J. King, series I, correspondence, box 2, March–August 1942, Operational Archives, NHC, Washington, D.C.

34. Beesly, *Very Special Intelligence*, 108.

35. Roger Winn, "Report of Visit to Washington," 3 June 1942. PRO: ADM 223/107, 2.

36. Ibid., 4. R. T. Barrett, "The Americans, the Navy Department and U-boat Tracking," paper written in 1946, with handwritten marginal comments and corrections by Roger Winn. PRO: ADM 223/286. The characterization of the lunch as "alcoholic" is Winn's own.

37. SRH 208, "United States Navy Submarine Warfare Reports, COMINCH to Admiralty," RG 457, NA, Washington, D.C. On Menzies's and Godfrey's objections to increasing SIGINT to the U.S. Navy, see Letter from "C" to the Prime Minister of 24 June 1941, PRO: HW 1/6, and DNI Memorandum to VCNS of 19 December 1941, PRO: ADM 205/9.

38. D.HIST. S. 1440-18, "OIC History," 1942, 6. Patrick Beesly, "Operational Intelligence and the Battle of the Atlantic: The Role of the Royal Navy's Submarine Tracking Room," in Boutilier, *RCN in Retrospect*, 185. NSHQ to OPNAV, 3 May 1942; NSHQ to Admiralty, 10 October 1941; file 1008-75-44, RG 24, vol. 3807, PARC.

39. "Western Approaches Convoy Instructions," pt. 300, quoted in Milner, *North Atlantic Run*, 60. John Terraine, *The U-boat Wars: 1916–1925* (New York: Henry Holt, 1989), 768.

40. The Admiralty, "Photographic Reconnaissance," PRO: ADM 223/84, 1.

41. Admiral Sir William James, "Operational Intelligence," 11 February 1937, PRO: ADM 223/84.

42. Hinsley, *British Intelligence*, 1:498–499. See also F. W. Winterbotham, *Secret and Personal* (London: William Kimber, 1969), 135–138, for the personal recollections of the chief of air intelligence of the Secret Intelligence Service on prewar SIS involvement.

43. PRO: ADM 223/84, 5.

44. "History of the U.S. Navy School of Photographic Interpretation," undated, Aviation History File, box 180, "Air/Ground Installations, Anacostia," Operational Archives, NHC, Washington, D.C.

252 Tracking the Axis Enemy

45. Constance Babington Smith, *Evidence in Camera: The Story of Photographic Intelligence in World War II* (London: Chatto and Windus, 1958), 145.

46. SPENAVO 130941 June 1941, Action to OPNAV. ALUSNA and SPENAVO London messages, September 1938–September 1941, file 1, folder 7, COMNAVEU Series I, Operational Archives, NHC, Washington, D.C.

47. SPENAVO 161330 June 1941, Action to OPNAV, Ibid.

48. "History of U.S. Navy School of Photographic Interpretation."

49. Hinsley, *British Intelligence*, 4:71. The authority for SIS involvement in refugee interrogations was, according to Hinsley, contained in CAB 93/2, which was not open to the public at the time of this writing.

50. M.R.D. Foot and J. M. Langley, *MI9: Escape and Evasion 1939–1945* (1979; reprint, London: Futura Publications, 1980), 13. "An escaper is someone who, having been captured, gets away; evader was never in enemy hands."

51. Head Foreign Intelligence Branch to Director of Naval Intelligence, memorandum of 27 June 1941, quoting Commander Ian Fleming, RNVR, who stated that "successful interrogation of prisoners of war, as practiced in the United Kingdom, is more of an art and not a science; that it depends, in obtaining successful results, upon the understanding and personality of trained interrogators." Box 228, RG 80, NA, Washington, D.C.

52. U.S. Naval Attaché London to Admiral Bailey's Committee, memorandum of 19 September 1940, file 20, Bailey Committee Memoranda 1940–1941, COMNAVEU Series II, Operational Archives, NHC, Washington, D.C.

53. Hinsley, *British Intelligence*, 2:33, 229.

54. Godfrey to Kirk, letter of 15 July 1941, box 228, RG 80, NA, Washington, D.C.

55. Hinsley, *British Intelligence*, 2:34. Brian Connell to Donald McLachlan, letter of 17 January 1967, McLachlan/Beesly file, MLBE 6/2, Churchill College Archives Center, Cambridge.

56. ONI Administrative History, 854.

57. U.S. Naval Attaché London to Admiral Bailey's Committee, memorandum of 19 September 1940, file 20, Bailey Committee Memoranda, 1940–1941, COMNAVEU Series II, Operational Archives, NHC, Washington, D.C.

58. OP-16-F to OP-16-F-9, memorandum of 2 July 1941, box 228, RG 80, NA, Washington, D.C.

59. "P/W Interrogation 1939–1945," undated, PRO: ADM 223/84, 53.

60. Ibid., 54, 55.

61. McLachlan, *Room 39*, 292.

62. S. J. Basset, "A Brief History of the Inter-Service Topographical Department (I.S.T.D.)," statement circulated as a Memorandum of Information by the U.S. Joint Intelligence Committee, 23 October 1943, entry 421, box 225, RG 165, Records of the War Department General and Special Staffs, NA, Washington, D.C., 1.

63. Godfrey to the Deputy Chief of the Naval Staff, minute of 21 June 1939, PRO: ADM 1/10218.

64. Beesly, *Very Special Admiral*, 211.

65. Basset, "Brief History of ISTD," 2.

66. Barry M. Katz, *Foreign Intelligence: Research and Analysis in the Office of Strategic Services 1942–1945* (Cambridge: Harvard University Press, 1989), 3. Katz (n. 2, chap. 1) gives as his source of information on the creation of OSS the official *War Report of the OSS*, which was declassified 17 July 1975, but he does not offer a page citation for the referenced quotation.

67. Ibid., xii. For an analysis of the impact of American scholars, especially those from Yale and the Ivy League, on OSS, see Robin W. Winks, *Cloak and Gown: Scholars in the Secret War 1939–1961* (New York: William Morrow, 1987).

68. Godfrey, *Memoirs*, 8:132.

69. COMNAVEU Administrative History, 125.

70. ONI Administrative History, 99. A Joint Intelligence Study Production Board flowchart is in entry 1, box 1, folder: JANIS, RG 226, Records of the Office of Strategic Services, NA, Washington, D.C.

71. Simpson, *Stark*, 118.

72. COMNAVEU Administrative History, 83.

73. Simpson, *Stark*, 136.

74. "FOLUS: British Liaison With COMNAVEU," file 54, COMNAVEU, British Liaison with, 1940–1943, COMNAVEU Series II, Operational Archives, NHC, Washington, D.C., 2.

75. Stark to Knox, letter of 3 June 1942. On occasion, Stark would write letters of general information to one person, then send copies to other friends. This copy has been preserved in the papers of Captain Harold D. Krick, USN, a former aide to Stark and family friend, and is in the possession of Barbara Krick Cooper, his daughter.

76. Alex Danchev, "Dill: Field-Marshal Sir John Dill," in *Churchill's Generals*, ed. John Keegan (New York: Grove Weidenfeld, 1991), 62.

77. "FOLUS: British Liaison With COMNAVEU," 3.

78. Ibid., 6.

79. Churchill to Stark, 13 March 1943, Stark papers, box A1, Correspondence, January–March 1943, Series II, Operational Archives, NHC, Washington, D.C. See also PRO: ADM 205/27 for the first sea lord's highly pragmatic reasoning behind the request.

80. W. Averell Harriman and Elie Abel, *Special Envoy to Churchill and Stalin, 1941–1946* (New York: Random House, 1975), 20.

81. "FOLUS: British Liaison With COMNAVEU," 7.

82. Churchill to Roosevelt, 15 April 1942, message serial no. 69, PRO: ADM 205/13, First Sea Lord's Records 1939–1945, correspondence with the Prime Minister January–May 1942.

83. King, Remarks to Officers Attending the 1 March 1943 Conference on Anti-Submarine Warfare, King Papers, box 3, Correspondence, March 1943, Series I, Operational Archives, NHC, Washington, D.C.

84. Libby to McDowell, 25 February 1942, box 40, Memos to/from British—1942, Series: Double Zero 1941–1946, Operational Archives, NHC, Washington, D.C.

85. Minutes of U.S. JCS 26th meeting, 28 July 1942, box 132, OSS 1942–1945, COMNAVEU Series II, Operational Archives, NHC, Washington, D.C.

86. Godfrey, Memorandum of Conversation with Cunningham, 22 June 1942, PRO: ADM 223/107.

87. Godfrey, minute of 10 August 1942, PRO: ADM 1/13497, Co-operation Between British and American Navies, 1942.

88. Cline, *Washington Command Post*, 164.

89. Alfred D. Chandler Jr. et al., eds, *The Papers of Dwight David Eisenhower: The War Years* (Baltimore: Johns Hopkins University Press, 1970), 1:421.

90. "History of AFHQ (Allied Forces Headquarters), Part One, August–December 1942," World War II Command File, box 192, Non-Navy Allied and Combined Commands, Operational Archives, NHC, Washington, D.C., 44–45.

91. Chandler, *Eisenhower Papers*, 1:447.

92. Samuel Eliot Morison, *Operations in North African Waters: October 1942–June 1943*, vol. 2 of *History of United States Naval Operations in World War II* (Boston: Little, Brown, 1950), 21, 33.

93. Ibid., 26, 237.

94. Hinsley, *British Intelligence*, 2:463.

95. Ibid., 2:475–476.

96. Andrew, *Her Majesty's Secret Service*, 15.

97. Godfrey to Chief of Staff, Mediterranean Fleet, 6 July 1939, PRO: ADM 1/10212, Intelligence Organization, Mediterranean Area.

98. Ibid.

99. Hinsley, *British Intelligence*, 2:478–482.

100. Ibid., 482.

Chapter 5. The Culmination

1. S. W. Roskill, *The Period of Balance*, vol. 2 of *The War at Sea 1939–1945* (London: HMSO, 1956), 485.

2. Samuel Eliot Morison, *The Battle of the Atlantic: September 1939–May 1943*, vol. 1 of *History of the United States Naval Operations in World War II* (Boston: Little, Brown, 1951), 407.

3. J. L. Granatstein, *Canada's War: The Politics of the Mackenzie King Government 1939–1945* (Toronto: Oxford University Press, 1975), 147–148. "Appreciation Western Atlantic Escorts—Organization," 29 January 1943, file S. 222-3-1, RG 24, vol. 11968, PARC.

4. NSHQ Ottawa to BAD Washington, 20 November 1942; BAD Washington to NSHQ Ottawa, late November 1942, file 282-1, RG 24, vol. 11976, PARC.

5. King to Nelles, message of 17 December 1942, file 282-1, RG 24, vol. 11976, PARC. Nelles to King, message of 15 January 1943, ibid. NSHQ to CTF 24, message of 16 Jan 1943, RG 24, vol. 12165 (messages), PARC. W.A.B. Douglas and Jürgen Rohwer, "'The Most Thankless Task' Revisited: Convoys, Escorts, and Radio Intelligence in the Western Atlantic, 1941–43," in Boutilier, *RCN in Retrospect*, 223. Milner, *North Atlantic Run*, 230.

6. M.S. 1017-10-39, "Development of Canadian Naval Policy," paragraph 33, file 9-4, RG 24, vol. 11963, PARC. DeMarbois, Biography, D.HIST 81/520/1480 DND, 471–472. "Naval Intelligence in Canada," Operational Intelligence, D.HIST. 81/520/1480, DND, 4–5. Minutes of the Atlantic Convoy Conference, 1–12 March 1943, Memorandum by the Chairman [King], RG 24, vol. 11968, PARC. Special sub-Committee on Communications [and] Operational Intelligence, Appendix A, ibid.

7. Knowles to Director of Naval History, letter of 23 October 1945, file 105, Knowles, Kenneth A., CAPT, USN, Report, 1946, COMNAVEU Series II, Operational Archives, NHC, Washington, D.C. Knowles was later selected by the director of naval history to be antisubmarine warfare historian for the Department of the Navy.

8. Samuel Eliot Morison, *The Atlantic Battle Won: May 1943–May 1945*, vol. 10 of *History of United States Naval Operations in World War II* (1956; reprint, Boston: Little, Brown, 1990), 12, 13.

9. Pound to Churchill, letter of 20 April 1943, PRO: ADM 205/32, First Sea Lord's Records 1939–1945, 1943—Misc. Correspondence. Also quoted in Stephen Roskill, *Churchill and the Admirals* (New York: William Morrow, 1978), 229.

10. Knowles to Director of Naval History, letter of 23 October 1945.

11. F-211 (Lt. John E. Parsons, USNR) to F-21 (Commander Kenneth A. Knowles, USN), memorandum, undated, box 10, SRMN-032, COMINCH File of Memoranda Concerning U-boat Tracking Operations, 2 January 1943–6 June 1945, RG 457, NA, Washington, D.C. Kenneth A. Knowles, "Ultra and the Battle of the Atlantic: An American View," in *Changing Interpretations and New Sources in Naval History: Papers From the Third United States Naval Academy History Symposium*, ed. Robert W. Love Jr. (New York: Garland, 1980), 448.

12. Michael Gannon, *Operation Drumbeat: The Dramatic True Story of Germany's First U-boat Attacks Along the American Coast in World War II* (New York: Harper and Row, 1990), 442 n. 5.

13. Knowles to Director of Naval History, 12 April 1946, file 105, Knowles, Kenneth A., CAPT, USN, Report 1946, COMNAVEU Series II, Operational Archives, NHC, Washington, D.C.

14. Redman (Op-20) to Horne (Vice Chief of Naval Operations), memorandum of 20 June 1942, SRH-268, "Advanced Intelligence Centers in the U.S. Navy," June 1942, RG 457, NA, Washington, D.C.

15. Knowles, "Ultra and the Battle of the Atlantic," 445.

16. Ronald Lewin, *Ultra Goes to War* (New York: McGraw-Hill, 1978), 64. According to Lewin, "Churchill himself, asking for Ultra papers, would say, 'Where are my eggs?': he had a way of referring to the people at Bletchley as 'the geese who laid golden eggs and never cackled.'"

17. Prime Minister to First Sea Lord, memorandum of 22 September 1942, PRO: ADM 205/14. Beesly, "Operational Intelligence Centre," 229.

18. Several sources exist for descriptions of the activities of the two submarine tracking rooms. On the American side, Parsons's memorandum on the functions of the "Secret Room" (see note 11) is of great value, as is Farago's description of

Knowles and the Tenth Fleet/COMINCH Staff's Atlantic Section (Farago, *Tenth Fleet*, 213–217). On the British side, Patrick Beesly's account (*Very Special Intelligence*, 167–171) remains definitive. More recently, Michael Gannon offered his portrait of a "normal" day in the British submarine tracking room that is clearly based on extensive research (*Operation Drumbeat*, 154–160).

19. F-211 to F-21, undated memorandum, box 10, SRMN-032, RG 457, NA, Washington, D.C.

20. COMINCH to Admiralty, 051330 June 1945, SRH-208, United States Navy Submarine Warfare Reports, COMINCH to Admiralty, RG 457, NA, Washington, D.C.

21. Roosevelt to Knox, handwritten memorandum, undated, but received by Knox on 16 August 1943, Knox Papers, box 4, General Correspondence 1943, Library of Congress, Washington, D.C. The underlining for emphasis was presumably done by FDR.

22. Farago, *Tenth Fleet*, 166, 167.

23. Knowles, "Ultra and the Battle of the Atlantic," 445. Julius A. Furer, *Administration of the Navy Department in World War II* (Washington, D.C.: Government Printing Office, 1959), figs. 5 and 8, depict the organization of the Office of the Chief of Naval Operations and that of the Headquarters, Commander in Chief, U.S. Fleet.

24. King and Whitehill, *Fleet Admiral King*, 471.

25. Hinsley, *British Intelligence*, 2:551.

26. Lewin, *Ultra Goes to War*, 58. For a detailed description of the operation of the bombes, see Gordon Welchman, *The Hut Six Story: Breaking the Enigma Codes* (New York: McGraw-Hill, 1982), appendix 1, 295 ff.

27. Kahn, *Seizing the Enigma*, 239. See also Burke, *Information and Secrecy*, for the history of development of the American machines.

28. Bradley F. Smith, *The Ultra-Magic Deals: And the Most Secret Special Relationship, 1940–1946* (Novato, Calif.: Presidio, 1992), 129. Kahn, *Seizing the Enigma*, 242. For a discussion of British reluctance to assist the United States in attacking German Enigma traffic, see Burke, *Information and Secrecy*, chap. 11.

29. Hinsley, *British Intelligence*, 2:553.

30. Rohwer, "Allied and Axis Radio Intelligence," 13.

31. Hinsley, *British Intelligence*, 2:554.

32. PRO: ADM 223/212, Admiralty Appreciation of the U-Boat Situation 1st August 1943. Morison, *Atlantic Battle Won*, 11. Roskill, *Navy at War*, 277.

33. Roskill, *Period of Balance*, 377.

34. Jürgen Rohwer, "Radio-Intelligence in the Battle of the Atlantic," in *The Missing Dimension: Governments and Intelligence Communities in the Twentieth Century*, ed. Christopher Andrew and David Dilks (Urbana: University of Illinois Press, 1984), 168. On the relative value of Ultra, see John Ferris, "Ralph Bennett and the Study of Ultra," *Intelligence and National Security* 6, no. 2 (1991), 473–486.

35. TG 21.14 Action Report of 10 September 1943, quoted in Williams, *Secret Weapon*, 218.

36. Marc Milner, *The U-boat Hunters: The Royal Canadian Navy and the Offen-*

sive Against Germany's Submarines (Annapolis, Md.: U.S. Naval Institute Press, 1994), 211.

37. Rohwer, "Allied and Axis Radio Intelligence," 24.

38. F. H. Hinsley, "The Influence of Ultra," in *Codebreakers*, ed. F. H. Hinsley and Alan Stripp (New York: Oxford University Press, 1993), 7.

39. Beesly, *Very Special Intelligence*, 110.

40. Dill to Cunningham, 15 November 1942, Cunningham letters 42–43, ADD MSS 52570, Cunningham Papers, British Library, London.

41. Arthur Bryant, *Turn of the Tide 1939–1943* (London: Collins, 1957), 541.

42. Forrest Pogue, *George C. Marshall: Organizer of Victory* (New York: Viking, 1973), 22.

43. Albert C. Wedemeyer, *Wedemeyer Reports!* (New York: Henry Holt, 1958), 179.

44. ONI Administrative History, 658.

45. Ibid., 98.

46. Ibid., 1478. Commander C. F. Baldwin, letter to Rear Admiral Train, DNI, of 26 August 1943, box 614, RG 80, NA, Washington, D.C., contains information on the JICA London proposal.

47. H. O. Dovey, "The Middle East Intelligence Centre," *Intelligence and National Security* 4 (October 1989), 802.

48. Zacharias to Major, letter of 27 January 1943, box 640, RG 80, NA, Washington, D.C.

49. Ellis M. Zacharias, *Secret Missions: The Story of an Intelligence Officer* (New York: G. P. Putnam's Sons, 1946), 301.

50. Ibid., 298.

51. Naval Liaison Officer with G-2 to ONI, memorandum of 3 July 1943, box 638, RG 80, NA, Washington, D.C.

52. ALUSNA Cairo to DNI, letter of 11 April 1942, box 296, RG 80, NA, Washington, D.C.

53. "A History of 30 Commando (Latterly Called 30 Assault Unit and 30 Advanced Unit)," undated, PRO: ADM 223/214, The 30th Assault Unit.

54. "Note by Godfrey dated 5.9.70," PRO: ADM 223/214.

55. "History of SIGINT Operations Undertaken by 30 Commando/30 AU." PRO: ADM 223/213, History of SIGINT Operations Undertaken by 30 Commando/30 AU,

56. Ibid.

57. "History of 30 Commando," PRO: ADM 223/214.

58. C. Morgan, "Seizure of French Cyphers," PRO: ADM 223/463, NID 9 and 17.

59. Ibid. In *British Intelligence in the Second World War*, Hinsley indicates that "copies of the French cyphers had been provided voluntarily by the commander of the [French] submarine *Narval* after her arrival at Malta and flown to the United Kingdom" (1:152, 153). However, the account of the theft of the ciphers is taken from a history of the British Naval Intelligence Division, on file at the Public Record Office, and is thought to be accurate.

60. Hinsley, *British Intelligence*, 1:154.

61. John Bryden, *Best Kept Secret: Canadian Secret Intelligence in the Second World War* (Toronto: Lester, 1993), 213.

62. Senior Naval Officer, JICA (North Africa) to ONI, 8 March 1943, Enclosure A (French memorandum for Major Delaney), box 644, RG 80, NA, Washington, D.C.

63. Officer-in-Charge, JICA, Navy Section, Casablanca to Lieutenant de Vaisseau Lux, French Liaison Officer (Bureau des Affaires Américaines), letter of 23 April 1943, box 644, RG 80, NA, Washington, D.C.

64. État Major, F.M.A. (Staff, French Naval Forces in Africa) to Officer in Charge, JICA, Navy Section, Casablanca, letter of 29 April 1943, box 644, RG 80, NA, Washington, D.C.

65. JICA North Africa to DNI, memorandum of 25 July 1943, box 640, RG 80, NA, Washington, D.C.

66. Hinsley, *British Intelligence*, 2:484.

67. David Hunt, *A Don at War*, rev. ed. (London: Frank Cass, 1990), 149.

68. Hinsley, *British Intelligence*, 2:584.

69. Kenneth Strong, *Intelligence at the Top: The Recollections of an Intelligence Officer* (London: Cassell, 1968), 81.

70. Dwight D. Eisenhower, *Crusade in Europe* (New York: Avon Books, 1968), 152.

71. Harry C. Butcher, *My Three Years With Eisenhower* (New York: Simon and Schuster, 1946), 278.

72. Chandler, *Eisenhower Papers*, 2:969, 1034.

73. Ibid., 2:971.

74. Strong, *Intelligence at the Top*, 81.

75. Eisenhower, *Crusade in Europe*, 194.

76. Henry Hewitt, "The Influence of Sea Power on the Victory in Europe," May 1945, quoted in Morison, *Operations in North African Waters*, 260.

77. Hinsley, *British Intelligence*, vol. 3, pt. 1, 232.

78. Samuel Eliot Morison, *Sicily-Salerno-Anzio: January 1943–June 1944*, vol. 9 of *History of United States Naval Operations in World War II* (Boston: Little, Brown, 1954), 37.

79. Andrew B. Cunningham, message of 2 July 1943, quoted in Morison, *Sicily-Salerno-Anzio*, 66.

80. Stephen E. Ambrose with Richard H. Immerman, *Ike's Spies: Eisenhower and the Espionage Establishment* (Garden City, N.Y.: Doubleday, 1981), 62.

81. Hinsley, *British Intelligence*, vol. 3, pt. 1, 85, 86.

82. Morison, *Sicily-Salerno-Anzio*, 23. Operation "Husky," PRO: ADM 223/209.

83. Hinsley, *British Intelligence*, vol. 3, pt. 1, 85, 86.

84. Morison, *Sicily-Salerno-Anzio*, 247.

85. Hinsley, *British Intelligence*, vol. 3, pt. 1, 110–113.

86. Chandler, *Eisenhower Papers*, 3:1552.

Chapter 6. Cracks in the Structure

1. First Sea Lord to First Lord, memorandum of 16 September 1942, PRO: ADM 205/20, Correspondence with the First Lord.

2. Beesly, *Very Special Admiral*, 231, 232.

3. Ewen Montagu, *Beyond Top Secret U* (London: Peter Davies, 1977), 23.

4. "Special Intelligence to Cunningham," file dated 8 September 1942, Godfrey Papers, box A (MS 81/05), National Maritime Museum Library, Greenwich, England. Subsequent comments attributed to Godfrey are, for the most part, drawn from his paper "Admiral Pound, Admiral Andrew Cunningham and Mr. Churchill," Dudley Pound Papers, DUPO 6/1, Churchill College Archives Center, Cambridge.

5. Beesly, *Very Special Admiral*, 232.

6. Pogue, *Marshall*, 21.

7. Beesly, *Very Special Admiral*, 233, 234.

8. Andrew, *Her Majesty's Secret Service*, 436.

9. Roskill, *Hankey*, 3:212, n. 2.

10. J. H. Godfrey, "Afterthoughts," PRO: ADM 223/619, The Navy and Naval Intelligence, 1939–1942.

11. "Notes on D.N.I.'s Visit to Washington, September–October 1942," 1 November 1942, PRO: ADM 223/107.

12. Ibid.

13. Ibid.

14. Dorwart, *Conflict of Duty*, 124, quoting Director of Naval Intelligence Walter S. Anderson.

15. "Notes on D.N.I.'s Visit to Washington," PRO: 223/107.

16. Churchill to First Lord and First Sea Lord, 9 March 1943, PRO: ADM 205/27, Correspondence with the Prime Minister, January–December 1943.

17. Rushbrooke to McLachlan, 16 June 1966, McLachlan and Beesly File 1/1, Churchill College Archives Center, Cambridge. On Rushbrooke as DNI, see Vice Admiral Ian Campbell's comments in MLBE 6/2.

18. Roskill, *Churchill and the Admirals*, 144.

19. Malcolm Muggeridge, "Book Review of a Very Limited Edition," *Esquire*, May 1966, 84, quoted in R. Harris Smith, *OSS: The Secret History of America's First Central Intelligence Agency* (Berkeley: University of California Press, 1972), 163.

20. Kermit Roosevelt, *The Overseas Targets*, vol. 2 of *War Report of the OSS* (1947; reprint, New York: Walker, 1976), 4.

21. COMNAVEU Administrative History, 127–128.

22. Simpson, *Stark*, 136.

23. Kittredge to Stark, memorandum of 4 March 1943, subject, "Organization and Plans of Resistance Movement in France," Stark Papers, Series II, box A1, "Correspondence April 1942–September 1943, Operational Archives, NHC, Washington, D.C. Colonel Haskill (OSS) to Commander Kittredge, 22 March 1943, "Informational Summaries of French Resistance Groups," folder

63, box 0050, entry 115, RG 226, Records of the Office of Strategic Services, NA, Washington, D.C.

24. Naval Attaché, Governments in Exile, London (Callan) to Director of Naval Intelligence, letter of 24 May 1943, box 638, RG 80, NA, Washington, D.C.

25. Navy Department (Op-16-FA-4), "Memorandum to Accompany Letter from Captain Callan," 16 June 1943, box 638, RG 80, NA, Washington, D.C.

26. SRH-153, Military Intelligence Service, War Department, Liaison Activities in the U.K. 1943–1945, box 25, RG 457, NA, Washington, D.C., 013–105. N.I.D. Section 12, Organisation and Duties, PRO: ADM 223/298.

27. War Department, "Proposed Operations by OSS in the European Theater, Comments on British C of S Recommendations, appendix to Enclosure B, JCS 305/D of 19 October 1943," folder ABC 361, box 357, entry 421, RG 165; Records of the War Department General and Special Staffs, NA, Washington, D.C.

28. Knox to Nimitz, letter of 5 May 1943, Secretary of the Navy Frank Knox Documents, box 6, folder 2, 31 December 1942–5 June 1943, Operational Archives, NHC, Washington, D.C.

29. NID 21, Historical Monograph, undated, PRO: ADM 223/90, Geographical Handbooks and Inter-Service Topographical Department.

30. ONI Administrative History, 484–485.

31. Navy Department, Memorandum for the Director, 6 July 1943, Subject: Liaison Trip to England, ONI Administrative History, 1360.

32. ONI Administrative History, 1361.

33. Henry M. Denham, quoted in McLachlan, *Room 39*, 189.

34. Henry M. Denham, "War Narrative, British Naval Attaché," Denham File 1, Churchill College Archives Center, Cambridge, 42.

35. Ibid., 10. Henry M. Denham, *Inside the Nazi Ring: A Naval Attaché in Sweden 1940–1945* (New York: Holmes and Meier, 1985), 28.

36. H.A.R. Philby, *My Silent War* (1968; reprint, New York: Ballantine Books, 1983), 49.

37. Hugh Trevor-Roper, *The Philby Affair: Espionage, Treason, and Secret Services* (London: William Kimber, 1968), 15.

38. ALUSNA Singapore 170225, dispatch of 18 November 1941 to OPNAV, box 55, RG 80, NA, Washington, D.C.

39. Stephen Roskill, *The Navy at War 1939–1945* (London: Collins, 1960), 125.

40. Montagu, *Beyond Top Secret U*, 90.

41. Director of Naval Intelligence to Director War Plans Division, memorandum of 16 April 1941, box 229, RG 80, NA, Washington, D.C.

42. ONI Administrative History, 530–531.

43. Beesly, *Very Special Admiral*, 142–143.

44. U.S. Naval Attaché Mexico City to Director of Naval Intelligence, letter of 4 November 1942, box 300, RG 80, NA, Washington, D.C.

45. Philby, *My Silent War*, 69.

46. Hinsley, *British Intelligence*, 4:148. J. C. Masterman, *The Double Cross System in the War of 1939 to 1945* (New Haven, Conn.: Yale University, 1972), 76.

47. Bickham Sweet-Escott, *Baker Street Irregular* (London: Methuen, 1965), 99.

48. Naval Intelligence Unit, Commander U.S. Naval Forces Northwest African Waters, to U.S. Naval Liaison Officer, Lisbon, Portugal, letter of 8 December 1943, box 647, RG 80, NA, Washington, D.C.

49. British Security Co-ordination, Washington, to Assistant Director of Naval Intelligence, letter of 9 September 1943, box 648, RG 80; Naval Intelligence Representative with Assistant Chief of Staff, G-2, War Department, to Director of Naval Intelligence, memorandum of 24 August 1943, box 647, RG 80; Hoover (FBI) to Train (DNI), letter of 6 July 1943, box 644, RG 80; Naval Intelligence Unit, Commander U.S. Naval Forces Northwest African Waters, to Director of Naval Intelligence, letter of 9 December 1943, box 647, RG 80, NA, Washington, D.C.

50. George F. Kennan, *Memoirs 1925–1950* (Boston: Little, Brown, 1967), 143.

Chapter 7. Interwar Faltering Steps

1. Edward S. Miller, *War Plan Orange: The U.S. Strategy to Defeat Japan, 1897–1945* (Annapolis, Md.: U.S. Naval Institute Press, 1991), 21.

2. John Costello, *The Pacific War* (New York: Rawson, Wade, 1981), 19.

3. John K. Fairbank, Edwin O. Reischauer, and Albert M. Craig, *East Asia: The Modern Transformation*, vol. 2 of *A History of East Asian Civilization* (Tokyo: Charles E. Tuttle, 1965), 219.

4. *Webster's Biographical Dictionary*, 1st ed. (Springfield, Mass.: G. & C. Merriam, 1957), 1448.

5. Costello, *Pacific War*, 8.

6. Kemp Tolley, *Yangtze Patrol: The U.S. Navy in China* (Annapolis, Md.: U.S. Naval Institute Press, 1971), 89, 90.

7. Joseph C. Grew, *Ten Years in Japan: A Contemporary Record Drawn From the Diaries and Private and Official Papers of Joseph C. Grew, United States Ambassador to Japan 1932–1942* (New York: Simon and Schuster, 1944), 234.

8. For details of U.S. Navy Plans Chief Captain Royal Ingersoll's inconclusive visit to London, see chapter 1.

9. Lewin, *American Magic*, 22, 23.

10. A. G. Denniston, "The Government Code and Cypher School Between the Wars," *Intelligence and National Security* 1 (January 1986), 54.

11. William F. Clarke, "Government Code and Cypher School: Its Foundation and Development With Special Reference to Its Naval Side," *Cryptologia* 11, no. 4 (October 1987), 221.

12. Lewin, *American Magic*, 18.

13. Clarke, "Government Code and Cypher School," 223.

14. Hinsley, *British Intelligence*, 1:40. PRO: Government Code and Cypher School: Far East Combined Bureau; Signals Intelligence Center in the Far East (HMS Anderson), (HW 4): HW 4/24, OIC and Special Intelligence Monographs, NID Archive, vol. 10A.

15. SRH-150, The Birthday of the Naval Security Group, RG 457, NA,

Washington, D.C., 3. For a rose-colored view of the U.S. Army's World War I cryptographic activities by one of its key players, see Herbert O. Yardley, *The American Black Chamber* (Indianapolis, Ind.: Bobbs-Merrill, 1931).

16. SRH-179, Radio Security Station Fourth Marine Regiment, Shanghai, China, in *Listening to the Enemy: Key Documents on the Role of Communications Intelligence in the War With Japan*, ed. Ronald H. Spector (Wilmington, Del.: Scholarly Resources, 1988), 28.

17. Safford to Director of Naval Communications, memorandum of 27 October 1924, ibid.

18. Laurence F. Safford, "A Brief History of Communications Intelligence in the United States," SRH-149, RG 457, NA, Washington, D.C., 4.

19. Ellis M. Zacharias to Commander in Chief, U.S. Asiatic Fleet, report of 28 November 1927, SRH-206, in Spector, *Listening to the Enemy*, 12–19.

20. "The Employment of Mobile Radio Intelligence Units by Commands Afloat During World War II," ibid., 77.

21. "The Far East Combined Bureau, Hongkong," PRO: ADM 223/494, British Intelligence in the Far East. John W. M. Chapman, "Pearl Harbor: The Anglo-Australian Dimension," *Intelligence and National Security* 4, no. 3 (July 1989), 456.

22. Air Chief Marshal Sir Robert Brooke-Popham, "Operations in the Far East," draft copy dated 8 July 1942, PRO: ADM/199/12.

23. Brooke-Popham, "Operations in the Far East," 7.

24. Barbara Winter, *The Intrigue Master: Commander Long and Naval Intelligence in Australia, 1913–1945* (Brisbane: Boolarong Press, 1995), 5. G. Hermon Gill, *Royal Australian Navy 1939–1942* (Canberra: Australian War Memorial, 1957), 71. Navy Department Melbourne to Acting Prime Minister, memorandum of 14 June 1918, file A 1608/1: B 15/1/1, Australian Archives, Canberra.

25. Frederick William Wheatley, "Unravelling of a German Code" (undated), Australian War Memorial [hereafter AWM] 252: A 228, Canberra, Australia.

26. "The Jellicoe Report, Summary," AWM 69: 23/29, Canberra.

27. David M. Horner, *High Command: Australia and Allied Strategy 1939–1945* (Canberra: Australian War Memorial, 1982), 224.

28. Gill, *RAN, 1939–1942*, 72. Winter, *Intrigue Master*, 12.

29. Winter, *Intrigue Master*, 26. For similar characterizations of Long, see "Papers of Cdr. G. M. Gill, Naval Historian," AWM: 3 DRL 6906, Canberra.

30. Report of Admiral of the Fleet Viscount Jellicoe of Scapa, "Naval Mission to New Zealand," August–October 1919, file EA-1: 85/1/20, pt. 1, NAHO, Wellington. "Pre War to 1942, New Zealand," PRO: ADM 223/494, Far East and Pacific History.

31. Admiralty to Commodore, New Zealand Squadron, letter of 23 April 1921; British Secretary of State for Dominion Affairs to the New Zealand Governor General, letter of 27 June 1925; Governor General to British Secretary of State for Dominion Affairs, letter of 29 December 1925; Commodore Commanding NZ Station to Naval Secretary, Wellington, memorandum of 15 March 1927, file N-1: 8/1/1, NAHO, Wellington.

32. "The Navy Department," file N/15/17, New Zealand Naval History, NAHO, Wellington. "Coast Watching," PRO: ADM 223/494.

33. NID paper dated 30 March 1940, PRO: ADM 223/495.

34. PRO: ADM 223/494.

35. New Zealand Chiefs of Staff Committee Paper, C.O.S./13 of 27 July 1938, file EA1: 84/3/37, NAHO, Wellington.

36. David Day, *The Great Betrayal: Britain, Australia & the Onset of the Pacific War 1939–1942* (New York: W. W. Norton, 1989).

37. Leutze, *Bargaining for Supremacy.*

38. DNI minute of 9 January 1934; Admiralty telegram to C-in-C China dated 12 January 1934; C-in-C China to Admiral Upham letter of 13 January 1934, PRO: ADM 116/3862, Naval Arrangements for War in the Far East.

39. Notes of a meeting held between Capt. Ingersoll, USN, Capt. R. Willson, USN (ALUSNA London), by Capt. Phillips, RN, Plans Division, Admiralty, 3 January 1938, PRO: ADM 116/3922, 46.

40. James R. Leutze, *A Different Kind of Victory: A Biography of Admiral Thomas C. Hart* (Annapolis, Md.: U.S. Naval Institute Press, 1981), 147.

41. Thomas C. Hart, memorandum, 1940, Papers of Admiral Thomas C. Hart, USN, folder, "Navy Miscellaneous 1939–1949," box 3, Operational Archives, NHC, Washington, D.C., 1.

42. Ibid., 2.

43. Hart to Stark, letter of 9 March 1940, Hart Papers, folder, "Stark and Hart 1939–1944," box 4, Operational Archives, NHC, Washington, D.C.

44. Leutze, *Different Kind of Victory,* 150.

45. Hart to Stark, letter of 7 June 1940, Hart Papers, folder, "Stark and Hart 1939–1944," box 4, Operational Archives, NHC, Washington, D.C.

46. Hart Diary, entry for 24 August 1939, quoted in Leutze, *Different Kind of Victory,* 152.

Chapter 8. Too Little, Too Late

1. Organization for National Security [NZ] to the Naval Secretary, Memorandum of 26 September 1939, file N-2: 30/21/1, pt. 1, NAHO, Wellington.

2. "Intelligence Conference with Captain Wylie, 4 January 1941, MP 1185/8/0, 1945/2/6; "Intelligence Liaison visit to Australia and New Zealand by Captain F. J. Wylie, R.N.," report dated 17 January 1941, MP 1185/8/0, 2021/5/529, Australian Archives, Melbourne.

3. Alan Stripp, *Codebreaker in the Far East* (London: Frank Cass, 1989), 96. John Prados, *Combined Fleet Decoded: The Secret History of American Intelligence and the Japanese Navy in World War II* (New York: Random House, 1995), 247.

4. ACNB to NZNB, Message of 9 April 1941, file N-2: 30/68/3, pt. 1; St. Aubyn to Chief of Naval Staff, Wellington, letter of 17 June 1941, file N-1: 13/18/61; Australian Naval Liaison Officer, Batavia to NZNB, 6 September 1941,

file N-1: 13/18/63, NAHO, Wellington. Long to Kennedy, letter of 27 October 1941, AWM 124: 4/292, Canberra.

5. Visit of NZ S.O. (O.& I.) to Melbourne, January 1940, N-2: 30/21/1, pt. 1, NAHO, Wellington.

6. CNS Wellington to St. Aubyn, letter of 12 March 1941, file N-2: 30/68/3, pt. 1; St. Aubyn to "Coops," letter of 26 April 1941, file N-1: 13/18/61, NAHO, Wellington.

7. "Combined Operational Intelligence Centre," file 188: 49 and file 69: 23/81, AWM, Canberra.

8. Long to Feldt, letter of 25 October 1940. file B 3476: 49C, AWM, Canberra.

9. Gill, *RAN, 1939–1942*, 420–421.

10. "Far East and Pacific History," PRO: ADM 223/494. Memorandum from the [N.Z.] Naval Secretary to the Minister of Defence of 16 August 1941, file EA-1: 85/1/11, NAHO, Wellington.

11. H. L. Shaw, "History of FECB (undated)," PRO: HW 4/25. Navy Department Minute to Director of Signals, RAAF, of 3 October 1941, AA 2969/1006 311/236G, Australian Archives, Canberra.

12. "Visit to Australia, Batavia and Singapore," report dated 9 June 1941, file N-1 22/2/48, NAHO, Wellington.

13. Samuel Eliot Morison, *The Rising Sun in the Pacific, 1931–April 1942*, vol. 3 of *History of United States Naval Operations in World War II* (Boston: Little, Brown, 1958), 53, n. 12.

14. Report of American-British-Dutch Conversations, Singapore, April 1941, Exhibit 50, PHA, *Hearings*, 1551.

15. The Chief of Naval Operations and the Chief of Staff, U.S. Army to the Special Naval Observer, London, and the Special Army Observer, London, letter of 3 July 1941, Exhibit 65, PHA, *Hearings*, 1678.

16. C. C. Bloch to H. E. Kimmel, letter of 19 March 1941, Bloch Papers, folder, "Husband E. Kimmel," box 2, Manuscript Division, Library of Congress, Washington, D.C.

17. Leutze, *Bargaining for Supremacy*, 263.

18. United States–British Staff Conversations, Report, Washington, D.C., 27 March 1941, Exhibit 49, PHA, *Hearings*, 1490.

19. The Chief of Naval Operations and the Chief of Staff, U.S. Army to the Special Naval Observer, London, and the Special Army Observer, London, letter of 3 July 1941, Exhibit 65, PHA, *Hearings*, 1677, 1678.

The observers were directed to inform the British chiefs of staff of the American chiefs' rejection of the Singapore report. It is unclear why the American chiefs chose to employ this rather unusual informational channel instead of the more customary one via the American military and naval attachés in London or the information exchange system newly authorized by the Anglo-American military chiefs in the ABC-1 conversations the previous month.

20. Ibid.

21. A summary of British proposals in the redrafted ADB-2 is contained in Admiralty to BAD, Washington, of 29 August 1941, passed to the Canadians and included in file S.213.3, RG 24, vol. 11967, PARC. The U.S. Navy's adverse reaction to the redraft is in GLEAM 150 of 11 October 1941, file S.213.4, ibid. British plans are in Admiralty to S.O. Force G [Phillips] message of 25 November 1941, file 213-3, ibid.

22. For detailed information on the Bailey Committee and the "Standardization of Arms" discussions, see chapter 2.

23. B.C.J. Fourteenth Meeting, United States Naval Co-operation, Minutes of Meeting held on Wednesday, 16th October (1940), PRO ADM 199/1159.

24. Leutze, *Different Kind of Victory*, 186.

25. British Embassy, Washington to Capt. Kirk (Director of Naval Intelligence), letter of 17 June 1941, Kirk Papers, folder, "Correspondence, Official and Personal 1939–1941," box 4, Operational Archives, NHC, Washington, D.C.

26. Quoted in Smith, "Admiral Godfrey's Mission," 448.

27. British Embassy, Washington to Capt. Kirk (Director of Naval Intelligence), letter of 17 June 1941, Kirk Papers, folder, "Correspondence, Official and Personal 1939–1941," box 4, Operational Archives, NHC, Washington, D.C.

28. Morison, *Rising Sun in the Pacific*, 49.

29. Lewin, *American Magic*, 47. Lewin comments in a footnote that "statements made by authorities like Safford and Layton before the Congressional Inquiry into the Pearl Harbor Attack amply confirm the extent of Anglo-American cooperation in this field before December 1941. Fabian testified that 'we had an established liaison with the British at Singapore' in evidence at the Hewitt Inquiry."

30. Hinsley, *British Intelligence*, 1:24.

31. Ibid., 1:40.

32. SRH-178, Radio Security Station Marine Detachment, Peiping, China, 1927–1935, RG 457, NA, Washington, D.C.

33. Spector, *Listening to the Enemy*, 9.

34. For details of the visit, see chapter 3.

35. Drea, *MacArthur's ULTRA*, 19.

36. A. Sinkov and Leo Rosen to Assistant Chief of Staff, G-2, report of 11 April 1941, SRH-145, RG 457, NA, Washington, D.C.

37. PRO: HW 4/25, Paymaster Captain H. L. Shaw, RN, "History of FECB" (undated).

38. Ibid.

39. Information developed from a telephonic interview with Captain Duane Whitlock, USN (ret.), who was assigned to Station CAST at the time of Burnett's visit and remained with the unit until after its evacuation from the Philippines in early 1942. Contrasting British information from Shaw, see "History of FECB," PRO: HW 4/25.

40. British observers with the U.S. Pacific Fleet, April 1941, file EA-1: 86/1/9, NAHO, Wellington. Admiralty to NSHQ, Ottawa, message of 20 November

1940, RG 24, vol. 11963, file N.M. O-160, PARC, Ottawa. John B. Hattendorf, ed., *On His Majesty's Service: Observations of the British Home Fleet From the Diary, Reports, and Letters of Joseph H. Wellings, Assistant U.S. Naval Attaché London, 1940–41* (Newport, R.I.: U.S. Naval War College, 1983).

41. Prime Minister, Canberra, to Prime Minister, Wellington, message of 1 November 1940; Casey to External Affairs, Canberra, telegram of 19 November 1940, file N-1: 22/4/47, NAHO, Wellington. Horner, *High Command*, 51.

42. "Instructions to Bailey, NZLO Washington," 16 July 1941, file N-1: 13/18/62; NZ Chief of Naval Staff to British Naval Observer to CINCPAC, letter of 12 May 1941, file N-1: 22/4/45, NAHO, Wellington.

43. SO(I), Wellington to U.S. Naval Observer, Wellington, memorandum of 31 July 1941; CINCPAC to Commander Parry, RN, memorandum of 2 August 1941; draft letter from SO(I) Wellington, to Commander Parry, RN, 30 August 1941, file N-2: 30/68/3, pt. 1, NAHO, Wellington.

44. ALUSNA & SPENAVO LONDON TO OPNAV, message, date-time group 140751 June 1941, folder 7, Secret/Confidential messages, May–June 1941, file 1, ALUSNA & SPENAVO London Messages, September 1938–September 1941, COMNAVEU Series I, Operational Archives, NHC, Washington , D.C.

45. OPNAV to ALUSNA & SPENAVO LONDON, message, date-time group 152120 July 1941, folder 9, Secret/Confidential messages, 4 July–15 July 1941, file 1, COMNAVEU Series I, Operational Archives, NHC, Washington, D.C.

46. ALUSNA & SPENAVO LONDON to OPNAV, message, date-time group 051443 August 1941; folder 11, Secret/Confidential messages, 29 July–17 August 1941; file 1, COMNAVEU Series I, Operational Archives, NHC, Washington, D.C.

47. British Secretary of State for Dominion Affairs to Prime Minister, Wellington, message of 2 September 1941, file N-2: 30/68/3, pt. 1, NAHO, Wellington.

48. CNO (Stark) to CINCAF (Hart), message, date-time group 012358, 2 December 1941, Navy Department, Strategic Plans Division Records, folder, "WPL-46, letters and dispatches, 12/40–12/41," Operational Archives, NHC, Washington, D.C.

49. Brooke-Popham to MacArthur, letter of 7 October 1941, General of the Army Douglas MacArthur, personal files, July 26–November 24, 1941, RG-2: USAFFE, reel #4, MacArthur Memorial Archives, Norfolk, Va.

50. Brink (U.S. Army Observer, Singapore) to MacArthur, message of 25 October 1941, ibid.

51. MacArthur to Brink, message of 30 October 1941, ibid.

52. MacArthur to Brink, message of 18 November 1941, ibid.

53. Morison, *Rising Sun in the Pacific*, 156.

54. Costello, *Pacific War*, 115. Martin Stephen, *The Fighting Admirals: British Admirals of the Second World War* (Annapolis, Md.: U.S. Naval Institute Press, 1991), 121–122.

55. Edwyn Gray, *Operation Pacific: The Royal Navy's War Against Japan* (Annapolis, Md.: U.S. Naval Institute Press, 1990), 22.

56. Leutze, *Different Kind of Victory*, 225.

57. Gray, *Operation Pacific*, 31.

58. Roberta Wohlstetter, *Pearl Harbor: Warning and Decision* (Stanford, Calif.: Stanford University Press, 1962), 272.

59. Morison, *Rising Sun in the Pacific*, 168–170.

60. Ibid., 174.

61. Not to be confused with Commander, later Captain, H. R. Sandwith, RN, who was DSD 9 in the Admiralty at much the same time and in the same line of work—D/F and "Y".

62. Loss of Singapore, February 1942, PRO: ADM 223/494, Far East and Pacific History, NID Archive vol. 40. For Burnett's confirmation of the warnings on Singapore, see John Ferris, "From Broadway House to Bletchley Park: The Diary of Malcolm Kennedy, 1934–46," *Intelligence and National Security* 4, no. 3 (July 1989), 441.

63. The last battle of Force Z is well described in Gray, *Operation Pacific*, chap. 3.

64. NZSM (Bailey) to Prime Minister (for CNS), message of 18 December 1941, RG 24, vol. 11979, file 141-8, PARC, Ottawa. Kennedy, Batavia, to DNIs Melbourne and Wellington, message of 18 December 1941, file N-1: 13/18/63, NAHO, Wellington.

65. Leutze, *Bargaining for Supremacy*, 266.

Chapter 9. Organizing for Cooperation

1. John Winton, *The Forgotten Fleet* (London: Michael Joseph, 1969), 19 n. 1.

2. Wavell to Churchill, signal of 21 February 1942, quoted in Ronald Lewin, *The Chief: Field Marshal Lord Wavell, Commander in Chief and Viceroy, 1939–1947* (New York: Farrar Straus Giroux, 1980), 139.

3. "ABDACOM," An Official Account of Events in the Southwest Pacific Command, January–February 1942, Section III, paragraph 12, Organization of Staff, (g) Intelligence Branch, PSF 1, Roosevelt Library.

4. "Evacuation of USN COMINT Personnel From Corregidor in WW II," SRH-207, RG 457, NA, Washington, D.C., 001. British Secretary of State for Dominion Affairs to Prime Minister, Wellington, telegram of 7 August 1942, EA-1: 84/3/1, pt. 1, NAHO, Wellington.

5. "Naval Security Group History to World War II," SRH-355, RG 457, NA, Washington, D.C.

6. In the U.S. Navy of 1942, men (since there were no women in the navy at that time) serving in the yeoman rate specialized in administrative and personnel matters and staffed ships' offices. In today's navy, persons performing duties similar to those of the yeomen at CAST would probably be designated communications technicians.

7. Clay Blair Jr., *Silent Victory: The U.S. Submarine War Against Japan*, vol. 1 (New York: J. B. Lippincott, 1975), 151, 171, 172.

8. "Evacuation of USN COMINT Personnel From Corregidor in WWII," SRH-207, RG 457, NA, Washington, D.C., 004.

9. Australian Naval Attaché, Washington, to CNS, message of 19 February 1942; CNS to Australian Legation, Washington, message of 23 February 1942, file A981: WAR 40, Australian Archives, Canberra.

10. In September 1941, the British Crown had approved the proposal that the New Zealand naval forces be designated the Royal New Zealand Navy.

11. Beasley to Long, letter of 15 January 1942; Naval Secretary to the Minister of Defence, minute of 13 January 1942; CNS Australia to CNS New Zealand 0314Z 18 Jan 1942, file N-2: 30/68/3, pt. 2, NAHO, Wellington.

12. Lieutenant Commander Beasley, "Narrative Report," dated 27 January 1942, N-2: 30/68/3, pt. 2, NAHO, Wellington.

13. BAD Washington message of 26 January 1942, RNZN War Diary, N-1: 14/2; Notes for NZ Liaison Officer, February 1942; CNS New Zealand to NZNB of 14 February 1942, N-1: 13/18/73, NAHO, Wellington.

14. NZLO, COMANZAC, to CNS, letter of 13 April 1942, N-1: 13/18/73, NAHO, Wellington.

15. Ronald H. Spector, *Eagle Against the Sun: The American War With Japan* (London: Penguin Books, 1984), 144.

16. Cline, *Washington Command Post*, 100–102, 378–379, gives details of the command structure for both the Pacific Ocean and the Southwest Pacific Areas.

17. ALUSNA Wellington letter to Deputy Chief of the Naval Staff dated 9 April 1942 and Deputy CNS reply thereto dated 10 April 1942, N-2: 8/11/14a; COMANZAC 0708Z/14, dated 14 April 1942, War Diary, N-1: 14/2, NAHO, Wellington.

18. Samuel Eliot Morison, *Coral Sea, Midway and Submarine Actions, May 1942–August 1942*, vol. 4 of *History of United States Naval Operations in World War II* (Boston: Little, Brown, 1950), 255.

19. G. Hermon Gill, *Royal Australian Navy 1942–1945* (Canberra: Australian War Memorial, 1968), 34.

20. COM 14 [Commandant Fourteenth Naval District, Hawaii] Combat Intelligence Bulletin No. 1, dated 16 January 1942, SRMD 009, "JICPOA/F-22 File of Administrative Letters/Correspondence, January 1942–September 1945," RG 457, NA, Washington, D.C., 010.

21. COMINCH 201730 January 1942, CINCPAC Command Summary, 179.

22. OPNAV 111852 February 1942, SRMD 009, RG 457, NA, Washington, D.C., 005.

23. "U.S. Intelligence Organisation in the Pacific," PRO: ADM 223/494, 5.

24. "HMS Anderson," PRO: HW4/24.

25. First Sea Lord to Ghormley [COMNAVEU], letter of 1 February 1942, PRO: ADM 205/19, Correspondence with U.S. Authorities.

26. COMINCH 011600 April 1942, CINCPAC Command Summary, 326.

27. United States Naval Liaison Office Colombo, Ceylon [Lammers], to Director of Naval Intelligence [Wilkinson], letter of 26 May 1942, folder A8-2/EF 13 (May–Jun), box 296, RG 80, NA, Washington, D.C.

28. Paul S. Dull, *A Battle History of the Imperial Japanese Navy (1941–1945)* (Annapolis, Md.: U.S. Naval Institute Press, 1978), 98, 99.

29. Morison, *Coral Sea*, 63.

30. Frederick Parker, "Cryptanalysis—Contributions and Controversy," paper delivered at a retrospective symposium on the Second World War, The Issue in Doubt, presented by the Admiral Nimitz Foundation, San Antonio, Tex., 26 March 1992, 268.

31. Dull, *Battle History*, 120.

32. John Costello, "Cryptanalysis—Contributions and Controversy," paper delivered at a retrospective symposium on the Second World War, The Issue in Doubt, presented by the Admiral Nimitz Foundation, San Antonio, Tex., 26 March 1992, 101.

33. Parker, "Cryptanalysis," 280.

34. *United States Naval Chronology, World War II* (Washington, D.C.: Government Printing Office, 1955), 27.

35. Mitsuo Fuchida and Masatake Okumiya, *Midway: The Battle That Doomed Japan, the Japanese Navy's Story* (Annapolis, Md.: U.S. Naval Institute Press, 1955), 232. FRUMEL Records—Midway, file B 5555 #4, Australian Archives, Melbourne.

36. Morison, *Coral Sea*, 81.

37. Roskill, *War at Sea*, 2:37, 38.

38. Gill, *RAN 1942–1945*, 59.

39. FRUMEL Records—Midway, 15 May, file B 5555 #4, Australian Archives, Melbourne; emphasis added.

40. Preface to "A Brief History of the G-2 Section GHQ, SWPA," RG 23, reel 924, MacArthur Memorial Archives, Norfolk, Va. Although this is a staff study, with the authors or the editor unnamed, the preface was almost certainly written by Willoughby himself and is certainly an accurate statement of his views.

41. Drea, *MacArthur's ULTRA*, 24. Blair, *Silent Victory*, 278, 79.

42. FRUMEL news memorandum for the month ending 15 February 1944 noted reassignments of liaison officers. SRH-275, Op-20-G File of Fleet Radio Unit Melbourne (FRUMEL), 28 June 1943–2 September 1945, RG 457, NA, Washington, D.C., 53.

43. D. M. Horner, "Special Intelligence in the South-West Pacific in World War II," *Australian Outlook* 32 (December 1978), 313. Drea, *MacArthur's ULTRA*, 20, 21.

44. Undated and unsigned report for the period summer 1942, PRO: ADM 223/297, "NID—Notes on and Extracts From Volumes of Papers Collected by Admiral Godfrey." Memo to General Akin dated 2 January 1943, file B 5435/1: 22, Australian Archives, Melbourne. Edward J. Drea, "Were the Japanese Army Codes Secure?" *Cryptologia* 19, no. 2 (April 1995), 130. The author is indebted to Mr. Drea for bringing this and other useful material to his attention.

45. S. D. Waters, *The Royal New Zealand Navy*, vol. of *Official History of New Zealand in the Second World War 1939–1945* (Wellington: War History Branch, Department of Internal Affairs, 1956). Gill, *RAN, 1942–1945*, 122. Morison, *Coral Sea*, 251, 266.

46. E. P. Forrestel, *Admiral Raymond A. Spruance, USN: A Study in Command* (Washington, D.C.: Government Printing Office, 1966), 63.

47. ARCTIC 220, dated 9 July 1942, AWM 124: 4/135, AWM, Canberra.

48. J. G. Coates, MP, to Admiral Halsey, letter of 31 October 1942, file EA-1: 59/2/12, pt. 1, NAHO, Wellington. Waters, *Royal New Zealand Navy*, 442, PRO: ADM 223/494.

49. Walter Lord, *Lonely Vigil: The Coastwatchers of the Solomons* (New York: Viking, 1977), 5, 6.

50. *Naval Staff History, Campaigns in the Solomons and New Guinea*, vol. 3 of *The War With Japan* (London: Admiralty, 1956), 33 n 1. Munroe Leaf's *Ferdinand the Bull* preferred to smell the flowers than to fight.

51. Gill, *RAN, 1942–1945*, 8.

52. Ibid., 122–123.

53. DNI Wellington, 2320Z/30 of 1 October 1942, New Zealand Navy War Diary, pt. 9, file N-1: 14/2, NAHO, Wellington. Long to Feldt, letter of 12 October 1942, file B 3476: 49C, Australian Archives, Melbourne.

54. *Naval Staff History, Campaigns in the Solomons and New Guinea*, 33.

55. "A Brief History of the G-2 Section," 39. Fleet Admiral William F. Halsey, quoted in F. A. Rhoades, *Diary of a Coastwatcher in the Solomons* (Fredericksburg, Tex.: Admiral Nimitz Foundation, 1982), back cover.

56. King to Commandant of the Marine Corps, endorsement dated 31 March 1942, to CMC letter dated 24 March 1942, box 293, RG 80, NA, Washington, D.C.

57. King to Nimitz, memorandum of 19 December 1942, enclosing a paper, "Establishment of Advanced Joint Intelligence Center," dated 16 December 1942, King Papers, Series I, Correspondence, box 3, December 1942, Operational Archives, NHC, Washington, D.C.

58. Holmes, *Double-Edged Secrets*, 36, 37.

59. SRH-020, "Narrative, Combat Intelligence Center, Pacific Ocean Area," box 8, RG 457, NA, Washington, D.C., 7.

60. Nimitz to King, letter of 28 May 1942, box 293, R 80, NA, Washington, D.C.

61. King to Director of Naval Intelligence, endorsement of 12 June 1942 to CINCPAC letter of 28 May 1942, SRMN-015, "The Establishment of Advanced Intelligence Centers, May 1942–August 1943," RG 457, NA, Washington, D.C., 4.

62. CINCPAC Command Summary, 670, SRH-020, RG 457, NA, Washington, D.C., 9.

63. Enclosure A to Vice Chief of Naval Operations letter, "Establishment of Advanced Intelligence Centers," of 8 September 1942, SRMN-015, RG 457, NA, Washington, D.C., 27.

Chapter 10. "Support" Vice "Cooperation"

1. Nimitz to King, letter of 13 December 1944, Papers of Fleet Admiral Chester W. Nimitz, file 19, Series XIII, Operational Archives, NHC, Washington, D.C.

2. Winton, *Forgotten Fleet*, 18.

3. Burnett, "Report of Visit to 'US Naval Radio Intelligence Centre,' Washington, 5 November–30 December 1942," PRO: ADM 223/297.

4. "Aide-Mémoire by Admiral Somerville," enclosure to letter from Stark to King, 22 June 1943, King Papers, Series I, box 3. Noble to King, letter of 22 July 1943, Double Zero 1941–1946 file, box 41, "Memo to/from British, 1943–1944," Operational Archives, NHC, Washington, D.C.

5. Comment by Commander in Chief United States Fleet, on Admiral Somerville's aide-Mémoire, dated 18 June 1943, King Papers, Series I, box 3, June 1943, Operational Archives, NHC, Washington, D.C.

6. "Notes on D.N.I.'s Visit to Washington, September October 1942," dated 1 November 1942, PRO: ADM 223/107.

7. Ibid.

8. Beasley to Long, letter of 22 March 1943, file N-2: 8/1/18, pt. 1; NZLO ComSoPac to NZNB, Memo #8 of 7 April 1943, file N-2: 8/6/23, NAHO, Wellington. PRO: ADM 223/297, N.I.D. vol. 42. "Far East and Pacific, III, Special," ADM 223/494.

9. Keith Jeffery, ed., "The Government Code and Cypher School: A Memorandum by Lord Curzon," *Intelligence and National Security* 1 (September 1986), 455.

10. Layton, *"And I Was There,"* 366–367, 420–422.

11. J.R.R. [probably Cdr. John R. Redman] to Director of Naval Communications, memorandum of 18 March 1943, SRMD-009, RG 457, NA, Washington, D.C., 030.

12. Memorandum for Op-20, dated 18 May 1943, ibid., 034–035.

13. OPNAV 080710 July 1944, to GC&CS and [British] Fleet Radio Unit Eastern Fleet, ibid., 171.

14. CINCPAC 080239 July 1944 to OPNAV, ibid.

15. DNC [director of naval communications] to Fleet Radio Unit Pacific [Pearl Harbor] 020333 August 1944, ibid., 196.

16. SRH-020, RG 457, NA, Washington, D.C., 13.

17. Memorandum for Op-20 dated 10 April 1943, SRMN-015, RG 457, NA, Washington, D.C., 38.

18. Officer-in-Charge, Advanced Intelligence Center, NorPac Area to CNO, letter of 5 November 1943, folder A7-5/AV–A7-5/EF, box 638, RG 80, NA, Washington, D.C.

19. Samuel Eliot Morison, *Breaking the Bismarcks Barrier, 22 July 1942–1 May 1944*, vol. 6 of *History of United States Naval Operations in World War II* (Boston: Little, Brown, 1950), 10, 11.

20. Minutes of the 128th Meeting of the Chiefs of Staff, 1 October 1943; Memorandum from the Ministry of Works to the Minister of Defence, 29 May 1944, file EA-1: 85-1-11, NAHO, Wellington.

21. Captain Laird to C.O.I.S. EF (undated), PRO: ADM 223/494.

22. Louis Morton, *Strategy and Command: The First Two Years*, vol. 10 of *The United States Army in World War II: The War in the Pacific* (Washington, D.C.: Department of the Army, 1962), 253.

23. "A Brief History of the G-2 Section," 75, 76.

24. Alan Powell, *War by Stealth: Australians and the Allied Intelligence Bureau 1942–1945* (Melbourne: Melbourne University Press, 1996).

25. MacArthur to Royle [Australian chief of naval staff], letter dated 2 July 1942, AWM 54: 423/6/5, Canberra. Powell, *War by Stealth,* 77.

26. Powell, *War by Stealth,* 332. Memo on the Duties of the Far Eastern Liaison Office prepared by its Director: Commander J.C.R. Proud, RANVR, dated 4 December 1943, AWM 3 DRL 6643: 2/56.5; CGS Australian Forces to Distribution, letter dated 5 July 1944, AWM 54: 423/2/31, Canberra. "Organization of FELO," dated June 1945, file A3269: T1, Australian Archives, Canberra.

27. Commander Allied Naval Forces (Kinkaid) to CINC, SWPA, letter of 23 December 1944, Australian Archives, A3269/1 N1 (vol. 1), Canberra. PRO: ADM 223/494.

28. CTF 71 (Admiral Christie) to Commander Seventh Fleet, letter of 12 November 1944, Australian Archives, A 3269/1 N1 (vol. 1), Canberra. Powell, *War by Stealth,* 170–173. G. B. Courtney, *Silent Feet: The History of 'Z' Special Operations 1942–1945* (Melbourne: R. J. & S. P. Austin, 1993), 139–145.

29. Allied Land Forces, SWPA, to CinC New Guinea Force, letter of 28 October 1942, AWM: 3 DRL 6643: 2/56.7, Canberra. "Allied Translation & Interpretation Section," PRO: ADM 223/494.

30. PRO: ADM 223/494.

31. Commander Southwest Pacific Force to Vice Chief of Naval Operations, letter of 25 November 1942, SRMN-015, RG 457, NA, Washington, D.C., 29, 30.

32. Seventh Fleet Letter 9L-44 of 18 May 1944, World War II Command file, box 277, "Fleets Numbered," folder: Seventh Fleet Letters 1944, Operational Archives, NHC, Washington, D.C. A copy of the same letter appears in Royal Australian Navy file B 3476: 159, Australian Archives, Melbourne.

33. McCollum, *Reminiscences,* 330–331.

34. "History of Intelligence Center Seventh Fleet," World War II Command File, box 277, folder: History of Intelligence Center Seventh Fleet, Operational Archives, NHC, Washington, D.C.

35. PRO: ADM 223/494.

36. PRO: ADM 223/297, ADM 223/494.

37. "Combined Operational Intelligence Centre," AWM 69: Item 23/81, Canberra.

38. Andrew Brown Cunningham, *A Sailor's Odyssey: The Autobiography of Admiral of the Fleet Viscount Cunningham of Hyndhope* (London: Hutchinson, 1951), 585. Correlli Barnett, *Engage the Enemy More Closely: The Royal Navy in the Second World War* (London: Hodder and Stoughton, 1991), 873.

39. Winton, *Forgotten Fleet,* 34.

40. President Roosevelt to Prime Minister, letter of 13 March 1944, quoted in Winston S. Churchill, *Closing the Ring,* vol. 5 of *The Second World War* (Boston: Houghton Mifflin, 1951), 578.

41. C. Julian Wheeler to Nimitz, letter of 13 November 1944, Double Zero file 1941–1946, folder 30, box 40, Operational Archives, NHC, Washington, D.C.

42. E. B. Potter, *Nimitz* (Annapolis, Md.: U.S. Naval Institute Press, 1976), 312.

43. Noble to Cunningham, letter of 12 January 1944, Papers of Admiral of the Fleet Sir Andrew B. Cunningham, ADD MSS 52571, letters 1943–1944, British Library.

44. *Naval Staff History, The Advance to Japan*, vol. 6 of *War With Japan* (London: Admiralty, 1959). British Source file, box 52, Operational Archives, NHC, Washington, D.C., 11.

45. Ibid, 14.

46. Stephen, *The Fighting Admirals*, 190.

47. Winston S. Churchill, *Triumph and Tragedy*, vol. 6 of *The Second World War* (Boston: Houghton Mifflin, 1953), 152. Cunningham, *Sailor's Odyssey*, 612.

48. McMorris to Nimitz, memorandum of 24 November 1944, Nimitz Papers, Series XIII, file 19, Operational Archives, NHC, Washington, D.C.

49. Wheeler to Nimitz, letter of 13 November 1944, Double Zero file 1941–1946, folder 30, box 40, Operational Archives, NHC, Washington, D.C.

50. Austin to Nimitz, memorandum of 8 December 1944, Double Zero file 1941–1946, folder 24, box 2, Operational Archives, NHC, Washington, D.C. "Report on Intelligence Conferences, Pearl Harbour, 17th. to 21st. December 1944"; Sheppard to Hillgarth, letter of 27th December 1944, PRO: ADM 223/495.

51. Holmes, *Double-Edged Secrets*, 204.

52. Samuel Eliot Morison, *Victory in the Pacific 1945*, vol. 14 of *History of United States Naval Operations in World War II* (Boston: Little, Brown, 1961), 106.

53. Somerville to King, letter of 8 March 1945, Double Zero file 1941–1946, folder 34, box 2, Operational Archives, NHC, Washington, D.C.

54. Joint Intelligence Committee to the Joint Chiefs of Staff, memorandum of 17 July 1944, Double Zero file 1941–1946, folder 138, box 37, Operational Archives, NHC, Washington, D.C.

55. S. W. Roskill, *The Offensive*, vol. 3, pt. 2 of *The War at Sea* (London: HMSO, 1961), 337. "Operation ICEBURG. Y Services Afloat," PRO: ADM 223/494.

56. One British intercept ("Y") group was embarked in HMS *King George V*, the fleet flagship, and one in HMS *Indomitable*, the aircraft carrier squadron commander's flagship. John Winton, *ULTRA in the Pacific* (Annapolis, Md.: U.S. Naval Institute Press, 1993), 217.

57. RADM Donald M. Showers, USN (ret.), "Oral History," unpublished ms., dated 18 September 1990, prepared by the Office of Naval Intelligence for transfer to the Naval Historical Center. Text of the Intelligence Agreement, Appendix I, to "Report on Intelligence Conferences, Pearl Harbour," dated 26 December 1944, PRO: ADM 223/495.

58. ADM 223/297; ADM 223/494.

59. Antony Best, "Constructing an Image: British Intelligence and Whitehall's Perception of Japan, 1931–1939," *Intelligence and National Security* 11, no. 3 (July 1996), 417. John W. M. Chapman, "Signals Intelligence Collaboration Among

the Tripartite Pact States on the Eve of Pearl Harbor," *Japan Forum* 3 (October 1991), 236. For information on German and Japanese liaison by submarine, see Allison W. Saville, "German Submarines in the Far East," *U.S. Naval Institute Proceedings* (August 1961), 80–92, and "Blockade Running Between Europe and the Far East by Submarine 1942–1944," report dated 1 December 1944, Ronald Lewin Papers, RLEW 5/3, Churchill College Archives Center, Cambridge.

60. Carl Boyd, *Hitler's Japanese Confidant: General Oshima Hiroshi and MAGIC Intelligence, 1941–1945* (Lawrence: University Press of Kansas, 1993), 37.

61. "Sigint Cooperation—A Warning," PRO: ADM 223/284. A.D.I. Science, "Air Technical Liaison Between Germany and Japan," Air Scientific Intelligence report #131 of 16 October 1944, Ronald Lewin Papers, RLEW 5/4, Churchill College Archives Center, Cambridge.

62. David Stevens, *U-boat Far From Home: The Epic Voyage of U-862 to Australia and New Zealand* (London: Allen and Unwin, 1997), 156, 157, provides an example of this type of SIGINT-initiated, antisubmarine operation.

63. "General Comments on Some of the Main Sources of BAY/HP.s," PRO: ADM 223/298.

64. E. B. Potter, *Bull Halsey* (Annapolis, Md.: U.S. Naval Institute Press, 1985), 345.

65. SRH-197, "U.S. Navy Communication Intelligence Organization, Liaison and Collaboration 1941–1945," RG 457, NA, Washington, D.C., 23–25.

66. "History of Intelligence Center Seventh Fleet," 4.

67. Holmes, *Double-Edged Secrets*, 215. Showers, "Oral History," 36.

68. PRO: ADM 223/494.

Chapter 11. Twilight of Cooperation

1. Forrest C. Pogue, *The Supreme Command*, vol. 4 of *The United States Army in World War II: The European Theater of Operations* (Washington, D.C.: Office of the Chief of Military History, Department of the Army, 1954), 15.

2. Roskill, *War at Sea*, vol. 3, pt. 2, 6.

3. Stephen, *Fighting Admirals*, 206. Robert W. Love Jr. and John Major, eds., *The Year of D-Day: The 1944 Diary of Admiral Sir Bertram Ramsay* (Hull, U.K.: University of Hull Press, 1994), details some of the pressures experienced by Ramsay as the scope of Overlord was enlarged and the irritations he felt from his American and British admirals as planning progressed.

4. Samuel Eliot Morison, *The Invasion of France and Germany 1944–1945*, vol. 11 of *History of United States Naval Operations in World War II* (Boston: Little, Brown, 1957), 29–30.

5. Chandler, *Eisenhower Papers*, 3:1654.

6. Strong, *Intelligence at the Top*, 127.

7. Pogue, *Supreme Command*, 71.

8. Strong, *Intelligence at the Top*, 133.

9. Pogue, *Supreme Command*, 71.

10. Hinsley, *British Intelligence* vol. 3, pt. 2, 751.

11. "Operations Overlord and Neptune," NID minute of 13 June 1944, PRO: ADM 223/287, NID vol. 51 concerning Overlord and Neptune.

12. "Remarks by Mr. Pritchett on Preparation of Intelligence for Overlord," PRO: ADM 223/287.

13. "Report by the Naval Commanders, Western Task Force," vol. 3 of "Report by the Allied Naval Commander-in-Chief Expeditionary Force on Operation 'Neptune,'" 13.

14. "Operations Overlord and Neptune," PRO: ADM 223/287.

15. Ibid.

16. Milner, *U-boat Hunters*, 135 ff.

17. Hinsley, *British Intelligence*, vol. 3, pt. 2, 750.

18. Ralph Bennett, *Ultra in the West: The Normandy Campaign 1944–45* (New York: Scribner's, 1979), 29.

19. Ambrose, *Ike's Spies*, 66.

20. Marshall to Eisenhower, letter of 15 March 1944, quoted ibid. Hinsley (*British Intelligence*, vol. 3, pt. 2, 781, footnote) claimed that just the opposite was the case—that the British SLUs presented Ultra to their commanders that had been "collated with other sources," whereas American SLUs handled Ultra "in isolation from other intelligence."

21. Hinsley, *British Intelligence*, vol. 3, pt. 2, 783.

22. Covering letter to "Report by the Allied Naval Commander-in-Chief Expeditionary Force on Operation 'Neptune,'" Appendix 3, 50.

23. "Provision, Collection and Dissemination of Intelligence," Naval Expeditionary Force Planning Memoranda of 10 April 1944, Operational Plans file, box: ANCXF (thru April 1944), Operational Archives, NHC, Washington, D.C.

24. Covering letter to "Report by the Allied Naval Commander-in-Chief Expeditionary Force on Operation 'Neptune,'" Appendix 3, 51–52.

25. The story of the E-boats' successes and their eventual destruction is well told in James Foster Tent's *E-boat Alert: Defending the Normandy Invasion Fleet* (Annapolis, Md.: U.S. Naval Institute Press, 1996), kindly brought to my attention by Michael Briggs, editor, University Press of Kansas.

26. Love and Major, *Year of D-Day*, 89.

27. Morison, *Invasion of France and Germany*, 35.

28. "Operations of the 30 Assault Unit," Annex B to vol. 1 of "Report by the Allied Naval Commander-in-Chief Expeditionary Force on Operation 'Neptune,'" 53.

29. "Report by the Naval Commanders, Western Task Force," vol. 3 of "Report by the Allied Naval Commander-in-Chief Expeditionary Force on Operation 'Neptune,'" 13. Wyman H. Packard, *A Century of U.S. Naval Intelligence* (Washington, D.C.: Department of the Navy, 1996), 429.

30. Maurice Matloff, *Strategic Planning for Coalition Warfare 1943–1944*, vol. 4 of *The United States Army in World War II: The War Department* (Washington, D.C.: Office of the Chief of Military History, Department of the Army, 1959), 490.

31. S. W. Roskill, *The Offensive 1st June 1942–14th August 1945*, vol. 3, pt. 2 of *The War at Sea 1939–1945* (London: HMSO, 1961), 86.

32. Morison, *Invasion of France and Germany*, 234.

33. Final Report of Commander Eighth Fleet on the Invasion of Southern France, Chap. 2, Intelligence, 29 November 1944, PRO: ADM 199/909, "The Invasion of Southern France," 163.

34. Ibid., 162.

35. Hinsley, *British Intelligence*, vol. 3, pt. 2, 479. Memo from Director of Plans, Canadian Naval Staff Headquarters to ACNS, 31 October 1944, file 1655-2, RG 24, vol. 8150, PARC. Interview of a former watchkeeper by the author. Roger Sarty, "The Limits of Ultra: The Schnorkel U-boat Offensive Against North America, November 1944–January 1945," *Intelligence and National Security* 12 (April 1997), 49.

36. Morison, *Invasion of France and Germany*, 326. Love and Major, *Year of D-Day*, 188 n 1.

37. Noble to Cunningham, letter of 12 January 1944, Cunningham, ADD MSS 52571, letters 1943–1944, British Library.

38. Noble to First Sea Lord, 24 January 1944; Noble to First Sea Lord, 30 January 1944; Minute from D. of P., Naval Staff to First Sea Lord dated 5 February 1944, Ibid.

39. Rushbrooke to Stark, letter of 30 January 1944; Stark to Rushbrooke, letter of 31 January 1944, Stark Papers, Series II, box A-2, file: Correspondence Jan–Feb 1944, Operational Archives, NHC, Washington, D.C.

40. Director of Scientific Research to DNI and Controller (R&D), paper of 12 April 1944; Director of Scientific Research to DNI, minute of 4 July 1944, PRO: ADM 116/5395.

41. Katz, *Foreign Intelligence*, 82, quoting William Langer, chief of R&A.

42. Gilbert to Hajo Holborn, et al., 28 November 1944, in Katz, *Foreign Intelligence*, 82.

43. "Distribution of U.S. J.I.C. Papers to the British J.I.C.," 10 March 1945, folder: ABC 344.8, Box 225, Entry 421, Record Group 165, Records of the War Department General and Special Staffs, NA, Washington, D.C.

44. Memorandum from the British naval attaché, Washington, of 3 August 1945, Minute from the DNI of 29 August 1945, PRO: 223/495, NID Archive vol. 41.

45. ALNAV #244 of 9 August 1945, forwarded to Admiralty on 14 September 1945 and circulated under a DNI Minute Sheet of 2 October 1945, PRO: ADM 223/495. Minute J.C.S. Slessor to VCAS, 16 July 1945, quoted in Richard Aldrich, "Imperial Rivalry: British and American Intelligence in Asia, 1942–46," *Intelligence and National Security* 3, no. 1 (January 1988), 55 n. 155.

46. Pogue, *Supreme Command*, 515.

47. James Bamford, *The Puzzle Palace: A Report on America's Most Secret Agency* (Boston: Houghton Mifflin, 1982), 308 ff. Smith, *Ultra-Magic Deals*, 220.

Chapter 12. In Retrospect

1. Knowles, "Ultra and the Battle of the Atlantic," 448.

Selected Bibliography

Documentary Sources

UNITED STATES
  National Archives
  Library of Congress
  Navy Historical Center, Operational Archives
  Naval Historical Foundation, Washington, D.C.
  Franklin D. Roosevelt Library, Hyde Park, N.Y.
  U.S. Naval War College, Newport, R.I.
  Nimitz Library, U.S. Naval Academy, Annapolis, Md.
  U.S. Naval Institute, Annapolis, Md.
  MacArthur Memorial Archives, Norfolk, Va.
GREAT BRITAIN
  Public Records Office, Kew
  Churchill Archives Centre, Cambridge University
  British Museum, London
  London University
  National Maritime Museum, Greenwich
  Naval Historical Branch, London
CANADA
  National Archives, Ottawa
  National Library, Ottawa
  Directorate of History, National Defence Headquarters, Ottawa
AUSTRALIA
  Australian Archives, ACT, Mitchell
  Australian Archives, Victoria, Melbourne
  National Library of Australia, Canberra
  Australian War Memorial, Canberra
NEW ZEALAND
  National Archives Head Office, Wellington.
  National Library of New Zealand, Wellington.

Official Histories and Documents

AUSTRALIA

Gill, G. Hermon. *Royal Australian Navy 1939–1942*. Canberra: Australian War Memorial, 1957.

———. *Royal Australian Navy 1942–1945*. Canberra: Australian War Memorial, 1968.

CANADA

Allan, C. E. "Building a Naval Operational Intelligence Centre 1939–1943." Unpublished ms. Department of National Defence, Directorate of History.

"Naval Intelligence in Canada." File 81/520/1480.

"Notes on the History of Operational Intelligence Centre in Canada." File S. 1440–18.

NEW ZEALAND

Waters, S. D. *The Royal New Zealand Navy*. Wellington: War History Branch, Department of Internal Affairs, 1956.

UNITED KINGDOM

Gwyer, J.M.A., and J.R.M. Butler. *Grand Strategy*. Vol. 3, *June 1941–August 1942*. London: HMSO, 1964.

Hinsley, F. H., E. E. Thomas, et al. *British Intelligence in the Second World War: Its Influence on Strategy and Operations*. 5 vols. London: HMSO, 1979–1990.

Naval Staff History. The Advance to Japan. Vol. 6 of *War With Japan*. London: Admiralty, 1959.

Naval Staff History. Campaigns in the Solomons and New Guinea. Vol. 3 of *The War With Japan*. London: Admiralty, 1956.

Naval Staff History. Home Waters and the Atlantic. London: Admiralty, 1961.

Roskill, S. W. *The War at Sea 1939–1945*. 3 vols. London: HMSO, 1954–1961.

UNITED STATES

Cline, Ray S. *Washington Command Post: The Operations Division*. Vol. 2 of *The United States Army in World War II: The War Department*. Washington, D.C.: Department of the Army, 1951.

Dziuban, Stanley W. *Military Relations Between the United States and Canada 1939–1945*. Vol. 5 of *The United States Army in World War II: Special Studies*. Washington, D.C.: Department of the Army, 1959.

Forrestel, E. P. *Admiral Raymond A. Spruance, USN: A Study in Command*. Washington, D.C.: Government Printing Office, 1966.

Furer, Julius A. *Administration of the Navy Department in World War II*. Washington, D.C.: Government Printing Office, 1959.

Matloff, Maurice. *Strategic Planning for Coalition Warfare 1943–1944*. Vol. 6 of *The United States Army in World War II: The War Department*. Washington, D.C.: Department of the Army, 1959.

Matloff, Maurice, and Edwin M. Snell. *Strategic Planning for Coalition Warfare 1941–1942*. Vol. 3 of *The United States Army in World War II: The War Department*. Washington, D.C.: Department of the Army, 1953.

Morison, Samuel Eliot. *History of the United States Naval Operations in World War II*. 15 vols. Boston: Little, Brown, 1947–1962.

Morton, Louis. *Strategy and Command: The First Two Years*. Vol. 11 of *The United States Army in World War II: The War in the Pacific*. Washington, D.C.: Department of the Army, 1962.

Packard, Wyman H. *A Century of U.S. Naval Intelligence*. Washington, D.C.: Navy Department, 1996.

Pogue, Forrest C. *The Supreme Command*. Vol. 4 of *The United States Army in World War II: The European Theater of Operations*. Washington, D.C.: Department of the Army, 1954.

Watson, Mark Skinner. *Chief of Staff: Prewar Plans and Preparations*. Vol. 2 of *The United States Army in World War II: The War Department*. Washington, D.C.: Department of the Army, 1950.

United States Congress. Joint Committee on the Investigation of the Pearl Harbor Attack. *Hearings*. Washington, D.C.: Government Printing Office, 1946.

United States Department of Defense. *The Magic Background of Pearl Harbor*. Washington, D.C.: Government Printing Office, 1978.

United States Department of State. *Foreign Relations of the United States, the Washington Conferences 1941–1942*. Washington, D.C.: Government Printing Office, 1968.

United States Naval Administration in World War II, Office of the Chief of Naval Operations, Office of Naval Intelligence. Washington, D.C.: Naval History Division, n.d.

United States Naval Chronology, World War II. Washington, D.C.: Government Printing Office, 1955.

Books and Chapters

Adams, Henry H. *Witness to Power: The Life of Fleet Admiral William D. Leahy*. Annapolis, Md.: U.S. Naval Institute Press, 1985.

Alsop, Stewart, and Thomas Braden. *Sub Rosa: The O.S.S. and American Espionage*. New York: Reynal and Hitchcock, 1946.

Ambrose, Stephen E., with Richard H. Immerman. *Ike's Spies: Eisenhower and the Espionage Establishment*. Garden City, N.Y.: Doubleday, 1981.

Andrew, Christopher. "Churchill and Intelligence." In *Leaders and Intelligence*, edited by Michael I. Handel. London: Frank Cass, 1989.

———. *Her Majesty's Secret Service: The Making of the British Intelligence Community*. New York: Viking, 1986.

Austin, Bernard L., Vice Admiral, USN. *Reminiscences*. Annapolis, Md.: U.S. Naval Institute Press, 1971.

Bamford, James. *The Puzzle Palace: A Report on America's Most Secret Agency*. Boston: Houghton Mifflin, 1982.

Barnett, Correlli. *Engage the Enemy More Closely: The Royal Navy in the Second World War*. London: Hodder and Stoughton, 1991.

Baylis, John. *Anglo-American Defence Relations 1939–1980: The Special Relationship*. New York: St. Martin's Press, 1980.

Beasly, Patrick. "British Naval Intelligence in Two World Wars—Some Similarities and Differences." In *Intelligence and International Relations*, edited by Christopher Andrew and Jeremy Noakes. Exeter Studies in History no. 15. Exeter: University of Exeter, 1987.

———. "Operational Intelligence and the Battle of the Atlantic: The Role of the Royal Navy's Submarine Tracking Room." In *The RCN in Retrospect 1910–1968*, edited by James A. Boutilier. Vancouver, B.C.: University of British Columbia Press, 1982.

———. *Room 40: British Naval Intelligence 1914–1918*. New York: Harcourt Brace Jovanovich, 1982.

———. *Very Special Admiral: The Life of Admiral J. H. Godfrey, CB*. London: Hamish Hamilton, 1980.

———. *Very Special Intelligence: The Story of the Admiralty's Operational Intelligence Centre 1939–1945*. London: Hamish Hamilton, 1977.

Bennett, Ralph. *Ultra in the West: The Normandy Campaign 1944–45*. New York: Scribner's, 1979.

Berle, Beatrice B., and Travis B. Jacobs, eds. *Navigating the Rapids, 1918–1971: The Papers of Adolf A. Berle*. New York: Harcourt Brace Jovanovich, 1973.

Blair, Clay Jr. *Silent Victory: The U.S. Submarine War Against Japan*. Philadelphia: J. B. Lippincott, 1975.

Boutilier, James A. Introduction to *The RCN in Retrospect, 1910–1968*, edited by James A. Boutilier. Vancouver, B.C.: The University of British Columbia Press, 1982.

Boyd, Carl. *Hitler's Japanese Confidant: General Oshima Hiroshi and MAGIC Intelligence, 1941–1945*. Lawrence: University Press of Kansas, 1993.

Brown, Anthony Cave. *The Last Hero: Wild Bill Donovan*. New York: Times Books, 1982.

Bryant, Arthur. *Turn of the Tide 1939–1943*. London: Collins, 1957.

Bryden, John. *Best Kept Secret: Canadian Secret Intelligence in the Second World War*. Toronto: Lester, 1993.

Burke, Colin. *Information and Secrecy: Vannevar Bush, Ultra, and the Other Memex*. Lanham, Md.: Scarecrow Press, 1994.

Burns, James MacGregor, *Roosevelt: The Lion and the Fox 1882–1940*. New York: Harcourt Brace Jovanovich, 1956.

Butcher, Harry C. *My Three Years With Eisenhower*. New York: Simon and Schuster, 1946.

Chandler, Albert D. Jr., et al., eds. *The Papers of Dwight David Eisenhower: The War Years*. Baltimore, Md.: Johns Hopkins University Press, 1970.

Churchill, Winston S. *The Second World War*. Vols 1–6. Boston: Houghton Mifflin, 1948–1953.

———. *The Hinge of Fate*, vol. 4 in *The Second World War*. Boston: Houghton Mifflin, 1950.

Colville, John. *The Fringes of Power: 10 Downing Street Diaries 1939–1955*. New York: W. W. Norton, 1985.

Costello, John. *The Pacific War*. New York: Rawson, Wade, 1981.

Courtney, G. B. *Silent Feet: The History of 'Z' Special Operations 1942–1945*. Melbourne: R. J. and S. P. Austin, 1993.

Cunningham, Andrew Brown. *A Sailor's Odyssey: The Autobiography of Admiral of the Fleet Viscount Cunningham of Hyndhope*. London: Hutchinson, 1951.

Dallek, Robert. *Franklin D. Roosevelt and American Foreign Policy, 1932–1945*. New York: Oxford University Press, 1979.

Dalton, Hugh. *The Fateful Years: Memoirs 1921–1945*. London: Frederick Muller, 1957.

Danchev, Alex. "Dill: Field-Marshal Sir John Dill." In *Churchill's Generals*, edited by John Keegan. New York: Grove Weidenfeld, 1991.

Day, David. *The Great Betrayal: Britain, Australia & the Onset of the Pacific War 1939–1942*. New York: W. W. Norton, 1989.

Denham, Henry M. *Inside the Nazi Ring: A Naval Attaché in Sweden 1940–1945*. New York: Holmes and Meier, 1985.

Dorwart, Jeffery M. *Conflict of Duty: The U.S. Navy's Intelligence Dilemma, 1919–1945*. Annapolis, Md.: U.S. Naval Institute Press, 1983.

———. *Office of Naval Intelligence: The Birth of America's First Intelligence Agency 1865–1918*. Annapolis, Md.: U.S. Naval Institute Press, 1979.

Douglas, W.A.B., and Jürgen Rohwer. "'The Most Thankless Task' Revisited: Convoys, Escorts, and Radio Intelligence in the Western Atlantic, 1941–43." In *The RCN in Retrospect, 1910–1968*, edited by James A. Boutilier. Vancouver, B.C.: University of British Columbia Press, 1982.

Drea, Edward J. *MacArthur's ULTRA: Codebreaking and the War Against Japan, 1942–1945*. Lawrence: University Press of Kansas, 1992.

Dull, Paul S. *A Battle History of the Imperial Japanese Navy (1941–1945)*. Annapolis, Md.: U.S. Naval Institute Press, 1978.

Dulles, Allen. *The Craft of Intelligence*. New York: Harper and Row, 1963.

Dyer, George C. *The Reminiscences of Vice Admiral George C. Dyer, USN*. Annapolis, Md.: U.S. Naval Institute Press, 1974.

Eisenhower, Dwight D. *Crusade in Europe*. New York: Avon Books, 1968.

Fairbank, John K., Edwin O. Reischauer, and Albert M. Craig. *East Asia: The Modern Transformation*. Tokyo: Charles E. Tuttle, 1965.

Farago, Ladislas. *The Tenth Fleet*. New York: Drum Books, 1986.

Feldt, Eric A. *The Coast Watchers*. New York: Bantam Books, 1979.

Foot, M.R.D., and J. M. Langley. *MI9: Escape and Evasion 1939–1945*. London: Futura Publications, 1980.

Fuchida, Mitsuo, and Masatake Okumiya. *Midway: The Battle That Doomed Japan, the Japanese Navy's Story*. Annapolis, Md.: U.S. Naval Institute Press, 1955.

Gannon, Michael. *Operation Drumbeat: The Dramatic True Story of Germany's First U-boat Attacks Along the American Coast in World War II*. New York: Harper and Row, 1990.

Gilbert, Martin. *The Second World War*. London: Weidenfeld and Nicolson, 1989.

Granatstein, J. L. *Canada's War: The Politics of the Mackenzie King Government 1939–1945*. Toronto: Oxford University Press, 1975.

Gray, Edwyn. *Operation Pacific: The Royal Navy's War Against Japan*. Annapolis, Md.: U.S. Naval Institute Press, 1990.

Grew, Joseph C. *Ten Years in Japan: A Contemporary Record Drawn From the Diaries and Private Papers of Joseph C. Grew, United States Ambassador to Japan 1932–1942*. New York: Simon and Schuster, 1944.

Handel, Michael I. "Leaders and Intelligence." In *Leaders and Intelligence*, edited by Michael I. Handel. London: Frank Cass, 1989.

Harriman, W. Averell, and Elie Abel. *Special Envoy to Churchill and Stalin, 1941–1946*. New York: Random House, 1975.

Hattendorf, John B., ed. *On His Majesty's Service: Observations of the British Home Fleet From the Diary, Reports, and Letters of Joseph H. Wellings, Assistant Naval Attache London, 1940–1941*. Newport, R.I.: U.S. Naval War College, 1983.

Hinsley, F. H. "The Influence of Ultra in the Second World War." In *Code-breakers: The Inside Story of Bletchley Park*, edited by F. H. Hinsley and Alan Stripp. New York: Oxford University Press, 1993.

Holmes, W. J. *Double-Edged Secrets: U.S. Naval Intelligence Operations in the Pacific During World War II*. Annapolis, Md.: U.S. Naval Institute Press, 1979.

Horner, David M. *High Command: Australia and Allied Strategy 1939–1945*. Canberra: Australian War Memorial, 1982.

Hull, Cordell. *The Memoirs of Cordell Hull*. New York: Macmillan, 1948.

Hunt, David. *A Don at War*. Rev. ed. London: Frank Cass, 1990.

Kahn, David. *The Codebreakers: The Story of Secret Writing*. New York: Macmillan, 1967.

———. *Seizing the Enigma: The Race to Break the German U-boat Codes*. Boston: Houghton Mifflin, 1991.

Katz, Barry M. *Foreign Intelligence: Research and Analysis in the Office of Strategic Services 1942–1945*. Cambridge: Harvard University Press, 1989.

Kennan, George F. *Memoirs 1925–1950*. Boston: Little, Brown, 1967.

Kimball, Warren F., ed. *Churchill and Roosevelt: The Complete Correspondence*. Princeton, N.J.: Princeton University Press, 1984.

King, Ernest J., and Walter Muir Whitehill. *Fleet Admiral King: A Naval Record*. New York: W. W. Norton, 1952.

Klachko, Mary, with David F. Trask. *Admiral William Shepherd Benson: First Chief of Naval Operations*. Annapolis, Md.: U.S. Naval Institute Press, 1987.

Knowles, Kenneth A. "Ultra and the Battle for the Atlantic: The American View." In *Changing Interpretations and New Sources in Naval History: Papers From the Third United States Naval Academy History Symposium*, edited by Robert W. Love Jr. New York: Garland, 1980.

Langer, William L., and S. Everett Gleason. *The Undeclared War 1940–1941*. New York: Harper and Brothers, 1952.

Layton, Edwin T. *"And I Was There": Pearl Harbor and Midway—Breaking the Secrets*. New York: William Morrow, 1985.

Leutze, James R. *Bargaining for Supremacy: Anglo-American Naval Collaboration 1937–1941*. Chapel Hill: University of North Carolina Press, 1977.

———. *A Different Kind of Victory: A Biography of Admiral Thomas H. Hart.* Annapolis, Md.: U.S. Naval Institute Press, 1981.

———, ed. *The London Journal of General Raymond E. Lee, 1940–1941.* Boston: Little, Brown, 1971.

Lewin, Ronald. *The American Magic: Codes, Ciphers and the Defeat of Japan.* New York: Farrar Straus Giroux, 1982.

———. *The Chief: Field Marshal Lord Wavell, Commander in Chief and Viceroy, 1939–1947.* New York: Farrar Straus Giroux, 1980.

———. *Ultra Goes to War.* New York: McGraw-Hill, 1978.

Loewenheim, Francis L., Harold D. Langley, and Manfred Jonas, eds. *Roosevelt and Churchill: Their Secret Wartime Correspondence.* New York: Saturday Review Press, 1975.

Lord, Walter. *Lonely Vigil: The Coastwatchers of the Solomons.* New York: Viking, 1977.

Love, Robert W. Jr., and John Major, eds. *The Year of D-Day: The 1944 Diary of Admiral Sir Bertram Ramsay.* Hull, U.K.: University of Hull Press, 1994.

Lund, W.G.D. "The Royal Canadian Navy's Quest for Autonomy in the North West Atlantic: 1941–43." In *The RCN in Retrospect, 1910–1968,* edited by James A. Boutilier. Vancouver, B.C.: University of British Columbia Press, 1982.

Masterman, J. C. *The Double Cross System in the War of 1939 to 1945.* New Haven, Conn.: Yale University Press, 1972.

McCollum, Arthur H. *Reminiscences.* Annapolis, Md.: U.S. Naval Institute Press, 1973.

McLachlan, Donald. *Room 39: A Study in Naval Intelligence.* New York: Atheneum, 1968.

Miller, Edward S. *War Plan Orange: The U.S. Strategy to Defeat Japan, 1897–1945.* Annapolis, Md.: U.S. Naval Institute Press, 1991.

Milner, Marc. *North Atlantic Run: The Royal Canadian Navy and the Battle for the Convoys.* Annapolis, Md.: U.S. Naval Institute Press, 1985.

———. *The U-boat Hunters: The Royal Canadian Navy and the Offensive Against Germany's Submarines.* Annapolis, Md.: U.S. Naval Institute Press, 1994.

Montagu, Ewen. *Beyond Top Secret U.* London: Peter Davies, 1977.

Morgan, William J., and Joye L. Leonhart. *A History of the Dudley Knox Center for Naval History.* Washington, D.C.: Dudley Knox Center for Naval History, 1981.

Parrish, Thomas. *The Ultra Americans: The U.S. Role in Breaking the Nazi Codes.* New York: Stein and Day, 1986.

Pearson, John. *Life of Ian Fleming.* New York: McGraw-Hill, 1966.

Philby, H.A.R. *My Silent War.* New York: Ballantine Books, 1983.

Pogue, Forrest. *George C. Marshall. Organizer of Victory, 1943–1945.* New York: Viking, 1973.

Potter, E. B. *Bull Halsey.* Annapolis, Md.: U.S. Naval Institute Press, 1985.

———. *Nimitz.* Annapolis, Md.: U.S. Naval Institute Press, 1976.

Powell, Alan. *War by Stealth: Australians and the Allied Intelligence Bureau 1942–1945*. Melbourne: Melbourne University Press, 1996.

Prados, John. *Combined Fleet Decoded: The Secret History of American Intelligence and the Japanese Navy in World War II*. New York: Random House, 1995.

Reynolds, David. *The Creation of the Anglo-American Alliance 1937–41: A Study in Competitive Co-operation*. Chapel Hill: University of North Carolina Press, 1982.

Rhoades, F. A. *Diary of a Coastwatcher in the Solomons*. Fredericksburg, Tex.: Admiral Nimitz Foundation, 1982.

Rohwer, Jürgen. "The Operational Use of 'ULTRA' in the Battle of the Atlantic." In *Intelligence and International Relations*, edited by Christopher Andrew and Jeremy Noakes. Exeter: University of Exeter, 1987.

———. "Radio-Intelligence in the Battle of the Atlantic." In *The Missing Dimension: Governments and Intelligence Communities in the Twentieth Century*, edited by Christopher Andrew and David Dilks. Urbana: University of Illinois Press, 1984.

Rohwer, Jürgen, and Gerhard Hümmelchen. *Chronology of the War at Sea 1939–1945: The Naval History of World War II*. Annapolis, Md.: U.S. Naval Institute Press, 1992.

Roosevelt, Kermit. *War Report of the OSS*. New York: Walker, 1976.

Roskill, Stephen. *Churchill and the Admirals*. New York: William Morrow, 1978.

———. *Hankey: Man of Secrets*. London: Collins, 1974.

———. *The Navy at War 1939–1945*. London: Collins, 1960.

Schlesinger, Arthur M. Jr. *The Coming of the New Deal*. Boston: Houghton Mifflin, 1958.

Schratz, Paul R. *Submarine Commander*. Lexington: University Press of Kentucky, 1988.

Sherwood, Robert E. *Roosevelt and Hopkins: An Intimate History*. New York: Harper and Brothers, 1948.

Simpson, B. Mitchell III. *Admiral Harold R. Stark: Architect of Victory, 1939–1945*. Columbia: University of South Carolina Press, 1989.

Smith, Bradley F. *Sharing Secrets With Stalin: How the Allies Traded Intelligence 1941–1945*. Lawrence: University Press of Kansas, 1996.

———. *The Ultra-Magic Deals: and the Most Secret Special Relationship, 1940–1960*. Novato, Calif.: Presidio, 1992.

Smith, Constance Babington. *Evidence in Camera: The Story of Photographic Intelligence in World War II*. London: Chatto and Windus, 1958.

Smith, R. Harris. *OSS: The Secret History of America's First Central Intelligence Agency*. Berkeley: University of California Press, 1972.

Spector, Ronald H. *Eagle Against the Sun: The American War With Japan*. London: Penguin Books, 1984.

———. *Listening to the Enemy: Key Documents on the Role of Communications Intelligence in the War With Japan*. Wilmington, Del.: Scholarly Resources, 1988.

Stephen, Martin. *The Fighting Admirals: British Admirals of the Second World War*. Annapolis, Md.: U.S. Naval Institute Press, 1991.

Stevens, David. *U-boat Far From Home: The Epic Voyage of U 862 to Australia and New Zealand*. London: Allen & Unwin, 1997.

Stripp, Alan. *Codebreaker in the Far East*. London: Frank Cass, 1989.

Strong, Kenneth. *Intelligence at the Top: The Recollections of an Intelligence Officer*. London: Cassell, 1968.

Sweet-Escott, Bickham. *Baker Street Irregular*. London: Methuen, 1965.

Tent, James Foster. *E-Boat Alert: Defending the Normandy Invasion Fleet*. Annapolis, Md.: U.S. Naval Institute Press, 1996.

Terraine, John. *The U-boat Wars, 1916–1945*. New York: Henry Holt, 1989.

Thomas, Edward. "The Evolution of the JIC System up to and During World War II." In *Intelligence and National Security*, edited by Christopher Andrew and Jeremy Noakes. Exeter Studies in History no. 15. Exeter: University of Exeter, 1987.

Tolley, Kemp. *Yangtze Patrol: The U.S. Navy in China*. Annapolis, Md.: U.S. Naval Institute Press, 1971.

Trevor-Roper, Hugh. *The Philby Affair: Espionage, Treason, and Secret Services*. London: William Kimber, 1968.

Tuchman, Barbara W. *The Zimmermann Telegram*. New York: Ballantine Books, 1979.

Wark, Wesley K. *The Ultimate Enemy: British Intelligence and Nazi Germany, 1933–1939*. Ithaca, N.Y.: Cornell University Press, 1985.

Wedemeyer, Alfred C. *Wedemeyer Reports!* New York: Henry Holt, 1958.

Weinberg, Gerhard L. *A World at Arms: A Global History of World War II*. New York: Cambridge University Press, 1994.

Welchman, Gordon. *The Hut Six Story: Breaking the Enigma Codes*. New York: McGraw-Hill, 1982.

Whitehead, Don. *The FBI Story: A Report to the People*. New York: Random House, 1956.

Williams, Kathleen B. *Secret Weapon: U.S. High-Frequency Direction Finding in the Battle of the Atlantic*. Annapolis, Md.: U.S. Naval Institute Press, 1996.

Winks, Robin W. *Cloak and Gown: Scholars in the Secret War 1939–1961*. New York: William Morrow, 1987.

Winter, Barbara. *The Intrigue Master: Commander Long and Naval Intelligence in Australia, 1913–1945*. Brisbane: Boolarong Press, 1995.

Winterbotham, F. W. *Secret and Personal*. London: William Kimber, 1969.

Winton, John. *The Forgotten Fleet*. London: Michael Joseph, 1969.

————. *ULTRA in the Pacific: How Breaking Japanese Codes and Cyphers Affected Naval Operations Against Japan*. Annapolis, Md.: U.S. Naval Institute Press, 1993.

Wohlstetter, Roberta. *Pearl Harbor: Warning and Decision*. Stanford, Calif.: Stanford University Press, 1962.

Yardley, Herbert O. *The American Black Chamber*. Indianapolis, Ind.: Bobbs-Merrill, 1931.

Zacharias, Ellis M. *Secret Missions: The Story of an Intelligence Officer*. New York: G. P. Putnam's Sons, 1946.

Articles and Papers

Aldrich, Richard. "Imperial Rivalry: British and American Intelligence in Asia, 1942–46." *Intelligence and National Security* 3, no. 1 (January 1988), 5–55.

Beesly, Patrick. "Operational Intelligence Centre, Naval Intelligence Division 1939–1945." *Naval Review* 63, pt. I (July 1975), 224–235; pt. II (October 1975), 314–324; 64, pt. III (January 1976), 44–52.

Best, Antony. "Constructing an Image: British Intelligence and Whitehall's Perception of Japan, 1931–1939." *Intelligence and National Security* 11, no. 3 (July 1996), 403–423.

Chapman, John W. M. "Pearl Harbor: The Anglo-Australian Dimension." *Intelligence and National Security* 4, no. 3 (July 1989), 451–460.

———. "Signals Intelligence Collaboration Among the Tripartite States on the Eve of Pearl Harbor." *Japan Forum* 3 (October 1991), 231–256.

Clarke, William F. "Government Code and Cypher School: Its Foundation and Development with Special Reference to Its Naval Side." *Cryptologia* 11, no. 4 (October 1987), 219–226.

Costello, John. "Cryptanalysis—Contributions and Controversy." Paper delivered at a retrospective symposium on the Second World War, The Issue in Doubt, presented by the Admiral Nimitz Museum, San Antonio, Tex., 26 March 1992.

Cowman, I. "Anglo-American Naval Relations in the Pacific 1937–1941." Ph.D. diss., University of London, 1989.

Currier, Prescott. "My 'Purple' Trip to England in 1941." *Cryptologia* 20 (July 1996), 193–201.

Denniston, A. G. "The Government Code and Cypher School Between the Wars." *Intelligence and National Security* 1 (January 1986), 48–70.

Dovey, H. O. "The Middle East Intelligence Centre." *Intelligence and National Security* 4 (October 1989), 800–812.

Drea, Edward J. "Were the Japanese Army Codes Secure?" *Cryptologia* 19, no. 2 (April 1995), 113–136.

Erskine, Ralph. "Naval Enigma: A Missing Link." *International Journal of Intelligence and Counterintelligence* 3 (winter 1989), 493–508.

Ferris, John. "From Broadway House to Bletchley Park: The Diary of Malcolm Kennedy, 1934–36." *Intelligence and National Security* 4, no. 3 (July 1989), 421–450.

———. "Ralph Bennett and the Study of Ultra." *Intelligence and National Security* 6, no. 2 (April 1991), 473–486.

Godfrey, John H. *Memoirs*. File GDFY 1/6. Cambridge: Churchill Archives Centre, 1965.

Horner, D. M. "Special Intelligence in the South-West Pacific Area in World War II." *Australian Outlook* 32 (December 1978), 310–327.

Ingersoll, Royal E. *Reminiscences*. New York: Oral History Research Office, Columbia University, 1965.

Jeffery, Keith, ed. "The Government Code and Cypher School: A Memorandum by Lord Curzon." *Intelligence and National Security* 1 (September 1986).

Kirk, Alan G. *Reminiscences*. New York: Oral History Research Office, Columbia University, 1962.

Kittredge, Tracy B. "United States–British Naval Cooperation, 1940–1945." Unpublished Ms., Naval Historical Center, Washington, D.C.

Packard, Wyman. "Notes on the Early History of Naval Intelligence in the United States." *ONI Review* 12 (April–May 1957), 169–175.

Parker, Frederick. "Cryptanalysis—Contributions and Controversy." Paper delivered at a retrospective symposium on the Second World War, The Issue in Doubt, presented by the Admiral Nimitz Museum, San Antonio, Tex., 26 March 1992.

Rohwer, Jürgen. "Allied and Axis Radio Intelligence in the Battle of the Atlantic: A Comparative Analysis." Paper delivered at the Thirteenth Military History Symposium, U.S. Air Force Academy, Colorado Springs, Colo., 12 October 1988.

St. John, Peter. "Canada's Accession to the Allied Intelligence Community 1940–1945." *Conflict Quarterly* 4, no. 4 (fall 1984), 5–21.

Sarty, Roger. "The Limits of Ultra: The Schnorkel U-boat Offensive Against North America, November 1944–January 1945." *Intelligence and National Security* 12 (April 1997), 44–68.

Saville, Allison W. "German Submarines in the Far East." *U.S. Naval Institute Proceedings* (August 1961), 80–92.

Smith, Bradley F. "Admiral Godfrey's Mission to America, June/July 1941." *Intelligence and National Security* 1 (September 1986), 441–450.

Wark, Wesley K. "Evolution of Military Intelligence in Canada." *Armed Forces and Society* 16 (Fall 1989), 77–98.

———. "In Search of a Suitable Japan: British Naval Intelligence in the Pacific Before the Second World War." *Intelligence and National Security* 1 (May 1986), 189–211.

Wells, A. R. "Studies in British Naval Intelligence 1880–1945." Ph.D. diss., University of London, 1972.

Index